Y0-BLZ-651

MEMOIRS OF AN
AMERICAN LADY

Painted by K. Macleay R.S.A. Engraved by H. Robinson.

Mrs Grant of Laggan.

BORN 1755.— DIED 1838.

From a Miniature painted in the 69th year of her Age.

MEMOIRS OF AN AMERICAN LADY
WITH SKETCHES OF MANNERS AND SCENES IN AMERICA AS THEY EXISTED PREVIOUS TO THE REVOLUTION

By MRS. ANNE GRANT

WITH UNPUBLISHED LETTERS
AND A MEMOIR OF MRS. GRANT
By JAMES GRANT WILSON

BOOKS FOR LIBRARIES PRESS
FREEPORT, NEW YORK

First Published 1901
Reprinted 1972

INTERNATIONAL STANDARD BOOK NUMBER:
0-8369-6771-2

LIBRARY OF CONGRESS CATALOG CARD NUMBER:
77-38354

PRINTED IN THE UNITED STATES OF AMERICA
BY
NEW WORLD BOOK MANUFACTURING CO., INC.
HALLANDALE, FLORIDA 33009

THIS EDITION
OF
AN ADMIRED AMERICAN CLASSIC,
WHICH FIRST APPEARED ALMOST A CENTURY AGO,
IS DEDICATED
BY THE AUTHOR'S GODSON
TO
MRS. JOHN V. L. PRUYN

CONTENTS OF PART ONE

	PAGE
PREFACE	ix
MEMOIR OF MRS. GRANT	xiii
INSCRIPTION	xxxvii

MEMOIRS OF AN AMERICAN LADY

INTRODUCTION 39

CHAPTER
- I. Origin of the Settlement of Albany 45
- II. The Five Nations — John and Philip Schuyler . 51
- III. Colonel Schuyler and Five Sachems visit England — Their Reception and Return 58
- IV. Colonel Schuyler and the Sachems — Literary Acquisitions — Manners of the Settlers . . . 64
- V. State of Religion among the Settlers — Sketch of the State of Society at New York 70
- VI. Description of Albany — Manner of Living there 75
- VII. Gentle Treatment of Slaves among the Albanians — Reflections on Servitude 80
- VIII. Education and Early Habits of the Albanians . . 88
- IX. First Adventures of the Indian Traders 96
- X. Marriages, Amusements, Rural Excursions, etc. . 110
- XI. Winter Amusements, etc. 119
- XII. Lay-Brothers — Miss Schuyler — Detached Indians 126
- XIII. Progress of Knowledge — Indian Manners . . . 135
- XIV. Marriage of Miss Schuyler — Description of the Flats 146
- XV. Philip Schuyler — His Management of the Indians 155
- XVI. Account of the Three Brothers 161

CONTENTS

		PAGE
XVII.	The House and Rural Economy of the Flats — Birds and Insects	165
XVIII.	Description of Colonel Schuyler's Barn . . .	174
XIX.	Military Preparations — Fidelity of the Mohawks	180
XX.	A Refractory Warrior — The Spirit pervading the New England Provinces	186
XXI.	Distinguishing Characteristics of the New York Colonists — Huguenots and Palatines . . .	191
XXII.	Adoption of Children Common in the Province — Madame's Visit to New York	195
XXIII.	Colonel Schuyler's Military Partiality — Indian Character falsely charged with Idleness . .	200
XXIV.	Progress of Civilization in Europe	207
XXV.	Independence of the Indians how first diminished	216
XXVI.	Attractions of the Indian Mode of Life — Account of a Settler among them	222
XXVII.	Indians attached by Conversion — Expedition of Mons. Barre — Ironical Sketch of an Indian .	229
XXVIII.	Christian Indians — Their Influence with the Mohawks	235
XXIX.	Madame's Adopted Children — Sister Susan .	243
XXX.	Death of Young Peter Schuyler — Society at the Flats	252
XXXI.	Hospitality — Achievements by the Negroes .	264
XXXII.	Resources of Madame — Provincial Customs .	271
XXXIII.	Followers of the Army — Resulting Inconveniences	279
XXXIV.	Arrival of a New Regiment — Domine Frielinghuysen	285
XXXV.	Plays Acted — Displeasure of the Domine . .	293
XXXVI.	Domine Frielinghuysen leaves his People . .	300

CONTENTS OF PART TWO

CHAPTER		PAGE
I.	Death of Colonel Philip Schuyler	1
II.	Mrs. Schuyler's Arrangements and Conduct after the Colonel's Death	7
III.	Mohawk Indians — Sir William Johnson	13
IV.	General Abercrombie — Death of Lord Howe	20
V.	Defeat at Ticonderoga — General Lee — Humanity of Madame	29
VI.	The Family of Madame's Sister — The Death of the Latter	35
VII.	Further Success of the British Arms — A Missionary — Cortlandt Schuyler	40
VIII.	Burning of the House at the Flats — Madame's Removal — Journey of the Author	47
IX.	Continuation of the Journey — Arrival at Oswego	57
X.	Benefit of Select Reading — Hunting Excursion	69
XI.	Gardening and Agriculture — Return of the Author to Albany	74
XII.	Madame's Family and Society Described	81
XIII.	Sir Jeffrey Amherst — Mutiny — Indian War	91
XIV.	Pontiac — Sir Robert Davers	99
XV.	Death of Captain Dalyell — Madame — Her Protégés	107
XVI.	Madame's Popularity — Exchange of Prisoners	117
XVII.	Return of the 55th Regiment to Europe — Privates sent to Pensacola	122
XVIII.	Property at Clarendon — Visionary Plans	128

CONTENTS

CHAPTER		PAGE
XIX.	Return to the Flats — Summer Amusements	142
XX.	Melancholy Presages — Turbulence of the People	147
XXI.	Settlers of a new Description — Madame's Chaplain	156
XXII.	Mode of conveying Timber in Rafts down the River	168
XXIII.	The Swamp — Patrick Coonie	172
XXIV.	Mrs. Schuyler's View of the Continental Politics	181
XXV.	Description of the breaking up of the Ice on Hudson's River	185
XXVI.	Departure from Albany — Origin of the State of Vermont	191
XXVII.	Prosperity of Albany — General Reflections	200
XXVIII.	Further Reflections — General Hamilton	211
XXIX.	Sketch of the Settlement of Pennsylvania	219
XXX.	Prospects brightening in America	228

APPENDIX

Letters to Dr. Joseph Green Cogswell	237
Correspondence between Mrs. Alexander Hamilton and Mrs. Grant	258
Letters to Mrs. Douglas Cruger, of New York	266
Letters to Mrs. Grant from Robert Southey and Others	271
"The Indian Widow," and Lines addressed to an American Lady	282
A List of Mrs. Anne Grant's Writings	287
INDEX	291

LIST OF ILLUSTRATIONS
PART ONE

Portrait of Mrs. Grant of Laggan, from a miniature painted in 1825 by K. Macleay, R.S.A. Engraved on steel by H. Robinson . . . . *Frontispiece*
Loch Laggan, Inverbess-shire, the early home of Mrs. Grant, where Queen Victoria and Prince Albert resided soon after their marriage. From a photograph 18
Fac-simile of note sent to Dr. Buchanan with a copy of "The American Lady." From the original in the possession of Mrs. William G. Rice, of Albany 25
An early portrait of Mrs. Grant 36
Portrait of Colonel Peter Schuyler. From a painting made in London in 1710 59
Portrait of King Hendrick, chief of the Five Nations . . 62
Map of the Flats on the banks of the Hudson, above Albany 149
Van Rensselaer Manor House, built in 1660, and replaced by another in 1765, which was removed a decade ago to Williamstown, Mass. The original manor house, erected by Jeremias Van Rensselaer, stood until 1840. From a drawing by Major Francis Pruyn 201

PART TWO

Portrait of Mrs. Grant after a painting by Sir John Watson Gordon. From a photograph received from Mrs. Annie Laggan Dewar, of Dunfermline, Scotland 1

LIST OF ILLUSTRATIONS

	PAGE
The Vanderhuyden Palace, erected on North Pearl Street in 1725. Introduced by Washington Irving in his story of "The Haunted House." From a water-color drawing	24
General Philip Schuyler's residence, built in 1760-61. In this historic mansion Washington, Layfayette, Franklin, and Burgoyne were entertained, and Alexander Hamilton and Elizabeth Schuyler were married in 1780 . .	45
Madame Schuyler's residence at the Flats. A front view. In this house Lord Howe was a guest when on his way to Ticonderoga, and to it he was brought back dead .	48
Fort Frederick, State Street, Albany, as seen in Colonial Days. From a painting in the possession of Mrs. J. V. L. Pruyn, of Albany	183
A fac-simile of Aunt Schuyler's signature, from her will .	196
The Schuyler Arms. From a painting in the possession of Mrs. Harriett Crosby Thompson of Troy	287

PREFACE

MRS. GRANT'S "Memoirs of an American Lady" has long been out of print, having become so scarce that the volume was almost unobtainable, and then only at an exorbitant price. By many it is believed that so charming a picture of Colonial life in New York nearly a century and a half ago, should not be permitted to pass away. It is not a romance nor a tale partly founded on reality, but it is an authentic record of facts, — a record which was much admired by Francis Jeffrey, Washington Irving, Sir Walter Scott, Robert Southey, William M. Thackeray,[1] and other great heirs of fame, one of whom praised the description of the breaking up of the ice in the Upper Hudson "as quite Homeric." George Bancroft said, "Your kinswoman, Mrs. Grant's, invaluable volume, should be in the library of every American lady."

[1] A presentation copy of the original edition of "The American Lady," received by the author of "Henry Esmond," from a member of Mrs. Grant's family, and now included in Major William H. Lambert's unequalled collection of Thackerayana, was among the "Great Thacker's" most highly prized literary treasures. The writer is the fortunate possessor of almost all her publications, being copies received from Mrs. Grant by his father, containing complimentary inscriptions.

PREFACE

In preparing a new edition of this genuine picture of our ancestors prior to the amazing changes produced by the Revolution, — a picture which Paulding informed me suggested "The Dutchman's Fireside," — it has been thought that some account of the good and gifted lady to whom the world is indebted for the Memoir of Mrs. Schuyler would be acceptable, as well as the numerous accompanying notes. A number of these were contributed to the edition of 1876, by Joel Munsell, the Albany antiquarian, while other notes were supplied two decades after that date, by the late George W. Schuyler. In the Appendix will be found a sheaf of Mrs. Grant's hitherto unpublished letters, addressed to Mrs. Alexander Hamilton and Dr. Joseph G. Cogswell between the years 1819–1834, that it is believed will enhance the value of the volume. A fine steel portrait of the author appears as a frontispiece. For the larger portion of the illustrations of ancient Albany that are included, the editor is indebted to the courtesy of Col. Augustus Pruyn, who made the photographs from which they are reproduced.

That Mrs. Grant should, in respect to persons and places, have made some slight errors in her admirable memoir of Mrs. Schuyler, is not surprising; the marvel is that so few appear in her pages, when it is remembered that the work was written nearly half a century after the occurrence of the events described, entirely from memory, and that too the recollections of a child between the age of three and

PREFACE

thirteen ! Mrs. Grant had neither the aid of letters, a diary, or data of any description in the preparation of the Memoir, which first appeared in London, in 1808, and was republished in Boston and New York during the following year. The last of the numerous editions printed since those dates in the new world and old, was issued in Albany precisely a quarter of a century ago.

J. G. W.

NEW YORK, *September*, 1901.

MEMOIR OF MRS. GRANT

MRS. ANNE GRANT, commonly styled of Laggan, to distinguish her from her friend and contemporary Mrs. Grant of Carron,[1] was born at Glasgow, February 21, 1755. Her father, Duncan MacVicar, who is described as a plain, brave, pious man, was an officer in the 77th infantry, a Highland regiment; her mother a descendant of the family of Stewart of Invernahyle. "My father," writes Mrs. Grant, "was born in the parish of Craignish, in Argyllshire, and was early left an orphan. He removed, when a young man, to Fort William in Inverness-shire, where he had some concern in farming along with his relation Captain MacVicar. In 1753, he married my mother, who was a grand-daughter of Mr. Stewart of Invernahyle, an ancient family in the neighboring county of Argyll. Sometime afterwards my parents removed to Glasgow." Her maternal grand-uncle, Alexander Stewart of Invernahyle, was the prototype of the Baron of Bradwardine in "Waverley." Sir Walter, in the introduction to a new edition in 1829,

[1] Mrs. Elizabeth Grant, author of "Roy's Wife of Aldivalloch."

says, "Stewart was a noble specimen of the old Highlander, far descended, gallant, courteous, and brave even to chivalry." Mrs. Grant, it may be mentioned, was one of the first to recognize his ideal representation in "Waverley," and to express the opinion that the work was written by Scott, who in her judgment was not, in that work, altogether just to her beloved Highlanders. "The only particular," writes Mrs. Grant, " of my infantine history that I remember to have heard related, took place in the streets of Glasgow, and I mention it to show at what an early age children observe and remember. My mother lived in the eastern extremity of the town: I suppose she often spoke to others, though not to me, of my father being in America, and might very probably point westward when describing in what direction the *New World* lay to some one who knew still less than myself of geography. Be that as it may, I certainly set off one Sunday evening when I was at most two years and eight months old, and walked deliberately by myself very nearly a mile to the western extremity of the Trongate; how much further I might have gone is not known. A lady looking out of a window saw with some surprise a child neatly dressed in white, with bare head and arms, walking alone and unattended in the middle of the street. She sent for me and asked me where I came from. I said 'mamma's house;' I could tell no more. She next questioned me where I was going. I answered in my imperfect manner that I was going to America to seek papa."[1]

Soon after this event, Mrs. MacVicar and her daughter sailed for the New World and settled at Claverack on the Hudson, where her husband was stationed with a party of Highlanders. Here Anne was taught to read by her mother, and learned to speak Dutch. An intelligent sergeant of the company made her a proficient in writing, and observing her eager thirst for knowledge presented his precocious little pupil with an appropriate soldier's gift, — even the poem of Wallace by the patriotic Scottish Homer, Blind Harry. The quaint and almost forgotten language in which this work is written, as well as its obsolete orthography, would have made it a sealed book to the half Scottish, half American child, had it not been for the kindness of the sergeant, who taught her to decipher words and to understand the meaning of the ancient minstrel. From this source she in part derived that enthusiastic love of her native land, "Where blooms the red heather and thistle sae green," which ever afterwards was a distinguishing feature in her character.

In 1760, Captain MacVicar, who had taken part in the disastrous expedition to Ticonderoga and been stationed at Oswego, was sent back to Claverack to conduct a company to the former place.

[1] "Mrs. Grant's Memoirs and Correspondence," 3 vols., London, 1844.

His wife and daughter accompanied the detachment on the picturesque and perilous journey through the wilderness to Oswego, concerning which Mrs. Grant remarks in her "Memoirs of an American Lady," "I am convinced that I thought more in that fortnight, that is, acquired more ideas and took more lasting impressions, than ever I did in the same space of time in my life." The commandant of the post was our old friend Major Duncan of Lundie,[1] whose portrait is given in Cooper's "Last of the Mohicans," and also by Mrs. Grant, who describes him as an experienced, humane, judicious yet obstinate officer, and somewhat of a humorist withal. In her sixth year Anne was familiar with the Old Testament, and read with eagerness and pleasure Milton's "Paradise Lost," a poem which has daunted so many youthful readers at the outset. Her talents, in the summer of 1762, attracted the attention of Madame Schuyler, with whom she resided at Albany for several years, acquiring during her sojourn among her hospitable friends an additional knowledge of the Dutch language at that day much spoken by many of the best families.

A few years after the conquest of Canada, Mac-Vicar resigned his position in the army, going on the half-pay list in 1765, and became a settler in Vermont, where he received a grant of land from the British government, to which he made large additions by purchase from his brother officers. While

[1] Afterwards Colonel Duncan, elder brother of Lord Camperdown.

here, his worth and agreeable manners won for him and his family the esteem of all the neighboring settlers. His career of prosperity was, however, interrupted by ill-health and low spirits, and in 1768 he decided to return to his native land. Anne accompanied her parents, and at the age of thirteen she left America never to see it again. Unfortunately for MacVicar, he took his departure from the country without disposing of his property, which, upon the breaking out of the Revolutionary War soon after, was confiscated by the new republican government. He was therefore compelled to depend chiefly upon his limited pay as a barrack-master of Fort Augustus, in Inverness-shire, to which position he had been appointed in 1773, and his daughter was no longer looked upon as a young American heiress.

With her journey from Glasgow to that place, which she could reach only by riding on horseback, commences the portion of Mrs. Grant's correspondence that was published under the title of "Letters from the Mountains." On the first evening after her arrival at the fort, she met the Rev. James Grant, the military chaplain, an accomplished scholar of somewhat romantic character, connected with several of the first families of the district. Her residence at Fort Augustus was terminated by her marriage to this gentleman in the year 1779, when they removed to the parish of Laggan, in Inverness-shire, to which Mr. Grant had been appointed.

On becoming the wife of a Highland clergyman, Mrs. Grant desired to aid her husband, but a difficulty opposed her progress at the outset. Although a Mac, she was not a Highlander, and she did not possess the most essential passport to a Highland heart, a knowledge of their language. Undeterred, however, by an obstacle which few Lowlanders comparatively except enthusiasts like Professor Blackie have ever surmounted, she, by great application, soon acquired a sufficient knowledge of Gaelic to converse freely with the people in their own tongue, and was successful in translating the poetry of the Highlands. One of her earliest translations, "The Aged Bard's Wish," is a composition of singular elegance and pathos, remarkable for certain allusions to the age and imagery of Ossian. With the Celtic language she studied the manners and feelings of the Highlanders, and was soon able to identify herself with the parishioners among whom her lot was cast; and they on their part appreciated these kind labors of a stranger with true Highland enthusiasm, and felt that she was their own countrywoman in heart and soul as well as in tongue and lineage. Mrs. Grant studied their "folklore," and was successful in relieving much distress among the peasantry of the surrounding district.

Her lines had fallen in pleasant places. In the simple life of a secluded Highland parish, many happy and tranquil years passed in Laggan, and

Loch Laggan, where Queen Victoria and Prince Albert resided soon after their Marriage

Mrs. Grant, the mother of twelve children, seemed destined to be one of those " of whom Fame speaks not " but

> " Gentle hearts rejoice
> Around their steps — till silently they die."

" The circles of our felicities," writes Sir Thomas Browne, "make short arches." Who shall question the wise axiom of the good old knight of Norwich? After four successive deaths in her family, Mr. Grant, who was constitutionally delicate, passed away in the year 1801,[1] and his widow was left with eight children dependent upon her exertions, while the manse, for more than a score of years her happy home, must be given up to his successor. On examining their affairs, Mrs. Grant found that she had been left in debt to a considerable amount, the scale of clerical and Highland hospitality on which the household had been conducted having greatly exceeded the amount of her husband's moderate stipend.

Among her many friends Mrs. Grant had long been known as a writer of verses, having in her ninth year essayed imitations of Milton, and composed several songs and poems while residing on the banks of the Clyde, before the family proceeded to Fort Augustus. " I had early," she writes, " dis-

---

[1] When the writer visited the parish of Laggan where the Rev. James Grant is buried, he found the good man's memory and that of his gifted wife were still cherished among the descendants of the warm-hearted Highlanders, who were so deeply attached to them during their twenty-one years' residence there.

covered a faculty for rhyming, scarcely worthy to be dignified with the name of poetry, but easy and fluent." Mrs. Grant was urged to collect and publish these productions with a view to aiding in the support of her family, and as an inducement three thousand subscribers were speedily obtained under the patronage of the celebrated Duchess of Gordon, one of whose summer seats was at Kinrara near Laggan. In 1803, "The Highlanders and other Poems" appeared in a well-printed octavo volume, the profits of which enabled Mrs. Grant to discharge the debts which had hung most heavily on her mind. Of a few songs which proceeded from her pen, only that charming one generally known from its melody as "The Blue Bells of Scotland" has outlived their author. The genius of Mrs. Grant was not lyrical; but in all her poetical productions there is a steady current of harmony and good sense, more indicative of the shrewd observer than the poet.

Perceiving from the surprising success of her poems a prospect of better maintaining her family by her literary efforts, Mrs. Grant sorrowfully abandoned the small farm near Laggan which she had leased after her husband's death, and removed to a sequestered spot in the neighborhood of Stirling. Besides her own family, including her mother, she had with her three girls from the West Indies, who were placed under her care. Her pecuniary resources were increased by the compensation which she received for this charge, and they continued to be so from a similar source for thirty years. Many young ladies were successively inmates of her family. The number was usually restricted to three or four, and the deep interest she felt in them and the affection which they retained for her contributed greatly to her happiness. The benefit which Mrs. Grant was expected to afford the fortunate inmates of her household was chiefly in forming their mind and manners, and at a later period an introduction into the Edinburgh literary society in which she moved. Among her many pupils was the mother of the late Duke of Argyll[1] and Miss Harriet Douglas[2] of New York, later Mrs. Douglas Cruger, with whom she maintained for many years a correspondence terminated only by her death. On one occasion the latter came down late to breakfast to Mrs. Grant's great annoyance, as she was fond of punctuality and showed her displeasure by not speaking. By way of atoning for her

---

[1] Writing from Inverary Castle on his return from a visit to the Marquis of Lorne, then Governor-General of Canada, the Duke says, "I have been reading, with unfeigned interest, your new edition of 'The American Lady,' for which I was indebted to you when we met in New York. Mrs. Grant possessed a powerful and sensitive mind, and her writings have afforded me both profit and pleasure, her admirable memoir of Mrs. Schuyler perhaps more than any other. Your account of the author adds value to the attractive volume."

[2] Sir John Watson Gordon's full-length portrait of Mrs. Grant was painted for Miss Douglas, and by her heirs presented in 1876, through George L. Schuyler of New York, to her daughter-in-law, Mrs. Grant, of Edinburgh. It is now the property of her son.

fault, Miss Douglas endeavored to be very agreeable, and to engage Mrs. Grant in conversation, when the old lady at length said,

"If I make a remark,
It will be of the lark." [1]

In 1806, Mrs. Grant's second work was published by the Longmans of London, entitled " Letters

[1] In a letter now before the writer, dated Rome, May 3, 1832, Miss Douglas sends Mrs. Grant an account of Sir Walter Scott, at that time in Italy with the vain hope of improving his shattered health : "Sir Walter Scott, who made us take a stirrup-cup with him the morning that we left Rome, goes the same way, *via* Venice, the Tyrol, and the Rhine, to Brussels, and it may be that he will overtake us, which would certainly be a great compensation for the delays that have occurred, to have the pleasure of his company and the benefit of his advice and judgment in these perplexing times [the cholera was then prevailing in portions of Europe]. He is brightened, I think, but not permanently bettered, by his journey. He did us the honor to take a drive with George [her brother, George Douglas, of New York] and myself, in the Appian Way, visiting the various tombs and curiosities that it offers. Sir Walter was with us from ten till four, and George amused him by repeating several extracts from his own poems, inspired by the quotations and anecdotes of his animated conversation. Afterward he went to see the portrait an American artist has been making of me, at his own request. It is to be yours during your lifetime, and you will receive it in a few weeks. The one by Sir William Beechy is still with him, and I do not know what I shall do about it, as every one condemns the likeness, and I shall have no opportunity of sitting for another.

"One morning when I was breakfasting with Sir Walter I received your last letter, and I read to him the portion where you say among the thousand and one reasons for your love and admiration of him was his charming Doric, so redolent of youth and its innocent enjoyments. I have no time to describe the royal wedding I attended at Naples last week, when the King's sister was married to the Prince of Spain. His Majesty graciously invited us to be present, although we had not then been presented."

from the Mountains," which had been written chiefly to her correspondents from the manse during a long series of years. They were so full of Highland scenery, character and legends, expressed in the happiest style of epistolary composition, that even with the omission of whatever was private or of a confidential character, they proved exceedingly popular and rapidly passed through several editions. "No person, I believe," wrote Mrs. Grant, "was so astonished at their success as myself;" and when another three hundred pounds was received for the second edition she said: "I calculate and wonder at my own wealth." As pleasant illustrations of the deep interest felt in the letters and their writer, it may be mentioned that three wealthy Scotch merchants of London, with whom Mrs. Grant had no previous acquaintance, sent her a present of three hundred pounds, and through the exertions of Miss Anne Cabot Lowell, Mrs. Josiah Quincy, and a few other ladies of Boston, also unknown to Mrs. Grant, an American edition of her "Letters from the Mountains" was published in that city, and a thousand dollars was remitted to her as the proceeds. In her

[1] This kind act was consummated chiefly through the efforts of Miss Lowell, whose brother John Lowell, Jr., became acquainted with Mrs. Grant during his residence of several years in Edinburgh, and left her a legacy of five thousand dollars as a mark of affectionate veneration for her character. Sir William Grant, Master of the Rolls, to whom this work was dedicated, bequeathed Mrs. Grant an annuity of £100 per annum. These legacies, combined with other sources of income during the later years of her long life, not only placed her in

brief autobiography Mrs. Grant mentions this unlooked for act of kindness in the following words: "Among the many singular events by which a quiet, secluded life has been diversified, one of the most remarkable was the benevolence and warmth of friendship which prompted an American lady of distinguished worth and talents to make a very uncommon exertion in behalf of the subject of this memoir. Meeting accidentally with the 'Letters from the Mountains,' this ardent and superior mind, not satisfied with warm approbation, and the elegant expression of these feelings to the author, actually, with the assistance of some friends, reprinted the work at Boston, and remitted the profits to the author. This lady, now beyond the reach of human praise, closed an exemplary life amidst her fondly attached friends and relations in 1811. She was daughter to the late eminent Judge Lowell, of New England."

Mrs. Grant's best-known work, begun in 1807 at the age of fifty-two, and issued by her friends the Messrs. Longman, of London, in the year following, is entitled "Memoirs of an American Lady." It consists, in addition to her youthful recollections of Margarita Schuyler, who married her cousin, Col. Philip Schuyler[1] of Albany, of descriptions of the simple manners of the descendants of the Dutch

easy circumstances, but permitted Mrs. Grant to gratify her generosity by giving to others.

[1] The distinguished Revolutionary general of the same name was a nephew of Mrs. Schuyler.

FACSIMILE OF NOTE ACCOMPANYING PRESENTATION COPY OF THE
SECOND LONDON EDITION OF "THE AMERICAN LADY"

settlers, sketches of the history of New York, and anecdotes of the Indians. What did not fall within her own personal experiences as a child she appears to have gleaned from the conversation of Mrs. Schuyler and others, and she seems to have forgotten nothing; for the quick-witted child had an observant eye and a mind like Macaulay's, which was

"Wax to receive, and marble to retain."

The volume concludes with two chapters of General Reflections, in which Mrs. Grant, who, like Mrs. Schuyler, was a staunch and true Tory, indulges in lugubrious prophecies of the moral, social, and intellectual future of the country. "What the loss of the Huguenots," she remarks, "was to commerce and manufactures in France, that of the loyalists was to religion, literature, and amenity in America." My excellent godmother should have lived to see our Centennial and Columbian expositions, or the later display of 1901, in Buffalo. A second edition of the work appeared in 1809, and was reprinted the same year in Boston and in New York.[1] Other editions appeared in the latter city in

[1] James K. Paulding, in a prefatory paragraph to his most popular work published in 1831, says, "The idea of the following tale was conceived on reading, many years ago, 'The Memoirs of an American Lady,' by Mrs. Grant, of Laggan; and the work partly finished about that time. The reader acquainted with the book referred to will perhaps wonder at the indiscretion of the author of 'The Dutchman's Fireside' in thus, as it were, provoking a comparison with one of the finest sketches of early American manners ever drawn."

1836 and 1846, also in Albany in 1876, while a third edition was published in London in 1817.

De Quincey accidentally encountered Mrs. Grant and one of her beautiful daughters in a stage-coach soon after the " Memoirs of an American Lady " first appeared. The charms of the daughter of course were not lost upon the enthusiastic temperament of the opium-eater; but the conversation of the mother seems to have impressed him more deeply. In his " Literary Reminiscences," written many years later, he tells us with much feeling: " Her kindness to me was particularly flattering, and to this day I retain the impression of the benignity which she — an established wit and just then receiving incense from all quarters — showed in her manners to me, — a person wholly unknown." In " Mrs. Fletcher's Autobiography " we also obtain occasional glimpses of Mrs. Grant. The author makes the following record at the time of the visit of George the Fourth to Edinburgh: " Mrs. Grant of Laggan, a great lover of kings, was of our party. The good old lady had, for this joyous occasion, put off her habitual black dress and robed herself in a salmon-colored satin, and with the rest of the party waved her handkerchief as the king appeared. They all had a good laugh at my expense, who, somewhat notorious for being no lover of kings, was actually detected shedding tears and waving my handkerchief, 'like the lave,' as the pageant passed."

In 1810 Mrs. Grant removed to Edinburgh,

and her residence there was frequented by Lord Jeffrey, Sir Walter Scott, Henry Mackenzie, "Christopher North," the "Ettrick Shepherd," and other magnates of the Scottish literary world. The year following she published her "Essays on the Superstitions of the Highlanders," — a work full of enthusiasm for the character of the people among whom she so long resided. So conspicuous was her pre-eminence in Gaelic literature by her beautiful translations,[1] and by her knowledge of the people, that the earlier volumes of the "Waverley Novels" were frequently attributed to her pen. Mrs. Grant's writings in prose and verse were among the first to draw attention to the romantic scenery and peculiar manners of the Scottish Highlanders, anticipating Walter Scott by more than a decade. It may be mentioned that when our author first met Scott, she thought his appearance "very unpromising and commonplace, yet though no gleam of genius animates his countenance, much of it appears in his conversation, which is rich, varied, easy, and animated."

"Eighteen Hundred and Thirteen," a metrical work, appeared in 1814, followed by her last literary production, entitled "Popular Models and Impressive Warnings for the Sons and Daughters of Industry," which was published in 1815. During the interval of twenty-three years between the publication of the last volume and her death, Mrs.

[1] *Vide* Wilson's "Poets and Poetry of Scotland," 2 vols., Harper's, 1876.

Grant's literary labors were no longer necessary for her support, but were taken up as recreation. They were confined chiefly to the composition of occasional verses, and to translations from the Gaelic. For one of these, a production of singular elegance and pathos, she in 1824 received the gold medal of the Highland Society. Her last poetical lines were written on her eighty-third birthday.

> "When all my earthly treasures fled,
> And grief bowed down my drooping head,
> Nor faith, nor hope, nor comfort fled.
> From bright abodes of peace and love
> New strength descended from above,
> To cheer me like the patriarch's dove.
> Now, though bereft of motion's powers,
> I pass no more through groves and flowers,
> But moveless waste the languid hours,
> While still the ethereal spark divine,
> And memory's ample store are mine,
> I neither suffer nor repine,
> But wait serene the final hour,
> Appointed by that Gracious Power,
> Who while those vials seemed of wrath,
> Shed countless blessings on my path."

No important events varied the even tenor of Mrs. Grant's life or circumstances till the year 1820, when she met with an unfortunate fall which produced permanent lameness, so that ever afterwards she was unable to move about without crutches or a cane. Five years later she received from the British government a pension of £100, in consideration of her literary talents, which, with the profits of her writings, the emolument from her pupils, and several legacies from friends, already mentioned, rendered her life free from pecuniary cares.

In 1827, her long series of domestic sorrows terminated in the loss of her only surviving daughter Mary, a pure and lovely character. A friend who visited her at this period wrote: "It was delightful to find you in old age, after such severe trials, so supported and strengthened by the power of God — not resigned merely, possessing not the calm benevolence of age alone; but all the kinder feelings in their freshness and flower, which, beautiful as they are in youth, become so much more deeply interesting when we know that care and sorrow have had no power to wither them, and that they will soon form part of that crown of glory which fadeth not. If we could have forgotten the blessings which God has for a time taken to himself and is reserving for you in his keeping, we might have thought of you only as one,

"'Whose cheerful day benevolence endears,
Whose night congratulating conscience cheers,
The general favorite, as the general friend.'"

Mrs. Grant survived her daughter nearly eleven years, and to the last her sympathies remained unchilled, and she continued to find pleasure in her conversational parties, as well as in receiving visitors, those from America being always most warmly welcomed. Her early attachment to her happy home on the Hudson remained unshaken to the end.

When my father saw her for the last time she was little changed in appearance from what her portrait painted eight years previous, and from which our engraving is taken, represents her, and was busily knitting, with two large volumes lying open before her in such a manner that she could turn to either and read without interrupting her accustomed work — when she remarked, "Willie, I should not feel any sorrow if I were deprived of all other books. These will suffice for my few remaining days." Mrs. Grant's companions were her Bible and Shakespeare. To the very end of her fourscore and almost four years, she was constantly adding to her wide field of knowledge as a means of usefulness: hers was the spirit of old Chaucer's Oxford scholar, —

"Gladly wolde he lerne, and gladly teche."

Mrs. Grant died at her residence in Manor Place, Edinburgh, November 7, 1838, retaining her faculties unimpaired to the last, and so gradually did her life depart that it may truthfully be said of her in the words of the poet:

"Of no distemper, of no blast she died,
But fell like Autumn fruit, that mellow'd long;
Even wonder'd at because she dropt no sooner.
Fate seemed to wind her up for fourscore years;
Yet freshly ran she on four summers more,
Till, like a clock worn out in eating time,
The wheels of weary life at last stood still."

In a letter announcing Mrs. Grant's death to my father, her son says: "My mother was entirely exempted from pain or suffering of any kind, bodily or mental, and she at last appeared to expire in a gentle slumber, leaving her features in the sweetest composure and confirming the assurance she gave us almost to the last that she suffered no pain. Her calmness and tranquillity in the prospect of death were what might have been expected from her firm and blameless life, and above all from her humble confidence in the pardoning mercy of God through the merits of our great Intercessor."

Mrs. Grant was buried beneath the shadows of the stately castle of Edinburgh, in what is known as the Auld West Kirk, and near her last resting-place is the grave of Thomas DeQuincey. From her tombstone we copied the following inscription:

>Sacred to the memory of
>Mrs. Anne Grant,
>Widow of the Rev. James Grant of Laggan
>In the county of Inverness,
>Who died at Edinburgh,
>7th November, 1838,
>aged 83.
>Endowed with the extraordinary energy of mind
>Her writings
>Illustrate the associations and scenes
>Of her eventful life.
>Her eminent virtues adorned its relations,
>Her Christian faith and fortitude sustained
>Its many severe afflictions
>In humble submission to
>The Will of God.

> Her numerous family of children,
> for whom she made
> Most meritorious and successful exertions,
> was by the will of a mysterious providence
> All cut off before herself
> except him who has made
> This Memorial
> Of his love and veneration.

The brilliant literary galaxy with glorious Sir Walter for its brightest star, which cast its splendor over the beautiful city of Edinburgh were almost all included among Mrs. Grant's friends and acquaintances, and many of the group were frequent visitors at her house. There also were to be met most of the educated Americans worth knowing, who passed through that famous city during more than a quarter of a century that the Northern Athens was Mrs. Grant's place of residence. Many of the latter became her attached friends and correspondents, as will be seen by the letters included in the appendix to this volume. Joanna Baillie, Southey, Wordsworth, Mrs. Hemans, the "sublime Mr. Hayley," as Thackeray calls him, and Campbell were also among her correspondents. "Your good old godmother," said Washington Irving, "was a great Tory, but always gave Americans a cordial welcome," and dear Dr. "Rab" Brown remarked at our last meeting in Edinburgh, "Mrs. Grant was one of the literary boasts of our city, universally known and respected."

MEMOIR OF MRS. GRANT xxxiii

"Mrs. Grant," remarks Lord Cockburn,[1] one of her Scottish contemporaries, "was a tall dark woman of very considerable intellect, great spirit, and the warmest benevolence. Her love of individual whigs, particularly of Jeffrey, in spite of her amusing horror of their principles, was honorable to the heart. She was always under the influence of an affectionate and delightful enthusiasm, which, unquenched by time or sorrow, survived the wreck of many domestic attachments and shed a glow over the close of a very protracted life. Both she and Mrs. Hamilton[2] were remarkable for the success of their literary conversational gatherings. Their evening parties had the greater merit from the smallness of their houses and of their means."

At the age of three score and ten Mrs. Grant began a sketch of her life, which contains a rapid view of the principal incidents of her career from her birth down to 1806, leaving the story of the last thirty years of her long and uneventful life to be told by another. This was lovingly done by her only surviving child, John P. Grant, W. S.,[3] who in 1844 issued a collection of her letters with a memoir, in three volumes. Revised editions of this delightful work appeared in 1845 and 1853,

[1] "Memorials of His Time," by Henry Cockburn, London, 1856.
[2] Mrs. Elizabeth Hamilton, author of "The Cottagers of Glenburnie."
[3] Mr. Grant died December 15, 1870, leaving a widow and four children, two of whom were sons in the service of the British Government. Mrs. J. P. Grant died in 1893, and their son Walter in 1897.

also from the press of the Longmans. A writer who was well acquainted with Mrs. Grant, remarks in a notice of the work, that "she was a woman of extraordinary good sense, and of uncommon powers of mind; whose letters, embracing a wide variety of subjects, are as truly valuable as those of any other writer, and likely to be of as permanent interest, and to afford as lasting gratification; but especially of a woman of great strength of character, formed by religious principle and penetrated by religious sentiment, the vital principle of whose moral being was faith in God and immortality, whose sympathies were warm and diffusive, and who was full of disinterested kindness."

We would gladly quote several passages from unpublished letters in our possession addressed to the late William Wilson and his wife, by Mrs. Grant, who gave her husband's name to their eldest son, and also some marked extracts from the published correspondence; but as the chorus to "Henry the Fifth" remarks—"time, numbers and due course of things cannot be here presented." Two good stories, however, we must quote, one of a very handsome and fashionable young gentleman whom Mrs. Grant did not know, who crossed a crowded drawing-room, seized her hand and kissed it, "thirty years and upwards," she says, "after anybody had thought of kissing my hand," and expressed to her the feeling which her poem, "The Highlanders," had awakened in him. The young stranger proved to be Colonel D'Este, son of the Duke of Sussex by his marriage with Lady Augusta Murray. Mrs. Grant continues, " I must not omit an anecdote better than my own about kissing. A young lady from England, very ambitious of distinction and thinking the outrageous admiration of genius was nearly as good as the possession of it, was presented to Sir Walter Scott, and had very nearly gone through the regular form of swooning sensibility on the occasion. Being afterwards introduced to the author, Henry Mackenzie, she bore it better and kissed his hand in admiring veneration. It is worth telling for the sake of Mr. Scott's comment. He said, 'did you ever hear the like of that English lass, to faint at the sight of a cripple clerk of session and kiss the dry withered hand of an old tax-gatherer.' "[1]

We cannot better conclude this brief memorial of Mrs. Grant than with the words of Sir Walter Scott, who thus characterizes her productions: " Her literary works, although composed amidst misfortune and privation, are written at once with simplicity and force, and uniformly bear the stamp of a virtuous and courageous mind, recommending to the reader that patience and fortitude which the writer herself practised in such an eminent degree. Her writings, deservedly popular in her own country, derive their success from the happy manner in

[1] Mr. Mackenzie held the office of comptroller of taxes for Scotland.

which, addressing themselves to the national pride of the Scottish people, they breathe a spirit at once of patriotism and of that candor which renders patriotism unselfish and liberal. We have no hesitation in attesting our belief that Mrs. Grant's writings have produced a strong and salutary effect upon her countrymen, who not only found recorded in them much of national history and antiquities which would otherwise have been forgotten; but found them combined with the soundest and best lessons of virtue and morality."

Jas. Grant Wilson.

New York, *September*, 1901.

AN EARLY PORTRAIT OF MRS. GRANT

TO THE RIGHT HONORABLE SIR WILLIAM GRANT, *Knt.*

Master of the Rolls

Sir;

IT is very probable that the friends, by whose solicitations I was induced to arrange in the following pages my early recollections, studied more the amusement I should derive from executing this task, than any pleasure they could expect from its completion.

The principal object of this work is to record the few incidents, and the many virtues, which diversified and distinguished the life of a most valued friend. Though no manners could be more simple, no notions more primitive than those which prevailed among her associates, the stamp of originality with which they were marked, and the peculiar circumstances in which they stood, both with regard to my friend, and the infant society to which they belonged, will, I flatter myself, give an interest with reflecting minds, even to this desultory narrative; and the miscellany of description, observation, and detail, which it involves.

If truth both of feeling and narration, which are its only merits, prove a sufficient counterbalance to carelessness, laxity, and incoherence of style, its prominent faults, I may venture to invite you, when you unbend from the useful and honorable labors to which your valuable time is devoted, to trace this feeble delineation of an excellent though unembellished character; and of the rapid pace with which an infant society has urged on its progress from virtuous simplicity to the dangerous " knowledge of good and evil," from tremulous imbecility to self-sufficient independence.

To be faithful, a delineation must necessarily be minute. Yet if this sketch, with all its imperfections, be honored by your indulgent perusal, such condescension of time and talent must certainly be admired, and may perhaps be imitated by others.

I am, Sir, very respectfully,
Your faithful humble servant,
THE AUTHOR.

LONDON, *October*, 1808.

PART ONE

MEMOIRS
OF
AN AMERICAN LADY

Introduction

To ———,

DEAR SIR,

OTHERS as well as you have expressed a wish to see a memoir of my earliest and most valuable friend.

To gratify you and them I feel many inducements, and see many objections.

To comply with any wish of yours is one strong inducement.

To please myself with the recollection of past happiness and departed worth is another; and to benefit those into whose hands this imperfect sketch may fall, is a third. For the authentic record of an exemplary life, though delivered in the most unadorned manner, or even degraded by poverty of style, or uncouthness of narration, has an attraction for the uncorrupted mind.

It is the rare lot of some exalted characters, by the united power of virtue and of talents, to soar above their fellow-mortals, and leave a luminous track behind, on which successive ages gaze with wonder and delight.

But the sweet influence of these benign stars, that now and then enlighten the page of history, is partial and unfrequent.

They to whom the most important parts on the stage of life are allotted, if possessed of abilities undirected by virtue, are too often

> "Wise to no purpose, artful to no end,"

that is really good and desirable.

They, again, where virtue is not supported by wisdom, are often, with the best intentions, made subservient to the short-sighted craft of the artful and designing. Hence, though we may be at times dazzled with the blaze of heroic achievement, or contemplate with a purer satisfaction those "awful fathers of mankind," by whom nations were civilized, equitable dominion established, or liberty restored: yet, after all, the crimes and miseries of mankind form such prominent features of the history of every country, that humanity sickens at the retrospect, and misanthropy finds an excuse amidst the laurels of the hero, and the deep-laid schemes of the politician:

> "And yet this partial view of things
> Is surely not the best." — *Burns.*

Where shall we seek the antidote to this chilling gloom left on the mind by these bustling intricate scenes, where the best characters, goaded on by

AN AMERICAN LADY

furious factions or dire necessity, become involved in crimes that their souls abhor?

It is the contemplation of the peaceful virtues in the genial atmosphere of private life, that can best reconcile us to our nature, and quiet the turbulent emotions excited by

"The madness of the crowd."

But vice, folly, and vanity are so noisy, so restless, so ready to rush into public view, and so adapted to afford food for malevolent curiosity, that the small still voice of virtue, active in its own sphere, but unwilling to quit it, is drowned in their tumult. This is a remedy, however,

"Not obvious, not obtrusive."

If we would counteract the baleful influence of public vice by the contemplation of private worth, we must penetrate into its retreats, and not be deterred from attending to its simple details by the want of that glare and bustle with which a fictitious or artificial character is generally surrounded.

But in this wide field of speculation one might wander out of sight of the original subject. Let me then resume it, and return to my objections. Of these the first and greatest is the dread of being inaccurate. Embellished facts, a mixture of truth and fiction, or what we sometimes meet with, a fictitious superstructure built on a foundation of reality, would be detestable on the score of bad taste, though no moral sense were concerned or consulted. 'T is walking on a river half frozen that betrays your footing every moment. By these repulsive artifices no person of real discernment is for a moment imposed upon. You do not know exactly which part of the narrative is false; but you are sure it is not all true, and therefore distrust what is genuine, where it occurs. For this reason a fiction, happily told, takes a greater hold of the mind than a narrative of facts, evidently embellished and interwoven with inventions.

I do not mean to discredit my own veracity. I certainly have no intention to relate anything that is not true. Yet in the dim distance of near forty years,[1] unassisted by written memorials, shall I not mistake dates, misplace facts, and omit circumstances that form essential links in the chain of narration? Thirty years since, when I expressed a wish to do what I am now about to attempt, how differently should I have executed it. A warm heart, a vivid imagination, and a tenacious memory, were then all filled with a theme which I could not touch without kindling into an enthusiasm, sacred at once to virtue and to friendship. Venerated friend of my youth, my guide, and my instructress, are then the dregs of an enfeebled mind, the worn affections of a wounded heart, the imperfect efforts of a decaying

[1] It will have been seen by the Memoir that Mrs. Grant was born in 1755, came to America in 1757, and returned to Scotland in 1768, at the age of 13; and that she wrote this work in 1808, at the age of 53.

memory, all that remain to consecrate thy remembrance, to make known thy worth, and to lay on thy tomb the offering of gratitude?

My friend's life, besides being mostly passed in unruffled peace and prosperity, affords few of those vicissitudes which astonish and amuse. It is from her relations, to those with whom her active benevolence connected her, that the chief interest of her story (if story it may be called) arises. This includes that of many persons, obscure indeed but for the light which her regard and beneficence reflected upon them. Yet without those subordinate persons in the drama, the action of human life, especially such a life as hers, cannot be carried on. Those can neither appear with grace, nor be omitted with propriety. Then, remote and retired as her situation was, the variety of nations and characters, of tongues and of complexions, with which her public spirit and private benevolence connected her, might appear wonderful to those unacquainted with the country and the times in which she lived; without a pretty distinct view of which my narrative would be unintelligible. I must be excused, too, for dwelling, at times, on the recollection of a state of society so peculiar, so utterly dissimilar to any other that I have heard, or read of, that it exhibits human nature in a new aspect, and is so far an object of rational curiosity, as well as a kind of phenomenon in the history of colonization. I forewarn the reader not to look for lucid order in the narration, or intimate connection between its parts. I have no authorities to refer to, no coeval witnesses of facts to consult. In regard to the companions of my youth, I sit like the "Voice of Cona," alone on the heath; and, like him too, must muse in silence, till at intervals the "light of my soul arises," before I can call attention to "a tale of other times," in which several particulars relative to my friend's ancestry must necessarily be included.

Chapter I

ORIGIN OF THE SETTLEMENT OF ALBANY

IT is well known that the province of New York, anciently called Munhattoes[1] by the Indians, was originally settled by a Dutch colony, which came from Holland, I think, in the time of Charles the Second. Finding the country to their liking, they were followed by others more wealthy and better informed. Indeed some of the early emigrants appear to have been people respectable both from their family and character. Of these the principal were the Cuylers, the Schuylers, the Rensselaers, the DeLanceys, the Cortlandts, the Timbrooks,[2] and

---

[1] It is not designed to notice for the purpose of rectifying or explaining all the discrepancies of nomenclature, chronology, and other matters, which Mrs. Grant, as she fears on the previous page she might, has fallen into in these pages. Not a few of them were common to the time she describes, but more recent investigations and discoveries have gradually developed a more correct knowledge.

The island of Manhattan, we learn from the *Albany Records*, was so called after the ancient name of the tribe of savages among whom the Dutch first settled themselves, but the appellation did not extend to the province.

[2] Dirk Wesselse Ten Broeck, the first of the name mentioned in the records, was known in public life as Dirk Wessels. He was the first acting Recorder under the charter of Albany, mayor 1696-97, and for many years a leading man in the colony. He died in 1717. His grandson, Dirk Ten Broeck, was mayor 1746-47, Abraham, a son of the last, was mayor 1779-83, and again 1796-98, and a general

the Beekmans, who have all of them been since distinguished in the late civil wars, either as persecuted loyalists or triumphant patriots. I do not precisely recollect the motives assigned for the voluntary exile of persons who were evidently in circumstances that might admit of their living in comfort at home, but am apt to think that the early settlers were those who adhered to the interest of the stadtholder's family, a party which, during the minority of King William, was almost persecuted by the high republicans. They who came over at a later period probably belonged to the party which opposed the stadtholder, and which was then in its turn depressed. These persons afterwards distinguished themselves by an aversion, almost amounting to antipathy, to the British army, and indeed to all the British colonists. Their notions were mean and contracted; their manners blunt and austere; and their habits sordid and parsimonious; as the settlement began to extend they retired, and formed new establishments, afterwards called Fishkill, Esopus, etc.

To the Schuylers, Cuylers, DeLanceys, Van Cortlandts, and a few others, this description did by no means apply. Yet they too bore about them the tokens of former affluence and respectability, such as family plate, portraits of their ancestors executed in a superior style, and great numbers of original paint-

of brigade in the Revolutionary War. His wife was Elizabeth, the only daughter of the sixth patroon of Rensselaerwyck, and aunt of the last, Patroon Stephen Van Rensselaer.

ings, some of which were much admired by acknowledged judges. Of these the subjects were generally taken from sacred history.

I do not recollect the exact time, but think it was during the last years of Charles the Second, that a settlement we then possessed at Surinam was exchanged for the extensive (indeed at that time boundless) province of Munhattoes,[1] which, in compliment to the then heir apparent, was called New York. Of the part of that country then explored, the most fertile and beautiful was situated far inland, on the banks of the Hudson river. This copious and majestic stream is navigable one hundred and seventy miles from its mouth for vessels of sixty or seventy tons burden.[2] Near the head of it, as a kind of barrier against the natives, and a central resort for traders, the foundation was laid of a town called

[1] Surinam was awarded to the Dutch at the peace of Westminster, after various reverses, while New York, for which it was exchanged, remained quietly in the hands of the English. The two nations however continued for more than a century to make Guiana a point of attack in time of war.

[2] The tonnage of the ancient sloops has been somewhat increased. The sloop in which Capt. Stewart Dean sailed from Albany to China in 1785, was 80 tons. The government made improvements in the navigation of the river after Albany became a port of entry, so that schooners of 200 tons were enabled to reach the city, and the Rochester steam boat, the largest vessel licensed at this port in 1836, of nearly 500 tons, made trips at low water. At a later day the Isaac Newton of 1400 tons was put on the river, and renewed efforts to increase the upward flow of the tide, in 1866, added nearly two feet to the surface. The altitude of Albany being but six or eight feet above that of New York, there are at all times three tides in the river, so great is the distance they have to ascend before reaching their utmost limit.

Oranienburgh,[1] and afterwards, by the British, Albany.

After the necessary precaution of erecting a small stockaded fort for security, a church was built in the centre of the intended town, which served in different respects as a kind of land-mark. A gentleman of the name of Van Rensselaer was considered as in a manner lord paramount of this city, a pre-eminence which his successor still enjoys, both with regard to the town and the lands adjacent. The original proprietor having obtained from the high and mighty states a grant of lands, which, beginning at the church, was twenty-four by forty-eight miles in size, forming a magnificent manor, including lands not only of the best quality of any in the province, but the most happily situated both for the purpose of commerce and agriculture. This great proprietor was looked up to as much as republicans in a new country could be supposed to look up to any one. He was called the patroon, a designation tantamount to lord of the manor. Yet in the distribution of these lands, the sturdy Belgian spirit of independence set limits to the power and profits of this lord of the forests, as he might then be called. None of these lands were either sold or alienated. The more wealthy settlers, as the

[1] It does not appear what name the Dutch may have given the locality. It was often alluded to as the Fuyck. Oranje is Dutch, but Fort Orange is English. I have not seen it elsewhere called Oranienburgh, although that would be a proper name — the city or fortress of Orange.

Schuylers,[1] Cuylers, etc., took very extensive leases of the fertile plains along the river, with boundless liberty of woods and pasturage, to the westward. The terms were, that the lease should hold while water runs and grass grows, and the landlord to receive the tenth sheaf of every kind of grain the ground produces. Thus ever accommodating the rent to the fertility of the soil, and changes of the seasons, you may suppose the tenants did not greatly fear a landlord, who could neither remove them, nor heighten their rents. Thus, without the pride of property, they had all the independence of proprietors. They were like German princes, who, after furnishing their contingent to the emperor, might make war on him when they chose. Besides the profits (yearly augmenting) which the patroon drew from his ample possessions, he held in his own hands an extensive and fruitful demesne. Yet preserving in a great measure the simple and frugal habits of his ancestors, his wealth was not an object of envy, nor a source of corruption to his fellow-citizens. To the northward of these bounds, and at the southern extremity also, the Schuylers and Cuylers held lands of their own. But the only other great landholders I remember, holding their land by those original tenures, were Phillips

---

[1] Philip (Pietersen) Schuyler bought his farm of several hundred acres and a large island about four miles north of Albany at a cost of 8,000 florins; and in recognition of the patroon's right he gave 40 bushels of wheat yearly.

and Cortlandt; their lands lay also on the Hudson's river, half way down to New York, and were denominated Phillip's and Cortlandt's manors.[1] At the time of the first settling of the country the Indians were numerous and powerful all along the river; but they consisted of wandering families, who, though they affixed some sort of local boundaries for distinguishing the hunting grounds of each tribe, could not be said to inhabit any place. The cool and crafty Dutch governors, being unable to cope with them in arms, purchased from them the most valuable tracts for some petty consideration. They affected great friendship for them; and, while conscious of their own weakness, were careful not to provoke hostilities; and they, silently and insensibly, established themselves to the west.

[1] Philipse, or Philipsen, a carpenter by trade, who founded a wealthy Dutch family. In 1674 a valuation of the estates of the principal inhabitants of New York was made, when that of Frederick Philipsen, the highest, was valued at 80,000 florins. A portion of this manor was sequestered by reason of the defection of the owner in the Revolution, who fled to England, and was allowed by that government about three hundred thousand dollars as compensation for his loss. The whole of the original property was at a later day estimated at over three millions of dollars. The Van Cortlandt manor is still in a measure intact, and known as such.

Chapter II

THE FIVE NATIONS — JOHN AND PHILIP SCHUYLER

ON the Mohawk river, about forty miles distant from Albany, there subsisted a confederacy of Indian tribes, of a very different character from those mentioned in the preceding chapter; too sagacious to be deceived, and too powerful to be eradicated. These were the once renowned Five Nations, whom any one, who remembers them while they were a people, will hesitate to call savages. Were *they* savages who had fixed habitations; who cultivated rich fields; who built castles (for so they called their not incommodious wooden houses, surrounded with palisadoes); who planted maize and beans, and showed considerable ingenuity in constructing and adorning their canoes, arms, and clothing? They who had wise though unwritten laws, and conducted their wars, treaties, and alliances with deep and sound policy; they whose eloquence was bold, nervous, and animated; whose language was sonorous, musical, and expressive; who possessed generous and elevated sentiments, heroic fortitude, and unstained probity: were these indeed savages? The difference

> " Of scent the headlong lioness between
> And hound sagacious, on the tainted green,"

is not greater than that of the Mohawks in point of civility and capacity, from other American tribes, among whom, indeed, existed a far greater diversity of character, language, etc., than Europeans seem to be aware of. This little tribute to the memory of a people who have been, while it soothes the pensive recollections of the writer, is not so foreign to the subject as it may at first appear. So much of the peace and safety of this infant community depended on the friendship and alliance of these generous tribes, and to conciliate and retain their affections so much address was necessary, that common characters were unequal to the task. Minds liberal and upright, like those I am about to describe, could alone excite that esteem, and preserve that confidence, which were essential towards retaining the friendship of those valuable allies.

From the time of the great rebellion, so many English refugees frequented Holland, that the language and manners of our country became familiar at the Hague, particularly among the stadtholder's party. When the province of New York fell under the British dominion, it became necessary that everybody should learn our language, as all public business was carried on in the English tongue, which they did the more willingly, as, after the revolution, the accession of the stadtholder to the English crown very much reconciled them to our government; still, however, the English was a kind of court language, little spoken, and imperfectly understood in the interior. Those who brought with them the French and English languages soon acquired a sway over their less enlightened fellow settlers. Of this number were the Schuylers and Cuylers, two families among whom intellect of the superior kind seemed an inheritance, and whose intelligence and liberality of mind, fortified by well-grounded principle, carried them far beyond the petty and narrow views of the rest. Habituated at home to centre all wisdom and all happiness in commercial advantages, they would have been very ill calculated to lay the foundation of an infant state in a country that afforded plenty and content, as the reward of industry, but where the very nature of the territory, as well as the state of society, precluded great pecuniary acquisitions. Their object here was taming savage nature, and making the boundless wild subservient to agricultural purposes. Commercial pursuits were a distant prospect; and before they became of consequence, rural habits had greatly changed the character of these republicans. But the commercial spirit, inherent in all true Batavians, only slept to wake again, when the avidity of gain was called forth by the temptation of bartering for any lucrative commodity. The furs of the Indians gave this occasion, and were too soon made the object of the avidity of petty traders. To the infant settlement at Albany the consequences of this short-sighted policy might have proved fatal, had not these patriotic leaders, by their example and influence, checked for a while such illiberal and dangerous practices. It is a fact singular and worth attending to, from the lesson it exhibits, that in all our distant colonies there is no other instance where a considerable town and prosperous settlement has arisen and flourished, in peace and safety, in the midst of nations disposed and often provoked to hostility: at a distance from the protection of ships, and from the only fortified city, which, always weakly garrisoned, was little fitted to awe and protect the whole province. Let it be remembered that the distance from New York to Albany is 160 miles; and that in the intermediate space, at the period of which I speak, there was not one town or fortified place. The shadow of a palisadoed fort[1] which then existed in Albany, was occupied by a single independent company, who did duty, but were dispersed through the town, working at various trades; so scarce indeed were artizans in this community, that a tradesman might in these days ask any wages he chose.

To return to this settlement, which evidently owed its security to the wisdom of its leaders, who always acted on the simple maxim that honesty is the best policy; several miles north from Albany a considerable possession, called the Flats, was inhabited by

[1] It may be worth noting that Captain Massey, who commanded this noneffective company for many years, was the father of Mrs. Lenox, an inestimable character, well known for her literary productions, and for being the friend and protégée of Doctor Johnson. — *Mrs. Grant.*

Colonel Philip Schuyler,[1] one of the most enlightened men in the province. This being a frontier, he would have found it a very dangerous situation had he not been a person of singular worth, fortitude, and wisdom. Were I not afraid of tiring my reader with a detail of occurrences which, taking place before the birth of my friend, might seem irrelevant to the present purpose, I could relate many instances almost incredible, of the power of mind displayed by this gentleman in governing the uninstructed without coercion or legal right. He possessed this species of power in no common degree; his influence, with that of his brother John Schuyler,[2] was exerted to conciliate the wandering tribes of Indians; and by fair traffic, for he too was a trader, and by fair liberal dealing, they attained their object. They also strengthened the league already formed with the five Mohawk nations, by procuring for them some assistance against their enemies, the Onondagoes of the lakes.[3]

[1] Col. Philip Schuyler, the husband of the American Lady, died about four years before Mrs. Grant, then a young girl, became acquainted with her. She doubtless heard the name Philip repeated often, and that of Col. Peter Schuyler who had died more than thirty years before, comparatively seldom. Philip had become fixed in her memory, and she sometimes uses it erroneously instead of Peter, as in this instance. It is clear from what follows agreeing with historical facts, that Col. Peter Schuyler is meant.

[2] John Schuyler was the youngest son of Philip Schuyler, the ancestor of one branch of the Schuyler family. He was the father of the American Lady, and the grandfather of General Philip Schuyler of the Revolution.

[3] The Iroquois, or Five Nations, consisted of the Mohawks,

Queen Anne had by this time succeeded to the stadtholder. The gigantic ambition of Louis the Fourteenth actuated the remotest parts of his extensive dominions; and the encroaching spirit of this restless nation began to discover itself in hostilities to the infant colony. A motive for which could scarce be discovered, possessing as they did already much more territory than they were able to occupy, the limits of which were undefined.[1] But the province of New York was a frontier; and, as such, a kind of barrier to the southern colonies. It began also to compete for a share of the fur trade, then very considerable, before the beavers were driven back from their original haunts. In short, the province daily rose in importance; and being in a great measure protected by the Mohawk tribes, the policy of courting their alliance, and impressing their minds with an exalted idea of the power and grandeur of the British empire, became obvious. I

Oneidas, Onondagas, Cayugas, and Senecas. It was probably the Hurons that Mrs. Grant had in mind as the antagonists of the New York Indians.

[1] The boundaries of farms and tracts were quite indefinite, and as they became cultivated all traces of the described bounds utterly ceased to be distinguishable. For instance, a farm now in the heart of the city of Albany, leased by the patroon to Isaac Casparse (that was Isaac the son of Caspar Halenbeck), is thus described in the lease: bounded on the north by the plain and the hill, on the east by the swamp, on the south by the Bever kil, and on the west by the woods. Nothing now remains but the creek to mark the boundaries of this tract, and that is arched over and used as a sewer. The hill was long since leveled, the swamp filled in and built upon, and the woods cleared up, and the area occupied by streets and a dense population.

cannot recollect the name of the governor at this time; but whoever he was, he, as well as the succeeding ones, visited the settlement at Albany, to observe its wise regulations, and growing prosperity, and to learn maxims of sound policy from those whose interests and happiness were daily promoted by the practice of it.

Chapter III

COLONEL SCHUYLER AND FIVE SACHEMS VISIT ENGLAND — THEIR RECEPTION AND RETURN

IT was thought advisable to bring over some of the heads of the tribes to England to attach them to that country : but to persuade the chiefs of a free and happy people, who were intelligent, sagacious, and aware of all probable dangers; who were strangers to all the maritime concerns, and had never beheld the ocean; to persuade such independent and high-minded warriors to forsake the safety and enjoyments of their own country, to encounter the perils of a long voyage, and trust themselves among entire strangers, and this merely to bind closer an alliance with the sovereign of a distant country — a female sovereign too ; a mode of government that must have appeared to them very incongruous ; this was no common undertaking, nor was it easy to induce these chiefs to accede to the proposal. The principal motive for urging it was to counteract the machinations of the French, whose emissaries in these wild regions had even then begun to style us, in effect, a nation of shop-keepers; and to impress the tribes dwelling in their boundaries with vast ideas of the power and

AN AMERICAN LADY

splendor of their *grand monarque,* while our sovereign, they said, ruled over a petty island, and was himself a trader. To counterwork those suggestions, it was thought requisite to give the leaders of the nation an adequate idea of our power, and the magnificence of our court. The chiefs at length consented, on this only condition, that their brother Philip,[1] who never told a lie, or spoke without thinking, should accompany them. However this gentleman's wisdom and integrity might qualify him for this employment, it by no means suited his placid temper, simple manners, and habits of life, at

---

[1] This event happening nearly half a century before Mrs. Grant was born, and nearly a century before this work was written, "unassisted by written memorials," the mistake of the name of Philip for Pieter is pardonable. It was Pieter, however, the eldest son of Philip, who figured in this episode. He was the first mayor of Albany in 1686, and twenty-four years later, in 1710, conducted these natives to England, arriving there in the time of Queen Anne and the *Spectator.* On this occasion his full length portrait was painted, and is still preserved among his descendants at the Flats, an engraving of which is here given, and some pleasant allusions are made to the event in the *Spectator* of that time.

Portrait of Col. Pieter Schuyler, painted in England, 1710.

once pastoral and patriarchal, to travel over seas, visit courts, and mingle in the bustle of a world, the customs of which were become foreign to those primitive inhabitants of new and remote regions. The adventure, however, succeeded beyond his expectation; the chiefs were pleased with the attention paid them, and with the mild and gracious manners of the queen, who at different times admitted them to her presence. With the good Philip she had many conversations, and made him some valuable presents, among which, I think, was her picture; but this with many others was lost, in a manner which will appear hereafter. Colonel Schuyler too was much delighted with the courteous affability of this princess; she offered to knight him, which he respectfully, but positively refused: and being pressed to assign his reasons, he said he had brothers and near relations in humble circumstances, who, already his inferiors in property, would seem as it were depressed by his elevation: and though it should have no such effect on his mind, it might be the means of awakening pride or vanity in the female part of his family. He returned, however, in triumph, having completely succeeded in his mission. The kings, as they were called in England, came back in full health, deeply impressed with esteem and attachment for a country which to them appeared the centre of arts, intelligence and wisdom; where they were treated with kindness and respect; and neither made the objects of perpetual exhibition,

AN AMERICAN LADY

nor hurried about to be continually distracted with a succession of splendid, and to them incomprehensible sights, the quick shifting of which rather tends to harass minds which have enough of native strength to reflect on what they see, without knowledge sufficient to comprehend it. It is to this childish and injudicious mode of treating those uncivilized beings, this mode of rather extorting from them a tribute to our vanity, than taking the necessary pains to inform and improve them, that the ill success of all such experiments since have been owing. Instead of endeavoring to conciliate them by genuine kindness, and by gradually and gently unfolding to them simple and useful truths, our manner of treating them seems calculated to dazzle, oppress and degrade them with a display of our superior luxuries and refinements: which, by the elevated and selfdenied Mohawk, would be regarded as unmanly and frivolous objects, and which the voluptuous and low-minded Otaheitean would so far relish, that the privation would seem intolerable, when he returned to his hogs and his cocoas. Except such as have been previously inoculated (a precaution which voyagers have rarely had the prudence or humanity to take), there is scarcely an instance of savages brought to Europe that have not died of the small-pox; induced either by the infection to which they are exposed from the indiscriminate crowds drawn about them or the alteration in their blood, which unusual diet, liquors, close air, and heated rooms, must necessarily produce.

The presents made to these adventurous warriors were judiciously adapted to their taste and customs. They consisted of showy habits, of which all these people are very fond, and arms made purposely in the form of those used in their own country. It was the fortune of the writer of these memoirs, more than thirty years after, to see that great warrior and faithful ally of the British crown the redoubted King Hendrick, then sovereign of the Five Nations, splendidly arrayed in a suit of light blue, made in an antique mode, and trimmed with broad silver lace ; which was probably an heirloom, in the family, presented to his father by his good ally, and sister, the female king of England.[1]

King Hendrick.

[1] King Hendrick, born 1680, killed 1755 at the battle of Lake George, as is well known, was not sovereign of the Five Nations, but was a chief of the Mohawk nation, who had been invested with the title of king, an unusual term for a leader among the Indians. Possibly it was another warrior similarly accoutered that Mrs. Grant saw at a later day ; for although King Hendrick returned with such a costume, and his portrait was painted in it in England during his visit, he had been a short time dead when Mrs. Grant arrived in the country.

AN AMERICAN LADY

I cannot exactly say how long Colonel Schuyler and his companions staid in England, but think they were nearly a year absent.[1] In those primeval days of the settlement, when our present rapid modes of transmitting intelligence were unknown, in a country so detached and inland as that at Albany, the return of these interesting travellers was like the first lighting of lamps in a city.

[1] These sachems or chiefs were all of the Mohawk nation, representing all of the Five Nations. They sailed for England in December, 1709, and had their first audience of Queen Anne on the 19th of the following April. On their stormy passage across the Atlantic one of them died, whence Mrs. Grant speaks of them as four in number. They left England on board a man-of-war, May 8, and arrived in Boston, Mass., July 15, 1710.

Chapter IV

COLONEL SCHUYLER AND THE SACHEMS — LITERARY ACQUISITIONS — MANNERS OF THE SETTLERS

THIS sagacious and intelligent patriot thus brought to the foot of the British throne, the high spirited rulers of the boundless wild, who, alike heedless of the power and splendor of distant monarchs, were accustomed to say, with Fingal, " sufficient for me is the desart, with all deer and woods." It may easily be supposed that such a mind as Philip's was equally fitted to acquire and communicate intelligence. He who had conversed with Addison, Marlborough, and Godolphin, who had gratified the curiosity of Oxford and Bolingbroke, of Arbuthnot and of Gay, with accounts of nature in her pristine garb, and of her children in their primitive simplicity; he who could do all this, no doubt received ample returns of various information from those best qualified to give it, and was besides a diligent observer. Here he improved a taste for literature, native to him, for it had not yet taken root in this uncultivated soil. He brought home the Spectator and the tragedy of Cato, Windsor Forest, Young's poem on the Last Day, and in short all the works then published of that constellation of wits which distinguished the last female reign. Nay more, and better, he brought Paradise Lost; which in after-times afforded such delight to some branches of his family, that to them

"Paradise, indeed, seemed opened in the wild."

But to return to our sachems, from whom we have too long digressed: when they arrived at Albany, they did not, as might be expected, hasten home to communicate their discoveries, or display their acquisitions. They summoned a congress there, not only of the elders of their own nation, but the chiefs of all those with whom they were in alliance. This solemn meeting was held in the Dutch church. In the present depressed and diminished state of these once powerful tribes, so few traces of their wonted energy remain, that it could scarce be credited, were I able to relate with what bold and flowing eloquence they clothed their conceptions; powerful reasoning, emphatic language, and graceful action, added force to their arguments, while they persuaded their adherents to renounce all connection with the tribes under the French influence; and form a lasting league, offensive and defensive, with that great queen whose mild majesty had so deeply impressed them: and the mighty people whose kindness had gratified, and whose power had astonished them, whose populous cities swarmed with arts and commerce, and in whose floating castles they had rode safely over the ocean.

I have seen a volume of the speeches of these Mohawks preserved by Colonel Schuyler; they were literally translated, so that the native idiom was preserved; which instead of appearing uncouth, seemed to add to their strength and sublimity.

When Colonel Schuyler returned from England, about the year 1709, his niece Catalina,[1] the subject of this narrative, was about seven years old; he had a daughter and sons, yet this child was early distinguished above the rest for docility, a great desire of knowledge, and an even and pleasing temper; this her uncle early observed. It was at that time very difficult to procure the means of instruction in those inland districts; female education of consequence was conducted on a very limited scale; girls learnt needlework (in which they were indeed both skilful and ingenious) from their mothers and aunts; they were taught too at that period to read, in Dutch, the Bible and a few Calvinist tracts of the

[1] Catalina was the youngest daughter of Capt. Johannes Schuyler, born March 5, 1704. Capt. Johannes was the youngest son of Philip Pietersen, and is noted for having led a successful expedition into Canada in 1690, at the age of 22. He was mayor of Albany 1703–6, and died July 27, 1747. His house on State Street, corner of South Pearl, built 1667, when recently taken down, was the oldest house in Albany. Catalyntje, as she was called, married Cornelis Cuyler, who was for a long time alderman of the second ward, and was mayor in 1742, to 1746, instead of Cornelis Schuyler, as is mentioned in some of the printed tables of the mayors. She was the younger sister of Madame Schuyler, the heroine of this work, who was Margaretta, born January 12, 1701. Papers bearing her signature are in existence, in which she signed her name *Margrita*, and tradition corroborates her identity as the daughter of Johannes Schuyler.

devotional kind. But in the infancy of the settlement few girls read English; when they did, they were thought accomplished; they generally spoke it, however, imperfectly, and few were taught writing. This confined education precluded elegance; yet, though there was no polish, there was no vulgarity. The dregs of the people, who subside to the bottom of the mass, are not only degraded by abject poverty, but so utterly shut out from intercourse with the more enlightened, and so rankled with envy at feeling themselves so, that a sense of their condition gradually debases their minds; and this degradation communicates to their manners, the vulgarity of which we complain. This more particularly applies to the lower class in towns, for mere simplicity, or even a rustic bluntness, I would by no means call vulgarity. At the same time these unembellished females had more comprehension of mind, more variety of ideas, more in short of what may be called original thinking, than could easily be imagined. Their thoughts were not like those of other illiterate women, occupied by the ordinary details of the day, and the gossiping tattle of the neighborhood. The life of new settlers, in a situation like this, where the very foundations of society were to be laid, was a life of exigencies. Every individual took an interest in the general welfare, and contributed their respective shares of intelligence and sagacity to aid plans that embraced important objects relative to the common good.

Every day called forth some new expedient, in which the comfort or advantage of the whole was implicated; for there were no degrees but those assigned to worth and intellect. This singular community seemed to have a common stock, not only of sufferings and enjoyments, but of information and ideas; some pre-eminence, in point of knowledge and abilities, there certainly was, yet those who possessed it seemed scarcely conscious of their superiority; the daily occasions which called forth the exertions of mind, sharpened sagacity, and strengthened character; avarice and vanity were there confined to very narrow limits; of money there was little; and dress was, though in some instances valuable, very plain, and not subject to the caprice of fashion. The wolves, the bears, and the enraged or intoxicated savages, that always hung threatening on their boundaries, made them more and more endeared to each other. In this calm infancy of society, the rigors of law slept, because the fury of turbulent passions, had not awakened it. Fashion, that capricious tyrant over adult communities, had not erected her standard; that standard to which the looks, the language, the very opinions of her subjects must be adjusted. Yet no person appeared uncouth, or ill bred, because there was no accomplished standard of comparison. They viewed no superior with fear or envy; and treated no inferior with contempt or cruelty; servility and insolence were thus equally unknown; perhaps they were less solicitous either to please or to shine than the members of more polished societies; because, in the first place they had no motive either to dazzle or deceive; and in the next, had they attempted it, they felt there was no assuming a character with success, where their native one was so well known. Their manners, if not elegant and polished, were at least easy and independent: the constant efforts necessary to extend their commercial and agricultural possessions prevented indolence; and industry was the certain path to plenty. Surrounded on all sides by those whom the least instance of fraud, insolence, or grasping meanness, would have rendered irreconcilable enemies, they were at first obliged to "assume a virtue if they had it not;" and every circumstance that renders virtue habitual, may be accounted a happy one. I may be told that the virtues I describe were chiefly those of situation. I acknowledge it. It is no more to be expected that this equality, simplicity, and moderation, should continue in a more advanced state of society, than that the sublime tranquillity, and dewy freshness, which adds a nameless charm to the face of nature, in the dawn of a summer's morning, should continue all day. Before increased wealth and extended territory these "wassel days" quickly receded; yet it is pleasing to indulge the remembrance of a spot, where peace and felicity, the result of a moral excellence, dwelt undisturbed, for, alas! hardly for a century.

Chapter V

STATE OF RELIGION AMONG THE SETTLERS—
SKETCH OF THE STATE OF SOCIETY AT NEW
YORK

I MUST finish this general outline, by saying something of that religion which gave stability and effect to the virtues of this infant society. Their religion, then, like their original national character, had in it little of fervor or enthusiasm: their manner of performing religious duties was regular and decent, but calm, and to more ardent imaginations might appear mechanical. None ever doubted of the great truths of revelation, yet few seemed to dwell on the result with that lively delight which devotion produces in minds of keener sensibility. If their piety, however, was without enthusiasm, it was also without bigotry; they wished others to think as they did, without showing rancor or contempt towards those who did not. In many individuals, whose lives seemed governed by the principles of religion, the spirit of devotion seemed to be quiescent in the heart, and to break forth in exigencies; yet that monster in nature, an impious woman, was never heard of among them.

Indeed it was on the females that the task of religious instruction generally devolved; and in all cases where the heart is interested, whoever teaches, at the same time learns.

Before I quit this subject, I must observe a singular coincidence; not only the training of children but of plants, such as needed peculiar care or skill to rear them, was the female province. Every one in town or country had a garden; but all the more hardy plants grew in the field, in rows, amidst the hills, as they were called, of Indian corn. These lofty plants sheltered them from the sun, while the same hoeing served for both; there cabbages, potatoes, and other esculent roots, with variety of gourds grew to a great size, and were of an excellent quality. Kidney-beans, asparagus, celery, great variety of salads and sweet herbs, cucumbers, etc., were only admitted into the garden, into which no foot of man intruded after it was dug in spring. Here were no trees, those grew in the orchard in high perfection; strawberries and many high flavored wild fruits of the shrub kind abounded so much in the woods, that they did not think of cultivating them in their gardens, which were extremely neat but small, and not by any means calculated for walking in. I think I yet see what I have so often beheld both in town and country, a respectable mistress of a family going out to her garden, in an April morning, with her great calash, her little painted basket of seeds, and her rake over her shoulder, to her garden labors. These were by no means figurative,

"From morn till noon, from noon till dewy eve."

A woman in very easy circumstances, and abundantly gentle in form and manners, would sow, and plant, and rake incessantly. These fair gardeners too were great florists: their emulation and solicitude in this pleasing employment, did indeed produce "flowers worthy of Paradise." These, though not set in "curious knots," were ranged in beds, the varieties of each kind by themselves; this, if not varied and elegant, was at least rich and gay. To the Schuylers this description did not apply; they had gardeners, and their gardens were laid out in the European manner.

Perhaps I should reserve my description of the manner of living in that country for that period, when, by the exertions of a few humane and enlightened individuals, it assumed a more regular and determinate form. Yet as the same outline was preserved through all the stages of its progression, I know not but that it may be the best to sketch it entirely, before I go further; that the few and simple facts which my narrative affords may not be clogged by explanations relative to the customs, or any other peculiarities which can only be understood by a previous acquaintance with the nature of the country, its political relations, and the manners of the people: my recollection all this while has been merely confined to Albany and its precincts. At New York there was always a governor, a few troops, and a kind of a little court kept; there too was a mixed, and in some degree, polished society. To this the accession of many families of French hugonots,[1] rather above the middling rank, contributed not a little: those conscientious exiles had more knowledge and piety than any other class of the inhabitants; their religion seemed indeed endeared to them by what they had suffered for adhering to it. Their number and wealth was such, as enabled them to build not only a street, but a very respectable church in the new city. In this place of worship service continued to be celebrated in the French language within my recollection, though the original congregation was by that time much blended in the mass of general society. It was the custom of the inhabitants of the upper settlement, who had any pretensions to superior culture or polish, among which number Col. Schuyler stood foremost, to go once in a year to New York, where all the lawcourts were held, and all the important business of the province transacted, here too they sent their children occasionally to reside with their relations, and to learn the more polished manners and language of the capital. The inhabitants of that city, on the

[1] Properly so written perhaps, because derived from Hugon, or Hugo, a heretic or conspirator, a term finally given to the French protestants of the sixteenth century, and now come to be written Huguenots.

other hand, delighted in a summer excursion to Albany. The beautiful and in some places highly singular banks of the river, rendering a voyage to its source both amusing and interesting, while the primitive manners of the inhabitants diverted the gay and idle, and pleased the thoughtful and speculative.

Let me now be indulged in drawing a picture of the abode of my childhood just as, at this time, it presents itself to my mind.

Chapter VI

DESCRIPTION OF ALBANY—MANNER OF LIVING THERE

THE city of Albany was stretched along the banks of the Hudson; one very wide and long street lay parallel to the river, the intermediate space between it and the shore being occupied by gardens. A small but steep hill rose above the centre of the town, on which stood a fort, intended (but very ill adapted) for the defense of the place, and of the neighboring country. From the foot of this hill, another street was built, sloping pretty rapidly down till it joined the one before mentioned that ran along the river. This street was still wider than the other; it was only paved on each side, the middle being occupied by public edifices. These consisted of a market place, a guard house, a town hall, and the English and Dutch churches. The English church, belonging to the episcopal persuasion, and in the diocese of the bishop of London, stood at the foot of the hill, at the upper end of the street. The Dutch church was situated at the bottom of the descent where the street terminated; two irregular streets, not so broad, but equally long, ran parallel to those, and a few even ones opened between them.

The town, in proportion to its population, occupied a great space of ground. This city, in short, was a kind of semi-rural establishment; every house had its garden, well, and a little green behind; before every door a tree was planted, rendered interesting by being coeval with some beloved member of the family; many of their trees were of a prodigious size and extraordinary beauty, but without regularity, every one planting the kind that best pleased him, or which he thought would afford the most agreeable shade to the open portico at his door which was surrounded by seats, and ascended by a few steps. It was in these that each domestic group was seated in summer evenings to enjoy the balmy twilight, or serenely clear moonlight. Each family had a cow, fed in a common pasture at the end of the town. In the evening they returned all together, of their own accord, with their tinkling bells hung at their necks, along the wide and grassy street, to their wonted sheltering trees, to be milked at their master's doors. Nothing could be more pleasing to a simple and benevolent mind than to see thus, at one view, all the inhabitants of a town, which contained not one very rich or very poor, very knowing or very ignorant, very rude or very polished individual; to see all these children of nature enjoying in easy indolence, or social intercourse,

"The cool, the fragrant, and the *dusky* hour,"

clothed in the plainest habits, and with minds as undisguised and artless. These primitive beings were dispersed in porches grouped according to similarity of years and inclinations. At one door young matrons, at another the elders of the people, at a third the youths and maidens, gaily chatting or singing together, while the children played round the trees, or waited by the cows, for the chief ingredient of their frugal supper, which they generally ate sitting on the steps in the open air. This picture, so familiar to my imagination, has led me away from my purpose, which was to describe the rural economy, and modes of living in this patriarchal city. At one end of the town, as I observed before, was a common pasture where all the cattle belonging to the inhabitants grazed together. A never-failing instinct guided each home to her master's door in the evening, there being treated with a few vegetables and a little salt, which is indispensably necessary for cattle in this country, they patiently waited the night; and after being milked in the morning, they went off in slow and regular procession to their pasture. At the other end of the town was a fertile plain along the river, three miles in length, and near a mile broad. This was all divided into lots, where every inhabitant raised Indian corn sufficient for the food of two or three slaves (the greatest number that each family ever possessed), and for his horses, pigs, and poultry: their flour and other grain they purchased from farmers in the vicinity. Above the town, a long stretch to the westward was occupied first by sandy hills, on which grew bilberries of uncommon size and flavor in prodigious quantities; beyond rise heights of a poor hungry soil, thinly covered with stunted pines, or dwarf oak. Yet in this comparatively barren tract, there were several wild and picturesque spots, where small brooks, running in deep and rich bottoms, nourished on their banks every vegetable beauty; there some of the most industrious early settlers had cleared the luxuriant wood from these charming little glens, and built neat cottages for their slaves, surrounded with little gardens and orchards, sheltered from every blast, wildly picturesque, and richly productive. Those small sequestered vales had an attraction that I know not how to describe, and which probably resulted from the air of deep repose that reigned there, and the strong contrast which they exhibited to the surrounding sterility. One of these was in my time inhabited by a hermit. He was a Frenchman, and did not seem to inspire much veneration among the Albanians. They imagined, or had heard, that he retired to that solitude in remorse for some fatal duel in which he had been engaged; and considered him as an idolator because he had an image of the virgin in his hut. I think he retired to Canada at last; but I remember being ready to worship him for the sanctity with which my imagination invested him, and being cruelly disappointed because I was not permitted to visit him. These cottages were in summer occupied by some of the negroes who cultivated the grounds about them, and served as a place of joyful liberty to the children of the family on holidays, and a nursery for the young negroes whom it was the custom to rear very tenderly, and instruct very carefully.

Chapter VII

GENTLE TREATMENT OF SLAVES AMONG THE ALBANIANS — REFLECTIONS ON SERVITUDE

IN the society I am describing, even the dark aspect of slavery was softened into a smile. And I must, in justice to the best possible masters, say, that a great deal of that tranquillity and comfort, to call it by no higher name, which distinguished this society from all others, was owing to the relation between master and servant being better understood here than in any other place. Let me not be detested as an advocate for slavery when I say that I think I have never seen people so happy in servitude as the domestics of the Albanians. One reason was (for I do not now speak of the virtues of their masters), that each family had few of them, and that there were no field negroes. They would remind one of Abraham's servants, who were all born in the house, which was exactly their case. They were baptized too, and shared the same religious instruction with the children of the family; and, for the first years, there was little or no difference with regard to food or clothing between their children and those of their masters.

When a negro-woman's child attained the age of three years, the first new year's day after, it was solemnly presented to a son or daughter, or other young relative of the family, who was of the same sex with the child so presented. The child to whom the young negro was given immediately presented it with some piece of money and a pair of shoes; and from that day the strongest attachment subsisted between the domestic and the destined owner. I have no where met with instances of friendship more tender and generous than that which here subsisted between the slaves and their masters and mistresses. Extraordinary proofs of them have been often given in the course of hunting or Indian trading, when a young man and his slave have gone to the trackless woods together, in the case of fits of the ague, loss of a canoe, and other casualties happening near hostile Indians. The slave has been known, at the imminent risk of his life, to carry his disabled master through trackless woods with labor and fidelity scarce credible; and the master has been equally tender on similar occasions of the humble friend who stuck closer than a brother; who was baptized with the same baptism, nurtured under the same roof, and often rocked in the same cradle with himself. These gifts of domestics to the younger members of the family, were not irrevocable: yet they were very rarely withdrawn. If the kitchen family did not increase in proportion to that of the master, young children were purchased from some family where they abounded, to furnish those attached servants to the rising progeny. They were never sold without consulting their mother, who, if expert and sagacious, had a great deal to say in the family, and would not allow her child to go into any family with whose domestics she was not acquainted. These negro-women piqued themselves on teaching their children to be excellent servants, well knowing servitude to be their lot for life, and that it could only be sweetened by making themselves particularly useful, and excelling in their department. If they did their work well, it is astonishing, when I recollect it, what liberty of speech was allowed to those active and prudent mothers. They would chide, reprove, and expostulate in a manner that we would not endure from our hired servants ; and sometimes exert fully as much authority over the children of the family as the parents, conscious that they were entirely in their power. They did not crush freedom of speech and opinion in those by whom they knew they were beloved, and who watched with incessant care over their interest and comfort. Affectionate and faithful as these home-bred servants were in general, there were some instances (but very few) of those who, through levity of mind, or a love of liquor or finery, betrayed their trust, or habitually neglected their duty. In these cases, after every means had been used to reform them, no severe punishments were inflicted at home. But the terrible sentence, which they

AN AMERICAN LADY 83

dreaded worse than death, was passed — they were sold to Jamaica. The necessity of doing this was bewailed by the whole family as a most dreadful calamity, and the culprit was carefully watched on his way to New York, lest he should evade the sentence by self-destruction.

One must have lived among those placid and humane people to be sensible that servitude, hopeless, endless servitude, could exist with so little servility and fear on the one side, and so little harshness or even sternness of authority on the other. In Europe, the footing on which service is placed in consequence of the corruptions of society, hardens the heart, destroys confidence, and embitters life. The deceit and venality of servants, not absolutely dishonest, puts it out of one's power to love or trust them. And if, in hopes of having people attached to us, who will neither betray our confidence, nor corrupt our children, we are at pains to rear them from childhood, and give them a religious and moral education; after all our labor, others of their own class seduce them away to those who can afford to pay higher for their services. This is not the case in a few remote districts. Where surrounding mountains seem to exclude the contagion of the world, some traces of fidelity and affection among domestics still remain. But it must be remarked, that, in those very districts, it is usual to treat inferiors with courtesy and kindness, and to consider those domestics who marry out of the family as holding a kind of relation to it, and still claiming protection. In short, the corruption of that class of people is, doubtless, to be attributed to the example of their superiors. But how severely are those superiors punished? Why this general indifference about home; why are the household gods, why is the sacred hearth so wantonly abandoned? Alas! the charm of home is destroyed, since our children, educated in distant seminaries, are strangers in the paternal mansion; and our servants, like mere machines, move on their mercenary track without feeling or exciting one kind or generous sentiment. Home, thus despoiled of all its charms, is no longer the scene of any enjoyment but such as wealth can purchase. At the same time we feel there a nameless cold privation, and conscious that money can coin the same enjoyments with more variety elsewhere, we substitute these futile and evanescent pleasures for that perennial spring of calm satisfaction, " without o'er flowing full," which is fed by the exercise of the kindly affections, and soon indeed must those stagnate where there are not proper objects to excite them. I have been forced into this painful digression by unavoidable comparisons. To return:

Amidst all this mild and really tender indulgence to their negroes, these colonists had not the smallest scruple of conscience with regard to the right by which they held them in subjection. Had that been the case, their singular humanity would have been incompatible with continued injustice. But the truth is, that of law the generality of those people knew little; and of philosophy, nothing at all. They sought their code of morality in the Bible, and there imagined they found this hapless race condemned to perpetual slavery; and thought nothing remained for them but to lighten the chains of their fellow Christians, after having made them such. This I neither "extenuate," nor "set down in malice," but merely record the fact. At the same time it is but justice to record also a singular instance of moral delicacy distinguishing this settlement from every other in the like circumstances: though from their simple and kindly modes of life, they were from infancy in habits of familiarity with these humble friends, yet being early taught that nature had placed between them a barrier, which it was in a high degree criminal and disgraceful to pass, they considered a mixture of such distinct races with abhorrence, as a violation of her laws. This greatly conduced to the preservation of family happiness and concord. An ambiguous race, which the law does not acknowledge; and who (if they have any moral sense, must be as much ashamed of their parents as these last are of them), are certainly a dangerous, because degraded part of the community. How much more so must be those unfortunate beings who stand in the predicament of the bat in the fable, whom both birds and beasts disowned? I am sorry to say that the progress of the British army, when it arrived, might be traced by a spurious and ambiguous race of this kind. But of a mulatto born before their arrival I only remember a single instance; and from the regret and wonder it occasioned, considered it as singular. Colonel Schuyler, of whom I am to speak, had a relation so weak and defective in capacity, that he never was intrusted with anything of his own, and lived an idle bachelor about the family. In process of time a favorite negro-woman, to the great offence and scandal of the family, bore a child to him, whose color gave testimony to the relation. The boy was carefully educated; and when he grew up, a farm was allotted to him well stocked and fertile, but in "depth of woods embraced," about two miles back from the family seat. A destitute white woman, who had somehow wandered from the older colonies, was induced to marry him; and all the branches of the family thought it incumbent on them now and then to pay a quiet visit to Chalk (for so, for some unknown reason, they always called him). I have been in Chalk's house myself, and a most comfortable abode it was; but considered him as a mysterious and anomalous being.

I have dwelt the longer on this singular instance of slavery existing devoid of its attendant horrors,

AN AMERICAN LADY

because the fidelity and affection resulting from a bond of union so early formed between master and servant, contributed so very much to the safety of individuals, as well as the general comfort of society, as will hereafter appear.

Chapter VIII

EDUCATION AND EARLY HABITS OF THE ALBANIANS

THE foundations both of friendship and still tenderer attachments were here laid very early by an institution which I always thought had been peculiar to Albany, till I found in Dr. Moore's View of Society on the Continent an account of a similar custom subsisting in Geneva. The children of the town were all divided into companies, as they called them, from five to six years of age, till they became marriageable. How those companies first originated, or what were their exact regulations, I cannot say; though I, belonging to none, occasionally mixed with several, yet always as a stranger, though I spoke their current language fluently. Every company contained as many boys as girls. But I do not know that there was any limited number; only this I recollect, that a boy and a girl of each company, who were older, cleverer, or had some other preëminence above the rest, were called heads of the company, and as such, obeyed by the others. Whether they were voted in, or attained their preëminence by a tacit acknowledgment of their superiority, I know not, but however it was attained it was never disputed. The company of little children had also their heads. All the children of the same age were not in one company; there were at least three or four of equal ages, who had a strong rivalry with each other; and children of different ages in the same family, belonged to different companies. Wherever there is human nature there will be a degree of emulation, strife, and a desire to lessen others, that we may exalt ourselves. Dispassionate as my friends comparatively were, and bred up in the highest attainable candor and innocence, they regarded the company most in competition with their own with a degree of jealous animosity. Each company, at a certain time of the year, went in a body to gather a particular kind of berries, to the hills. It was a sort of annual festival, attended with religious punctuality. Every company had an uniform for this purpose; that is to say, very pretty light baskets made by the Indians, with lids and handles, which hung over the arm, and were adorned with various colors. One company would never allow the least degree of taste to the other in this instance; and was sure to vent its whole stock of spleen in decrying the rival baskets. Nor would they ever admit that the rival company gathered near so much fruit on these excursions as they did. The parents of these children seemed very much to encourage this manner of marshalling and dividing themselves. Every child was permitted to entertain the whole company on its birth-day, and once besides, during winter and spring. The master and mistress of the family always were bound to go from home on these occasions, while some old domestic was left to attend and watch over them, with an ample provision of tea, chocolate, preserved and dried fruits, nuts, and cakes of various kinds, to which was added cider or a syllabub, for these young friends met at four, and did not part till nine or ten, and amused themselves with the utmost gaiety and freedom in any way their fancy dictated. I speak from hearsay; for no person that does not belong to the company is ever admitted to these meetings: other children or young people visit occasionally and are civilly treated, but they admit of no intimacies beyond their company. The consequence of these exclusive and early intimacies was, that, grown up, it was reckoned a sort of apostasy to marry out of one's company. And indeed it did not often happen. The girls, from the example of their mothers, rather than any compulsion, became very early notable and industrious, being constantly employed in knitting stockings, and making clothes for the family and slaves; they even made all the boys' clothes. This was the more necessary, as all articles of clothing were extremely dear. Though all the necessaries of life, and some luxuries abounded, money, as yet, was a scarce commodity. This industry was the more to be admired, as children were here indulged to a degree that, in our vitiated state of society, would have rendered them good for nothing. But there, where ambition, vanity, and the more turbulent passions were scarce awakened; where pride, founded on birth, or any external preëminence, was hardly known; and where the affections flourished fair and vigorous, unchecked by the thorns and thistles with which our minds are cursed in a more advanced state of refinement, affection restrained parents from keeping their children at a distance, and inflicting harsh punishments. But then they did not treat them like apes or parrots; by teaching them to talk with borrowed words and ideas, and afterwards gratifying their own vanity by exhibiting these premature wonders to company, or repeating their sayings. They were tenderly cherished, and early taught that they owed all their enjoyments to the divine source of beneficence, to whom they were finally accountable for their actions; for the rest they were very much left to nature, and permitted to range about at full liberty in their earliest years, covered in summer with some slight and cheap garb, which merely kept the sun from them, and in the winter with some warm habit, in which convenience only was consulted. Their dress of ceremony was never put on but when their *company* was assembled. They were extremely fond of their children; but luckily for the latter, never dreamed of being vain of their immature wit and parts, which accounts, in some measure for the great scarcity of coxcombs among them. The children returned the fondness of their parents with such tender affection, that they feared giving them pain as much as ours do punishment, and very rarely wounded their feelings by neglect, or rude answers. Yet the boys were often wilful and giddy at a certain age, the girls being sooner tamed and domesticated.

These youths were apt, whenever they could carry a gun (which they did at a very early period), to follow some favorite negro to the woods, and, while he was employed in felling trees, range the whole day in search of game, to the neglect of all intellectual improvement, and contract a love of savage liberty which might, and in some instances did, degenerate into licentious and idle habits. Indeed, there were three stated periods in the year when, for a few days, young and old, masters and slaves, were abandoned to unruly enjoyment, and neglected every serious occupation for pursuits of this nature.

We who occupy countries fully inhabited can form no idea of the multitude of birds and animals that nature provides to consume her waste fertility in those regions unexplored by man. In the interior of the province the winter is much colder than might be supposed, from the latitude in which it lies, which is only 43 degrees 36 minutes, from the keen north winds which blow constantly for four or five months over vast frozen lakes and snowy tracts, in the direction of Canada. The snow too lies very deep; but when once they are visited by the south wind in March, its literally warm approach dissolves the snow like magic; and one never sees another wintry day till the season of cold returns. These southern winds seem to flow in a rapid current, uninterrupted by mountains or other obstacles, from the burning sands of the Floridas, Georgia, and the Carolinas, and bring with them a degree of warmth, that appears no more the natural result of the situation, than the intense cold of winter does in that season.

Along the sea banks, in all these southern provinces, are low sandy lands, that never were or will be inhabited, covered with the berry-bearing myrtle, from which wax is extracted fit for candles. Behind these banks are woods and unwholesome swamps of great extent. The myrtle groves formerly mentioned afford shelter and food to countless multitudes of pigeons in winter, when their fruit is in season; while wild geese and ducks, in numbers nearly as great, pass the winter in the impenetrable swamps behind. Some time in the month of April, a general emigration takes place to the northward, first of the geese and ducks, and then of the pigeons; they keep the direction of the sea coast till they come to the mouths of the great rivers, and then follow their course till they reach the great lakes in the interior, where nature has provided for them with the same liberality as in their winter haunts. On the banks of these lakes there are large tracts of ground covered with a plant taller and more luxuriant than the wild carrot, but something resembling it, on the seeds of which the pigeons feed all the summer, while they are breeding and rearing their young. When they pass in spring, which they always do in the same track, they go in great numbers, and are very fat. Their progression northward and southward begins always about the vernal and autumnal equinoxes; and it is this that renders the carnage so great when they pass over inhabited districts.[1] They begin to fly in the dawn, and are never seen after nine or ten o'clock in the morning, possibly feeding and resting in the woods all the rest of the day. If the morning be dry and windy, all the fowlers (that is every body) are disappointed, for then they fly so high that no shot can reach them: but in a cloudy morning the carnage is incredible; and it is singular that their removal falls out at the times of the year that the weather (even in this serene climate) is generally cloudy. This

[1] The immense flocks of pigeons that formerly came down from the north after the season of incubation in such numbers as sometimes to darken the atmosphere like a passing cloud, have long since ceased to be witnessed in the valleys of the Hudson and the Connecticut. Geese and ducks also appear in diminished numbers, and are more frequently heard making their passage by night, and are not so often seen in the unbroken form of their flight, which is that of a harrow, or the letter A.

migration, as it passed by, occasioned, as I said before, a total relaxation from all employments, and a kind of drunken gaiety, though it was rather slaughter than sport; and, for above a fortnight, pigeons in pies and soups, and every way they could be dressed, were the food of the inhabitants. These were immediately succeeded by wild geese and ducks, which concluded the carnival for that season, to be renewed in September. About six weeks after the passage of these birds, sturgeon of a large size, and in great quantity, made their appearance in the river. Now the same ardor seemed to pervade all ages in pursuit of this new object. Every family had a canoe; and on this occasion all were launched; and these persevering fishers traced the course of the sturgeon up the river, followed them by torch light, and often continued two nights upon the water, never returning till they had loaded their canoes with this valuable fish, and many other very excellent in their kinds, that come up the river at the same time. The sturgeon not only furnished them with good part of their food in the summer months, but was pickled or dried for future use or exportation.

Chapter IX

FIRST ADVENTURES OF THE INDIAN TRADERS

TO return to the boys, as all young men were called here till they married. Thus early trained to a love of sylvan sports, their characters were unfolded by contingencies. In this infant society penal laws lay dormant, and every species of coercion was unknown.

Morals, founded on Christianity, were fostered by the sweet influence of the charities of life. The reverence which children in particular had for their parents, and the young in general for the old, was the chief bond that held society together. This veneration being founded on esteem, certainly could only have existed thus powerfully in an uncorrupted community. It had, however, an auxiliary no less powerful.

Here, indeed, it might with truth be said,

"Love breath'd his infant sighs from anguish free."

In consequence of this singular mode of associating together little exclusive parties of children of both sexes, which has been already mentioned, endearing intimacies, formed in the age of playful innocence, were the precursors of more tender attachments.

These were not wrought up to romantic enthusiasm, or extravagant passion, by an inflamed imagination, or by the fears of rivalry, or the artifices of coquetry, yet they had power sufficient to soften the manners and elevate the character of the lover.

I know not if this be the proper place to observe, how much of the general order of society, and the happiness of a people depends on marriage being early and universal among them; but of this more hereafter. The desire (undiverted by any other passion) of obtaining the object of their affection, was to them a stimulus to early and severe exertion. The enamored youth did not listlessly fold his arms and sigh over his hopeless or unfortunate passion. Of love not fed by hope they had not an idea. Their attachments originated at too early an age, and in a circle too familiar to give room for those first-sight impressions of which we hear such wonders. If the temper of the youth was rash and impetuous, and his fair one gentle and complying, they frequently formed a rash and precipitate union without consulting their relations, when perhaps the elder of the two was not above seventeen. This was very quietly borne by the parties aggrieved. The relations of both parties met, and with great calmness consulted on what was to be done. The father of the youth or the damsel, which ever it was who had most wealth, or fewest children, brought home the young couple: and the new married man immediately set about a trading adventure, which was renewed every season, till he had the means of providing a home of his own. Meantime the increase of the younger family did not seem an inconvenience, but rather a source of delight to the old people; and an arrangement begun from necessity was often continued through choice for many years after. Their tempers, unruffled by the endless jealousies and competitions incident to our mode of life, were singularly placid, and the love of offspring, where children were truly an unmixed blessing, was a common sentiment which united all the branches of the family and predominated over every other. The jarring and distrust, the petulance and *egotism*, which, distinct from all weightier considerations, would not fail to poison concord, were different families to dwell under one roof here, were there scarcely known. It is but justice to our acquired delicacy of sentiment to say, that the absence of refinement contributed to this tranquillity. These primitive people, if they did not gather the flowers of cultivated elegance, were not wounded by the thorns of irritable delicacy: they had neither artificial wants, nor artificial miseries. In short, they were neither too wise to be happy, nor too witty to be at rest.

Thus it was in the case of unauthorized marriages. In the more ordinary course of things, love, which makes labor light, tamed these young hunters, and transformed them into diligent and laborious traders, for the nature of their trade included very severe labor. When one of the *boys* was deeply smitten, his fowling-piece and fishing rod were at once relinquished. He demanded of his father forty or at most fifty dollars, a negro boy and a canoe; all of a sudden he assumed the brow of care and solicitude, and began to smoke, a precaution absolutely necessary to repel aguish damps, and troublesome insects. He arrayed himself in a habit very little differing from that of the aborigines, into whose bounds he was about to penetrate, and in short commenced Indian trader; that strange amphibious animal, who uniting the acute senses, strong instincts, and unconquerable patience and fortitude of the savage, with the art, policy, and inventions of the European, encountered, in the pursuit of gain, dangers and difficulties equal to those described in the romantic legends of chivalry.

The small bark canoe in which this hardy adventurer embarked himself, his fortune, and his faithful *squire* (who was generally born in the same house, and predestined to his service), was launched amidst the tears and prayers of his female relations, amongst whom was generally included his destined bride, who well knew herself to be the motive of this perilous adventure.

The canoe was entirely filled with coarse strouds and blankets, guns, powder, beads, etc., suited to the various wants and fancies of the natives; one pernicious article was never wanting, and often made a great part of the cargo. This was ardent spirits, for which the natives too early acquired a relish, and the possession of which always proved dangerous, and sometime fatal to the traders. The Mohawks bringing their furs and other peltry habitually to the stores of their wonted friends and patrons, it was not in that easy and safe direction that these trading adventures extended. The canoe generally steered northward towards the Canadian frontier. They passed by the flats and stonehook in the outset of their journey. Then commenced their toils and dangers at the famous water-fall called the Cohoes, ten miles above Albany, where three rivers,[1] uniting their streams into one, dash over a rocky shelf, and falling into a gulf below with great violence, raise clouds of mist bedecked with splendid rainbows. This was the Rubicon which they had to pass before they plunged into pathless woods, ingulphing swamps, and lakes, the opposite shores of which the eye could not reach. At the Cohoes on account of the obstruction formed by the torrent, they unloaded their canoe, and carried

[1] It is *below* the Cohoes falls that the Mohawk becomes several streams, and debouches into the Hudson at four points, after meandering about and forming numerous islands, among which the American army constructed fortifications of earth, to further impede the progress of the British army, if it should force the American lines at Stillwater. Traces of these earthworks are still distinguishable on Van Schaick's and Haver Islands.

it above a mile further upon their shoulders, returning again for the cargo, which they were obliged to transport in the same manner. This was but a prelude to labors and dangers, incredible to those who dwell at ease. Further on, much longer carrying places frequently recurred: where they had the vessel and cargo to drag through thickets impervious to the day, abounding with snakes and wild beasts, which are always to be found on the side of the rivers.[1]

Their provision of food was necessarily small, for fear of overloading the slender and unstable conveyance already crowded with goods. A little dried beef and Indian corn meal was their whole stock, though they formerly enjoyed both plenty and variety. They were in a great measure obliged to depend upon their own skill in hunting and fishing, and the hospitality of the Indians; for hunting, indeed, they had small leisure, their time being sedulously employed in consequence of the obstacles that retarded their progress. In the slight and fragile canoes, they often had to cross great lakes, on which the wind raised a terrible surge. Afraid

[1] These ancient mynheers, with wonderful perseverance and courage, were forced in those voyages to breast the downward and devious current of the Mohawk, with its rifts, falls and portages, descend into Oneida Lake, and follow its outlet to Oswego; course along the winding shores of Ontario and Erie to Detroit; up that river to St. Clair; and along the shores of Huron, crossing Saginaw bay to Mackinac, where they traded with the Indian for his furs; then with infinite labor to retrace their route to Pearl Street, laden with riches so hardly earned as often to reduce them to early decrepitude.

of going into the track of the French traders, who were always dangerous rivals, and often declared enemies, they durst not follow the direction of the river St. Lawrence; but, in search of distant territories and unknown tribes, were wont to deviate to the east and southwest, forcing their painful way towards the source of "rivers unknown to song," whose winding course was often interrupted with shallows and oftener still by fallen trees of great magnitude lying across, which it was requisite to cut through with their hatchets before they could proceed. Small rivers which wind through fertile valleys, in this country, are peculiarly liable to this obstruction. The chestnut and hickory grow to so large a size in this kind of soil, that in time they become top heavy, and are then the first prey to the violence of the winds; and thus falling form a kind of accidental bridge over these rivers.

When the toils and dangers of the day were over, the still greater terrors of the night commenced. In this, which might literally be styled the howling wilderness, they were forced to sleep in the open air, which was frequently loaded with the humid evaporation of swamps, ponds, and redundant vegetation. Here the axe must be again employed to procure the materials of a large fire even in the warmest weather. This precaution was necessary that the flies and musquitoes might be expelled by the smoke, and that the wolves and bears might be deterred by the flame from encroaching on their place of rest. But the light which afforded them protection created fresh disturbance.

> "Loud as the wolves on Orca's stormy steep,
> Howl to the roarings of the northern deep,"

the American wolves howl to the fires kindled to affright them, watching the whole night on the surrounding hills to keep up a concert which truly "rendered night hideous:" meanwhile the bullfrogs, terrible though harmless, and smaller kinds of various tones and countless numbers, seemed all night calling to each other from opposite swamps, forming the most dismal assemblage of discordant sounds. Though serpents abounded very much in the woods, few of them were noxious. The rattlesnake, the only dangerous reptile, was not so frequently met with as in the neighboring provinces, and the remedy which nature has bestowed as an antidote to his bite was very generally known. The beauties of rural and varied scenery seldom compensated the traveller for the dangers of his journey. "In the close prison of innumerable boughs," and on ground thick with underwood, there was little of landscape open to the eye. The banks of streams and lakes no doubt afforded a rich variety of trees and plants: the former of a most majestic size, the latter of singular beauty and luxuriance; but otherwise they only travelled through a grove of chestnuts or oak, to arrive at another of maple, or poplar, or a vast stretch of pines and other evergreens. If by chance they arrived at a hill crowned with cedars, which afforded some command of prospect, still the gloomy and interminable forest, only varied with different shades of green, met the eye which ever way it turned, while the mind, repelled by solitude so vast, and silence so profound, turned inward on itself. Nature here wore a veil rich and grand, but impenetrable: at least this was the impression it was likely to make on an European mind; but a native American, familiar from childhood with the productions and inhabitants of the woods, sought the nuts and wild fruits with which they abounded, the nimble squirrel in all its varied forms, the architect beaver, the savage racoon, and the stately elk, where we should see nothing but awful solitudes untrod by human foot. It is inconceivable how well these young travellers, taught by their Indian friends, and the experimental knowledge of their fathers, understood every soil and its productions. A boy of twelve years old would astonish you with his accurate knowledge of plants, their properties, and their relation to the soil and to each other. " Here (said he), is a wood of red oak, when it is " grubbed up this will be loam and sand, and make " good Indian corn ground. This chestnut wood " abounds with strawberries, and is the very best " soil for wheat. The poplar wood yonder is not " worth clearing; the soil is always wet and cold. " There is a hickory wood, where the soil is always " rich and deep, and does not run out; such and "such plants that dye blue, or orange, grow under "it."

This is merely a slight epitome of the wide views of nature that are laid open to these people from their very infancy, the acquisition of this kind of knowledge being one of their first amusements, yet those who were capable of astonishing you by the extent and variety of this local skill, in objects so varied and so complicated, never heard of a petal, corolla, or stigma in their lives, nor even of the strata of that soil with the productions and properties of which they were so intimately acquainted.

Without compass, or guide of any kind, the traders steered through these pathless forests. In those gloomy days when the sun is not visible, or in winter, when the falling snows obscured his beams, they made an incision on the bark on the different sides of a tree; that on the north was invariably thicker than the other, and covered with moss in much greater quantity. And this never failing indication of the polar influence, was to those sagacious travellers a sufficient guide. They had indeed several subordinate monitors. Knowing so well as they did the quality of the soil by the trees or plants most prevalent, they could avoid a swamp, or approach with certainty to a river or high ground if such was their wish, by means that to us would seem incomprehensible. Even the savages seldom visited these districts, except in the dead of winter;

they had towns, as they called their summer dwellings, on the banks of the lakes and rivers in the interior, where their great fishing places were. In the winter, their grand hunting parties were in places more remote from our boundaries, where the deer and other larger animals took shelter from the neighborhood of man. These single adventurers sought the Indians in their spring haunts as soon as the rivers were open; there they had new dangers to apprehend. It is well known that among the natives of America, revenge was actually a virtue, and retaliation a positive duty : while faith was kept with these people they never became aggressors. But the Europeans, by the force of bad example, and strong liquors, seduced them from their wonted probity. Yet from the first their notion of justice and revenge was of that vague and general nature, that if they considered themselves injured, or if one of their tribe had been killed by an inhabitant of any one of our settlements, they considered any individual of our nation as a proper subject for retribution. This seldom happened among our allies; never indeed, but when the injury was obvious, and our people very culpable. But the avidity of gain often led our traders to deal with Indians, among whom the French possessed a degree of influence, which produced a smothered animosity to our nation. When at length, after conquering numberless obstacles, they arrived at the place of their destination, these daring adventurers found occasion for no little address, patience, and indeed courage, before they could dispose of their cargo, and return safely with the profits.

The successful trader had now laid the foundation of his fortune, and approved himself worthy of her for whose sake he encountered all these dangers. It is utterly inconceivable, how even a single season, spent in this manner, ripened the mind, and changed the whole appearance, nay the very character of the countenance of these demi-savages, for such they seem on returning from among their friends in the forests. Lofty, sedate, and collected, they seem masters of themselves, and independent of others; though sun-burnt and austere, one scarce knows them till they unbend. By this Indian likeness, I do not think them by any means degraded. One must have seen these people (the Indians I mean), to have any idea what a noble animal man is, while unsophisticated. I have been often amused with the descriptions that philosophers, in their closets, who never in their lives saw man but in his improved or degraded state, give of uncivilized people; not recollecting that they are at the same time uncorrupted. Voyagers, who have not their language, and merely see them transiently, to wonder and be wondered at, are equally strangers to the real character of man in a social, though unpolished state. It is no criterion to judge of this state of society by the roaming savages (truly such) who are met with on these inhospitable coasts where nature is niggardly of her gifts, and where the skies frown continually on her hard-fated children. For some good reason to us unknown, it is requisite that human beings should be scattered through all habitable space, "till gradual life goes out beneath the pole:" and to beings so destined, what misery would result from social tenderness and fine perceptions. Of the class of social beings (for such indeed they were) of whom I speak, let us judge from the traders who know their language and customs, and from the adopted prisoners who have spent years among them. How unequivocal, how consistent is the testimony they bear to their humanity, friendship, fortitude, fidelity, and generosity; but the indulgence of the recollections thus suggested have already led me too far from my subject.

The joy that the return of these youths occasioned was proportioned to the anxiety their perilous journey had produced. In some instances the union of the lovers immediately took place before the next career of gainful hardships commenced. But the more cautious went to New York in winter, disposed of their peltry, purchased a larger cargo, and another slave and canoe. The next year they laid out the profits of their former adventures in flour and provisions, the staple of the province; this they disposed of at the Bermuda islands, where they generally purchased one of those light sailing, cedar schooners, for building of which those islanders are famous, and proceeding to the leeward islands loaded it with a cargo of rum, sugar and molasses.

They were now ripened into men, and considered as active and useful members of society, possessing a stake in the common weal.

The young adventurer had generally finished this process by the time he was one, or at most, two and twenty. He now married, or if married before, which pretty often was the case, brought home his wife to a house of his own. Either he kept his schooner, and loading her with produce, sailed up and down the river all summer, and all winter disposed of the cargoes he obtained in exchange to more distant settlers; or he sold her, purchased European goods, and kept a store. Otherwise he settled in the country, and became as diligent in his agricultural pursuits as if he had never known any other.

Chapter X

MARRIAGES, AMUSEMENTS, RURAL EXCURSIONS, ETC.

IT was in this manner that the young colonist made the transition from boyhood to manhood; from the disengaged and careless bachelor, to the provident and thoughtful father of a family; and thus was spent that period of life so critical in polished society to those whose condition exempts them from manual labor. Love, undiminished by any rival passion, and cherished by innocence and candor, was here fixed by the power of early habit, and strengthened by similarity of education, tastes, and attachments. Inconstancy, or even indifference among married couples was unheard of, even where there happened to be a considerable disparity in point of intellect. The extreme affection they bore their mutual offspring was a bond that for ever endeared them to each other. Marriage in this colony was always early, very often happy, and very seldom indeed interested. When a man had no son, there was nothing to be expected with a daughter, but a well brought up female slave, and the furniture of the best bed-chamber. At the death of her father she obtained another division of his effects, such as he thought she needed or deserved, for there was no rule in these cases.

Such was the manner in which those colonists began life: nor must it be thought that those were mean or uninformed persons. Patriots, magistrates, generals, those who were afterwards wealthy, powerful and distinguished, all, except a few elder brothers, occupied by their possessions at home, set out in the same manner; and in after life, even in the most prosperous circumstances, they delighted to recount the "humble toils and destiny obscure" of their early years.

The very idea of being ashamed of anything that was neither vicious nor indecent never entered an Albanian head. Early accustomed to this noble simplicity, this dignified candor, I cannot express the contempt and disgust I felt at the shame of honorable poverty, the extreme desire of concealing our real condition, and appearing what we are not, that peculiarly characterizes, I had almost said disgraces, the northern part more particularly of this island. I have often wondered how this vile sentiment, that undermines all true greatness of mind, should prevail more here than in England, where wealth, beyond a doubt, is more respected, at least preponderates more over birth, and heart, and mind, and many other valuable considerations. As a people we certainly are not sordid, why then should we descend to the meanness of being ashamed of our condition, while we have not done anything to degrade ourselves? Why add a sting to poverty, and a plume to vanity, by the poor transparent artifice that conceals nothing, and only changes pity into scorn?

Before I quit the subject of Albanian manners, I must describe their amusements, and some other peculiarities in their modes of life. When I say their amusements, I mean those in which they differed from most other people. Such as they had in common with others require no description. They were exceedingly social, and visited each other very frequently, beside the regular assembling together in porches every fine evening. Of the more substantial luxuries of the table they knew little, and of the formal and ceremonious parts of good breeding still less.

If you went to spend a day anywhere, you were received in a manner we should think very cold. No one rose to welcome you; no one wondered you had not come sooner, or apologized for any deficiency in your entertainment. Dinner, which was very early, was served exactly in the same manner as if there were only the family. The house indeed was so exquisitely neat and well regulated, that you could not surprise them; and they saw each other so often and so easily, that intimates made no difference. Of strangers they were shy: not by any means from want of hospitality, but from a consciousness that people who had little to value themselves on but their knowledge of the modes and

AN AMERICAN LADY

ceremonies of polished life, disliked their sincerity, and despised their simplicity. If you showed no insolent wonder, but easily and quietly adopted their manners, you would receive from them not only very great civility, but much essential kindness. Whoever has not common sense and common gratitude enough to pay this tribute of accommodation to those among whom he is destined for the time to live, must of course be an insulated, discontented being; and come home railing at the people whose social comforts he disdained to partake. After sharing this plain and unceremonious dinner, which might, by the bye, chance to be a very good one, but was invariably that which was meant for the family, tea was served in at a very early hour. And here it was that the distinction shown to strangers commenced. Tea here was a perfect regale; accompanied by various sort of cakes unknown to us, cold pastry, and great quantities of sweetmeats and preserved fruits of various kinds, and plates of hickory and other nuts ready cracked. In all manner of confectionery and pastry these people excelled; and having fruit in great abundance, which costs them nothing, and getting sugar home at an easy rate, in return for their exports to the West Indies, the quantity of these articles used in families, otherwise plain and frugal, was astonishing. Tea was never unaccompanied with some of these petty articles; but for strangers a great display was made. If you staid supper, you were sure of a most substantial though plain one. In this meal they departed, out of compliment to the strangers, from their usual simplicity. Having dined between twelve and one you were quite prepared for it. You had either game or poultry roasted, and always shell-fish in the season: you had also fruit in abundance. All this with much neatness, but no form. The seeming coldness with which you were first received, wore off by degrees. They could not accommodate their topics to you, and scarcely attempted it. But the conversation of the old, though limited in regard to subjects, was rational and easy, and had in it an air of originality and truth not without its attractions. That of the young was natural and playful yet full of localities, which lessened its interest to a stranger, but which were extremely amusing when you became one of the initiated.

Their amusements were marked by a simplicity which, to strangers, appeared rude and childish (I mean those of the younger class). In spring, eight or ten of the young people of one company, or related to each other, young men and maidens, would set out together in a canoe on a kind of rural excursion, of which amusement was the object. Yet so fixed were their habits of industry, that they never failed to carry their work-baskets with them, not as a form, but as an ingredient necessarily mixed with their pleasures. They had no attendants; and steered a devious course of four, five, or perhaps more miles, till they arrived at some of the beautiful islands with which this fine river abounded, or at some sequestered spot on its banks, where delicious wild fruits, or particular conveniences for fishing, afforded some attraction. There they generally arrived by nine or ten o'clock, having set out in the cool and early hour of sunrise. Often they met another party going, perhaps, to a different place, and joined them, or induced them to take their route. A basket with tea, sugar, and the other usual provisions for breakfast, with the apparatus for cooking it; a little rum and fruit for making cool weak punch, the usual beverage in the middle of the day, and now and then some cold pastry, was the sole provision; for the great affair was to depend on the sole exertions of the *boys*, in procuring fish, wild ducks, etc., for their dinner. They were all, like Indians, ready and dexterous with the axe, gun, etc. Whenever they arrived at their destination they sought out a dry and beautiful spot opposite to the river, and in an instant with their axes cleared so much superfluous shade or shrubbery as left a semicircular opening, above which they bent and twined the boughs, so as to form a pleasant bower, while the girls gathered dried branches, to which one of the youths soon set fire with gun powder, and the breakfast, a very regular and cheerful one, occupied an hour or two; the young men then set out to fish, or perhaps shoot birds, and the maidens sat busily down to their work, singing and conversing with all the ease and gaiety the bright serenity of the atmosphere and beauty of the surrounding scene were calculated to inspire. After the sultry hours had been thus employed, the *boys* brought their tribute from the river or the wood, and found a rural meal prepared by their fair companions, among whom were generally their sisters and the chosen of their hearts. After dinner they all set out together to gather wild strawberries, or whatever other fruit was in season; for it was accounted a reflection to come home empty handed. When wearied of this amusement, they either drank tea in their bower, or, returning, landed at some friend's on the way, to partake of that refreshment. Here, indeed,

"Youth's free spirit, innocently gay,
Enjoyed the most that innocence could give."

Another of their summer amusements was going to the bush, which was thus managed: a party of young people set out in little open carriages, something in the form of a gig, of which every family had one; every one carried something with him, as in these cases there was no hunting to add provision. One brought wine for negus, another tea and coffee of a superior quality, a third a pigeon pie; in short, every one brought something, no matter how trifling, for there was no emulation about the extent of the contribution. In this same bush, there were spots to which the poorer members of the community retired, to work their way with patient industry, through much privation and hardship, compared to the plenty and comfort enjoyed by the rest. They perhaps could only afford to have one negro woman, whose children as they grew up, became to their master a source of plenty and ease; but in the meantime the good man wrought hard himself, with a little occasional aid sent him by his friends. He had plenty of the necessaries of life, but no luxuries. His wife and daughter milked the cows and wrought at the hay, and his house was on a smaller scale than the older settlers had theirs, yet he had always one neatly furnished room, a very clean house, with a pleasant portico before it, generally a fine stream beside his dwelling, and some Indian wigwams near it. He was wood-surrounded, and seemed absolutely to live in the bosom of nature, screened from all the artificial ills of life; and those spots cleared of incumbrances, yet rich in native luxuriance, had a wild originality about them not easily described. The young parties, or sometimes elder ones, who set out on this woodland excursion, had no fixed destination, they went generally in the forenoon, and when they were tired of going on the ordinary road, turned into the *bush*, and whenever they saw an inhabited spot, with the appearance of which they were pleased, went in with all the ease of intimacy, and told them they were come to spend the afternoon there. The good people, not in the least surprised at this incursion, very calmly opened the reserved apartments, or if it were very hot, received them in the portico. The guests produced their stores, and they boiled their tea-kettle, and provided cream, nuts, or any peculiar dainty of the woods which they chanced to have; and they always furnished bread and butter, which they had excellent of their kinds. They were invited to share the collation, which they did with great ease and frankness; then dancing, or any other amusement that struck their fancy, succeeded. They sauntered about the bounds in the evening, and returned by moonlight. These good people felt not the least embarrassed at the rustic plainness of everything about them; they considered themselves as on the way, after a little longer exertion of patient industry, to have every thing that the others had; and their guests thought it an agreeable variety in this abrupt manner to visit their sequestered abodes.

Chapter XI

WINTER AMUSEMENTS, ETC.

IN winter, the river, frozen to a great depth, formed the principal road through the country, and was the scene of all those amusements of skating and sledge races, common to the north of Europe. They used in great parties to visit their friends at a distance, and having an excellent and hardy breed of horses, flew from place to place over the snow or ice in these sledges with incredible rapidity, stopping a little while at every house they came to, and always well received, whether acquainted with the owners or not. The night never impeded these travellers, for the atmosphere was so pure and serene, and the snow so reflected the moon and starlight, that the nights exceeded the days in beauty.

In town all the *boys* were extravagantly fond of a diversion that to us would appear a very odd and childish one. The great street of the town, in the midst of which, as has been formerly mentioned, stood all the churches and public buildings, sloped down from the hill on which the fort stood, towards the river; between the buildings was an unpaved carriage road, the foot-path beside the houses being the only part of the street which was paved. In winter this sloping descent, continued for more than a quarter of a mile, acquired firmness from the frost, and became extremely slippery. Then the amusement commenced. Every boy and youth in town, from eight to eighteen, had a little low sledge, made with a rope like a bridle to the front, by which it could be dragged after one by the hand. On this one or two at most could sit, and this sloping descent being made as smooth as a looking glass, by sliders' sledges, etc., perhaps a hundred at once set out in succession from the top of this street, each seated in his little sledge with the rope in his hand, which, drawn to the right or left, served to guide him. He pushed it off with a little stick, as one would launch a boat; and then, with the most astonishing velocity, precipitated by the weight of the owner, the little machine glided past, and was at the lower end of the street in an instant. What could be so delightful in this rapid and smooth descent I could never discover; though in a more retired place, and on a smaller scale, I have tried the amusement; but to a young Albanian, sleighing as he called it, was one of the first joys of life, though attended by the drawback of walking to the top of the declivity dragging his sledge every time he renewed his flight, for such it might well be called. In the managing this little machine some dexterity was necessary; an unskillful Phæton was sure to fall. The conveyance was so low, that a fall was attended with little danger, yet with much disgrace, for an universal laugh from all sides assailed the fallen charioteer. This laugh was from a very full chorus, for the constant and rapid succession of this procession, where every one had a brother, lover, or kinsman, brought all the young people in town to the porticos, where they used to sit wrapt in furs till ten or eleven at night, engrossed by this delectable spectacle. What magical attraction it could possibly have, I never could find out; but I have known an Albanian, after residing some years in Britain, and becoming a polished fine gentleman, join the sport, and slide down with the rest. Perhaps, after all our laborious refinements in amusement, being easily pleased is one of the great secrets of happiness, as far as it is attainable in this " frail and feverish being."

Now there remains another amusement to be described, which I mention with reluctance, and should scarce venture to mention at all had I not found a precedent for it among the virtuous Spartans. Had Lycurgus himself been the founder of their community, the young men could scarce have stolen with more alacrity and dexterity. I could never conjecture how the custom could possibly originate among a set of people of such perfect and plain integrity. But thus it was. The young men now and then spent a convivial evening at a tavern together, where, from the extreme cheapness of liquor, their bills (even when they committed an occasional excess) were very moderate. Either to lessen the expense of the supper, or from the pure love of what they styled frolic (Anglicè mischief), they never failed to steal either a roasting pig or a fat turkey for this festive occasion. The town was the scene of these depredations, which never extended beyond it. Swine and turkeys were reared in great numbers by all the inhabitants. For those they brought to town in winter, they had an appropriate place at the lower end of the garden, in which they were locked up. It is observable, that these animals were the only things locked up about the house, for this good reason, that nothing else ran the least risk of being stolen. The dexterity of the theft consisting in climbing over very high walls, watching to steal in when the negroes went down to feed the horse or cow, or making a clandestine entrance at some window or aperture; breaking up doors was quite out of rule, and rarely ever resorted to. These exploits were always performed in the darkest nights; if the owner heard a noise in his stables, he usually ran down with a cudgel, and laid it without mercy on any culprit he could overtake. This was either dexterously avoided or patiently borne. To plunder a man, and afterwards offer him any personal injury, was accounted scandalous; but the turkeys or pigs were never recovered. In some instances a whole band of these young plunderers would traverse the town, and carry off such a prey as would afford provision for many jovial nights. Nothing was more common than to find one's brothers or nephews amongst these pillagers.

Marriage was followed by two dreadful privations: a married man could not fly down the street in a little sledge, or join a party of pig stealers, without outraging decorum. If any of their confederates married, as they frequently did, very young, and were in circumstances to begin housekeeping, they were sure of an early visit of this nature from their old confederates. It was thought a great act of gallantry to overtake and chastise the robbers. I recollect an instance of one young married man, who had not long attained to that dignity, whose turkeys screaming violently one night, he ran down to chastise the aggressors; he overtook them in the fact: but finding they were his old associates, could not resist the force of habit, joined the rest in another exploit of the same nature, and then shared his own turkey at the tavern. There were two inns in the town, the masters of which were " honorable men; " yet these pigs and turkeys were always received and dressed without questioning whence they came. In one instance, a young party had in this manner provided a pig, and ordered it to be roasted at the King's Arms; another party attacked the same place whence this booty was taken, but found it already rifled. This party was headed by an idle mischievous young man, who was the Ned Poins of his fraternity; well guessing how the stolen roasting pig was disposed of, he ordered his friends to adjourn to the rival tavern, and went himself to the King's Arms.[1] Inquiring in the kitchen (where a pig was roasting) who supped there, he soon arrived at certainty: then taking an opportunity when there was no one in the kitchen but the cook-maid, he sent for one of the jovial party, who were at cards up stairs. During her absence, he cut the string by which the pig was suspended, laid it in the dripping pan, and through the quiet and dark streets of that sober city, carried it safely to the other tavern: where, after finishing the roasting, he and his companions prepared to regale themselves. Meantime the pig was missed at the King's Arms; and it was immediately concluded, from the dexterity and address with which this trick was performed, that no other but the Poins aforesaid could be the author of it. A new stratagem was now devised to outwit this stealer of the stolen. An adventurous youth of the despoiled party laid down a parcel of shavings opposite to the other tavern, and setting them in a blaze, cried fire! a most alarming sound here, where such accidents were too frequent. Every one rushed out of the house, where supper had been just served. The dexterous purveyor, who had occasioned all this disturbance, stole in, snatched up the dish with

[1] This tavern was on the north-west corner of Green and Beaver Streets, the sign of which bore the effigy of King George. One of the early outbursts of patriotism in the Revolution spent its fury in wresting this obnoxious emblem of royalty from its hangings, and it was burnt in State Street.

the pig in it, stole out again by the back door, and feasted his companions with the recovered spoils.

These were a few idle young men, the sons of avaricious fathers, who, grudging to advance the means of pushing them forward by the help of their own industry to independence, allowed them to remain so long unoccupied, that their time was wasted, and habits of conviviality at length degenerated in those of dissipation. These were not only pitied and endured, but received with a degree of kindness and indulgence that was wonderful. They were usually a kind of wags, went about like privileged persons, at whose jests no one took offence; and were in their discourse and style of humor, so much like Shakespeare's clowns, that on reading that admirable author, I thought I recognized my old acquaintances. Of these, however, I saw little, the society admitted at my friend's being very select.

Chapter XII

LAY-BROTHERS — MISS SCHUYLER— DETACHED INDIANS

BEFORE I quit this attempt to delineate the members of which this community was composed, I must mention a class of aged persons, who, united by the same recollections, pursuits, and topics, associated very much with each other, and very little with a world which they seemed to have renounced. They might be styled lay-brothers, and were usually widowers, or persons, who, in consequence of some early disappointment, had remained unmarried. These were not devotees who had, as was formerly often the case in Catholic countries, run from the extreme of licentiousness to that of bigotry. They were generally persons who were never marked as being irreligious or immoral; and just as little distinguished for peculiar strictness, or devotional fervor. These good men lived in the house of some relation, where they had their own apartments to themselves; and only occasionally mixed with the family. The people of the town lived to a great age; ninety was frequently attained; and I have seen different individuals of both sexes who had reached an hundred. These ancients seemed to place all their delight in pious books and devotional exercises particularly in singing psalms, which they would do in their own apartments for hours together. They came out and in like ghosts, and were treated in the same manner; for they never spoke unless when addressed, and seemed very careless of the things of this world, like people who had got above it. Yet they were much together, and seemed to enjoy each other's conversation. Retrospection on the scenes of early life, anticipation of that futurity so closely veiled from our sight, and discussions regarding different passages of holy writ seemed their favorite themes. They were mild and benevolent, but abstracted, and unlike other people. Their happiness, for happy I am convinced they were, was of a nature peculiar to themselves, not obvious to others. Others there were not deficient in their attention to religious duties, who living in the bosom of their families, took an active and cheerful concern to the last in all that amused or interested them; and I never understood that the lay-brothers, as I have chosen to call them, blamed them for so doing. One of the first Christian virtues, charity, in the most obvious and common sense of the word, had little scope. Here a beggar was unheard of. People, such as I have described in the *bush*, or going there, were no more considered as objects of pity, than we consider an apprentice as such for having to serve his time before he sets up for himself. In such cases, the wealthier, because older settlers, frequently gave a heifer or colt each to a new beginner, who set about clearing land in their vicinity. Orphans were never neglected; and from their early marriages, and the casualties their manner of life subjected them to, these were not unfrequent. You never entered a house without meeting children. Maidens, bachelors, and childless married people, all adopted orphans, and all treated them as if they were their own.

Having given a sketch, that appears to my recollection (aided by subsequent conversations with my fellow travellers) a faithful one, of the country and its inhabitants, it is time to return to the history of the mind of Miss Schuyler, for by no other circumstances than prematurity of intellect, and superior culture, were her earliest years distinguished. Her father,[1] dying early, left her very much to the tuition of his brother.[2] Her uncle's frontier situation made him a kind of barrier to the settlement; while the powerful influence, that his knowledge of nature and of character, his sound judgment and unstained integrity, had obtained over both parties, made him the bond by which the aborigines were united with the colonists. Thus, little leisure was

[1] The author's memory was at fault. The father of Miss Schuyler survived his brother, Col. Peter S., twenty-three years.

[2] Col. Peter Schuyler, Member of the King's Council. His niece sometimes accompanied him to the capitol (New York) to visit among her friends and relatives, who were quite numerous in that city. The voyage from Albany frequently occupied several days.

left him for domestic enjoyments, or literary pursuits, for both of which his mind was peculiarly adapted. Of the leisure time he could command, however, he made the best use; and soon distinguishing Catalina [1] as the one amongst his family to whom nature had been most liberal, he was at the pains to cultivate her taste for reading, which soon discovered itself by procuring for her the best authors in history, divinity, and belles-lettres; in this latter branch her reading was not very extensive; but then the few books of this kind that she possessed were very well chosen; and she was early and intimately familiar with them. What I remember of her, assisted by comparisons since made with others, has led me to think that extensive reading, superficial and indiscriminate, such as the very easy access to books among us encourages, is not at an early period of life favorable to solid thinking, true taste, or fixed principle. Whatever she knew, she knew to the bottom; and the reflections, which were thus suggested to her strong discerning mind, were digested by means of easy and instructive conversation. Colonel Schuyler had many relations in New York; and the governor and other ruling characters there carefully cultivated the acquaintance of a person so well qualified to instruct and inform them on certain points as he was. Having considerable dealings in the fur trade too, he went every winter to the capital for a short time,

[1] Margaretta.

to adjust his commercial concerns, and often took his favorite niece along with him, who, being of an uncommon quick growth and tall stature, soon attracted attention by her personal graces, as well as by the charms of her conversation. I have been told, and should conclude from a picture I have seen drawn when she was fifteen, that she was in her youth very handsome. Of this few traces remained when I knew her: excessive corpulence having then overloaded her majestic person, and entirely changed the aspect of a countenance once eminently graceful. In no place did female excellence of any kind more amply receive its due tribute of applause and admiration than here, for various reasons: First, cultivation and refinement were rare. Then, as it was not the common routine that women should necessarily have such and such accomplishments, pains were only taken on minds strong enough to bear improvements without becoming conceited or pedantic. And lastly, as the spur of emulation was not invidiously applied, those who acquired a superior degree of knowledge considered themselves as very fortunate in having a new source of enjoyment opened to them. But never having been made to understand that the chief motive of excelling was to dazzle or outshine others, they no more thought of despising their less fortunate companions, than of assuming preëminence for discovering a wild plum-tree or bee-hive in the woods, though, as in the former

AN AMERICAN LADY

case, they would have regarded such a discovery as a benefit and a pleasure; their acquisitions, therefore, were never shaded by affectation. The women were all natives of the country, and few had more than domestic education. But men, who possessed the advantages of early culture and usage of the world, daily arrived on the continent from different parts of Europe. So that if we may be indulged in the inelegant liberty of talking commercially of female elegance, the supply was not equal to the demand. It may be easily supposed that Miss Schuyler met with due attention; who, even at this early age, was respected for the strength of her character, and the dignity and composure of her manners. Her mother,[1] whom she delighted to recollect, was mild, pious and amiable; her acknowledged worth was chastened by the utmost diffidence. Yet accustomed to exercise a certain power over the minds of the natives, she had great influence in restraining their irregularities, and swaying their opinions. From her knowledge of their language, and habit of conversing with them, some detached Indian families resided for a while in summer in the vicinity of houses occupied by the more wealthy and benevolent inhabitants. They generally built a slight wigwam under shelter of the orchard fence on the

[1] Her mother was the only daughter of Dr. Abraham Staats, an early immigrant, and sister of Dr. Samuel Staats, member of the King's Council.

shadiest side; and never were neighbors more harmless, peaceable and obliging; I might truly add, industrious: for in one way or other they were constantly occupied. The women and their children employed themselves in many ingenious handicrafts, which, since the introduction of European arts and manufactures, have greatly declined. Baking trays, wooden dishes, ladles and spoons, shovels and rakes, brooms of a peculiar manufacture, made by splitting a birch block into slender but tough filaments: baskets of all kinds and sizes, made of similar filaments, enriched with the most beautiful colors, which they alone knew how to extract from vegetable substances, and incorporate with the wood. They made also of the birch bark (which is here so strong and tenacious, that cradles and canoes are made of it), many receptacles for holding fruit and other things curiously adorned with embroidery, not inelegant, done with the sinews of deer, and leggans[1] and moquesans,[2] a very comfortable and highly ornamented substitute for shoes and stockings, then universally used in winter among the men of our own people. They had also a beautiful manufacture of deer-skin, soft-

[1] Leggins, a long gaiter for protecting the ankle and leg, spoken of in Capt. Thomas Anbury's book of travels as country boots.

[2] Moccasins, a shoe or cover for the foot, made of deer skin or other soft leather, without a sole, and ornamented on the upper side; the customary shoe worn by the American Indians. Some of these discrepancies of orthography may not be chargeable to the author, but possibly are what are known as *typographical errors.*

ened to the consistence of the finest chamois leather, and embroidered with beads of wampum, formed like bugles; these, with great art and industry, they formed out of shells, which had the appearance of fine white porcelain, veined with purple. This embroidery showed both skill and taste, and was among themselves highly valued. They had belts, large embroidered garters, and many other ornaments, formed, first of sinews, divided to the size of coarse thread, and afterwards, when they obtained worsted thread from us, of that material, formed in a manner which I could never comprehend. It was neither knitted nor wrought in the manner of net, nor yet woven; but the texture was formed more like an officer's sash than anything I can compare it to. While the women and children were thus employed, the men sometimes assisted them in the more laborious part of their business, but oftener occupied themselves in fishing on the rivers, and drying or preserving, by means of smoke, in sheds erected for the purpose, sturgeon and large eels, which they caught in great quantities, and of an extraordinary size, for winter provision.

Boys on the verge of manhood, and ambitious to be admitted into the hunting parties of the ensuing winter, exercised themselves in trying to improve their skill in archery, by shooting birds, squirrels, and racoons. These petty huntings helped to support the little colony in the neighborhood, which however derived its principal subsistence from an exchange of their manufactures with the neighboring family for milk, bread, and other articles of food.

The summer residence of these ingenious artisans promoted a great intimacy between the females of the vicinity and the Indian women, whose sagacity and comprehension of mind were beyond belief.

It is a singular circumstance, that though they saw the negroes in every respectable family not only treated with humanity, but cherished with parental kindness, they always regarded them with contempt and dislike, as an inferior race, and would have no communication with them. It was necessary then that all conversations should be held, and all business transacted with these females, by the mistress of the family. In the infancy of the settlement the Indian language was familiar to the more intelligent inhabitants, who found it very useful, and were, no doubt, pleased with its nervous and emphatic idiom, and its lofty and sonorous cadence. It was indeed a noble and copious language, when one considers that it served as the vehicle of thought to a people whose ideas and sphere of action we should consider as so very confined.

Chapter XIII

PROGRESS OF KNOWLEDGE — INDIAN MANNERS

CONVERSING with those interesting and deeply reflecting natives, was to thinking minds no mean source of entertainment. Communication soon grew easier; for the Indians had a singular facility in acquiring other languages; the children I well remember, from experimental knowledge, for I delighted to hover about the wigwam, and converse with those of the Indians, and we very frequently mingled languages. But to return: whatever comfort or advantage a good and benevolent mind possesses, it is willing to extend to others. The mother of my friend, and other matrons, who like her experienced the consolations, the hopes, and the joys of Christianity, wished those inestimable natives to share in their pure enjoyments.

Of all others these mild and practical Christians were the best fitted for making proselytes. Unlike professed missionaries, whose zeal is not always seconded by judgment, they did not begin by alarming the jealousy with which all manner of people watch over their hereditary prejudices. Engaged in active life, they had daily opportunities of demonstrating the truth of their religion by its influence upon their conduct. Equally unable and unwilling to enter into deep disquisitions or polemical arguments, their calm and unstudied explanations of the essential doctrines of Christianity, were the natural results which arose out of their ordinary conversation. To make this better understood, I must endeavor to explain what I have observed in the unpolished society, that occupies the wild and remote regions of different countries. Their conversation is not only more original, but, however odd the expression may appear, more philosophical than that of persons equally destitute of mental culture in more populous districts. They derive their subjects of reflection and conversation more from natural objects, which lead minds, possessing a certain degree of intelligence, more forward to trace effects to their causes. Nature there, too, is seen arrayed in virgin beauty and simple majesty. Its various aspects are more grand and impressive. Its voice is more distinctly heard, and sinks deeper into the heart. These people, more dependent on the simples of the fields and the wild fruits of the woods; better acquainted with the forms and instincts of the birds and beasts, their fellow denizens in the wild; and more observant of every constellation and every change in the sky, from living so much in the open air, have a wider range of ideas than we are aware of. With us, art every where combats nature, opposes her plainest dictates, and too often conquers her. The poor are so confined to the spot where their occupations lie, so engrossed by their struggles for daily bread, and so surrounded by the works of man, that those of their Creator are almost excluded from their view, at least form a very small part of the subjects that engross their thoughts. What knowledge they have is often merely the husks and orts that fall from the table of their superiors, which they swallow without chewing.

Many of those who are one degree above the lowest class, see nature in poetry, novels, and other books, and never think of looking for her any where else; like a person amused by seeing the reflection of the starry heavens or shifting clouds in a calm lake, never lifting his eyes to those objects of which he sees the imperfect though resembling pictures.

Those who live in the undisguised bosom of tranquil nature, and whose chief employment it is, by disencumbering her of waste luxuriance, to discover and improve her latent beauties, need no borrowed enthusiasm to relish the sublime and graceful features. The venerable simplicity of the sacred scriptures, has something extremely attractive for a mind in this state. The soul, which is the most familiar with its Creator, in his works, will be always the most ready to recognize him in his word. Conversations which had for their subject the nature and virtues of plants, the extent and boundaries of woods and lakes, and the various operations of instinct in animals, under those circumstances where they are solely directed by it, and the distinct customs and manners of various untutored nations, tended to expand the mind, and teach it to aspire to more perfect intelligence. The untaught reasoners of the woods could not but observe that the Europeans knew much that was concealed from them, and derived many benefits and much power from that knowledge. Where they saw active virtue keep pace with superior knowledge, it was natural to conclude that persons thus beneficially enlightened, had clearer and ampler views of that futurity, which to them only dimly gleamed through formless darkness. They would suppose, too, that those illuminated beings had some means of approaching nearer to that source of light and perfection from which wisdom is derived, than they themselves had attained. Their minds being thus prepared by degrees, these pious matrons (probably assisted by those laybrothers of whom I have spoken) began to diffuse the knowledge of the distinguishing doctrines of Christianity among the elderly and well-intentioned Indian women. These did not by any means receive the truth without examination: the acuteness of intellect which discovered itself in their objections (of which I have heard many striking instances) was astonishing; yet the humble and successful instruments of enlightening those sincere and candid people, did by no means take to themselves any merit in making proselytes. When they found their auditors disposed to listen diligently to the truth, they sent them to the clergymen of the place, who instructed, confirmed, and baptized them. I am sorry that I have not a clear and distinct recollection of the exact manner, or the numbers, etc., of these first converts, of whom I shall say more hereafter; but I know that this was the usual process. They were, however, both zealous and persevering, and proved the means of bringing many others under the law of love, to which it is reasonable to suppose the safety of this unprotected frontier was greatly owing at that crisis, that of the first attacks of the French. The Indian women, who, from motives of attachment to particular families, or for the purpose of carrying on the small traffic already mentioned, were wont to pass their summers near the settlers, were of detached and wandering families, who preferred this mode of living to the labor of tilling the ground, which entirely devolved upon the women among the five nations. By tilling the ground I would not be understood to mean any settled mode of agriculture, requiring cattle, enclosures, or implements of husbandry. Grain made but a very subordinate part of their subsistence, which was chiefly derived from fishing and hunting. The little they had was maize; this with kidney beans and tobacco, the only plants they cultivated, was sowed in some very pleasant fields along the Mohawk river, by the women, who had no implements of tillage but the hoe, and a kind of wooden spade. These fields lay round their *castles,* and while the women were thus employed, the men were catching and drying fish by the rivers or on the lakes. The younger girls were much busied during summer and autumn, in gathering wild fruits, berries, and grapes, which they had a peculiar mode of drying to preserve them for the winter. The great cranberry they gathered in abundance, which, without being dried, would last the whole winter, and was much used by the settlers. These dried fruits were no luxury; a fastidious taste would entirely reject them. Yet, besides furnishing another article of food, they had their use, as was evident. Without some antiseptic, they who lived the whole winter on animal food, without a single vegetable, or anything of the nature of bread, unless now and then a little maize, which they had the art of boiling down to softness in ley of wood-ashes, must have been liable to that great scourge of northern nations in their primitive state, the scurvy, had not this simple dessert been a preservative against it. Rheumatisms, and sometimes agues affected them, but no symptom of any cutaneous disease was ever seen on an Indian.

The stragglers from the confines of the orchards did not fail to join their tribes in winter; and were zealous, and often successful in spreading their new opinions. Indians supposed that every country had its own mode of honoring the great spirits, to whom all were equally acceptable. This had, on one hand, the bad effect of making them satisfied with their own vague and undefined notions; and on the other, the good one of making them very tolerant of those of others. If you do not insult their belief (for mode of worship they have scarce any), they will hear you talk of yours with the greatest patience and attention. Their good breeding in this respect, was really superlative. No Indian ever interrupted any, the most idle talker: but when they concluded, he would deliberately, methodically, and not ungracefully answer or comment upon all they had said, in a manner which showed that not a word had escaped him.

Lady Mary Montague ludicrously says, that the court of Vienna was the paradise of old women; and that there is no other place in the world where a woman past fifty excites the least interest. Had her travels extended to the interior of North America, she would have seen another instance of this inversion of the common mode of thinking. Here a woman never was of consequence, till she had a son old enough to fight the battles of his country: from that date she held a superior rank in society; was allowed to live at ease, and even called to consultations on national affairs. In savage and warlike countries, the reign of beauty is very short, and its influence comparatively limited. The girls in childhood had a very pleasing appearance; but excepting their fine hair, eyes and teeth, every external grace was soon banished by perpetual drudgery, carrying burdens too heavy to be borne, and other slavish employments considered beneath the dignity of the men. These walked before, erect and graceful, decked with ornaments, which set off to advantage the symmetry of their well formed persons, while the poor women followed, meanly attired, bent under the weight of the children and utensils they carried everywhere with them; and disfigured and degraded by ceaseless toils. They were very early married; for a Mohawk had no other servant but his wife; and whenever he commenced hunter, it was requisite that he should have some one to carry his load, cook his kettle, make his moquesans, and above all, produce the young warriors who were to succeed him in the honors of the chase, and of the tomahawk. Wherever man is a mere hunter, woman is a mere slave. It is domestic intercourse that softens man, and elevates woman; and of that there can be little, where the employments and amusements are not in common: the ancient Caledonians honored the fair; but then, it is to be observed, they were fair huntresses, and moved, in the light of their beauty, to the hill of roes; and the culinary toils were entirely left to the rougher sex. When the young warrior above alluded to made his appearance, it softened the cares of his mother; who well knew that when he grew up, every deficiency in tenderness to his wife would be made up in superabundant duty and affection to her. If it were possible to carry filial veneration to excess, it was done here; for all other charities were absorbed in it. I wonder this system of depressing the sex in their early years to exalt them when all their juvenile attractions were flown, and when mind alone can distinguish them, has not occurred to our modern reformers. The Mohawks took good care not to admit their women to share their prerogatives, till they approved themselves good wives and mothers.

This digression, long as it is, has a very intimate connection with the character of my friend; who early adopted the views of her family, in regard to those friendly Indians, which greatly enlarged her mind, and ever after influenced her conduct. She was, even in childhood, well acquainted with their language, opinions, and customs; and, like every other person, possessed of a liberality or benevolence of mind, whom chance had brought acquainted with them, was exceedingly partial to those high-souled and generous natives. The Mohawk language was early familiar to her; she spoke Dutch and English with equal ease and purity; was no stranger to the French tongue; and could (I think) read German. I have heard her speak it. From the conversations which her active curiosity led her to hold with native Africans brought into her father's family, she was more intimately acquainted with the customs, manners, and government of their native country, than she could have been, by reading all that was ever written on the subject. Books are, no doubt, the granaries of knowledge: but a diligent, inquiring mind, in the active morning of life, will find it strewed like manna over the face of the earth; and need not, in all cases, rest satisfied with intelligence accumulated by others, and tinctured with their passions and prejudices. Whoever reads Homer or Shakespeare may daily discover that they describe both nature and art from their own observation. Consequently you see the images, reflected from the mirror of their great minds, differing from the descriptions of others, as the reflection of an object in all its colors and proportions from any polished surface, does from a shadow on a wall, or from a picture drawn from recollection. The enlarged mind of my friend, and her simple yet easy and dignified manners, made her readily adapt herself to those with whom she conversed, and every where command respect and kindness: and, on a nearer acquaintance, affection followed; but she had too much sedateness and independence to adopt those caressing and insinuating manners, by which the vain and the artful so soon find their way into shallow minds. Her character did not captivate at once, but gradually unfolded itself; and you had always something new to discover. Her style was grave and masculine, without the least embellishment; and at the same time so pure, that everything she said might be printed without correction, and so plain, that the most ignorant and most inferior persons were never at a loss to comprehend it. It possessed, too, a wonderful flexibility; it seemed to rise and fall with the subject. I have not met with a style which, to a noble and uniform simplicity, united such variety of expression. Whoever drinks knowledge pure at its sources, solely from a delight in filling the capacities of a large mind, without the desire of dazzling or outshining others; whoever speaks for the sole purpose of conveying to other minds those ideas, from which he himself has received pleasure and advantage, may possess this chaste and natural style: but it is not to be acquired by art or study.

Chapter XIV

MARRIAGE OF MISS SCHUYLER — DESCRIPTION OF THE FLATS

MISS S. had the happiness to captivate her cousin Philip,[1] eldest son of her uncle, who was ten years older than herself, and was *in all respects* to be accounted a suitable, and in the worldly sense, an advantageous match for her. His father was highly satisfied to have the two

---

[1] This Col. Philip was the eldest son of Col. Peter Schuyler and his wife, Maria Van Rensselaer, baptized January 15, 1696, and but five years older than his cousin whom he married. His mother was the daughter of Jeremiah Van Rensselaer, and a granddaughter of the first patroon of Rensselaerwyck. He died February 16, 1758, and his monument is the oldest and most conspicuous one in the family burial ground at the Flats, resting horizontally upon pillars, and bearing the following inscription.

In Memory of
COL[NL]. PHILIP SCHUYLER,
A Gentleman who was Improved
in Several publick employments
in which he Acted with integrity,
he was singularly hospitable,
a Sincere friend, kind Master,
a most tender Husband ;
he Liv'd Respected and died greatly Lamented.
Feb. 16th, 1758, Aged 62 years.

Madame Schuyler was buried by his side, but the metal tablet on the monument marking her grave is gone. It is to be replaced by a new tablet.

objects on whom he had bestowed so much care and culture united, but did not live to see this happy connection take place. They were married in the year 1719, when she was in the eighteenth year of her age.[1] When the old colonel died, he left considerable possessions to be divided among his children, and from the quantity of plate, paintings, etc., which they shared, there is reason to believe he must have brought some of his wealth from Holland, as in those days people had little means of enriching themselves in new settlements. He had also considerable possessions in a place near the town, now called Fishkill,[2] about twenty miles below Albany.[3] His family residence, however, was at the Flats, a fertile and beautiful plain on the banks of the river. He possessed about two miles on a stretch of that rich and level champain. This possession was bounded on the east by the river Hudson, whose high banks overhung the stream and its pebbly strand, and were both adorned and defended by elms (larger than ever I have seen in any other place), decked with natural festoons of wild grapes, which abound along the banks of this noble stream. These lofty elms

[1] They were married December 29, 1720, and Col. Peter Schuyler died February 19, 1724.

[2] Miss Schuyler's father had a large and valuable tract of land on the Fishkill at Saratoga, fifty miles above Albany, and the father of Philip Schuyler had a large landed property at Kinderhook and in its neighborhood, below Albany.

[3] Query, Catskill? Fishkill is 100 miles from Albany.

were left when the country was cleared to fortify the banks against the masses of thick ice which make war upon them in spring, when the melting snows burst this glassy pavement, and raise the waters many feet above their usual level. This precaution not only answers that purpose, but gratifies the mind by presenting to the eye a remnant of wild magnificence of nature amidst the smiling scenes produced by varied and successful cultivation. As you came along by the north end of the town, where the patroon had his seat, you afterwards passed by the enclosures of the citizens, where, as formerly described, they planted their corn, and arrived at the Flats, Col. Schuyler's possession.[1] On the right you saw the river in all its beauty, there above a mile broad. On the opposite side the view was bounded by steep hills, covered with lofty pines, from which a waterfall descended,[2] which not only gave animation to the

[1] In the last century, the road passed down in front of the patroon's mansion, to the river, and followed its bank northward to Stillwater, where the troops took bateaux. This ancient road was known as the king's highway. In front of Madame Schuyler's house those armies annually passed to the theatre of war on Lake Champlain, and sometimes encamped on the ground now occupied by the southern portion of West Troy.

"No. 2. Old Schuyler House" was the residence of the American Lady. Above and to the left lived Peter (Pedrom) Schuyler. (P. P. Schuyler was a son of the latter.) To the left of P. P. Schuyler resided Jeremiah Schuyler. His house was subsequently occupied by his grandson, Abraham N. Cuyler. Southeast of No. 2 is the island Mrs. Grant describes so graphically.

[2] This waterfall, known as the Wynant's kill, became, half a cen-

MAP OF THE FLATS ABOVE ALBANY.

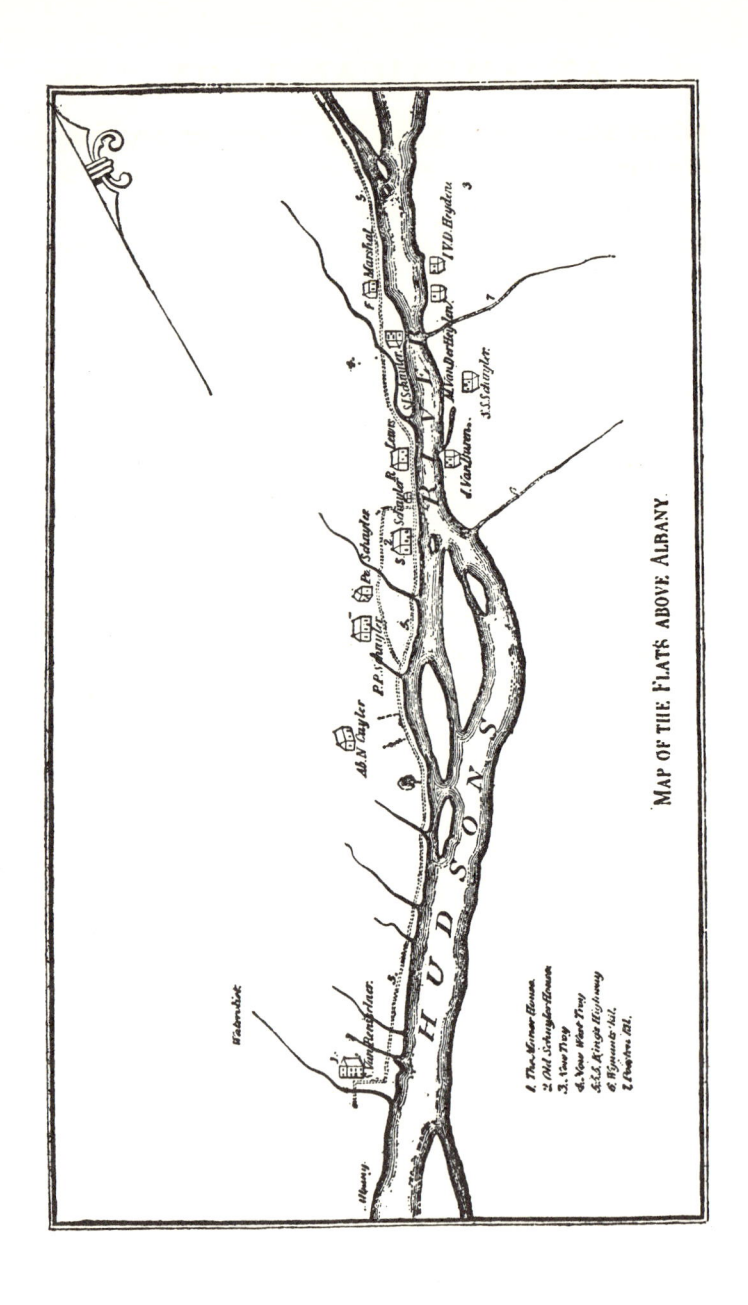

AN AMERICAN LADY 149

sylvan scene, but was the best barometer imaginable, foretelling by its varied and intelligible sounds every approaching change, not only of the weather, but of the wind. Opposite to the grounds lay an island, above a mile in length, and about a quarter in breadth, which also belonged to the colonel: exquisitely beautiful it was, and though the haunt I most delighted in, it is not in my power to describe it. Imagine a little Egypt, yearly overflowed, and of the most redundant fertility. This charming spot was at first covered tury ago, the site of the Albany nail works, whose fires light the skies by night, and send up pillars of smoke by day. The island has acquired a considerable altitude since the time of Mrs. Grant's residence there, and is otherwise changed, being in fact two islands, a narrow creek running between them.

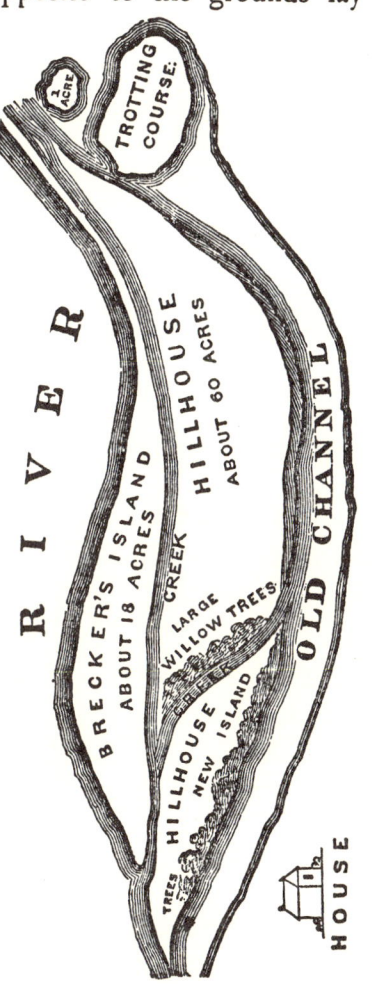

with wood, like the rest of the country, except a long field in the middle where the Indians had probably cultivated maize; round this was a broad shelving border, where the grey and the weeping willows, the bending osier, and numberless aquatic plants not known in this country, were allowed to flourish in the utmost luxuriance, while within, some tall sycamores and wild fruit trees towered above the rest. Thus was formed a broad belt, which in winter proved an impenetrable barrier against the broken ice, and in summer was the haunt of numberless birds and small animals, who dwelt in perfect safety, it being impossible to penetrate it. Numberless were the productions of this luxuriant spot; never was a richer field for a botanist; for though the ice was kept off, the turbid waters of the spring flood overflowed it annually, and not only deposited a rich sediment, but left the seeds of various plants swept from the shores it had passed by. The centre of the island, which was much higher than the sides, produced, with a slight degree of culture, the most abundant crops of wheat, hay, and flax. At the end of this island, which was exactly opposite to the family mansion, a long sand-bank extended: on this was a very valuable fishing-place, of which a considerable profit might be made. In summer, when the water was low, this narrow stripe (for such it was) came in sight, and furnished an amusing spectacle; for there the bald or white-headed eagle (a large picturesque bird, very frequent in this country), the ospray, the heron, and the curlew, used to stand in great numbers in a long row, like a military arrangement, for a whole summer day, fishing for perch and a kind of fresh-water herring which abounded there. At the same season a variety of wild ducks, who bred on the shores of the island (among which was a small white diver of an elegant form), led forth their young to try their first excursion. What a scene have I beheld on a calm summer evening! There indeed were "fringed banks" richly fringed, and wonderfully variegated; where every imaginable shade of color mingled, and where life teemed prolific on every side. The river, a perfect mirror, reflecting the pine-covered hills opposite; and the pliant shades that bend without a wind, round this enchanting island, while hundreds of the white divers, sawbill ducks with scarlet heads, teal, and other aquatic birds, sported at once on the calm waters. At the discharge of a gun from the shore, these feathered beauties all disappeared at once, as if by magic, and in an instant rose to view in different places.

How much they seemed to enjoy that life which was so new to them; for they were the young broods first led forth to sport upon the waters. While the fixed attitude and lofty port of the large birds of prey, who were ranged upon the sandy shelf, formed an inverted picture in the same clear mirror, and were a pleasing contrast to the playful multitude around. These they never attempted to disturb, well aware of the facility of escape which their old retreats afforded them. Such of my readers as have had patience to follow me to this favorite isle, will be, ere now, as much bewildered as I have often been myself on its luxuriant shores. To return to the southward, on the confines of what might then be called an interminable wild, rose two gently sloping eminences, about half a mile from the shore. From each of these a large brook descended, bending through the plain, and having their course marked by the shades of primeval trees and shrubs left there to shelter the cattle when the ground was cleared. On these eminences, in the near neighborhood and full view of the mansion at the Flats, were two large and well built dwellings, inhabited by Colonel Schuyler's two younger sons, Peter and Jeremiah. To the eldest was allotted the place inhabited by his father, which, from its lower situation and level surface, was called the Flats. There was a custom prevalent among the new settlers something like that of gavelkind; they made a pretty equal division of lands among their younger sons. The eldest, by preëminence of birth, had a larger share, and generally succeeded to the domain inhabited by his father, with the slaves, cattle, and effects upon it.

This, in the present instance, was the lot of the eldest son of that family whose possessions I have been describing. His portion of land on the shore of the river was scarcely equal in value to those of his brother, to whose possessions the brooks I have mentioned formed a natural boundary, dividing them from each other, and from his. To him was allotted the costly furniture of the family, of which paintings, plate, and china constituted the valuable part; everything else being merely plain and useful. They had also, a large house in Albany, which they occupied occasionally.

I have neglected to describe in its right place the termination or back ground of the landscape I have such delight in recollecting. There the solemn and interminable forest was varied here and there by rising grounds, near streams where birch and hickory, maple and poplar, cheered the eye with a lighter green, through the prevailing shade of dusky pines. On the border of the wood, where the trees had been thinned for firing, was a broad shrubbery all along, which marked the edges of the wood above the possessions of the brothers as far as it extended.

This was formed of sumac, a shrub with leaves continually changing color through all the varieties from blending green and yellow to orange tawney, and adorned with large lilac-shaped clusters of bright scarlet grains, covered with pungent dust of a sharp flavor, at once saline and acid. This the Indians used as salt to their food, and for the dyeing of different colors. The red glow, which was the general result of this natural border, had a fine effect, thrown out from the dusky shades which towered behind.

To the northward, a sandy tract, covered with low pines, formed a boundary betwixt the Flats and Stonehook,[1] which lay further up the river.

[1] Steenhoek was in front of the plat now occupied by the Arsenal, and the Steenhoek kill is still seen issuing from the government grounds, draining the swamp in the rear.

Chapter XV

PHILIP SCHUYLER — HIS MANAGEMENT OF THE INDIANS

PHILIP SCHUYLER, who on the death of his father, succeeded to the inheritance I have been describing, was a person of a mild, benevolent character, and an excellent understanding, which had received more culture than was usual in that country. But whether he had returned to Europe, for the purpose of acquiring knowledge in the public seminaries there, or had been instructed by any of the French protestants, who were sometimes retained in the principal families for such purposes, I do not exactly know; but am led rather to suppose the latter, from the connection which always subsisted between that class of people and the Schuyler family.

When the intimacy between this gentleman and the subject of these memoirs took place she was a mere child; for the colonel, as he was soon after called, was ten years older than she. This was singular there, where most men married under twenty. But his early years were occupied by momentous concerns; for, by this time, the public safety began to be endangered by the insidious wiles of the French Canadians, to whom our frontier settlers began to be formidable rivals in the fur trade, which the former wished to engross. In process of time, the Indians, criminally indulged with strong liquors by the most avaricious and unprincipled of the traders, began to have an insatiable desire for them, and the traders' avidity for gain increased in the same proportion.

Occasional fraud on the one hand gave rise to occasional violence on the other. Mutual confidence decayed, and hostility betrayed itself, when intoxication laid open every thought. Some of our traders were, as the colonists alleged, treacherously killed in violation of treaties solemnly concluded between them and the offending tribes.

The mediation and protection of the Mohawk tribes were as usual appealed to. But these shrewd politicians saw evident the value of their protection to an unwarlike people, who made no effort to defend themselves; and who, distant from the source of authority, and contributing nothing to the support of government, were in a great measure neglected. They began also to observe, that their new friends were extending their possessions on every side, and conscious of their wealth and increasing numbers, did not assiduously cultivate the good will of their faithful allies as formerly. These nations, savage as we may imagine them, were as well skilled in the arts of negotiation as the most polite Europeans. They waged perpetual war with each other about their hunting grounds; each tribe laying claim to some vast wild territory destined for that purpose, and divided from other districts by boundaries which we should consider as merely ideal, but which they perfectly understood. Yet these were not so distinctly defined as to preclude all dispute; and a casual encroachment on this imaginary deer park, was a sufficient ground of hostility; and this, not for the value of the few deer or bears which might be killed, but that they thought their national honor violated by such an aggression. That system of revenge, which subsisted with equal force among them all, admitted of no sincere conciliation till the aggrieved party had obtained at least an equal number of scalps and prisoners for those that they had lost. This bloody reckoning was not easily adjusted. After a short and hollow truce, the remaining balance on either side afforded a pretext for new hostility, and time to solicit new alliances; for which last purpose much art and much persuasive power of eloquence were employed.

But the grand mystery of Indian politics was the flattery, the stratagem, and address employed in detaching other tribes from the alliance of their enemies. There could not be a stronger proof of the restless and turbulent nature of ambition than these artful negotiations, the consequence of perpetual hostility, where one would think there was so little ground for quarrel; and that amongst a people who individually, were by no means quarrelsome or covetous, and seemed in their private transactions with each other, impressed with a deep sense of moral rectitude; who reasoned soundly, reflected deeply, and acted in most cases consequentially. Property there was none, to afford a pretext for war, excepting a little possessed by the Mohawks, which they knew so well how to defend, that their boundaries were never violated; "For their awe and their fear was upon all the nations round about." Territory could not be the genuine subject of contention in these thinly peopled forests, where the ocean and the pole were the only limits of their otherwise boundless domain. The consequence attached to the authority of chiefs, who, as such, possessed no more property than others, and had not power to command a single vassal for their own personal benefit, was not such as to be the object of those wars. Their chief privilege was that of being first in every dangerous enterprise. They were loved and honored, but never, that I have heard of, traduced, envied, or removed from their painful preëminence.

The only way in which these wars can be accounted for, is, first, from the general depravity of our nature, and from a singularly deep feeling of injury, and a high sense of national honor. They were not the hasty outbreakings of savage fury, but were commenced in the most solemn and deliberate manner; and not without a prelude of remonstrances, from the aggrieved party, and attempts to soothe and conciliate from the other. This digression must not be considered as altogether from the purpose. To return to the Indians, whose history has its use in illustrating that of mankind: they now became fully sensible of the importance they derived from the increased wealth and undefended state of the settlement. They discovered too, that they held the balance between the interior settlements of France and England, which, though still distant from each other, were daily approximating.

The Mohawks, though always brave and always faithful, felt a very allowable repugnance to expose the lives of their warriors in defence of those who made no effort to defend themselves; who were neither protected by the arms of their sovereign, nor by their own courage. They came down to hold a solemn congress, at which the heads of the Schuyler and Cuyler families assisted; and where it was agreed that hostilities should be delayed for the present, the hostile nations pacified by concessions and presents, and means adopted to put the settlement in a state of defence against future aggressions.

On all such occasions, when previously satisfied with regard to the justice of the grounds of quarrel, the Mohawks promised their hearty coöperation. This they were the readier to do, as their young brother Philip (for so they styled Colonel Schuyler) offered not only to head such troops as might be raised for this purpose, but to engage his two brothers, who were well acquainted with the whole frontier territory, to serve on the same terms. This was a singular instance of public spirit in a young patriot, who was an entire stranger to the profession of arms; and whose sedate equanimity of character was adverse to every species of rashness or enthusiasm. Meantime the provisions of the above-mentioned treaty could not be carried into effect, till they were ratified by the assembly at New York, and approved by the governor. Of this there was little doubt; the difficulty was to raise and pay the troops. In the interim, while steps were taking to legalize the project, in 1719, the marriage betwixt Colonel Schuyler and his cousin took place under the happiest auspices.

Chapter XVI

ACCOUNT OF THE THREE BROTHERS

COLONEL Schuyler and his two brothers all possessed a superior degree of intellect, and uncommon external advantages. Peter, the only one remaining when I knew the family, was still a comely and dignified looking old gentleman; and I was told his brothers were at least equal to him in this respect. His youngest brother Jeremiah,[1] who was much beloved for a disposition, frank, cheerful and generous to excess, had previously married a lady from New York; with whom he obtained some fortune: a thing then singular in that country. This lady, whom, in her declining years, I knew very well, was the daughter of a wealthy and distinguished family of French protestants. She was lively, sensible, and well informed.

Peter,[2] the second, was married to a native of Albany. She died early; but left behind two children; and the reputation of much worth and

[1] Peter and Jeremiah Schuyler were twins, and baptized in the church January 12, 1698, the youngest of the children of Col. Peter, whom the Indians called Quidor. Peter junior married Catharine Groesbeck, and Jeremiah married Susanna ———, a Huguenot lady of New York. Jeremiah was buried at the Flats in 1753, but Peter was living September, 1771.

[2] Peter the third, not the second. See note on p. 253.

great attention to her conjugal and maternal duties. All these relations lived with each other, and with the new married lady, in habits of the most cordial intimacy and perfect confidence. They seemed, indeed, actuated by one spirit; having in all things similar views and similar principles. Looking up to the colonel as the head of the family, whose worth and affluence reflected consequence upon them all, they never dreamt of envying either his superior manners, or his wife's attainments, which they looked upon as a benefit and ornament to the whole.

Soon after their marriage they visited New York, which they continued to do once a year in the earlier period of their marriage, on account of their connection in that city, and the pleasing and intelligent society that was always to be met with there, both on account of its being the seat of government, and the residence of the commander-in-chief on the continent, who was then necessarily invested with considerable power and privileges, and had, as well as the governor for the time being, a petty court assembled round him. At a very early period a better style of manners, greater ease, frankness, and polish prevailed at New York, than in any of the neighboring provinces. There was, in particular, a Brigadier-general Hunter,[1] of whom I have heard Mrs. Schuyler talk a great deal, as coinciding with

[1] Robert Hunter succeeded Francis Lovelace as governor of New York in 1709, and was governor of Jamaica, in 1728.

her husband successively, in their plans either of defence or improvement. He, I think, was then governor; and was as acceptable to the Schuylers for his colloquial talents and friendly disposition, as estimable for his public spirit and application to business, in which respects he was not equalled by any of his successors. In his circle the young couple were much distinguished. There were too among those leading families, the Livingstons and Rensselaers, friends connected with them both by blood and attachment. There was also another distinguished family to whom they were allied, and with whom they lived in cordial intimacy; these were the De Lanceys, of French descent, but, by subsequent intermarriages, blended with the Dutch inhabitants. Of these there were very many then in New York, as will be hereafter explained; but as these conscientious exiles were persons allied in religion to the primitive settlers, and regular and industrious in their habits, they soon mingled with and became a part of that society, which was enlivened by their sprightly manners, and benefited by the useful arts they brought along with them. In this mixed society, which must have had attraction for young people of superior, and, in some degree, cultivated intellect, this well-matched pair took great pleasure; and here, no doubt, was improved that liberality of mind and manners which so much distinguished them from the less enlightened inhabitants of their native city. They were so much caressed in New York, and found so many charms in the intelligent and comparatively polished society of which they made a part there, that they had at first some thoughts of residing there. These, however, soon gave way to the persuasions of the colonel, with whom they principally resided till his death, which happened 1721,[1] two years after. This union was productive of all that felicity which might be expected to result from entire congeniality not of sentiment only, but of original dispositions, attachments, and modes of living and thinking. He had been accustomed to consider her as a child with tender endearment. She had been used to look up to him from infancy as the model of manly excellence; and they drew knowledge and virtue from the same fountain, in the mind of that respectable parent whom they equally loved and revered.

[1] He seems to have been buried 22 September, 1724. See Pearson's "Early Settlers of Albany," also note 1 on p. 147.

Chapter XVII

THE HOUSE AND RURAL ECONOMY OF THE FLATS — BIRDS AND INSECTS

I HAVE already sketched a general outline of that pleasant home to which the colonel was now about to bring his beloved.

Before I resume my narrative, I shall indulge myself in a still more minute account of the premises, the mode of living, etc., which will afford a more distinct idea of the country; all the wealthy and informed people of the settlement living on a smaller scale, pretty much in the same manner. Be it known, however, that the house I had so much delight in recollecting, had no pretension to grandeur, and very little to elegance. It was a large brick house of two or rather three stories (for there were excellent attics), besides a sunk story, finished with the exactest neatness. The lower floor had two spacious rooms, with large light closets; on the first there were three rooms, and in the upper one four. Through the middle of the house was a very wide passage, with opposite front and back doors, which in summer admitted a stream of air peculiarly grateful to the languid senses. It was furnished with chairs and pictures like a summer parlor.

Here the family usually sat in hot weather, when there were no ceremonious strangers.

Valuable furniture (though perhaps not very well chosen or assorted) was the favorite luxury of these people; and in all the houses I remember, except those of the brothers, who were every way more liberal, the mirrors, the paintings, the china, but above all, the state bed, were considered as the family seraphim, secretly worshiped, and only exhibited on very rare occasions. But in Col. Schuyler's family the rooms were merely shut up to keep the flies, which in that country are an absolute nuisance, from spoiling the furniture.[1] Another motive was, that they might be pleasantly cool when opened for company. This house had also two appendages common to all those belonging to persons in easy circumstances there. One was a large portico at the door, with a few steps leading up to it, and floored like a room; it was open at the sides, and had seats all round. Above was either a slight wooden roof, painted like an awning, or a covering of lattice-work, over which a transplanted vine spread its luxuriant leaves and numerous clusters. These, though small, and rather too acid till sweetened by the frost, had a beautiful appearance. What gave an air of liberty and safety to these rustic porticoes, which always produced in my mind a sensation of pleasure that I know not

[1] They still preserve at the house of Mr. Stephen Schuyler, some of the furniture of Madame Schuyler.

how to define, was the number of little birds domesticated there. For their accommodation there was a small shelf built round, where they nestled, sacred from the touch of slaves and children, who were taught to regard them as the good genii of the place, not to be disturbed with impunity.

I do not recollect sparrows there,[1] except the wood-sparrow. These little birds were of various kinds peculiar to the country; but the one most frequent and familiar was a pretty little creature, of a bright cinnamon color, called a wren, though little resembling the one to which we give that name, for it is more sprightly, and flies higher. Of these and other small birds, hundreds gave and received protection around this hospitable dwelling. The protection they received consisted merely in the privilege of being let alone. That which they bestowed was of more importance than any inhabitant of Britain can imagine. In these new countries,

[1] English sparrows, as they are commonly called, were introduced into Albany about the year 1865, where they were tenderly cherished and fed, as the enemy of worms that infested shade trees in unusual number and variety. Their popularity was seriously diminished, however, when it was discovered that they had driven away the wrens, blue-birds, robins, and other familiar birds, whose cheerful notes had been substituted by the single harsh and monotonous chirp of their successors. Out of the city precincts a different reception awaited them. There the husbandman, jealous of his grain fields, saluted the sparrow with the shot-gun. Their presence soon began to be regarded in the city as an unequal exchange for the popular songsters that had been driven away, and their habits to be attended with unpleasant annoyance.

where man has scarce asserted his dominion, life swarms abundant on every side; the insect population is numerous beyond belief, and the birds that feed on them are in proportion to their abundance. In process of time, when their sheltering woods are cleared, all these recede before their master, but not before his empire is fully established. These minute aërial foes are more harassing than the terrible inhabitants of the forest, and more difficult to expel. It is only by protecting, and in some sort domesticating, these little winged allies, who attack them in their own element, that the conqueror of the lion and tamer of the elephant can hope to sleep in peace, or eat his meals unpolluted. While breakfasting or drinking tea in the airy portico, which was often the scene of these meals, birds were constantly gliding over the table with a butterfly, grasshopper, or cicada in their bills, to feed their young, who were chirping above. These familiar inmates brushed by without ceremony, while the chimney swallow, the martin, and other hirundines in countless numbers darted past in pursuit of this aërial population, while the fields resounded with the ceaseless chirping of many gay insects unknown to our more temperate summers. These were now and then mingled with the animated and not unpleasing cry of the tree-frog, a creature of that species, but of a light slender form, almost transparent, and of a lively green; it is dry to the touch, and has not the dank moisture of its aquatic relations; in short it is a pretty lively creature, with a singular and cheerful note. This loud and not unpleasing insect chorus, with the swarms of gay butterflies in constant motion, enliven scenes to which the prevalence of woods, rising "shade above shade" on every side, would otherwise give a still and solemn aspect. Several objects, which with us are no small additions to the softened changes and endless charms of rural scenery, it must be confessed are wanting there. No lark welcomes the sun that rises to gild the dark forests and gleaming lakes of America; no mellow thrush or deep-toned blackbird warbles through these awful solitudes, or softens the balmy hour of twilight with

" The liquid language of the *groves*."

Twilight itself, the mild and shadowy hour, so soothing to every feeling, every pensive mind; that soft transition from day to night, so dear to peace, so due to meditation, is here scarce known, at least only known to have its shortness regretted. No daisy hastens to meet the spring, or embellishes the meads in summer; here no purple heath exhales its wholesome odor, or decks the arid waste with the chastened glow of its waving bells. No *bonny* broom, such as enlivens the narrow vales of Scotland with gaudy bloom, nor flowering furze with its golden blossoms, defying the cold blasts of early spring, animate their sandy wilds. There the white-blossomed sloe does not forerun the orchard's bloom, nor the pale primrose shelter its modest head beneath the tangled shrubs. Nature, bountiful yet not profuse, has assigned her various gifts to various climes, in such a manner that none can claim a decided preëminence; and every country has peculiar charms, which endear it to the natives beyond any other. I have been tempted by lively recollections into a digression rather unwarrantable. To return:

At the back of the large house was a smaller and lower one, so joined to it as to make the form of a cross. There one or two lower and smaller rooms below, and the same number above, afforded a refuge to the family during the rigors of winter, when the spacious summer rooms would have been intolerably cold, and the smoke of prodigious wood fires would have sullied the elegantly clean furniture. Here, too, was a sunk story, where the kitchen was immediately below the eating parlor, and increased the general warmth of the house. In summer the negroes resided in slight outer kitchens, where food was dressed for the family. Those who wrought in the fields, often had their simple dinner cooked without, and ate it under the shade of a great tree. One room I should have said, in the greater house only, was opened for the reception of company; all the rest were bed-chambers for their accommodation, while the domestic friends of the family occupied neat little bedrooms in the attics, or in the winter house.

This house contained no drawing-room; that was an unheard-of luxury; the winter rooms had carpets; the lobby had oil-cloth painted in lozenges, to imitate blue and white marble. The best bedroom was hung with family portraits, some of which were admirably executed; and in the eating room, which, by the bye, was rarely used for that purpose, were some fine scripture paintings; that which made the greatest impression on my imagination, and seemed to be universally admired, was one of Esau coming to demand the anticipated blessing; the noble manly figure of the luckless hunter, and the anguish expressed in his comely though strong-featured countenance, I shall never forget. The house fronted the river, on the brink of which, under shades of elm and sycamore, ran the great road towards Saratoga, Stillwater, and the northern lakes; a little simple avenue of morella cherry trees, enclosed with a white rail, led to the road and river, not three hundred yards distant. Adjoining to this, on the south side, was an enclosure, subdivided into three parts, of which the first was a small hay field, opposite the south end of the house; the next, not so long, a garden; and the third, by far the largest, an orchard. These were surrounded by simple deal fences. Now let not the genius that presides over pleasure-grounds, nor any of his elegant votaries, revolt with disgust while I mention the unseemly ornaments which were exhibited on the stakes to which the deals of these same fences were bound. Truly they consisted of the skeleton heads of horses and cattle in as great numbers as could be procured, stuck upon the above said poles. This was not mere ornament either, but a most hospitable arrangement for the accommodation of the small familiar birds before described. The jaws are fixed on the pole, and the skull uppermost. The wren, on seeing a skull thus placed, never fails to enter by the orifice, which is too small to admit the hand of an infant, lines the pericranium with small twigs and horse hair, and there lays her eggs in full security. It is very amusing to see the little creature carelessly go out and in at this little aperture, though you should be standing immediately beside it. Not satisfied with providing these singular asylums for their feathered friends, the negroes never fail to make a small round hole in the crown of every old hat they can lay their hands on, and nail it to the end of the kitchen, for the same purpose. You often see in such a one, at once, thirty or forty of these odd little domicils, with the inhabitants busily going out and in.

Besides all these salutary provisions for the domestic comfort of the birds, there was, in clearing the way for their first establishment, a tree always left in the middle of the back yard, for their sole emolument: this tree being purposely pollarded at midsummer, when all the branches were full of sap. Wherever there had been a branch the decay of the inside produced a hole; and every hole was the habitation of a bird. These were of various kinds; some of which had a pleasing note, but on the whole, their songsters are far inferior to ours. I rather dwell on these minutiæ, as they not only mark the peculiarities of the country, but convey very truly the image of a people not too refined for happiness, which, in the process of elegant luxury, is apt to die of disgust.

Chapter XVIII

DESCRIPTION OF COLONEL SCHUYLER'S BARN

ADJOINING to the orchard was the most spacious barn I ever beheld; which I shall describe for the benefit of such of my readers as have never seen a building constructed on a plan so comprehensive. This barn, which, as will hereafter appear, answered many beneficial purposes besides those usually allotted for such edifices, was of a vast size, at least an hundred feet long, and sixty wide. The roof rose to a very great height in the midst, and sloped down till it came within ten feet of the ground, when the walls commenced; which, like the whole of this fabric, was formed of wood. It was raised three feet from the ground, by beams resting on stone; and on these beams were laid in the middle of the building a very massive oak floor. Before the door was a large sill, sloping downwards, of the same materials. About twelve feet in breadth on each side of this capacious building were divided off for cattle; on one side ran a manger, at the above mentioned distance from the wall, the whole length of the building, with a rack above it; on the others were stalls for the other cattle, running also the whole length of the building. The cattle and horses stood with their hinder parts to the wall, and their heads projecting towards the threshing floor. There was a prodigious large box or open chest in one side built up, for holding the corn after it was thrashed; and the roof, which was very lofty and spacious, was supported by large cross beams; from one to the other of these was stretched a great number of long poles, so as to form a sort of open loft, on which the whole rich crop was laid up. The floor of those parts of the barn, which answered the purposes of a stable and cow-house, was made of thick slab deals, laid loosely over the supporting beams. And the mode of cleaning those places was by turning the boards, and permitting the dung and litter to fall into the receptacles left open below for the purpose: from thence, in spring they were often driven down the river, the soil in its original state not requiring the aid of manure. In the front[1] of this vast edifice there were prodigious folding doors, and two others that opened behind.

Certainly never did cheerful rural toils wear a more exhilarating aspect than while the domestics were lodging the luxuriant harvest in this capacious repository. When speaking of the doors, I should have mentioned that they were made in the gable ends; those in the back equally large, to correspond with those in the front; while on each side of the

[1] By the front is meant the gable end, which contains the entrance. — *Mrs. Grant.*

great doors were smaller ones, for the cattle and horses to enter. Whenever the corn or hay was reaped or cut, and ready for carrying home, which in that dry and warm climate happened in a very few days, a wagon loaded with hay, for instance, was driven into the midst of this great barn, loaded also with numberless large grasshoppers, butterflies, and cicadas, who came along with the hay. From the top of the wagon, this was immediately forked up into the loft of the barn, in the midst of which was an open space left for the purpose; and then the unloaded wagon drove, in rustic state, out of the great door at the other end. In the meantime every member of the family witnessed, or assisted in this summary process; by which the building and thatching of stacks was at once saved; and the whole crop and cattle were thus compendiously lodged under one roof.

The cheerfulness of this animated scene was much heightened by the quick appearance, and vanishing of the swallows; who twittered among their high-built dwellings in the roof. Here, as in every other instance, the safety of these domestic friends was attended to; and an abode provided for them. In the front of this barn were many holes, like those of a pigeon-house, for the accommodation of the martin:[1] that being the species

[1] The martin, the largest of the swallow family, has disappeared from this locality. Seventy years ago elevated boxes were provided for their accommodation in rearing their young at many residences in

to which this kind of home seems most congenial; and, in the inside of the barn, I have counted above fourscore at once. In the winter, when the earth was buried deep in new fallen snow, and no path fit for walking in was left, this barn was like a great gallery, well suited for that purpose; and furnished with pictures, not unpleasing to a simple and contented mind. As you walked through this long area, looking up, you beheld the abundance of the year treasured above you; on one side the comely heads of your snorting steeds presented themselves arranged in seemly order; on the other, your kine displayed their meeker visages, while the perspective on either, was terminated by heifers and fillies no less interesting. In the midst, your servants exercised the flail; and even, while they threshed out the straw, distributed it to the expectants on both sides; while the "liberal handful" was occasionally thrown to the many colored poultry on the hill. Winter itself never made this abode of life and plenty cold or cheerless. Here you might walk and view all your subjects, and their means of support, at one glance; except, indeed, the sheep, for whom a large and commodious building was erected very near the barn: the roof of which was furnished with a loft large enough to contain hay sufficient for their winter's food.

city and country. They appeared about the middle of April, and having reared two broods during the summer, departed about the third week in August for a warmer winter climate.

Col. Schuyler's barn was by far the largest I have ever seen: but all of them, in that country, were constructed on the same plan, furnished with the same accommodation, and presented the same cheering aspect. The orchard, as I formerly mentioned, was on the south side of the barn; on the north, a little farther back towards the wood, which formed a dark screen behind this smiling scene, there was an enclosure, in which the remains of the deceased members of the family were deposited. A field of pretty large extent, adjoining to the house on that side, remained uncultivated, and unenclosed; over it were scattered a few large apple trees of a peculiar kind; the fruit of which was never appropriated. This piece of level and productive land, so near the family mansion, and so adapted to various and useful purposes, was never made use of: but left open as a public benefit.

From the known liberality of this munificent family, all Indians, or new settlers, on their journey, whether they came by land or water, rested here. The military, in passing, always formed a camp on this common; and here the Indian wigwams were often planted; here all manner of garden stuff, fruit, and milk, were plentifully distributed to wanderers of all descriptions. Every summer, for many years, there was an encampment, either of regular or provincial troops, on 'this common: and often when the troops proceeded northward, a little colony of helpless women and children, belonging to them, was left in a great measure dependent on the compassion of these worthy patriarchs; for such the brothers might be justly called.

Chapter XIX

MILITARY PREPARATIONS — FIDELITY OF THE MOHAWKS

THE first year of the colonel's marriage was chiefly spent in New York, and in visits to the friends of his bride and other relations. The following years they spent at home; surrounded daily by his brothers, and their families, and other relatives, with whom they maintained the most affectionate intercourse. The colonel, however (as I have called him by anticipation), had, at this time, his mind engaged by public duties of the most urgent nature. He was a member of the colonial assembly; and, by a kind of hereditary right, was obliged to support that character of patriotism, courage, and public wisdom, which had so eminently distinguished his father. The father of Mrs. Schuyler, too, had been long mayor of Albany;[1] at that time an office of great importance: as including, within itself, the entire civil power exercised over the whole settlement as well as the town, and having attached to it a sort of patriarchal authority; for the people, little ac-

---

[1] He was mayor from 1703 to 1706. His son Johannis Jr., held the office 1742-3.

quainted with coercion, and by no means inclined to submit to it, had, however, a profound reverence, as is generally the case in the infancy of society, for the families of their first leaders; whom they had looked up to merely as knowing them to possess superior worth, talent and enterprise. In a society, as yet uncorrupted, the value of this rich inheritance can only be diminished by degradation of character, in the representative of a family thus self-ennobled; especially if he be disinterested. This, though apparently a negative quality, being the one of all others that, combined with the higher powers of mind, most engages affection in private and esteem in public life. This is a shield that blunts the shafts which envy never fails to level at the prosperous, even in old establishments; where, from the very nature of things, a thousand obstructions rise in the upward path of merit, and a thousand temptations appear to mislead it from its direct road; and where the rays of opinion are refracted by so many prejudices of contending interests and factions. Still, if any charm can be found to fix that fleeting phantom popularity, this is it; it would be very honorable to human nature, if this could be attributed to the pure love of virtue; but alas! multitudes are not made up of the wise or the virtuous. Yet the very unselfishness of our nature inclines us to love and trust those who are not likely to desire any benefit from us in return for those they confer. Other vices may be, if not social, in some degree gregarious: but even the avaricious hate avarice in all but themselves.

Thus, inheriting unstained integrity, unbounded popularity, a cool, determined spirit, and ample possessions, no man had fairer pretensions to unlimited sway, in the sphere in which he moved, than the colonel; but of this, no man could be less desirous. He was too wise and too happy to solicit authority; and yet too public-spirited and too generous to decline it, when any good was to be done or any evil resisted; from which no private benefit resulted to himself.

Young as his wife was, and much as she valued the blessing of their union, and the pleasure of his society, she showed a spirit worthy of a Roman matron; in willingly risking all her happiness, even in that early period of her marriage, by consenting to his assuming a military command; and leading forth the provincial troops against the common enemy; who had now become more boldly dangerous than ever. Not content with secretly stimulating the Indian tribes, who were their allies, and enemies to the Mohawks, to acts of violence, the French Canadians, in violation of existing treaties, began to make incursions on the slightest pretexts. It was no common warfare in which the colonel was about to engage; but the duties of entering on vigorous measures for the defence of the country, became not only obvious but urgent.

No other person but he had influence enough to produce any cohesion among the people of that district, or any determination, with their own arms and at their own cost, to attack the common enemy. As formerly observed, this had hitherto been trusted to the five confederate Mohawk nations; who, though still faithful to their old friends, had too much sagacity and observation, and indeed too strong a native sense of rectitude to persuade their young warriors to go on venturing their lives in defence of those, who, from their increased power and numbers, were able to defend themselves with the aid of their allies. Add to this, that their possessions were on all sides daily extending; and that they, the Albanians, were carrying their trade for furs, etc., into the deepest recesses of the forests, and towards those great lakes which the Canadians were accustomed to consider as the boundaries of their dominions; and where they had Indians whom they were at great pains to attach to themselves, and to inspire against us and our allies.

Colonel Schuyler's father had held the same rank in a provincial corps formerly: but in his time, there was a profound peace in the district he inhabited; though from his resolute temper, and knowledge of public business, and of the different Indian languages, he was selected to head a regiment raised in the Jerseys and the adjacent bounds, for the defence of the back frontiers of Pennsylvania, New England, etc. Colonel Philip Schuyler was the first who raised a corps in the interior of the province of New York; which was not only done by his personal influence, but occasioned him a considerable expense, though the regiment was paid by the province, the province also furnishing arms and military stores; their service being, like that of all provincials, limited to the summer half year.[1]

The governor and chief commander came up to Albany to view and approve the preparations making for this interior war, and to meet the congress of Indian sachems; who on that occasion, renewed their solemn league with their brother the great king. Colonel Schuyler, being then the person they most looked up to and confided in, was their proxy on this occasion in ratifying an engagement to which they ever adhered with singular fidelity. And mutual presents brightened the chain of amity, to use their own figurative language.

The common and the barn, at the Flats, were

[1] After the treaty of Utrecht, 1713, there was peace between England and France about thirty years, during which time their American colonies enjoyed repose. In the meantime the French of Canada built Fort St. Frederick at Crown Point on Lake Champlain, and made other preparations for future hostilities. About 1743, during the war of the Austrian Succession, so called, the colonies were again in arms. Fort St. Frederick was a standing menace to New York and New England, and they organized an army for its capture. Col. Philip Schuyler, commanding the Albany militia, took part in the military preparations for the expedition. His cousin, Col. Peter Schuyler of New Jersey, and not his father, who had been dead several years, commanded a regiment, and was required to defend the frontiers of his state and of Pennsylvania.

fully occupied, and the hospitable mansion, as was usual on all public occasions, overflowed. There the general, his aid-de-camps, the sachems, and the principal officers of the colonel's regiment, were received; and those who could not find room there of the next class, were accommodated by Peter and Jeremiah. On the common was an Indian encampment: and the barn and orchard were full of the provincials. All these last brought as usual their own food; but were supplied by this liberal family with every production of the garden, dairy, and orchard. While the colonel's judgment was exercised in the necessary regulations for this untried warfare, Mrs. Schuyler, by the calm fortitude she displayed in this trying exigence, by the good sense and good breeding with which she accommodated her numerous and various guests, and by those judicious attentions to family concerns, which, producing order and regularity through every department without visible bustle and anxiety, enable the mistress of a family to add grace and ease to hospitality, showed herself worthy of her distinguished lot.

Chapter XX

A REFRACTORY WARRIOR — THE SPIRIT PERVADING THE NEW ENGLAND PROVINCES

WHILE these preparations were going on, the general [1] [Gov. Shirley] was making every effort of the neighborhood to urge those who had promised assistance, to come forward with their allotted quotas.

On the other side of the river, not very far from the Flats, lived a person whom I shall not name; though his conduct was so peculiar and characteristic of the times, that his anti-heroism is on that sole account worth mentioning. This person lived in great security and abundance, in a place like an earthly paradise, and scarcely knew what it was to have an ungratified wish, having had considerable wealth left to him; and from the simple and domestic habits of his life, had formed no desires beyond it, unless indeed it were the desire of being

[1] The courage, ability and energy of Gov. Shirley were not eminently appreciated in New York. Yet his acts are abundantly recorded in the volumes of the documentary history of that colony. He has found an ardent vindicator in Samuel G. Drake, in the "Particular History of the French and Indian War" (1870), in which his civil and military services are set forth advantageously, and he is characterized as one of the ablest of the colonial governors.

thought a brave man, which seemed his greatest ambition: he was strong, robust, and an excellent marksman; talked loud, looked fierce, and always expressed the utmost scorn and detestation of cowardice. The colonel applied to him, that his name, and the names of such adherents as he could bring, might be set down in the list of those who were to bring their quota, against a given time, for the general defence; with the request he complied. When the rendezvous came on, this talking warrior had changed his mind, and absolutely refused to appear; the general sent for him, and warmly expostulated on his breach of promise; the bad example, and the disarrangement of plan which it occasioned: the culprit spoke in a high tone, saying, very truly "that the general was possessed of no legal means of coercion; that every one went or staid as they chose; and that his change of opinion on that subject rendered him liable to no penalty whatever." Tired of this sophistry, the enraged general had recourse to club law; and seizing a cudgel, belabored this recreant knight most manfully; while several Indian sachems, and many of his own countrymen and friends, coolly stood by; for the colonel's noted common was the scene of his assault. Our poor neighbor (as he long after became) suffered this dreadful bastinado, unaided and unpitied; and this example, and the subsequent contempt under which he labored (for he was ever after styled captain, and he did not refuse the title), was said to have an excellent effect in preventing such retrograde motions in subsequent campaigns.[1] The provincial troops, aided by the faithful Mohawks, performed their duty with great spirit and perseverance. They were, indeed, very superior to the ignorant, obstinate, and mean-souled beings, who, in after times, brought the very name of provincial troops into discredit; and were actuated by no single motive but that of avoiding the legal penalty then affixed to disobedience, and enjoying the pay and provisions allotted to them by the province or the mother country, I cannot exactly say which. Afterwards, when the refuse of mankind were selected, like Falstaff's soldiers, and raised much in the same way, the New York troops still maintained their respectability. This superiority might, without reproaching others, be in some measure accounted for from incidental causes. The four New England provinces were much earlier

[1] Above thirty years after, when the writer of these pages lived with her family at the Flats, the hero of this little tale used very frequently to visit her father, a veteran officer ; and being a great talker, war and politics were his incessant topics. There was no campaign or expedition proposed but what he censured and decided on ; proposing methods of his own, by which they might have been much better conducted ; in short Parolles with his drum was a mere type of our neighbor. Her father long wondered how kindly he took to him, and how a person of so much wealth and eloquence should dwell so obscurely, and shun all the duties of public life ; till at length we discovered that he still loved to talk arrogantly of war and public affairs, and pitched upon him for a listener, as the only person he could suppose ignorant of his disgrace. Such is human nature ! and so incurable is human vanity ! ! — *Mrs. Grant.*

settled, assumed sooner the forms of a civil community, and lived within narrower bounds; they were more laborious; their fanaticism, which they brought from England in its utmost fervor, long continued its effervescence, where there were no pleasures, or indeed lucrative pursuits, to detach their mind from it, and long after that genuine spirit of piety, which, however narrowed and disfigured, was still sincere, had in a great measure evaporated; enough of the pride and rigor of bigotry remained to make them detest and despise the Indian tribes, as ignorant heathen savages. The tribes, indeed, who inhabited their district, had been so weakened by an unsuccessful warfare with the Mohawks, and were so every way inferior to them, that after the first establishment of the colony, and a few feeble attacks successfully repulsed, they were no longer enemies to be dreaded, or friends to be courted. This had an unhappy effect with regard to those provinces; and to the different relations in which they stood with respect to the Indian, some part of the striking difference in the moral and military character of these various establishments must be attributed.

The people of New England left the mother country, as banished from it by what they considered oppression; came over foaming with religious and political fury, and narrowly missed having the most artful and able of demagogues, Cromwell himself, for their leader and guide. They might be compared to lava, discharged by the fury of internal combustion, from the bosom of the commonwealth, while inflamed by contending elements. This lava, every one acquainted with the convulsions of nature must know, takes a long time to cool; and when at length it is cooled, turns to a substance hard and barren, that long resists the kindly influence of the elements, before its surface resumes the appearance of beauty and fertility. Such were the almost literal effects of political convulsions, aggravated by a fiery and intolerant zeal for their own mode of worship, on these self-righteous colonists.

These preliminary remarks on the diversity of character in those neighboring provinces lead the way, in the meantime, to a discrimination, the effects of which have become interesting to the whole world.

Chapter XXI

DISTINGUISHING CHARACTERISTICS OF THE NEW YORK COLONISTS — HUGUENOTS AND PALATINES

BUT to return to the superior moral and military character of the New York populace. It was in the first place owing to a well-regulated piety, less concerned about forms than essentials. Next, to an influx of other than the original settlers, which tended to render the general system of opinion more liberal and tolerant. The French protestants, driven from their native land by intolerant bigotry, had lived at home excluded alike from public employments and fashionable society. Deprived of so many resources that were open to their fellow subjects, and forced to seek comfort in piety and concord for many privations, self-command and frugality had been in a manner forced upon them; consequently they were not so vain or so volatile as to disgust their new associates; while their cheerful tempers, accommodating manners, and patience under adversity, were very prepossessing.

These additional inhabitants, being such as had suffered real and extreme hardships for conscience sake, from absolute tyranny and the most cruel intolerance, rejoiced in the free exercise of a pure and rational religion, and in the protection of mild and equitable laws, as the first of human blessings; which privation had so far taught them to value, that they thought no exertion too great to preserve them. I should have formerly mentioned, besides the French refugees already spoken of, during the earliest period of the establishment of the British sovereignty in this part of the continent, a great number of the protestants, whom the fury of war and persecution on religious accounts had driven from the Palatinate, during the successful and desolating period of the wars carried on against that unhappy country by Louis the Fourteenth. The subdued and contented spirit, the simple and primitive manners, and frugal, industrious habits of these genuine sufferers for conscience sake, made them an acquisition to any society which received them, and a most suitable infusion among the inhabitants of this province; who, devoted to the pursuits of agriculture and the Indian trade, which encouraged a wild romantic spirit of adventure, little relished those mechanical employments, or that petty yet necessary traffic in shops, etc., to which part of every regulated society must needs devote their attention. These civic toils were left to those patient and industrious exiles; while the friendly intercourse with the original natives had strongly tinctured the first colonists with many of their habits and modes of thinking. Like them, they delighted in hunting; that image of war, which so generally, where it is the prevalent amusement, forms the body to athletic force and patient endurance, and the mind to daring intrepidity. It was not alone the timorous deer or feeble hare that were the objects of their pursuit; nor could they in such an impenetrable country attempt to rival the fox in speed or subtlety. When they kept their "few sheep in the wilderness," the she bear, jealous for her young, and the wolf, furious for prey, were to be encountered for their protection. From these allies too, many who lived much among them had learnt that fearless adherence to truth, which exalts the mind to the noblest kind of resolution. The dangers they were exposed to of meeting wandering individuals, or parties of hostile Indians, while traversing the woods in their sporting or commercial adventures, and the necessity that sometimes occurred of defending their families by their own personal prowess, from the stolen irruptions of detached parties of those usually called the French Indians, had also given their minds a warlike bent; and as a boy was not uncommonly trusted at nine or ten years of age with a light fowlingpiece, which he soon learned to use with great dexterity, few countries could produce such dexterous marksmen, or persons so well qualified for conquering those natural obstacles of thick woods and swamps, which would at once baffle the most determined European. It was not only that they were strong of limb, swift of foot, and excellent marksmen — the hatchet was as familiar to them as the musket; and an amateur, who had never cut wood but for his diversion, could hew down a tree with a celerity that would astonish and abash a professed wood-cutter in this country; in short, when means or arguments could be used powerful enough to collect a people so uncontrolled and so uncontrollable, and when headed by a leader whom they loved and trusted, so much as they did Col. Schuyler, a well armed body of New York provincials had nothing to dread but an ague or an ambuscade, to both of which they were much exposed on the banks of the lakes, and amidst the swampy forests, through which they had to penetrate in pursuit of an enemy of whom they might say with the Grecian hero, that "they wanted but daylight to conquer him." This first essay in arms of those provincials, under the auspices of their brave and generous leader, succeeded beyond their hopes. This is all I can recollect of it. Of its destination I only know that it was directed against some of those establishments which the French began to make within the British boundaries. The expedition only terminated with the season. The provincials brought home Canadian prisoners, who were kept on their parole in the houses of the three brothers, and became afterwards their friends; and the Five Nations brought home Indian prisoners, most of whom they adopted, and scalps enough to strike awe into the adverse nations, who were for a year or two afterwards pretty quiet.

Chapter XXII

ADOPTION OF CHILDREN COMMON IN THE PROVINCE — MADAME'S VISIT TO NEW YORK

MRS. SCHUYLER had contributed all in her power to forward this expedition: but was probably hurt, either by the fatigue of receiving so many friends, or the anxiety produced by parting with them under such circumstances; for soon after the colonel's departure she was delivered of a dead child, which event was followed by an alarming illness; but she wished the colonel to be kept in ignorance of it, that he might give his undivided attention to the duties in which he was engaged. Providence, which doubtless had singled out this benevolent pair to be the parents of many who had no natural claim upon their affection, did not indulge them with any succeeding prospects of a family of their own. This privation, not a frequent one in this colony, did not chill the minds or narrow the hearts of people, who, from this circumstance, found themselves more at liberty to extend their beneficence, and enlarged that circle which embraced the objects of their love and care. This indeed was not singular during that reign of natural feeling which preceded the prevalence of artificial modes in this primitive district. The love of offspring is certainly one of the strongest desires that the uncorrupted mind forms to itself in a state of comparative innocence. Affecting indifference on this subject is the surest proof of a disposition either callous, or led by extreme vanity to pretend insensibility to the best feelings of nature.

To a tie so exquisitely tender, the pledge and bond of connubial union; to that bud of promised felicity, which always cheers with the fragrance of hope the noon-day of toil or care, and often supports with the rich cordial of filial love and watchful duty the evening of our decline, what mind can be indifferent. No wonder the joys of paternity should be highly relished where they were so richly flavored; where parents knew not what it was to find a rebel or a rival in a child; first, because they set the example of simplicity, of moderation, and of seeking their highest joys in domestic life; next, because they quietly expected and calmly welcomed the evening of life; and did not, by an absurd desire of being young too long, inspire their offspring with a premature ambition to occupy their place. What sacrifices have I not seen made to filial piety! How many respectable (though not young) maidens, who without pretending a dislike to marriage, have rejected men whom their hearts approved, because they would not forsake, during her lifetime, a widowed mother, whose sole comfort they were?

For such children who, that hopes to grow old, would not wish? A consideration which the most polished manners of Europe teach us to banish as far as possible from our minds. We have learned to check this natural sentiment, by finding other objects for those faculties of our minds, which nature intended to bless and benefit creatures born to love us, and to enlarge our affections by exciting them. If this stream, which so naturally inclines to flow downwards, happened to be checked in its course for want of the usual channel, these adepts in the science of happiness immediately formed a new one, and liked their canal as well as a river, because it was of their own making. To speak without a metaphor, whoever wanted a child adopted one; love produced love, and the grafted scion very often proved an ornament and defence to the supporting stock. But then the scion was generally artless and graceful. This is a part of the manners of my old friends which I always remember with delight; more particularly as it was the invariable custom to select the child of a friend who had a numerous family. The very animals are not devoid of that mixture of affection and sagacity, which suggests a mode of supplying his great desideratum. Next to that prince of cats, the famous cat of Whittington, I would place the cat recorded by Dr. White in his curious natural history, who when deprived of her young, sought a parcel of deserted leverets to suckle and to fondle. What an example!

The following year produced a suspension of hostilities between the provinces and the Canadians. The colonel went to New York to attend his duty, being again chosen a member of the colonial assembly. Mrs. Schuyler accompanied him; and being improved both in mind and manners since her marriage, which, by giving her a more important part to act, had called forth her powers, she became the centre of a circle by no means inelegant or uninformed; for society was there more various and more polished than in any other part of the continent, both from the mixture of settlers, formerly described, and from its being situated in a province most frequently the seat of war, and consequently forming the head-quarters of the army, which, in point of the birth and education of the candidates for promotion, was on a very different footing from what it has been since. It was then a much narrower range, and the selection more attended to. Unless a man, by singular powers or talent, fought his way from the inferior ranks, there was hardly an instance of a person getting even a subaltern's commission whose birth was not at least genteel, and who had not interest and alliances. There were not so many lucrative places under government. The wide field of adventure since opened in the East was scarcely known; a subaltern's pay was more adequate to the maintenance of a gentleman; and the noblest and most respected families had no other way of providing for such younger brothers, as were not bred to any learned profession but by throwing them into the army. As to morals, this did not perhaps much mend the matter. These officers might in some instances be thoughtless, and even profligate, but they were seldom ignorant or low bred ; and that rare character called a finished gentleman, was not unfrequently to be found among the higher ranks of them; who had added experience, reading, and reflection to their original stock of talents and attainments.

Chapter XXIII

COLONEL SCHUYLER'S MILITARY PARTIALITY — INDIAN CHARACTER FALSELY CHARGED WITH IDLENESS

IT so happened that a succession of officers, of the description mentioned in the preceding chapter, were to be ordered upon the service which I have been detailing; and whether in New York or at home, they always attached themselves particularly to this family, who, to the attractions of good breeding and easy intelligent conversation, added the power, which they preëminently possessed, of smoothing the way for their necessary intercourse with the independent and self-righted settlers, and instructing them in many things essential to promote the success of the pursuits in which they were about to engage. It was one of Aunt Schuyler's many singular merits, that, after acting for a time a distinguished part in this comparatively refined society, where few were so much admired and esteemed, she could return to the homely good sense and primitive manners of her fellow citizens at Albany, free from fastidiousness and disgust. Few indeed, without study or design, ever better understood the art of being happy, and

Van Rensselaer Manor House, built in 1660

making others so. Being gay is another sort of thing; gaiety, as the word is understood in society, is too often assumed, artificial, and produced by such an effort, that in the midst of laughter, "the heart is indeed sad." Very different are the smiles that occasionally illume the placid countenance of cheerful tranquillity. They are the emanations of a heart at rest: in the enjoyment of that sunshine of the breast, which is set forever to the restless votaries of mere amusement.

According to the laudable custom of the country they took home a child, whose mother had died in giving her birth, and whose father was a relation of the colonel's. This child's name was either Schuyler or Cuyler, I do not exactly remember which;[1] but I remember her many years after as Mrs. Vander Poolen; when, as a comely contented looking matron, she used to pay her annual visit to her benefactress, and send her ample presents of such rural dainties as her abode afforded. I have often heard her warm in her praises; saying how useful, how modest, and how affectionate she had been; and exulting in her comfortable settlement, and the plain worth, which made her a blessing to her family. From this time to her aunt's death, above fifty years afterwards, her house was never without one, but much oftener two children, whom

[1] Maria, a sister of Aunt Schuyler's husband, married Abraham Staats. They had three children, Peter, Barent and Annatje. Peter died young, and Annatje married Johannes Van der Poel.

this exemplary pair educated with parental care and kindness. And whenever one of their protégés married out of the house, which was generally at a very early age, she carried with her a female slave, born and baptized in the house, and brought up with a thorough knowledge of her duty, and an habitual attachment to her mistress; besides the usual present of the furniture of a chamber, and a piece of plate, such as a tea-pot, tankard, or some such useful matter, which was more or less valuable as the protégé was more or less beloved: for though Aunt Schuyler had great satisfaction from the characters and conduct of all her adopted, there were, no doubt, degrees of merit among them, of which she was better able to judge than if she had been their actual mother.

There was now an interval of peace, which gave these philanthropists more leisure to do good in their own way. They held a three-fold band of kindness in their hands, by which they led to the desirable purpose of mutual advantage, three very discordant elements, which were daily becoming more difficult to mingle and to rule; and which yet were the more dependent on each other for mutual comfort, from the very causes which tended to disunite them.

In the first place, the Indians began to assume that unfavorable and uncertain aspect, which it is the fate of man to wear in the first steps of his progress from that state where he is a being at once warlike and social, having few wants, and being able, without constant labor or division of ranks, to supply them; where there is no distinction, save that attained by superior strength of mind and body; and where there are no laws, but those dictated by good sense, aided by experience, and enforced by affection, this state of life may be truly called the reign of the affections: the love of kindred and of country ruling paramount, unrivalled by other passions, all others being made subservient to these. Vanity, indeed, was in some degree flattered; for people wore ornaments, and were at no small pains to make them. Pride existed: but was differently modified from what we see it; every man was proud of the prowess and achievements of his tribe collectively; of his personal virtues he was not proud, because we excel but by comparison; and he rarely saw instances of the opposite vices in his own nation, and looked on others with unqualified contempt.

When any public benefit was to be obtained, or any public danger to be averted, their mutual efforts were all bent to one end; and no one knew what it was to withhold his utmost aid, nor indeed could in that stage of society have any motive for doing so. Hence, no mind being contracted by selfish cares, the community were but as one large family, who enjoyed or suffered together. We are accustomed to talk, in parrot phrase, of indolent savages; and to be sure, in warm climates, and where the state of man is truly savage, that is to say, unsocial, void of virtue and void of comforts, he is certainly an indolent being; but that individual, in a cold climate, who has tasted the sweets of social life, who knows the wants that arise from it, who provides for his children in their helpless state, and where taste and ingenuity are so much improved, that his person is not only clothed with warm and seemly apparel, but decorated with numerous and not inelegant ornaments; which from the scarcity and simplicity of his tools, he has no ready or easy mode of producing: when he has not only found out all these wants, which he has no means of supplying but by his individual strength, dexterity, and ingenuity, industry must be added, ere they can be all regularly gratified. Very active and industrious, in fact, the Indians were in their original state; and when we take it into consideration, that beside all these occupations, together with their long journeys, wars and constant huntings and fishing, their leisure was occupied not only by athletic but studious games, at which they played for days together with unheard of eagerness and perseverance, it will appear they had very little of that lounging time, for which we are so apt to give them credit. Or if a chief occasionally after fatigue, of which we can form no adequate idea, lay silent in the shade, those frisking Frenchmen who have given us most details concerning them, were too restless themselves to subdue their skipping spirits to the recollection, that a Mohawk had no study or arm chair wherein to muse and cogitate; and that his schemes of patriotism, his plans of war, and his eloquent speeches, were all like the meditations of Jacques, formed "under the greenwood tree." Neither could any man lounge on his sofa, while half a dozen others were employed in shearing the sheep, preparing the wool, weaving and making his coat, or in planting the flax for his future linen, and flaying the ox for his future shoes; were he to do all this himself, he would have little leisure for study or repose. And all this and more the Indian did, under other names and forms. So that idleness, with its gloomy followers *ennui* and suicide, were unknown among this truly active people: yet that there is a higher state of society cannot be denied; nor can it be denied that the intermediate state is a painful and enfeebling one.

Man, in a state of nature, is taught by his more civilized brethren a thousand new wants before he learns to supply one. Thence barter takes place; which in the first stage of progression is universally fatal to the liberty, the spirit, and the comforts of an uncivilized people.

In the east, where the cradle of our infant nature was appointed, the clime was genial, its productions abundant, and its winters only sufficient to consume the surplus, and give a welcome variety to the seasons. There man was either a shepherd or a hunter, as his disposition led; and that perhaps in the same family. The meek spirit of Jacob delighted in tending his father's flocks; while the more daring and adventurous Esau traced the wilds of Mount Seir, in pursuit both of the fiercer animals who waged war upon the fold, and the more timorous who administered to the luxury of the table.

The progress of civilization was here gradual and gentle; and the elegant arts seem to have gone hand in hand with the useful ones. For we read of bracelets and ear-rings sent as tokens of love, and images highly valued and coveted; while even agriculture seemed in its infancy.

Chapter XXIV

PROGRESS OF CIVILIZATION IN EUROPE

POPULATION extending to the milder regions of Europe, brought civilization along with it; so that it is only among the savages (as we call our ancestors of the north) that we can trace the intermediate state I have spoken of. Amongst them, one regular gradation seems to have taken place; they were first hunters and then warriors. As they advanced in their knowledge of the arts of life, and acquired a little property, as much of pastoral pursuits as their rigorous climate would allow, without the aid of regular agriculture, mingled with their wandering habits. But, except in a few partial instances, from hunters they became conquerors: the warlike habits acquired from that mode of life raising their minds above patient industry, and teaching them to despise the softer arts that embellish society. In fine, their usual process was to pass to civilization through the medium of conquest. The poet says,

> "With noble scorn the first fam'd Cato viewed
> Rome learning arts from Greece which she subdued."

The surly censor might have spared his scorn, for doubtless science, and the arts of peace were by far the most valuable acquisitions resulting from their conquest of that polished and ingenious people. But when the savage hunters of the north became too numerous to subsist on their deer and fish, and too warlike to dread the conflict with troops more regularly armed, they rushed down, like a cataract, on their enfeebled and voluptuous neighbors; destroyed the monuments of art, and seemed for a time to change the very face of nature. Yet dreadful as were the devastations of this flood, let forth by divine vengeance to punish and to renovate, it had its use in sweeping away the hoarded mass of corruption with which the dregs of mankind had polluted the earth. It was an awful, but a needful process; which, in some form or other, is always renewed when human degeneracy has reached its ultimatum. The destruction of these feeble beings, who, lost to every manly and virtuous sentiment, crawl about the rich property which they have not sense to use worthily, or spirit to defend manfully, may be compared to the effort nature makes to rid herself of the noxious brood of wasps and slugs, cherished by successive mild winters. A dreadful frost comes; man suffers, and complains; his subject animals suffer more, and all his works are for a time suspended: but this salutary infliction purifies the air, meliorates the soil and destroys millions of lurking enemies, who would otherwise have consumed the productions of the earth, and deformed the face of nature. In these barbarous irruptions, the monuments of art, statues, pictures, temples, and palaces, seem to be most lamented. From age to age the virtuosi of every country have reëchoed to each other their feeble plaints over the lost works of art; as if that had been the heaviest sorrow in the general wreck; and as if the powers that produced them had ceased to exist. It is over the defaced image of the divine Author, and not merely the mutilated resemblance of his creatures, that the wise and virtuous should lament! We are told that in Rome there were as many statues as men: had all these lamented statues been preserved would the world be much wiser or happier? a sufficient number remain as models to future statuaries, and memorials of departed art and genius. Wealth, directed by taste and liberality, may be much better employed in calling forth, by due encouragement, that genius which doubtless exists among our cotemporaries, than in paying exorbitantly the vender of fragments.

> "Mind, mind alone, bear witness earth and heav'n!
> The living fountains in itself contains
> Of beauteous and sublime."

And what has mind achieved, that, in a favorable conjuncture, it might not again aspire to? The lost arts are ever the theme of classical lamentation; but the great and real evil was the loss of the virtues which protected them; of courage, fortitude, honor, and patriotism; in short, of the whole manly character. This must be allowed, after the dreadful tempest of subversion was over, to have been in some degree restored in the days of chivalry: and it is equally certain that the victors learnt from the vanquished many of the arts that support life, and all those which embellish it. When their manners were softened by the aid of a mild and charitable religion, this blended people assumed that undefined power, derived from superior valor and superior wisdom, which has so far exalted Europe over all the regions of the earth. Thus, where a bold and warlike people subdue a voluptuous and effeminate one, the result is, in due time, an improvement of national character. In similar climes and circumstances to those of the primeval nations in the other hemisphere, the case has been very different. There, too, the hunter, by the same gradation became a warrior; but first allured by the friendship which sought his protection; then repelled by the art that coveted and encroached on his territories; and lastly by the avarice that taught him new wants, and then took an undue advantage of them; they neither wished for our superfluities, nor envied our mode of life; nor did our encroachments much disturb them, as they receded into their trackless coverts as we approached from the coast. But though they scorned our refinements; and though our government, and all the enlightened minds amongst us, dealt candidly and generously with all such as were not set on by our enemies to injure us, the blight of European vices, the mere consequence of private greediness and fraud, proved fatal to our very friends. As I formerly observed, the nature of the climate did not admit of the warriors passing through the medium of a shepherd's life to the toils of agriculture. The climate, though extremely warm in summer, was so severe in winter, and that winter was so long, that it required no little labor to secure the food for the animals which were to be maintained; and no small expense in that country to procure the implements necessary for the purpose of agriculture. In other countries, when a poor man has not wherewithal to begin farming, he serves another; and the reward of his toil enables him to set up for himself. No such resource was open to the Indians, had they even inclined to adopt our modes. No Indian ever served another, or received assistance from any one except his own family. 'T is inconceivable, too, what a different kind of exertion of strength it requires to cultivate the ground, and to endure the fatigues of the chase, long journeys, etc. To all that induces us to labor they were indifferent. When a governor of New York was describing to an Indian the advantages that some one would derive from such and such possessions; "Why," said he, with evident surprise, "should any man desire to possess more than he uses?" More appeared to his untutored sense an incumbrance.

I have already observed how much happier they

considered their manner of living than ours; yet their intercourse with us daily diminished their independence, their happiness, and even their numbers. In the new world this fatality has never failed to follow the introduction of European settlers; who, instead of civilizing and improving, slowly consume and waste; where they do not, like the Spaniards, absolutely destroy and exterminate the natives. The very nature of even our most friendly mode of dealing with them was pernicious to their moral welfare; which, though too late, they well understood, and could as well explain. Untutored man, in beginning to depart from that life of exigencies, in which the superior acuteness of his senses, his fleetness and dexterity in the chase, are his chief dependence, loses so much of all this before he can become accustomed to, or qualified for our mode of procuring food by patient labor, that nothing can be conceived more enfeebled and forlorn than the state of the few detached families remaining of vanished tribes, who having lost their energy, and even the wish to live in their own manner, were slowly and reluctantly beginning to adopt ours. It was like that suspension of life which takes place in the chrysalis of insects, while in their progress towards a new state of being. Alas! the indolence with which we reproach them, was merely the consequence of their commercial intercourse with us; and the fatal passion for strong liquors which resulted from it. As the fabled enchanter, by waving his magic wand, chains up at once the faculties of his opponents, and renders strength and courage useless; the most wretched and sordid trader, possessed of this master-key to the appetites and passions of these hard-fated people, could disarm those he dealt with of all their resources, and render them dependent — nay dependent on those they scorned and hated. The process was simple; first, the power of sending, by mimic thunder, an unseen death to a distant foe, which filled the softer inhabitants of the southern regions with so much terror, was here merely an object of desire and emulation; and so eagerly did they adopt the use of fire-arms, that they soon became less expert in using their own missile weapons. They could still throw the tomahawk with such an unerring aim, that, though it went circling through the air towards its object, it never failed to reach it. But the arrows, on which they had formerly so much depended, were now considered merely as the weapons of boys, and only directed against birds.

Thus was one strong link forged in the chain of dependence; next, liquor became a necessity, and its fatal effects who can detail! But to make it still clearer, I have mentioned the passion for dress, in which all the pride and vanity of this people were centred. In former days this had the best effect, in being a stimulus to industry. The provision requisite for making a splendid appearance at the winter meetings for hunting and the national congress, occupied the leisure hours of the whole summer. The beaver skins of the last year's hunting were to be accurately dressed, and sewed together, to form that mantle which was as much valued, and as necessary to their consequence, as the pelice of sables to that of an eastern bashaw. A deer skin, or that of a bear, or beaver, had their stated price. The boldest and most expert hunter had most of these commodities to spare, and was therefore most splendidly arrayed. If he had a rival, it was in him whose dexterous ingenuity in fabricating the materials of which his own dress was composed, enabled him to vie with the hero of the chase.

Thus superior elegance in dress was not, as with us, the distinction of the luxurious and effeminate, but the privilege and reward of superior courage and industry; and became an object worthy of competition. Thus employed, and thus adorned, the sachem or his friends found little time to indulge the stupid indolence we have been accustomed to impute to them.

Another arduous task remains uncalculated: before they became dependent on us for the means of destruction, much time was consumed in forming their weapons; in the construction of which no less patience and ingenuity were exercised than in that of their ornaments: and those too were highly embellished, and made with great labor out of flints, pebbles and shells. But all this system of employment was soon overturned by their late acquaintance with the insidious arts of Europe; to the use of whose manufactures they were insensibly drawn in, first by their passion for fire-arms, and finally by their fatal appetite for liquor. To make this more clear, I shall insert a dialogue, such as, if not literally, at least in substance, might pass betwixt an Indian warrior and a trader.

Chapter XXV

INDEPENDENCE OF THE INDIANS HOW FIRST DIMINISHED

INDIAN. — Brother, I am come to trade with you; but I forewarn you to be more moderate in your demands than formerly.

Trader. — Why, brother, are not my goods of equal value with those you had last year?

Indian. — Perhaps they may; but mine are more valuable because more scarce. The great spirit who has withheld from you strength and ability to provide food and clothing for yourselves, has given you cunning and art to make guns and provide scaura;[1] and by speaking smooth words to simple men, when they have swallowed madness, you have by little and little purchased their hunting grounds, and made them corn lands. Thus the beavers grow more scarce, and deer flies farther back; yet after I have reserved skins for my mantle, and the clothing of my wife, I will exchange the rest.

Trader. — Be it so, brother: I came not to wrong you, or take your furs against your will. It is true the beavers are few, and you go further for them. Come, brother, let us deal fair first, and smoke

[1] Scaura is the Indian name for rum. — *Mrs. Grant.*

friendly afterwards. Your last gun cost fifty beaver skins; you shall have this for forty; and you shall give marten and racoon skins in the same proportion for powder and shot.

Indian. — Well, brother, that is equal. Now for two silver bracelets, with long pendant ear-rings of the same, such as you sold to Cardarani in the sturgeon [1] month last year, how much will you demand?

Trader. — The skins of two deer for the bracelets, and those of two fawns for the ear-rings.

Indian. — That is a great deal; but wampum grows scarce, and silver never rusts. Here are the skins.

Trader. — Do you buy any more? Here are knives, hatchets, and beads of all colors.

Indian. — I will have a knife and a hatchet; but must not take more; the rest of the skins will be little enough to clothe the women and children, and buy wampum. Your beads are of no value, no warrior who has slain a wolf will wear them.[2]

Trader. — Here are many things good for you, which you have not skins to buy; here is a looking-glass, and here is a brass kettle, in which your

[1] The Indians appropriate a month to catch fish or animals, which is at that time the predominant object of pursuit; as the bear month, the beaver month, etc. — *Mrs. Grant.*

[2] Indians have a great contempt, comparatively, for the beads we send them; which they consider as only fit for those plebeians who cannot by their exertions win any better. They estimate them compared with their own wampum, as we do pearls compared with paste. — *Mrs. Grant.*

woman may boil her maize, her beans, and above all her maple sugar. Here are silver broaches, and here are pistols for the youths.

Indian. — The skins I can spare will not purchase them.

Trader. — Your will determines, brother; but next year you will want nothing but powder and shot, having already purchased your gun and ornaments. If you will purchase from me a blanket to wrap round you, a shirt and blue stroud for under garments to yourself and your woman; and the same for leggings, this will pass the time, and save you the great labor of dressing the skins, making the thread, etc., for your clothing; which will give you more fishing and shooting time, in the sturgeon and bear months.

Indian. — But the custom of my fathers!

Trader. — You will not break the custom of your fathers, by being thus clad for a single year. They did not refuse those things which were never offered to them.

Indian. — For this year, brother, I will exchange my skins; in the next I shall provide apparel more befitting a warrior. One pack alone I will reserve to dress for a future occasion. The summer must not find a warrior idle.

The terms being adjusted and the bargain concluded, the trader thus shows his gratitude for liberal dealing.

Trader. — Corlaer has forbid bringing scaura to

steal away the wisdom of the warriors; but we white men are weak and cold; we bring kegs for ourselves, lest death arise from the swamps. We will not sell scaura; but you shall taste some of ours in return for the venison with which you have feasted us.

Indian. — Brother, we will drink moderately.

A bottle was then given to the warrior by way of present, which he was advised to keep long; but found it irresistible. He soon returned with the reserved pack of skins, earnestly urging the trader to give him beads, silver broaches, and above all scaura, to their full amount. This, with much affected reluctance at parting with the private stock, was at last yielded. The warriors now, after giving loose for a while to frantic mirth, began the war-whoop, made the woods resound with infuriate howlings; and having exhausted their dear bought draught, probably determined, in contempt of that probity which at all other times they rigidly observed, to plunder the instrument of their pernicious gratification. He, well aware of the consequences, took care to remove himself and his goods to some other place; and a renewal of the same scene ensued. Where, all this time, were the women, whose gentle counsels might have prevented these excesses? Alas! unrestrained by that delicacy which is certainly one of the best fruits of refinement, they shared in them, and sunk sooner under them. A long and deep sleep generally succeeded; from which they awoke in a state of dejection and chagrin, such as no Indian had ever experienced under any other circumstance. They felt as Milton describes Adam and Eve to have done after their transgression. Exhausted and forlorn, and stung with the consciousness of error and dependence, they had neither the means nor the desire of exercising their wonted summer occupations with spirit. Vacancy produced languor, and languor made them again wish for the potion which gave temporary cheerfulness.[1] They carried their fish to the next fort or habitation to barter for rum. This brought on days of frenzy, succeeded by torpor. When again roused by want to exertion, they saw the season passing without the usual provision; and by an effort of persevering industry, tried to make up for past negligence; and then, worn out by exertion, sunk into supine indolence, till the approach of winter called them to hunt the bear; and the arrival of that (their busy season), urged on their distant excursions in pursuit of deer. Then they resumed their wonted character, and became what they used to be; but conscious that acquired tastes and wants, which they had lost the habit of supplying themselves, would throw them again on the traders for clothing, etc., they were themselves out-straining every sinew to procure enough of peltry to answer their purpose, and to gratify their newly acquired appetites. Thus the energy, both

[1] From Peter Schuyler, brother to the colonel, I have heard many such details. — *Mrs. Grant.*

of their characters and constitutions, was gradually undermined; and their numbers as effectually diminished, as if they had been wasted by war.

The small-pox was also so fatal to them, that whole tribes on the upper lakes have been entirely extinguished by it. Those people being in the habit of using all possible means of closing the pores of the skin, by painting and anointing themselves with bears' grease, to defend them against the extremity of cold, to which their manner of life exposed them; and not being habitually subject to any cutaneous disease, the small-pox rarely rises upon them; from which it may be understood how little chance they had of recovering. All this I heard Aunt Schuyler relate, whose observations and reflections I merely detail.

Chapter XXVI

ATTRACTIONS OF THE INDIAN MODE OF LIFE —ACCOUNT OF A SETTLER AMONG THEM

IN this wild liberty, habits of probity, mutual confidence, and constant variety, there was an undefinable charm, that, while they preserved their primitive manners, wrought in every one who dwelt for any time amongst them.

I have often heard my friend speak of an old man, who, being carried away in his infancy by some hostile tribe who had slain his parents, was rescued very soon after by a tribe of friendly Indians, who, from motives of humanity, resolved to bring him up among themselves, that he might, in their phrase, "learn to bend the bow, and speak truth." When it was discovered, some years after, that he was still living, his relations claimed him; and the community wished him to return and inherit his father's lands, now become more considerable. The Indians were unwilling to part with their protégé; and he was still more reluctant to return. This was considered as a bad precedent; the early settlers having found it convenient in several things regarding hunting, food, etc., to assimilate, in some degree, with the Indians; and the young men occasionally, at that early period, joining their hunting and fishing parties. It was considered as a matter of serious import to reclaim this young alien; lest others should be lost to the community and to their religion by following his example. With difficulty they forced him home; where they never could have detained him, had they not carefully and gradually inculcated into his mind the truths of Christianity. To those instructions even his Indian predilections taught him to listen; for it was the religion of his fathers, and venerable to him as such: still, however, his dislike of our manners was never entirely conquered, nor was his attachment to his foster fathers ever much diminished. He was possessed of a very sound intellect, and used to declaim with the most vehement eloquence against our crafty and insidious encroachments on our old friends. His abhorrence of the petty falsehoods to which custom has too well reconciled us, and those little artifices which we all occasionally practise, rose to a height fully equal to that felt by Gulliver. Swift and this other misanthrope, though they lived at the same time, could not have had any intercourse, else one might have supposed the invectives which he has put into the mouth of Gulliver, were borrowed from this demi-savage; whose contempt and hatred of selfishness, meanness, and duplicity, were expressed in language worthy of the dean. Insomuch, that years after I had heard of this singular character, I thought, on reading Gulliver's asperities after returning from Houyhnhnmland, that 1 had met my old friend again. One really does meet with characters that fiction would seem too bold in portraying. This original had an aversion to liquor, which amounted to abhorrence; being embittered by his regret at the mischief resulting from it to his old friends, and rage at the traders for administering the means of depravity. He never could bear any seasoning to his food; and despised luxury in all its forms.

For all the growing evils I have been describing, there was only one remedy, which the sagacity of my friend and her other self soon discovered; and their humanity as well as principle led them to try all possible means of administering. It was the pure light and genial influence of Christianity alone that could cheer and ameliorate the state of these people, now, from a concurrence of circumstances scarcely to be avoided in the nature of things, deprived of the independence habitual to their own way of life, without acquiring in its room any of those comforts which sweeten ours. By gradually and gently unfolding to them the views of a happy futurity, and the means by which depraved humanity was restored to a participation of that blessing; pride, revenge, and the indulgence of every excess of passion or appetite being restrained by the precepts of a religion ever powerful where it is sincere; their spirits would be brought down from the fierce pride which despises improvement to adopt such of our modes, as would enable them to incorporate in time with our society, and procure for themselves a comfortable subsistence, in a country no longer adapted to supply the wants of the houseless rangers of the forest.

The narrow policy of many looked coldly on this benevolent project. Hunters supplied the means of commerce, and warriors those of defence; and it was questionable whether a Christian Indian would hunt or fight as well as formerly. This, however, had no power with those in whom Christianity was any thing more than a name. There were already many Christian Indians; and it was very encouraging, that not one, once converted, had ever forsaken the strict profession of their religion, or ever, in a single instance, abandoned themselves to the excesses so pernicious to their unconverted brethren. Never was the true spirit of Christianity more exemplified than in the lives of those comparatively few converts, who about this time amounted to more than two hundred. But the tender care and example of the Schuylers coöperating with the incessant labors of a judicious and truly apostolic missionary, some years after greatly argumented their numbers in different parts of the continent: and to this day, the memory of David Brainard, the faithful laborer alluded to, is held in veneration in those districts that were blessed with his ministry. He did not confine it to one people or province, but travelled from place to place to disseminate the gospel to new converts, and confirm and cherish the truth already planted. The first foundation of that church had, however, as I formerly mentioned, been laid long ago: and the examples of piety, probity, and benevolence set by the worthies at the Flats, and a few more, were a very necessary comment on the doctrines to which their assent was desired.

The great stumbling block which the missionaries had to encounter with the Indians (who, as far as their knowledge went, argued with great acuteness and logical precision), was the small influence which our religion seemed to have over many of its professors. "Why," said they, "if the book of truth, that shows the way to happiness, and bids all men do justice, and love one another, is given both to Corlaer and Onnonthio,[1] does it not direct them both in the same way? Why does Onnonthio worship, and Corlaer neglect, the mother of the blessed one? And why do the missionaries blame those for worshiping things made with hands, while the priests tell the praying nation,[2] that Corlaer and his people have forsaken the worship of his forefathers: besides, how can people, who believe that God and good spirits view and take an interest in

[1] Corlaer was the title given by them to the governor of New York; and was figuratively used for the governed, and Onnonthio for those of Canada, in the same manner. — *Mrs. Grant.*

[2] Praying nation was a name given to a village of Indians near Montreal, who professed the Roman catholic faith. — *Mrs. Grant.*

all their actions, cheat and dissemble, drink and fight, quarrel and backbite, if they believe the great fire burns for those who do such things? If we believed what you say, we should not exchange so much good for wickedness, to please an evil spirit who would rejoice at our destruction." .... To this reasoning it was not easy to oppose any thing that would carry conviction to untutored people, who spoke from observation and the evidence of the senses; to which could only be opposed scripture texts, which avail not till they are believed; and abstract reasoning, extremely difficult to bring to the level of an unlearned understanding. Great labor and perseverance wrought on the minds of a few, who felt conviction, as far as it is to be ascribed to human agency, flow from the affectionate persuasions of those whom they visibly beheld earnest for their eternal welfare; and when a few had thus yielded,[1] the peace and purity of their lives, and the sublime enjoyment they seemed to derive from the prospects their faith opened into futurity, was an inducement to others to follow the same path.

[1] Some of them have made such a proficiency in practical religion as ought to shame many of us, who boast the illuminating aids of our native Christianity. Not one of these Indians has been concerned in those barbarous eruptions which deluged the frontiers of our southwestern provinces with the blood of so many innocents, of every age and sex. At the commencement of these ravages, they flew into the settlements, and put themselves into the protection of government. The Indians no sooner became Christians, than they openly professed their loyalty to King George; and therefore, to contribute to their conversion was as truly politic as nobly Christian. — *Mrs. Grant.*

This, abstractedly from religious considerations of endless futurity, is the true and only way to civilization; and to the blending together the old and new inhabitants of these regions. National pride, rooted prejudices, ferocity and vindictive hatred, all yield before a change that new-moulds the whole soul, and furnishes men with new fears and hopes, and new motives for action.

Chapter XXVII

INDIANS ATTACHED BY CONVERSION — EXPEDITION OF MONS. BARRE — IRONICAL SKETCH OF AN INDIAN

UPON the attachment the Indians had to our religion was grafted the strongest regard to our government, and the greatest fidelity to the treaties made with us. I shall insert a specimen of Indian eloquence, illustrative of this last; not that I consider it by any means so rich, impressive, or sublime as many others that I could quote, but as containing a figure of speech rarely to be met with among savage people, and supposed by us incompatible with the state of intellectual advancement to which they have attained. I mean a fine and well supported irony. About the year 1696,[1] Mons. Barre, the commander of the French forces in Canada, made a kind of inroad, with a warlike

[1] De la Barre made an attempt to invade the Seneca country in 1684. He crossed Lake Ontario from Fort Frontenac (Kingston) and landed in the country of the Onondagas, some distance east of Oswego. The Indian sachems visited him, and after seeing his hopeless condition with an army wasted and dying, they made him an ironical speech, as seen on page 154. He was recalled the following year. In 1696 the Count de Frontenac made war on the Onondaga nation, and destroyed their village.

design, into the precincts claimed by our Mohawk allies; the march was tedious, the French fell sick, and many of their Indians deserted them. The wily commander, finding himself unequal to the meditated attack, and that it would be unsafe to return through the lakes and woods, while in hourly danger of meeting enemies so justly provoked, sent to invite the sachems to a friendly conference: and, when they met, asserted, in an artful speech, that he and his troops had come with the sole intention of settling old grievances, and smoking the calumet of peace with them. The Indians, not imposed on by such pretences, listened patiently to his speech, and then made the answer which the reader will find in the notes.[1] It is to be observed, that who-

[1] "Onnonthio, I honor you; and all the warriors that are with me likewise honor you. Your interpreter has finished his speech, I begin mine. My words make haste to reach your ears; hearken to them, Yonnondio. You must have believed, when you left Quebec, that the sun had burnt up all the forests which made our country so inaccessible to the French; or that the lakes had so far overflowed their banks, that they had surrounded our castles, and that it was impossible for us to get out of them. Yes, Yonnondio, surely you have dreamt so; and the curiosity of seeing so great a wonder has brought you so far. Now you are undeceived, since I and the warriors here present are come to assure you, that the Hurons, Onondagoes, and Mohawks are yet alive. I thank you in their name for bringing back into their country the calumet, which your predecessor received from their hands. It was happy for you that you left under ground that murdering hatchet, which has been so often dyed with the blood of the French. Hear, Onnonthio, I do not sleep; I have my eyes open; and the sun that enlightens me discovers to me a great captain, at the head of his soldiers, who speaks as if he were dreaming. He says that he only came to the lake to smoke out of the great calumet with the Five Nations; but Connaratego says that he sees the contrary; that it was

ever they considered as the ruling person for the time being in Canada, they styled Onnonthio; to knock them on the head, if sickness had not weakened the arms of the French. I see Onnonthio raving in a camp of sick men, whose lives the great spirit has saved by inflicting this sickness upon them. Hear, Onnonthio, our women had taken their clubs; our children and old men had carried their bows and arrows into the heart of your camp, if our warriors had not disarmed them, and kept them back, when your messenger came to our castles. It is done, and I have said it. Hear, Yonnondio, we plundered none of the French, but those who carried guns, powder, and ball to the wolf and elk tribes, because those arms might have cost us our lives. Herein we follow the example of the Jesuits, who stave all the kegs of rum brought to the castles where they are, lest the drunken Indians should knock them on the head. Our warriors have not beavers enough to pay for all those arms that they have taken; and our old men are not afraid of the war. This belt preserves my words. We carried the English into our lakes, to trade with the wolf and elk tribes, as the praying Indians brought the French to our castles, to carry on a trade, which the English say is theirs. We are born free. We neither depend on Onnonthio nor Corlaer; we may go where we please. If your allies be your slaves, use them as such; command them to receive no other but your people. This belt preserves my words. We knocked the Connecticut Indians and their confederates on the head because they had cut down the trees of peace, which were the limits of our country. They had hunted beavers on our lands, contrary to the customs of all Indians, for they have left none alive. They have killed both male and female. They brought the Sathanas into our country to take part with them, after they had formed ill designs against us; we have done less than they merited.

"Hear, once more, the words of the Five Nations. They say that when they buried the hatchet at Cardaraqui (in the presence of your predecessor), in the middle of the fort [Detroit], they planted the tree of peace in the same place, to be there carefully preserved; that instead of an abode for soldiers, that fort might be a rendezvous for merchants; that in place of arms and ammunition, only peltry and goods should enter there.

"Hear, Yonnondio, take care for the future that so great a number of soldiers as appear there do not choke the tree of peace, planted in so small a fort. It will be a great loss after having so easily taken root,

while the governor of New York they always called Corlaer.

Twice in the year the new converts came to Albany to partake of the sacrament, before a place of worship was erected for themselves. They always spent the night, or oftener two nights, before their joining in this holy rite at the Flats: which was their general rendezvous from different quarters. There they were cordially received by the three brothers, who always met together at this time to have a conference with them on subjects the most

<blockquote>
if you should stop its growth, and prevent its covering your country and ours with its branches. I assure you, in the name of the Five Nations, that our warriors shall dance to the calumet of peace under its leaves, and shall remain quiet on their mats ; and that they shall never dig up the hatchet till Corlaer or Onnonthio, either jointly or separately attack the country which the great spirit had given to our ancestors. This belt preserves my words, and this other the authority which the Five Nations have given me." Then, Garangula, addressing himself to Mons. de Main, who understood his language, and interpreted, spoke thus : " Take courage, friend, you have spirits ; speak, explain my words, omit nothing. Tell all that your brethren and friends say to Onnonthio, your governor, by the mouth of Garangula, — who loves you, and desires you to accept of this present of beaver, and take part with me in my feast, to which I invite you. This present of beaver is sent to Yonnondio on the part of the Five Nations."

Mons. Barre returned to his fort much enraged at what he had heard ; Garangula feasted the French officers, and then went home ; and Mons. Barre set out on his way towards Montreal ; and as soon as the general, with the few soldiers that remained in health, had embarked, the militia made their way to their own habitations without order or discipline. Thus a chargeable and fatiguing expedition meant to strike the terror of the French name into the stubborn hearts of the Five Nations, ended in a scold between a French general and an old Indian. — *Colden's History of the Five Nations*, page 68.
</blockquote>

important to their present and future welfare. These devout Indians seemed all impressed with the same feelings, and moved by the same spirit. They were received with affectionate cordiality, and accommodated in a manner quite conformable to their habits, in the passage, porch, and offices; and so deeply impressed were they with a sense of the awful duty that brought them there, and the rights of friendship and hospitality, and at this period become so much acquainted with our customs, that though two hundred communicants, followed by many of their children, were used to assemble on these occasions, the smallest instance of riot or impropriety was not known amongst them. They brought little presents of game, or of their curious handicrafts, and were liberally and kindly entertained by their good brother Philip, as they familiarly called him. In the evening they all went apart to secret prayer; and in the morning, by dawn of day, they assembled before the portico; and their entertainers, who rose early to enjoy, unobserved, a view of their social devotion, beheld them with their mantles drawn over their heads, prostrate on the earth, offering praises and fervent supplications to their Maker. After some time spent in this manner, they arose, and seated in a circle on the ground, with their heads veiled as formerly, they sang an hymn, which it was delightful to hear, from the strength, richness, and sweet accord of their uncommonly fine voices; which every one that ever heard this sacred chorus, however indifferent to the purport of it, praised as incomparable. The voices of the female Indians are particularly sweet and powerful. I have often heard my friend dwell with singular pleasure on the recollection of those scenes, and of the conversations she and the colonel used to hold with the Indians, whom she described as possessed of very superior powers of understanding; and in their religious views and conversations, uniting the ardor of proselytes with the firm decision and inflexible steadiness of their national character. It was on the return of those new Christians to the Flats, after they had thus solemnly sealed their profession, that these wise regulations for preserving peace and good will between the settlers (now become confident and careless from their numbers) and the Indians, jealous with reason of their ancient rites, were concluded.

Chapter XXVIII

CHRISTIAN INDIANS — THEIR INFLUENCE WITH THE MOHAWKS

THE influence these converts had obtained over the minds of those most venerated for wisdom among their countrymen, was the medium through which this patriot family, in some degree, controlled the opinions of that community at large, and kept them faithful to the British interests. Every two or three years there was a congress held, by deputies from New York, who generally spoke to the Indians by an interpreter; went through the form of delivering presents from their brother the great king, redressing petty grievances, smoking the calumet of peace, and delivering belts, the pledges of amity. But these were mere public forms: the real terms of this often renewed amity having been previously digested by those who far better understood the relations subsisting between the contracting parties, and the causes most likely to interrupt their union. Colonel Schuyler, though always ready to serve his country in exigencies, did not like to take upon himself any permanent responsibility, as a superintendent of Indian affairs, as it might have diminished that private influence which arose from the general veneration for his character, and from a conviction that the concern he took was voluntary and impartial; neither did he choose to sacrifice that domestic peace and leisure, which he so well knew how to turn to the best account, being convinced that by his example and influence, as a private gentleman, he had it in his power to do much good of a peculiar kind, which was incompatible with the weight and bustle of public affairs, or with that hospitality which, as they managed it, was productive of so many beneficial effects. I have already shown how, by prudent address and kind conciliation, this patriotic pair soothed and attached the Indians to the British interest. As the country grew more populous, and property more abundant and more secure, the face of society in this inland region began to change. They whose quiet and orderly demeanor, devotion, and integrity did not much require the enforcement of laws, began now to think themselves above them. To a deputed authority, the source of which lay beyond the Atlantic, they paid little deference; and from their neighbors of New Hampshire and Connecticut, who bordered on their frontiers, and served with them in the colonial wars, they had little to learn of loyalty or submission. These people they held in great contempt, both as soldiers and statesmen; and yet, from their frequent intercourse with those who talked of law and politics in their peculiar uncouth dialect incessantly, they insensibly adopted many of their notions. There is a certain point of stable happiness at which our imperfect nature merely seems to arrive; for the very materials of which it is formed contain the seeds of its destruction. This was the case here: that peaceful and desirable equality of conditions, from which so many comforts resulted, in process of time occasioned an aversion to superiors, to whom they were not accustomed, and an exaggerated jealousy of the power which was exercised for their own safety and comfort. Their manners unsophisticated, and their morals in a great measure uncorrupted, led them to regard with unjustifiable scorn and aversion those strangers who brought with them the manners of more polished, though less pure, communities. Proud of their haughty bluntness, which daily increased with their wealth and security, they began to consider respectful and polite behavior as a degree of servility and duplicity; while they revolted at the power exercised over themselves, and very reluctantly made the exertions necessary for their own protection, they showed every inclination to usurp the territories of their Indian allies; and use to the very utmost the power they had acquired over them, by supplying their wants.

At the liberal table of Aunt Schuyler, where there was always intelligence, just notions, and good breeding to be met with, both among the owners and their guests, many had their prejudices softened down, their minds enlarged, and their manners improved. There they met British officers of rank and merit, and persons in authority; and learnt that the former were not artificial coxcombs, nor the latter petty tyrants, as they would otherwise be very apt to imagine. Here they were accustomed to find authority respected on the one hand, and on the other to see the natural rights of man vindicated, and the utmost abhorrence expressed of all the sophistry by which the credulous were misled by the crafty, to have a code of morality for their treatment of heathens, different from that which directed them in their dealing with Christians. Here a selection of the best and worthiest, of the different characters and classes we have been describing, met; and were taught, not only to tolerate, but to esteem each other; and it required the calm, temperate wisdom, and easy versatile manners of my friend to bring this about. It is, when they are called to act in a new scene, and among people different from any they had known or imagined, that the folly of the wise and the weakness of the strong become discernable.

Many officers justly esteemed, possessed of capacity, learning, and much knowledge, both of the usages of the world, and the art of war, from the want of certain habitudes, which nothing but experience can teach, were disqualified for the warfare of the woods; and from a secret contempt with which they regarded the blunt simplicity and plain appearance of the settlers, were not amenable to their advice on these points. They were not aware how much they were to depend on them for the means of carrying on their operations; and by rude or negligent treatment so disgusted them, that they withheld the horses, oxen, wagons, etc., which were to be paid for, merely to show their independence; well knowing the dreaded and detested military power, even if coercive measures were resorted to, would have no chance for redress in their courts; and even the civil authorities were cautious of doing any thing so unpopular as to decide in favor of the military. Thus, till properly instructed, those bewildered strangers were apt to do the thing of all others that annihilates a feeble authority; threaten where they could not strike, and forfeit respect where they could not enforce obedience: a failure of this kind clogged and enfeebled all their measures; for without the hearty coöperation of the inhabitants in furnishing prerequisites, nothing could go on in a country without roads, or public vehicles, for the conveyance of their warlike stores. Another rock they were apt to run upon was, a neglect of the Indians, whom they neither sufficiently feared as enemies, nor valued as friends: till taught to do so by maturer judgments. Of this, Braddock's defeat was an instance; he was brave, experienced, and versed in all military science: his confidence in which, occasioned the destruction of himself and his army. He considered those counsels that warned him, how little manœuvres or numbers would avail in the close prison of innumerable boughs, as the result of feeble caution; and marched his army to certain ruin, in the most brave and scientific manner imaginable. Upon certain occasions there is no knowledge so valuable as that of our own ignorance.

At the Flats, the self-righted boor learned civilization and subordination: the high bred and high spirited field officer gentleness, accommodation, and respect for unpolished worth and untaught valor. There, too, the shrewd and deeply reflecting Indian learnt to respect the British character, and to confide in that of the settlers; by seeing the best specimens of both acting candidly towards each other, and generously to himself.

My friend was most particularly calculated to be the coadjutor of her excellent consort, in thus subduing the spirits of different classes of people, strongly disposed to entertain a repulsive dislike of each other, and by leading them to the chastened enjoyment of the same social pleasure, under the auspices of those, whose good will they were all equally convinced of, she contrived to smooth down asperities, and assimilate those various characters, in a manner that could not be done by any other means.

Accustomed from childhood, both from the general state of society, and the enlarged minds of her particular associates, to take liberal views of everything, and to look forward on all occasions to consequences, she steadily followed her wise and

AN AMERICAN LADY

benevolent purposes, without being attracted by petty gratifications, or repelled by petty disgusts. Neither influenced by female vanity, or female fastidiousness, she might very truly say of popularity, as Falstaff says of Worcester's rebellion, " it lay in her way and she found it:" for no one ever took less pains to obtain it; and if the weight of solid usefulness and beneficence had not, as it never fails to do in the long run, forced approbation, her mode of conducting herself, though it might greatly endear her to her particular associates, was not conciliating to common minds. The fact was, that, though her benevolence extended through the whole circle of those to whom she was known, she had too many objects of importance in view to squander time upon imbecility and insignificance. Nor could she find leisure for the routine of ordinary visits, or inclination for the insipidity of ordinary chit-chat.

If people of the description here alluded to, could forward any plan advantageous to the public, or to any of those persons in whom she was particularly interested, she would treat them occasionally with much civility: for she had all the power of superior intellect without the pride of it: but could not submit to a perpetual sacrifice to forms and trifles. This, in her, was not only justifiable, but laudable; yet it is not mentioned as an example, because a case can very rarely occur, where the benefit resulting to others, from making one's own path, and forsaking the ordinary road, can be so essential; few ever can have a sphere of action so peculiar or so important as hers; and very few indeed have so sound a judgment to direct them in choosing, or so much fortitude to support them in pursuing, a way of their own.

In ordinary matters, where neither religion nor morality is concerned, it is much safer to trust to the common sense of mankind in general, than to our own particular fancy. Singularity of conduct or opinion is so often the result of vanity or affectation, that whoever ventures upon it ought to be a person whose example is looked up to by others. A person too great to follow, ought to be great enough to lead. But though her conversation was reserved for those she preferred, her advice, compassion, and good offices were always given where most needed.

Chapter XXIX

MADAME'S ADOPTED CHILDREN — SISTER SUSAN

YEARS passed away in this manner, varied only by the extension of that protection and education which they gave to a succession of nephews and nieces of the colonel or Mrs. Schuyler. These they did not take from mere compassion, as all their relations were in easy circumstances; but influenced by various considerations, such as, in some cases, the death of the mother of the children, or perhaps the father; in others, where their nieces or nephews married very early, and lived in the houses of their respective parents, while their young family increased before they had a settled home; or in instances where, from the remote situations in which the parents lived, they could not so easily educate them. Indeed the difficulty of getting a suitable education for children, whose parents were ambitious for their improvement, was great; and a family so well regulated as hers, and frequented by such society, was in itself an academy, both for the best morals and manners. When people have children born to them, they must submit to the ordinary lot of humanity; and if they have not the happiness of meeting with many good qualities to cultivate and rejoice over, there is nothing left for them but to exert themselves to the utmost to reform and ameliorate what will admit of improvement. They must carefully weed and prop; if the soil produce a crop both feeble and redundant, affection will blind them, to many defects; imperious duty will stimulate them, and hope, soothing, however deceitful, will support them. But when people have the privilege, as in this case, of choosing a child, they are fairly entitled to select the most promising. This selection I understood always to have been left to Aunt Schuyler; and it appeared, by the event, to have been generally a happy one. Fifteen, either nephews or nieces, or the children of such, who had been under her care, all lived to grow up and go out into the world: all acted their parts so as to do credit to the instruction they had received, and the example they looked up to. Besides these, they had many whom they brought for two or three years to their house to reside; either because the family they came from was at the time crowded with younger children, or because they were at a time of life when a year or two spent in such society as was there assembled, might not only form their manners, but give a bias to their future character.

About the year 1730, they brought home a nephew of the colonel's, whose father having a large family, and having, to the best of my recollection, lost his wife, entirely gave over the boy to the protection of his relation. This boy was his uncle's god-son, and called Philip[1] after him. He was a great favorite in the family; for though apparently thoughtless and giddy, he had a very good temper, and quick parts; and was upon the whole an ingenious, lively, and amusing child. He was a very great favorite, and continued to be so in some measure, when he grew up.

There were other children, whose names and relation to my friends I do not remember, in the house at the same time; but none that staid so long, or were so much talked of as this. There certainly never were people who received so much company, made so respectable a figure in life, and always kept so large a family about them with so little tumult or bustle, or indeed at so moderate an expense. What their income was I cannot say; but am sure it could not have been what we should think adequate to the good they did, and the hospitality and beneficence which they practised: for the rents of land were then of so little value, that though they possessed a considerable estate in another part of the country, only very moderate profits could result from it; but, indeed, from the simplicity of dress, etc., it was easier; though in that respect, too, they preserved a kind of dignity, and went beyond others in the materials, though

[1] Colonel Schuyler's sister Gertrude married Johannes Lansing, and had a large family. It was her son Philip here referred to.

not the form of their apparel. Yet their principal expense was a most plentiful and well ordered table, quite in the English style: which was a kind of innovation: but so many strangers frequented the houses of the three brothers, that it was necessary to accommodate themselves to the habit of their guests.

Peter being in his youth an extensive trader, had spent much time in Canada, among the noblesse there; and had served in the continental levies. He had a fine commanding figure, and quite the air and address of a gentleman, and was, when I knew him, an old man.

Intelligent and pleasing in a very high degree, Jeremiah had too much familiar kindness to be looked up to like his brother. Yet he also had a very good understanding, great frankness and affability, and was described by all who knew him, as the very soul of cordial friendship and warm benevolence. He married a polished and well educated person, whose parents (French protestants) were people of the first fashion in New York, and had given with her a good fortune, a thing very unusual in that country. They used in the early years of their marriage, to pay a visit every winter to their connections at New York, who passed part of every summer with them. This connection, as well as that with the Flats, gave an air of polish, and a tincture of elegance to this family beyond others; and there were few so gay and social.

This cheerfulness was supported by a large family, fourteen, I think, of very promising children. These, however, inheriting from their mother's family a delicate constitution, died one after another as they came to maturity : one only, a daughter, lived to be married ; but died after having had one son and one daughter.[1]

I saw the mother of this large family, after outliving her own children, and a still greater number of brothers and sisters, who had all settled in life, prosperous and flourishing, when she married ; I saw her a helpless bed-ridden invalid ; without any remaining tie, but a sordid grasping son-in-law, and two grandchildren, brought up at a distance from her.

With her, too, I was a great favorite, because I listened with interest to her details of early happiness, and subsequent woes and privations ; all of which she described to me with great animation, and the most pathetic eloquence. How much a patient listener, who has sympathy and interest to bestow on a tale of wo, will hear ! and how affecting is the respect and compassion even of an artless child, to a heart that has felt the bitterness of neglect, and known what it was to pine in solitary sadness ! Many a bleak day have I walked a mile to visit this blasted tree, which the storm of calamity had stripped of every leaf ! and surely in the house of sorrow the heart is made better.

[1] Three of Jeremiah Schuyler's daughters were married, but died before their mother, leaving small families.

From this chronicle of past times, I derived much information respecting our good aunt; such as she would not have given me herself. The kindness of this generous sister-in-law was indeed the only light that shone on the declining days of Sister Susan, as she was wont affectionately to call her. What a sad narrative would the detail of this poor woman's sorrows afford! which, however, she did not relate in a querulous manner; for her soul was subdued by affliction, and she did not "mourn as those that have no hope." One instance of self-accusation I must record. She used to describe the family she left as being no less happy, united, and highly prosperous, than that into which she came: if, indeed, she could be said to leave it, going as she did for some months every year to her mother's house, whose darling she was, and who, being only fifteen years older than herself, was more like an elder sister, united by fond affection.

She went to New York to lie in, at her mother's house, of her four or five first children; her mother at the same time having children as young as hers: and thus caressed at home by a fond husband, and received with exultation by the tenderest parents; young, gay, and fortunate, her removals were only variations of felicity; but gratified in every wish, she knew not what sorrow was, nor how to receive the unwelcome stranger when it arrived. At length she went down to her father's as usual, to lie in of her fourth child, which died when it was eight days old.

She then screamed with agony, and told her mother, who tried by pious counsel to alleviate her grief, that she was the most miserable of human beings; for that no one was capable of loving their child so well as she did hers, and could not think by what sin she had provoked this affliction: finally, she clasped the dead infant to her bosom, and was not, without the utmost difficulty, persuaded to part with it; while her frantic grief outraged all decorum. After this, said she, "I have seen my thirteen grown-up children, and my dear and excellent husband, all carried out of this house to the grave: I have lost the worthiest and most affectionate parents, brothers and sisters, such as few ever had; and however my heart might be pierced with sorrow, it was still more deeply pierced with a conviction of my own past impiety and ingratitude; and under all this affliction I wept silently and alone; and my outcry or lamentation was never heard by mortal." What a lesson was this!

This once much loved and much respected woman, have I seen sitting in her bed, where she had been long confined, neglected by all those whom she had known in her better days, excepting Aunt Schuyler, who, unwieldy and unfit for visiting as she was, came out two or three times in the year to see her, and constantly sent her kindly tokens of remembrance. Had she been more careful to preserve her independence, and had she accommodated herself more to the plain manners of the people she lived among, she might in her adversity have met with more attention; but too conscious of her attainments, lively, regardless, and perhaps vain, and confident of being surrounded and admired by a band of kinsfolk, she was at no pains to conciliate others; she had, too, some expensive habits; which, when the tide of prosperity ebbed, could meet with little indulgence among a people who never entertained an idea of living beyond their circumstances.

Thus, even among those unpolished people, one might learn how severely the insolence of prosperity can be avenged on us, even by those we have despised and slighted; and who perhaps were very much our inferiors in every respect: though both humanity and good sense should prevent our mortifying them, by showing ourselves sensible of that circumstance.

This year was a fatal one to the families of the three brothers. Jeremiah, impatient of the uneasiness caused by a wen upon his neck, submitted to undergo an operation: which, being unskillfully performed, ended fatally, to the unspeakable grief of his brothers and of aunt, who was particularly attached to him, and often dwelt on the recollection of his singularly compassionate disposition, the generous openness of his temper, and peculiar warmth of his affections. He, indeed, was "taken away from the evil to come;" for of his large family, one after the other went off, in consequence of the weakness of their lungs; which withstood none of the ordinary diseases of small-pox, measles, etc., till in a few years, there was not one remaining.

These were melancholy inroads on the peace of her, who might truly be said, to "watch and weep, and pray for all;" for nothing could exceed our good aunt's care and tenderness for this feeble family; who seemed flowers which merely bloomed to wither in their prime; for they were, as is often the case with those who inherit such disorders, beautiful, with quickness of comprehension, and abilities beyond their age.

Chapter XXX

DEATH OF YOUNG PETER SCHUYLER — SOCIETY AT THE FLATS

ANOTHER very heavy sorrow followed the death of Jeremiah; Peter, being the eldest brother, his son, as I formerly mentioned, was considered and educated as heir to the colonel. It was Peter's house that stood next to the colonel's; their dwelling being arranged according to their ages, the youth was not in the least estranged from his own family (who were half a mile off), by his residence in his uncle's, and was peculiarly endeared to all the families (who regarded him as the future head of their house), by his gentle manners and excellent qualities. With all these personal advantages, which distinguished that comely race, and which give grace and attraction to the unfolding blossoms of virtue, at an early age he was sent to a kind of college, then established in New Jersey; and he was there instructed, as far as in that place he could be. He soon formed an attachment to a lady still younger than himself, but so well brought up, and so respectably connected, that his friends were greatly pleased with the marriage, early as it was, and his father, with the highest satisfaction, received the

young couple into the house. There they were
the delight and ornament of the family, and lived
amongst them as a common blessing. The first
year of their marriage a daughter was born to them,
whom they named Cornelia; and the next, a son
whom they called Peter.[1] The following year,
which was the same that deprived them of their
brother Jeremiah, proved fatal to a great many
children and young people, in consequence of an
endemial disease, which every now and then used
to appear in the country, and made great havoc.
It was called the purple or spotted fever, and was
probably of the putrid kind: be that as it may, it
proved fatal to this interesting young couple.
Peter, who had lost his wife but a short time
before, was entirely overwhelmed by this stroke:
a hardness of hearing, which had been gradually
increasing before, deprived him of the consolations
he might have derived from society. He encouraged his second son to marry; shut himself up for
the most part in his own apartment; and became,
in effect, one of those lay brothers I have formerly
described. Yet, when time had blunted the edge
of this keen affliction, many years after, when we
lived at the Flats, he used to visit us: and though

---

[1] Peter Schuyler, third of the name, married Gertrude, daughter of John Schuyler, Jr., and sister of Philip S., the future major-general. He died September, 1753, leaving a widow and two children. His daughter Cornelia married Walter Livingston of the Manor; and his son Peter married Gertrude Lansing. His widow subsequently married Dr. John Cochran, surgeon-general of the Revolutionary Army.

he did not hear well, he conversed with great spirit, and was full of anecdote and information. Meanwhile, Madame did not sink under this calamity, though she felt it as much as her husband, but supported him; and exerted herself to extract consolation from performing the duties of a mother to the infant who was now become the representative of the family. Little Peter [1] was accordingly brought home, and succeeded to all that care and affection of which his father had formerly been the object, while Cornelia was taken home to Jersey, to the family of her maternal grandfather,[2] who was a distinguished person in that district. There she was exceedingly well educated, became an elegant and very pleasing young woman, and was happily and most respectably married before I left the country, as was her brother very soon after. They are still living; and Peter, adhering to what might be called, eventually the safer side, during the war with the mother country, succeeded undisturbed to his uncle's inheritance.

All these new cares and sorrows did not in the least abate the hospitality, the popularity, or the public spirit of these truly great minds. Their dwelling, though in some measure become a house of mourning, was still the rendezvous of the wise

[1] Peter Schuyler, fourth of the name, was a man of considerable prominence, and was State Senator several terms. He died January, 1792, leaving no children.

[2] Her step-father, Dr. John Cochran, lived for a time in New Brunswick, N. J.

and worthy, the refuge of the stranger, and an academy for deep and sound thinking, taste, intelligence, and moral beauty. There the plans for the public good were digested by the rulers of the province, who came, under the pretext of a summer excursion for mere amusement. There the operations of the army, and the treaties of peace or alliance with various nations, were arranged; for there the legislators of the state, and the leaders of the war, were received, and mixed serious and important counsels with convivial cheerfulness, and domestic ease and familiarity. 'T is not to be conceived how essential a point of union, a barrier against license, and a focus, in which the rays of intellect and intelligence were concentrated (such as in this family), were to unite the jarring elements of which the community was composed, and to suggest to those who had power without experience, the means of mingling in due proportions its various materials for the public utility. Still, though the details of family happiness were abridged, the spirit that produced it continued to exist, and to find new objects of interest. A mind elevated by the consciousness of its own powers, and enlarged by the habitual exercise of them, for the great purpose of promoting the good of others, yields to the pressure of calamity, but sinks not under it; particularly when habituated, like these exalted characters, to look through the long vista of futurity towards the final accomplishment of the designs of Providence. Like a diligent gardener, who, when his promising young plants are blasted in full strength and beauty, though he feels extremely for their loss, does not sit down in idle chagrin, but redoubles his efforts to train up their successors to the same degree of excellence. Considering the large family she (Madame) always had about her, of which she was the guiding star as well as the informing soul, and the innocent cheerfulness which she encouraged and enjoyed; considering, too, the number of interesting guests whom she received, and that complete union of minds, which made her enter so intimately into all the colonel's pursuits, it may be wondered how she found time for solid and improved reading; because people, whose time is so much occupied in business and society, are apt to relax, with amusing trifles of the desultory kind, when they have odd half hours to bestow on literary amusements. But her strong and indefatigable mind never loosened its grasp; ever intent on the useful and the noble, she found little leisure for what are indeed the greatest objects of feeble characters. After the middle of life she went little out; her household, long since arranged by certain general rules, went regularly on, because every domestic knew exactly the duties of his or her place, and dreaded losing it, as the greatest possible misfortune. She had always with her some young person, "who was unto her as a daughter;" who was her friend and companion; and bred up in such a manner as to qualify her for being such; and one of whose duties it was to inspect the state of the household, and " report progress," with regard to the operations going on in the various departments. For no one better understood, or more justly estimated, the duties of housewifery. Thus, those young females, who had the happiness of being bred under her auspices, very soon became qualified to assist her, instead of encroaching much on her time. The example and conversation of the family in which they lived, was to them a perpetual school for useful knowledge, and manners easy and dignified, though natural and artless. They were not indeed embellished, but then they were not deformed by affectation, pretensions, or defective imitations of fashionable models of nature. They were not indeed bred up "to dance, to dress, to roll the eye, or troul the tongue;" yet they were not lectured into unnatural gravity, or frozen reserve. I have seen those of them that were lovely, gay, and animated, though in the words of an old familiar lyric,

"Without disguise or art, like flowers that grace the wild,
  Their sweets they did impart whene'er they spoke or smiled."

Two of those to whom this description particularly applies, still live; and still retain not only evident traces of beauty, but that unstudied grace and dignity which is the result of conscious worth and honor, habituated to receive the tribute of general respect. This is the privilege of minds which are always in their own place, and neither stoop to solicit applause from their inferiors, nor strive to rise to a fancied equality with those whom nature or fortune have placed beyond them.

Aunt was a great manager of her time, and always contrived to create leisure hours for reading; for that kind of conversation which is properly styled gossiping, she had the utmost contempt. Light, superficial reading, such as merely fills a blank in time, and glides over the mind without leaving an impression, was little known there; for few books crossed the Atlantic but such as were worth carrying so far for their intrinsic value. She was too much accustomed to have her mind occupied with objects of real weight and importance, to give it up to frivolous pursuits of any kind. She began the morning with reading the scriptures. They always breakfasted early, and dined two hours later than the primitive inhabitants, who always took that meal at twelve. This departure from the ancient customs was necessary in this family, to accommodate the great numbers of British as well as strangers from New York, who were daily entertained at her liberal table. This arrangement gave her the advantage of a longer forenoon to dispose of. After breakfast she gave orders for the family details of the day, which, without a scrupulous attention to those minutæ which fell more properly under the notice of her young friends, she always regulated in the most judicious manner, so as to prevent all appearance of hurry and confusion. There was such a rivalry among domestics, whose sole ambition was her favor; and who had been so trained up from infancy, each to their several duties, that excellence in each department was the result both of habit and emulation; while her young protégés were early taught the value and importance of good housewifery, and were sedulous to little matters of decoration and elegance, which her mind was too much engrossed to attend to; so that her household affairs, ever well regulated, went on in a mechanical kind of progress, that seemed to engage little of her attention, though her vigilant and overruling mind set every spring of action in motion. Having thus easily and speedily arranged the details of the day, she retired to read in her closet, where she generally remained till about eleven; when, being unequal to distant walks, the colonel and she, and some of her elder guests, passed some of the hotter hours among those embowering shades of her garden, in which she took great pleasure. Here was their lyceum; here questions in religion and morality, too weighty for table talk, were leisurely and coolly discussed; and plans of policy and various utility arranged. From this retreat they adjourned to the portico; and while the colonel either retired to write, or went to give directions to his servants, she sat in this little tribunal, giving audience to new settlers, followers of the army left in hapless dependence, and others who wanted assistance or advice, or hoped she would intercede with the colonel for something more peculiarly in his way, he having great influence with the colonial government. At the usual hour her dinner-party assembled, which was generally a large one; and here I must digress from the detail of the day to observe, that, looking up as I always did to Madame with admiring veneration, and having always heard her mentioned with unqualified applause, I look often back to think what defects or faults she could possibly have to rank with the sons and daughters of imperfection, inhabiting this transitory scene of existence, well knowing, from subsequent observation of life, that error is the unavoidable portion of humanity. Yet of this truism, to which every one will readily subscribe, I can recollect no proof in my friend's conduct, unless the luxury of her table might be produced to confirm it. Yet this, after all, was but comparative luxury. There was more choice and selection, and perhaps more abundance at her table, than at those of the other primitive inhabitants, yet how simple were her repasts compared to those which the luxury of the higher ranks in this country offer to provoke the sated appetite. Her dinner-party generally consisted of some of her intimate friends or near relations; her adopted children, who were inmates for the time being; and strangers sometimes invited, merely as friendless travellers, on the score of hospitality, but often welcomed for some time as stationary visitors, on account of worth or talents, that gave value to their society; and, lastly, military guests, selected with some discrimination on account of the young friends, whom they wished not only to protect, but cultivate by an improving association. Conversation here was always rational, generally instructive, and often cheerful. The afternoon frequently brought with it a new set of guests. Tea was always drank early here; and as I have formerly observed, was attended with so many petty luxuries of pastry, confectionery, etc., that it might well be accounted a meal by those whose early and frugal dinners had so long gone by. In Albany it was customary, after the heat of the day was past, for the young people to go in parties of three or four, in open carriages, to drink tea at an hour or two's drive from town. The receiving and entertaining this sort of company generally was the province of the younger part of the family; and of these parties many came in summer evenings to the Flats, when tea, which was very early, was over. The young people, and those who were older, took their different walks, while Madame sat in her portico, engaged in what might comparatively be called light reading, essays, biography, poetry, etc., till the younger party set out on their return home, and her domestic friends rejoined her in her portico, where, in warm evenings, a slight repast was sometimes brought; but they more frequently shared the last and most truly social meal within.

Winter made little difference in her mode of occupying her time. She then always retired to her closet to read at stated periods.

In conversation she certainly took delight, and peculiarly excelled; yet did not in the least engross it, or seem to dictate. On the contrary, her thirst for knowledge was such, and she possessed such a peculiar talent for discovering the point of utility in all things, that from every one's discourse she extracted some information, on which the light of her mind was thrown in such a direction, as made it turn to account. Whenever she laid down her book she took up her knitting, which neither occupied her eyes nor attention, while it kept her fingers engaged; thus setting an example of humble diligence to her younger protégés. In this employment she had a kind of tender satisfaction, as little children, reared in the family, were the only objects of her care in this respect. For those, she constantly provided a supply of hosiery till they were seven years old; and, after that, transferred her attention to some younger favorite. In her earlier days, when her beloved colonel could share the gaieties of society, I have been told they both had a high relish for innocent mirth, and every species of humorous pleasantry; but in my time there was a chastened gravity in her discourse, which, however, did not repulse innocent cheerfulness, though it dashed all manner of levity, and that flippancy which great familiarity sometimes encourages amongst young people, who live much together. Had Madame, with the same good sense, the same high principle, and general benevolence towards young people, lived in society such as is to be met with in Britain, the principle upon which she acted would have led her to have encouraged in such society more gaiety and freedom of manners. As the regulated forms of life in Britain set bounds to the ease that accompanies good breeding, and refinement, generally diffused, supplies the place of native delicacy, where that is wanting, a certain decent freedom is both safe and allowable. But amid the simplicity of primitive manners, those bounds are not so well defined. Under these circumstances, mirth is a romp, and humor a buffoon; and both must be kept within strict limits.

Chapter XXXI

HOSPITALITY — ACHIEVEMENTS BY THE NEGROES

THE hospitalities of this family were so far beyond their apparent income, that all strangers were astonished at them. To account for this, it must be observed that, in the first place, there was perhaps scarce an instance of a family possessing such uncommonly well trained, active, and diligent slaves as that I describe. The set that were staid servants, when they married, had some of them died off by the time I knew the family; but the principal roots from whence the many branches, then flourishing, sprung, yet remained. These were two women, who had come originally from Africa while very young; they were most excellent servants, and the mothers or grand-mothers of the whole set, except one white-wooled negro man; who, in my time, sat by the chimney and made shoes for all the rest. The great pride and happiness of these sable matrons were, to bring up their children to dexterity, diligence, and obedience. Diana being determined that Maria's children should not excel hers in any quality, which was a recommendation to favor; and Maria equally resolved that her brood, in the race of excellence, should outstrip Diana's. Never was a more fervent competition. That of Phillis and Brunetta, in the Spectator, was a trifle to it; and it was extremely difficult to decide on their respective merits; for though Maria's son Prince, cut down wood with more dexterity and dispatch than any one in the province, the mighty Cæsar, son of Diana, cut down wheat and threshed it, better than he. His sister Betty, who, to her misfortune, was a beauty of her kind, and possessed wit equal to her beauty, was the best seamstress and laundress, by far, I have ever known; and plain unpretending Rachel, sister to Prince, wife to Titus, alias Tyte, and head cook, dressed dinners that might have pleased Apicius. I record my old humble friends by their real names, because they allowedly stood at the head of their own class; and distinction of every kind should be respected. Besides, when the curtain drops, or indeed long before it falls, 't is perhaps more creditable to have excelled in the lowest parts, than to have fallen miserably short in the higher. Of the inferior personages, in this dark drama I have been characterizing, it would be tedious to tell: suffice it, that besides filling up all the lower departments of the household, and cultivating to the highest advantage a most extensive farm, there was a thoroughbred carpenter and shoemaker, and an universal genius who made canoes, nets, and paddles; shod horses, mended implements of husbandry, managed the fishing, in itself no small department, reared hemp and tobacco, and spun both; made cider, and tended wild horses, as they call them; which it was his province to manage and to break. For every branch of the domestic economy, there was a person allotted, educated for the purpose; and this society was kept immaculate, in the same way that the Quakers preserve the rectitude of theirs; and indeed, in the only way that any community can be preserved from corruption; when a member showed symptoms of degeneracy, he was immediately expelled, or in other words, more suitable to this case, sold. Among the domestics, there was such a rapid increase, in consequence of their marrying very early, and living comfortably without care, that if they had not been detached off with the young people brought up in the house, they would have swarmed like an overstocked hive.

The prevention of crimes was so much attended to in this well-regulated family, that there was very little punishment necessary; none that I ever heard of, but such as Diana and Maria inflicted on their progeny, with a view to prevent the dreaded sentence of expulsion; notwithstanding the petty rivalry between the branches of the two original stocks, intermarriages between the Montagues and Capulets of the kitchen, which frequently took place, and the habit of living together under the same mild, though regular government, produced a general cordiality and affection among all the members of the family, who were truly ruled by the law of love: and even those who occasionally differed about trifles, had an unconscious attachment to each other, which showed itself on all emergencies. Treated themselves with care and gentleness, they were careful, and kind, with regard to the only inferiors and dependents they had, the domestic animals. The superior personages in the family, had always some good property to mention, or good saying to repeat of those whom they cherished into attachment, and exalted into intelligence; while they, in their turn, improved the sagacity of their subject animals, by caressing and talking to them. Let no one laugh at this; for whenever a man is at ease and unsophisticated, where his native humanity is not extinguished by want, or chilled by oppression, it overflows to inferior beings; and improves their instincts, to a degree incredible to those who have not witnessed it. In all mountainous countries, where man is more free, more genuine, and more divided into little societies much detached from others, and much attached to each other, this cordiality of sentiment, this overflow of good will take place. The poet says,

"Humble love, and not proud reason,
Keeps the door of heaven."

This question must be left for divines to determine; but sure am I that humble love, and not proud reason, keeps the door of earthly happiness, as far as it is attainable. I am not going, like the admirable Crichton, to make an oration in praise of ignorance; but a very high degree of refinement certainly produces a quickness of discernment, a niggard approbation, and a fastidiousness of taste, that find a thousand repulsive and disgusting qualities mingled with those that excite our admiration, and would (were we less critical) produce affection. Alas! that the tree should so literally impart the knowledge of good and evil; much evil and little good. It is time to return from this excursion, to the point from which I set out.

The Princes and Cæsars of the Flats had as much to tell of the sagacity and attachments of the animals, as their mistress related of their own. Numberless anecdotes that delighted me in the last century, I would recount; but fear I should not find my audience of such easy belief as I was; nor so convinced of the integrity of my informers. One circumstance I must mention, because I well know it to be true. The colonel had a horse which he rode occasionally, but which oftener travelled with Mrs. Schuyler in an open carriage. At particular times, when bringing home hay or corn, they yoked Wolf, for so he was called, in a wagon; an indignity to which, for a while, he unwillingly submitted. At length, knowing resistance was in vain, he had recourse to stratagem; and whenever he saw Tyte marshalling his cavalry for service, he swam over to the island; the umbrageous and tangled border of which I formerly mentioned: there he fed with fearless impunity till he saw the boat approach; whenever that happened he plunged into the thicket, and led his followers such a chase, that they were glad to give up the pursuit. When he saw from his retreat that the work was over, and the fields bare, he very coolly returned. Being, by this time, rather old, and a favorite, the colonel allowed him to be indulged in his dislike to drudgery. The mind which is at ease, neither stung by remorse, nor goaded by ambition or other turbulent passions, nor worn with anxiety for the supply of daily wants, nor sunk into languor by stupid idleness, forms attachments and amusements, to which those exalted by culture would not stoop, and those crushed by want and care could not rise. Of this nature was the attachment to the tame animals which the domestics appropriated to themselves, and to the little fanciful gardens where they raised herbs or plants of difficult culture, to sell and give to their friends. Each negro was indulged with his great squirrel, or musk rat; or perhaps his beaver, which he tamed and attached to himself, by daily feeding and caressing him in the farm-yard. One was sure about all such houses, to find these animals, in whom their masters took the highest pleasure. All these small features of human nature must not be despised for their minuteness. To a good mind they afford consolation.

Science, directed by virtue, is a godlike enlargement of the powers of human nature; and exalted rank is so necessary a finish to the fabric of society, and so invariable a result from its regular establishment, that in respecting those, whom the divine wisdom has set above us, we perform a duty such as we expect from our own inferiors; which helps to support the general order of society. But so very few in proportion to the whole can be enlightened by science, or exalted by situation, that a good mind draws comfort from discovering even the petty enjoyments permitted to those in the state we consider most abject and depressed.

Chapter XXXII

RESOURCES OF MADAME — PROVINCIAL CUSTOMS

IT may appear extraordinary, with so moderate an income, as could in those days be derived even from a considerable estate in that country, how Madame found means to support that liberal hospitality, which they constantly exercised. I know the utmost they could derive from their lands, and it was not much: some money they had, but nothing adequate to the dignity, simple as it was, of their style of living, and the very large family they always drew around them. But with regard to the plenty, one might almost call it luxury, of their table, it was supplied from a variety of sources, that rendered it less expensive than could be imagined. Indians, grateful for the numerous benefits they were daily receiving from them, were constantly bringing the smaller game, and, in winter and spring, loads of venison. Little money passed from one hand to another in the country; but there was constantly, as there always is in primitive abodes, before the age of calculation begins, a kindly commerce of presents. The people of New York and Rhode Island, several of whom were wont to pass a part of the summer with the colonel's family, were loaded with all the productions of the farm and river, when they went home. They again never failed, at the season, to send a large supply of oysters, and all other shell-fish, which at New York abounded; besides great quantities of tropical fruit, which, from the short run between Jamaica and New York, were there almost as plenty and cheap as in their native soil. Their farm yielded them abundantly all that in general a musket can supply; and the young relatives who grew up about the house, were rarely a day without bringing some supply from the wood or the stream. The negroes, whose business lay frequently in the woods, never willingly went there, or any where else, without a gun, and rarely came back empty handed. Presents of wine, then a very usual thing to send to friends to whom you wished to show a mark of gratitude, came very often, possibly from the friends of the young people who were reared and instructed in that house of benediction; as there were no duties paid for the entrance of any commodity there, wine, rum, and sugar, were cheaper than can easily be imagined; and in cider they abounded.

The negroes of the three truly united brothers, not having home employment in winter, after preparing fuel, used to cut down trees, and carry them to an adjoining saw-mill, where in a very short time, they made great quantities of planks, staves, etc., which is usually styled lumber, for the West India market. And when a ship load of their flour, lumber, and salted provisions were accumulated, some relative, for their behoof, freighted a vessel, and went out to the West Indies with it. In this Stygian schooner, the departure of which was always looked forward to with unspeakable horror, all the stubborn or otherwise unmanageable slaves were embarked, to be sold by way of punishment. This produced such salutary terror, that preparing the lading of this fatal vessel generally operated a temporary reform at least. When its cargo was discharged in the West Indies, it took in a cargo of wine, rum, sugar, coffee, chocolate, and all other West India productions, paying for whatever fell short of the value, and returning to Albany, sold the surplus to their friends, after reserving to themselves a most liberal supply of all the articles thus imported. Thus they had not only a profusion of all the requisites for good house-keeping, but had it in their power to do what was not unusual there in wealthy families, though none carried it so far as these worthies.

In process of time, as people multiplied, when a man had eight or ten children to settle in life, and these marrying early, and all their families increasing fast, though they always were considered as equals, and each kept a neat house and decent outside, yet it might be that some of them were far less successful than others, in their various efforts to support their families; but these deficiencies were supplied in a quiet and delicate way, by presents of every thing a family required, sent from all their connections and acquaintances; which, where there was a continual sending back and forward of sausages, pigs, roasting pieces, etc., from one house to another, excited little attention : but when aunt's West Indian cargo arrived all the families of this description within her reach, had an ample boon sent them of her new supply.

The same liberal spirit animated her sister, a very excellent person, who was married to Cornelius Cuyler,[1] then mayor of Albany; who had been a most successful Indian trader in his youth, and had acquired large Indian possessions, and carried on an extensive commercial intercourse with the traders of that day, bringing from Europe quantities of those goods that best suited them, and sending back their peltry in exchange; he was not only wealthy, but hospitable, intelligent, and liberal-minded, as appeared by his attachment to the army; which was, in those days, the distinguishing feature of those who in knowledge and candor were beyond others. His wife had the same considerate and prudent generosity, which ever directed the humanity of her sister; though, having a large family, she could not carry it to so great an extent.

If this maternal friend of their mutual relatives could be said to have a preference among her own,

[1] Cornelius Cuyler was the son of Johannes Cuyler and his wife Elsie, daughter of Dirk Wesselse Ten Broeck.

and her husband's relations, it was certainly to this family. The eldest son Philip, who bore her husband's name, was on that and other accounts, a particular favorite; and was, I think, as much with them in childhood, as his attention to his education, which was certainly the best the province could afford, would permit.

Having become distinguished through all the northern provinces, the common people, and the inferior class of the military, had learned from the Canadians who frequented her house, to call aunt, Madame Schuyler: but by one or other of these appellations she was universally known: and a kindly custom prevailed, for those who were received into any degree of intimacy in her family, to address her as their aunt, though not in the least related. This was done oftener to her than others, because she excited more respect and affection; but it had in some degree the sanction of custom. The Albanians were sure to call each other aunt or cousin, as far as the most strained construction would carry those relations. To strangers they were indeed very shy at first, but extremely kind; when they not only proved themselves estimable, but by a condescension to their customs, and acquiring a smattering of their language, ceased to be strangers, then they were in a manner adopted; for the first seal of cordial intimacy among the young people was to call each other cousin; and thus in an hour of playful or tender intimacy I have known it more than once begin : " I think you like me well enough, and I am sure I like you very well ; come, why should not we be cousins?" "I am sure I should like very well to be your cousin, for I have no cousins of my own where I can reach them." " Well, then you shall be my cousin, for ever and ever." In this uncouth language, and in this artless manner, were these leagues of amity commenced. Such an intimacy was never formed unless the object of it were a kind of favorite with the parents, who immediately commenced uncle and aunt to the new cousin. This, however, was a high privilege, only to be kept by fidelity and good conduct. If you exposed your new cousin's faults, or repeated her minutest secrets, or by any other breach of constancy lost favor, it was as bad as refusing a challenge ; you were coldly received every where, and could never regain your footing in society.

Aunt's title, however, became current every where, and was most completely confirmed in the year 1750, when she gave with more than common solemnity a kind of annual feast, to which the colonel's two brothers, and his sisters, aunt's sister, Mrs. Cornelius Cuyler, and their families, with several other young people related to them, assembled. This was not given on a stated day, but at a time when most of these kindred could be collected. This year I have often heard my good friend commemorate, as that on which the family stock of happiness felt the first diminution. The feast was made, and attended by all the collateral branches, consisting of fifty-two, who had a claim by marriage or descent, to call the colonel and my friend uncle and aunt, besides their parents. Among these were reckoned three or four grandchildren of their brothers. At this grand gala there could be no less than sixty persons, but many of them were doomed to meet no more; for the next year the small-pox, always peculiarly mortal here (where it was improperly treated in the old manner), broke out with great virulence, and raged like a plague; but none of those relatives whom Mrs. Schuyler had domesticated suffered by it; and the skill which she had acquired from the communications of the military surgeons who were wont to frequent her house, enabled her to administer advice and assistance, which essentially benefited many of the patients in whom she was particularly interested; though even her influence could not prevail on people to have recourse to inoculation. The patriarchal feast of the former year, and the humane exertions of this, made the colonel and his consort appear so much in the light of public benefactors, that all the young regarded them with a kind of filial reverence, and the addition of uncle and aunt was become confirmed and universal, and was considered as an honorary distinction. The ravages which the small-pox made this year among their Mohawk friends, was a source of deep concern to these revered philanthropists; but this was an evil not to be remedied by any ordinary means. These people being accustomed from early childhood to anoint themselves with bear's grease, to repel the innumerable tribes of noxious insects in summer, and to exclude the extreme cold in winter, their pores are so completely shut up, that the small-pox does not rise upon them, nor have they much chance of recovery from any acute disease; but, excepting the fatal infection already mentioned, they are not subject to any other but the rheumatism, unless in very rare instances. The ravages of disease this year operated on their population as a blow, which it never recovered; and they considered the small-pox in a physical, and the use of strong liquors in a moral sense, as two plagues which we had introduced among them, for which our arts, our friendship, and even our religion, were a very inadequate recompense.

Chapter XXXIII

FOLLOWERS OF THE ARMY—RESULTING INCONVENIENCES

TO return to the legion of commissaries, etc. These em-ployments were at first given to very inferior people; it was seen, however, that as the scale of military operations and erections increased, these people were enriching themselves, both at the expense of the king and the inhabitants; whom they frequently exasperated into insolence, or resistance, and then used that pretext to keep in their own hands the payments to which these people were entitled. When their wagons and slaves were pressed into the service, it was necessary to employ such persons from the first. The colonel and the mayor, and all whom they could influence, did all they could to alleviate an evil that could not be prevented, and was daily aggravating disaffection. They found, as the importance of these offices increased, it would conduce more to the public good, by larger salaries to induce people to accept them who were gentlemen, and had that character to support; and who, being acquainted with the people and their language, knew best how to qualify and soften, and where to apply, so as least to injure or irritate. Some young men, belonging to the country, were at length prevailed on to accept two or three of these offices; which had the happiest effect, in conciliating and conquering the aversion that existed against the regulars.

Among the first of the natives who engaged in those difficult employments, was one of aunt's adopted sons, formerly mentioned; Philip Schuyler of the pasture,[1] as he was called, to distinguish him from the other nephew; who, had he lived, would have been the colonel's heir. He appeared merely a careless good humored young man. Never was any one so little what he seemed, with regard to ability, activity, and ambition, art, enterprise, and perseverance, all of which he possessed in an uncommon degree, though no man had less the appearance of these qualities; easy, complying, and good humored, the conversations, full of wisdom and sound policy, of which he had been a seemingly inattentive witness, at the Flats, only slept in his recollection, to wake in full force when called forth by occasion.

A shrewd and able man, who was, I think, a brigadier[2] in the service, was appointed quartermaster general, with the entire superintendence of

[1] "Philip Schuyler of the pasture" refers to the future general. He married Catharine, daughter of Col. John Van Rensselaer of Claverack. His residence at this time was south of Albany, overlooking the fields in which the citizens pastured their cows.

[2] General Bradstreet, who built the house then occupied by his friend, Philip Schuyler.

all the boats, buildings, etc., in New York, the Jerseys, and Canadian frontier. He had married, when very young, a daughter of Colonel Rensselaer. Having at the time no settled plan for the support of a young family, he felt it incumbent on him to make some unusual exertion for them. Colonel Schuyler and his consort not only advised him to accept an inferior employment in this business, but recommended him to the Brigadier Bradstreet, who had the power of disposing of such offices, which were daily growing in importance. They well knew that he possessed qualities which might not only render him an useful servant to the public, but clear his way to fortune and distinction. His perfect command of temper, acuteness, and dispatch in business, and in the hour of social enjoyment, easily relapsing into all that careless frank hilarity and indolent good humor, which seems the peculiar privilege of the free and disencumbered mind, active and companionable, made him a great acquisition to any person under whom he might happen to be employed. This the penetration of Bradstreet soon discovered; and he became not only his secretary and deputy, but in a short time after, his ambassador, as one might say: for before Philip Schuyler was twenty-two, the general, as he was universally styled, sent him to England to negotiate some business of importance with the board of trade and plantations. In the meanwhile some other young men, natives of the country, accepted employments in the same department, by this time greatly extended. Averse as the country people were to the army, they began to relish the advantage derived from the money which that body of protectors, so much feared and detested, expended among them. This was more considerable than might at first be imagined. Government allowed provisions to the troops serving in America; without which they could not indeed have proceeded through an uninhabited country; where even in such places as were inhabited, there were no regular markets, no competition for supply; nothing but exorbitant prices could tempt those people who were not poor, and found a ready market for all their produce in the West-Indies. Now having a regular supply of such provisions as are furnished to the fleet, they had no occasion to lay out their money for such things; and rather purchased the produce of the country, liquors, etc., for which the natives took care to make them pay very high; an evil which the Schuylers moderated as much as possible, though they could not check it entirely. This provision system was a very great, though necessary evil; for it multiplied contractors, commissaries and store-keepers without end. At a distance from the source of authority, abuses increase, and redress becomes more difficult; which is of itself a sufficient argument against the extension of dominion. Many of those new comers were ambiguous characters, originally from the old country (as expatriated Britons fondly call their native land), but little known in this, and not happy specimens of that they had left. These satellites of delegated power had all the insolence of office, and all that avidity of gain, which a sudden rise of circumstances creates in low and unprincipled minds; and they, from the nature of their employment, and the difficulty of getting provisions transported from place to place, were very frequently the medium of that intercourse carried on between the military and the natives: and did not by any means contribute to raise the British character in their estimation.

I dwell the more minutely on all these great, though necessary evils, which invariably attend an army in its progress through a country which is the theatre of actual war, that the reader may be led to set a just value on the privileges of this highly favored region; which, sitting on many waters, sends forth her thunders through the earth; and while the farthest extremes of the east and west bend to her dominion, has not for more than half a century heard the sound of hostility within her bounds. Many unknown persons, who were in some way attached to the army, and resolved to live by it in some shape, set up as traders; carried stores suited to military consumption along with them, and finally established themselves as merchants in Albany. Some of these proved worthy characters, however; and intermarrying with the daughters of the citizens, and adopting in some degree their sober manners, became in process of time estimable members of society. Others, and indeed the most part of them, rose like exhalations, and obtaining credit by dint of address and assurance, glittered for a time; affecting showy and expensive modes of living, and aping the manners of their patrons. These, as soon as peace diminished their military establishment, and put an end to that ferment and fluctuation, which the actual presence of war never fails to excite, burst like bubbles on the surface of the subsiding waves, and astonished the Albanians with the novel spectacle of bankruptcy and imprisonment. All this gradually wrought a change on the face of society; yet such was the disgust which the imputed licentiousness, foppery, and extravagance of the officers, and the pretensions unsupported by worth or knowledge of their apes and followers, produced, that the young persons, who first married those ambiguous new comers, generally did so without the consent of their parents; whose affection for their children, however, soon reconciled them.

Chapter XXXIV

ARRIVAL OF A NEW REGIMENT — DOMINE FRIELINGHUYSEN

A REGIMENT came to town about this time, the superior officers of which were younger, more gay, and less amenable to good counsel than those who used to command the troops, which had formerly been placed on this station. They paid their visits at the Flats, and were received; but not as usual, cordially; neither their manners nor morals being calculated for that meridian. Part of the Royal Americans, or independent companies, had at this time possession of the fort; some of these had families: and they were in general persons of decent morals, and a moderate and judicious way of thinking, who, though they did not court the society of the natives, expressed no contempt for their manners or opinions. The regiment I speak of, on the contrary turned those plain burghers into the highest ridicule, yet used every artifice to get acquainted with them. They wished in short to act the part of very fine gentlemen; and the gay and superficial in those days were but too apt to take for their model the fine gentlemen of the detestable old comedies; which good taste has now very properly exploded; and at which, in every stage of society, the uncorrupted mind must have felt infinite disgust. Yet forms arrayed in gold and scarlet, and rendered more imposing by an air of command and authority, occasionally softened down into gentleness and submission; and by that noisy gaiety which youthful inexperience mistakes for happiness, and that flippant petulance, which those who knew not much of the language, and nothing at all of the world, mistook for wit, were very ensnaring. Those dangerously accomplished heroes made their appearance at a time when the English language began to be more generally understood; and when the pretensions of the merchants, commissaries, etc., to the stations they occupied were no longer dubious. Those polished strangers now began to make a part of general society. At this crisis it was that it was found necessary to have recourse to billets. The superior officers had generally been either received at the Flats, or accommodated in a large house which the colonel had in town. The manner in which the hospitality of that family was exercised, the selection which they made of such as were fitted to associate with the young persons who dwelt under their protection, always gave a kind of tone to society; and held out a light to others.

Madame's sister, as I before observed, was married to the respectable and intelligent magistrate, who administered justice, not only to the town, but to the whole neighborhood. In their house, also, such of the military were received, and entertained, as had the sanction of her sister's approbation. This judicious and equitable person, who in the course of trading in early life upon the lakes, had undergone many of the hardships, and even dangers, which awaited the military in that perilous path of duty, knew well what they had to encounter in the defence of a surly and self-righted race, who were little inclined to show them common indulgence: far less gratitude. He judged equitably between both parties; and while with the most patriotic steadiness he resisted every attempt of the military to seize anything with a high hand, he set the example himself, and used every art of persuasion to induce his countrymen to every concession that could conduce to the ease and comfort of their protectors. So far at length he succeeded, that when the regiment to which I allude arrived in town, and showed in general an amiable and obliging disposition, they were quartered in different houses; the superior officers being lodged willingly by the most respectable of the inhabitants, such as, not having large families, had room to accommodate them. The colonel and Madame happened, at the time of these arrangements, to be at New York.

In the meanwhile society began to assume a new aspect; of the satellites, which on various pretexts, official and commercial, had followed the army, several had families, and those began to mingle more frequently with the inhabitants: who were as yet too simple to detect the surreptitious tone of lax morals and second-handed manners, which prevailed among many of those who had but very lately climbed up to the stations they held, and in whose houses the European modes and diversions were to be met with; these were not in the best style, yet even in that style they began to be relished by some young persons, with whom the power of novelty prevailed over that of habit; and in a few rare instances, the influence of the young drew the old into a faint consent to these attempted innovations; but with many the resistance was not to be overcome.

In this state of matters, one guardian genius watched over the community with unremitting vigilance. From the original settlement of the place there had been a succession of good quiet clergymen, who came from Holland to take the command of this expatriated colony. These good men found an easy charge, among a people with whom the external duties of religion were settled habits, which no one thought of dispensing with; and where the primitive state of manners, and the constant occupation of the mind in planting and defending a territory where everything was, as it were, to be new created, was a preservation to the morals. Religion being never branded with the reproach of imputed hypocrisy, or darkened by the frown of austere bigotry, was venerated even by those who were content to glide thoughtless down the stream of time, without seriously considering whither it was conveying them till sorrow or sickness reminded them of the great purpose for which they were indulged with the privilege of existence.

The domines, as these people called their ministers, contented themselves with preaching in a sober and moderate strain to the people; and, living quietly in the retirement of their families, were little heard of but in the pulpit; and they seemed to consider a studious privacy as one of their chief duties. Domine Frielinghuysen,[1] however, was not contented with this quietude, which he seemed to consider as tending to languish into indifference. Ardent in his disposition, eloquent in his preaching, animated and zealous in his conversation, and frank

[1] Theodorus Frielinghuysen was the eldest son of Rev. Jacobus Theodorus Frielinghuysen, a native of West Friesland, who came over in 1720, and settled in New Jersey. His five sons became pastors of churches, and his two daughters married pastors. Domine Frielinghuysen came to Albany in 1746; he published a catechism in the Dutch tongue, the second edition of which was issued by Weyman in New York in 1748. His lot was cast in the midst of a violent controversy among the clergy on the subject of ordination, the older clergy insisting upon the rite being performed in Holland. A bitter dispute was carried on fifteen years, disturbing the peace of neighborhoods, dividing families, and rending the churches into factions. Houses of worship were locked up, ministers were assaulted in the discharge of their functions, and Sunday profaned by scenes of violence and mobs. The party which opposed separation were called conferentie, the other coetus. The dispute was not settled till 1772. Of course the domine was an actor in the scene.

and popular in his manners, he thought it his duty to awaken in every breast that slumbering spirit of devotion, which he considered as lulled by security, or drooping in the meridian of prosperity, like tender plants in the blaze of sunshine. These he endeavored to refresh by daily exhortation, as well as by the exercise of his public duties. Though rigid in some of his notions, his life was spotless, and his concern for his people warm and affectionate; his endeavors to amend and inspire them with happier desires and aims, were considered as the labor of love, and rewarded by the warmest affection, and the most profound veneration; and what to him was of much more value, by a growing solicitude for the attainment of that higher order of excellence which it was his delight to point out to them. But while he thus incessantly "allured to brighter worlds, and led the way," he might perhaps insensibly have acquired a taste of dominion, which might make him unwilling to part with any portion of that most desirable species of power, which subjects to us, not human actions only, but the will which directs them. A vulgar ambition contents itself with power to command obedience, but the more exalted and refined ambition aims at a domination over mind. Hence the leaders of a sect, or even those who have powers to awake the dying embers of pious fervor, sway the hearts of their followers in a manner far more gratifying to them, than any enjoyment to be derived from temporal power. That this desire should unconsciously gain ground in a virtuous and ardent mind, is not wonderful; when one considers how the best propensities of the human heart are flattered, by supposing that we only sway the minds of others, to incline them to the paths of peace and happiness, and derive no other advantage from this tacit sovereignty, but that of seeing those objects of affectionate solicitude grow wiser and better.

To return to the apostolic and much beloved Frielinghuysen. The progress which this regiment made in the good graces of his flock, and the gradual assimilation to English manners of a very inferior standard, alarmed and grieved the good man not a little; and the intelligence he received from some of the elders of his church, who had the honor of lodging the more dissipated subalterns, did not administer much comfort to him. By this time the Anglomania was beginning to spread. A sect arose among the young people, who seemed resolved to assume a lighter style of dress and manners, and to borrow their taste in those respects from their new friends. This bade fair soon to undo all the good pastor's labors. The evil was daily growing; and what, alas, could Domine Frielinghuysen do but preach! This he did earnestly, and even angrily, but in vain. Many were exasperated but none reclaimed. The good domine, however, had those who shared his sorrows and resentments; the elder and wiser heads of families, indeed a great majority of the primitive inhabitants, were steadfast against innovation. The colonel of the regiment, who was a man of fashion and family, and possessed talents for both good and evil purposes, was young and gay; and being lodged in the house of a very wealthy citizen, who had before, in some degree, affected the newer modes of living, so captivated him with his good breeding and affability, that he was ready to humor any scheme of diversion which the colonel and his associates proposed. Under the auspices of this gallant commander, balls began to be concerted, and a degree of flutter and frivolity to take place, which was as far from elegance as it was from the honest artless cheerfulness of the meetings usual among them. The good domine more and more alarmed, not content with preaching, now began to prophesy; but like Cassandra, or to speak as justly, though less poetically, like his whole fraternity, was doomed always to deliver true predictions to those who never heeded them.

Chapter XXXV

PLAYS ACTED — DISPLEASURE OF THE DOMINE

NOW the very ultimatum of degeneracy, in the opinion of these simple good people, was approaching; for now the officers, encouraged by the success of all their former projects for amusement, resolved to new fashion and enlighten those amiable novices whom their former schemes had attracted within the sphere of their influence; and, for this purpose, a private theatre was fitted up, and preparations made for acting a play; except the Schuylers and their adopted family, there was not perhaps one of the natives who understood what was meant by a play. And by this time, the town, once so closely united by intermarriages and numberless other ties, which could not exist in any other state of society, were divided into two factions: one consisting almost entirely of such of the younger class, as, having a smattering of New York education, and a little more of dress and vivacity, or perhaps levity, than the rest, were eager to mingle in the society, and adopt the manner of those strangers. It is but just, however, to add, that only a few of the more estimable were included in this number; these, however they might have been captivated with novelty and plausibility, were too much attached to their older relations to give them pain, by an intimacy with people to whom an impious neglect of duties the most sacred was generally imputed, and whose manner of treating their inferiors, at that distance from the control of higher powers, was often such as to justify the imputation of cruelty, which the severity of military punishments had given rise to. The play, however, was acted in a barn, and pretty well attended, notwithstanding the good domine's earnest charges to the contrary. It was *The Beaux Stratagem;* no favorable specimen of the delicacy or morality of the British theatre; and as for the wit it contains, very little of that was level to the comprehension of the novices who were there first initiated into a knowledge of the magic of the scene, yet they "laughed consumedly," as Scrub says, and actually did so, "because they were talking of him." They laughed at Scrub's gestures and appearance; and they laughed very heartily at seeing the gay young ensigns, whom they had been used to dance with, flirting fans, displaying great hoops, and, with painted cheeks and colored eye-brows, sailing about in female habiliments. This was a jest palpable and level to every understanding; and it was not only an excellent good one, but lasted a long while; for every time they looked at them when restored to their own habits, they laughed anew at the recollection of their late masquerade. " It is much," says Falstaff, "that a lie with a grave face, and a jest with a sad brow, will do with a fellow who never had the ache in his shoulders." One need only look back to the first rude efforts at comic humor which delighted our fathers, to know what gross and feeble jests amuse the mind, as yet a stranger to refinement. The loud and artless mirth so easily excited in a good-humored child, the *naïveté* of its odd questions and ignorant wonder, which delight us while associated with innocence and simplicity, would provoke the utmost disgust if we met with them where we look for intelligence and decorous observances. The simplicity of primitive manners, in what regards the petty amusements, and minute attentions, to which we have become accustomed, is exactly tantamount to that of childhood; it is a thing which, in our state of society, we have no idea of. Those who are from their depressed situation ignorant of the forms of polished life, know, at least, that such exist; and either awkwardly imitate them, or carefully avoid committing themselves, by betraying their ignorance. Here, while this simplicity (which by the bye, was no more vulgar than that of Shakespeare's Miranda), with its concomitant purity, continued unbroken by foreign modes, it had all the charm of undesigning childhood; but when half education and ill supported pretensions took place of this sweet attraction, it assumed a very different aspect, it was no longer simplicity, but vulgarity. There are things that every one feels and no one can describe; and this is one of them.

But to return to our Mirandas and their theatrical heroes: the fame of their exhibitions went abroad, and opinions were formed of them no way favorable to the actors or to the audience. In this region of reality, where rigid truth was always undisguised, they had not learned to distinguish between fiction and falsehood. It was said that the officers, familiar with every vice and every disguise, had not only spent a whole night in telling lies in a counterfeited place, the reality of which had never existed, but that they were themselves a lie, and had degraded manhood, and broke through an express prohibition in scripture, by assuming female habits; that they had not only told lies, but cursed and swore the whole night; and assumed the characters of knaves, fools, and robbers, which every good and wise man held in detestation, and no one would put on unless they felt themselves easy in them. Painting their faces, of all other things, seemed most to violate the Albanian ideas of decorum, and was looked upon as the most flagrant abomination. Great and loud was the outcry produced by it. Little skilled in sophistry, and strangers to all the arts " that make the worse appear the better reason," the young auditors could only say "that indeed it was very amusing; made them laugh heartily, and did harm to nobody."

So harmless, indeed, and agreeable did this entertainment appear to the new converts of fashion, that *The Recruiting Officer* was given out for another night, to the great annoyance of M. Frielinghuysen, who invoked heaven and earth to witness and avenge this contempt, not only of his authority, but, as he expressed it, of the source from whence it was derived. Such had been the sanctity of this good man's life, and the laborious diligence and awful earnestness with which he inculcated the doctrines he taught, that they had produced a correspondent effect, for the most part, on the lives of his hearers, and led them to regard him as the next thing to an evangelist; accustomed to success in all his undertakings, and to " honor, love, obedience, troops of friends," and all that gratitude and veneration can offer to its most distinguished object, this rebellion against his authority, and contempt of his opinion (once the standard by which every one's judgment was regulated), wounded him very deeply. The abhorrence with which he inspired the parents of the transgressors, among whom were many young men of spirit and intelligence, was the occasion of some family disagreements, a thing formerly scarcely known. Those young people, accustomed to regard their parents with implicit reverence, were unwilling to impute to them unqualified harshness, and therefore removed the blame of a conduct so unusual to their spiritual guide; "and while he thought, good easy man, full surely his greatness was a ripening, nipt his root." Early one Monday morning, after the domine had, on the preceding day, been peculiarly eloquent on the subject of theatrical amusements, and pernicious innovations, some unknown person left within his door a club, a pair of old shoes, a crust of black bread, and a dollar. The worthy pastor was puzzled to think what this could mean; but had it too soon explained to him. It was an emblematic message, to signify the desire entertained of his departure. The stick was to push him away, the shoes to wear on the road, and the bread and money a provision for his journey. These symbols appear, in former days, to have been more commonly used, and better understood than at present; for instance, we find that when Robert Bruce, afterwards king of Scotland, was in a kind of honorable capacity in the court of England; when his friend, the earl of Gloucester, discovered that it was the intention of the king to imprison him in the tower, lest he should escape to Scotland and assert his rights, unwilling by word or writing to discover what had passed in council, and at the same time desirous to save his friend, he sent him a pair of gilt spurs and twelve crowns, and ordered the servant to carry them to him as returning what he had formerly borrowed from him. This mysterious gift and message was immediately understood; and proved the means of restoring Bruce, and with him the laws and liberty of his native kingdom. Very different, however, was the effect produced by this *mal àpropos* symbol of dislike. Too conscious, and too fond of popularity, the pastor languished under a sense of imaginary degradation, grew jealous, and thought every one alienated from him because a few giddy young people were stimulated by momentary resentments to express disapprobation in this vague and dubious manner. Thus, insensibly, do vanity and self-opinion mingle with our highest duties. Had the domine, satisfied with the testimony of a good conscience, gone on in the exercise of his duty, and been above allowing little personal resentments to mingle with his zeal for what he thought right, he might have felt himself far above an insult of this kind; but he found to his cost, that "a habitation giddy and unsure hath he that buildeth on the fickle heart" of the unsteady, wavering multitude.

Chapter XXXVI

DOMINE FRIELINGHUYSEN LEAVES HIS PEOPLE

MADAME now returned to town with the colonel; and finding this general disorder and division of sentiments with regard to the pastor, as well as to the adoption of new modes, endeavored, with her usual good sense, to moderate and heal. She was always of opinion that the increase of wealth should be accompanied with a proportionate progress in refinement and intelligence; but she had a particular dislike to people's forsaking a respectable plainness of dress and manners for mere imperfect imitation, and inelegant finery. She knew too well the progress of society to expect, that, as it grew wealthy and numerous, it would retain its pristine purity; but then she preferred a " gradual abolition " of old habits, that people, as they receded from their original modes of thinking and living, might rather become simply elegant, than tawdrily fine; and though she all along wished, in every possible way, to promote the comfort of the brave men to whom the country owed so much, she by no means thought an indiscriminate admission of those strangers among the youth of the place, so unpractised in the ways of the world, an advisable measure; she was particularly displeased with the person in whose house the colonel of the regiment lodged, for so entirely domesticating a showy stranger, of whose real character he knew so little. Liberal and judicious in her views, she did not altogether approve the austerity of the domine's opinions, nor the vehemence of his language; and, as a Christian, she still less approved his dejection and concern at the neglect or rudeness of a few thoughtless young persons. In vain the colonel and Madame soothed and cheered him with counsel and kindness; night and day he mused on the imagined insult; nor could the joint efforts of the most respectable inhabitants prevent his heart from being corroded with the sense of imagined unkindness. At length he took the resolution of leaving those people so dear to him, to visit his friends in Holland, promising to return in a short time, whenever his health was restored, and his spirits more composed. A Dutch ship happened about this time to touch at New York, on board of which the domine embarked; but as the vessel belonging to Holland was not expected to return, and he did not, as he had promised, either write or return in an English ship, his congregation remained for a great while unsupplied, while his silence gave room for the most anxious and painful conjectures; these were not soon removed, for the intercourse with Holland was not frequent or direct. At length, however, the sad reality was but too well ascertained. This victim of lost popularity had appeared silent and melancholy to his shipmates, and walked constantly on deck. At length he suddenly disappeared, leaving it doubtful whether he had fallen overboard by accident, or was prompted by despair to plunge into eternity. If this latter was the case, it must have been the consequence of a temporary fit of insanity; for no man had led a more spotless life, and no man was more beloved by all that were intimately known to him. He was, indeed, before the fatal affront, which made such an undue impression on him, considered as a blessing to the place; and his memory was so beloved, and his fate so regretted, that this, in addition to some other occurrences falling out about the same time, entirely turned the tide of opinion, and rendered the thinking as well as the violent party, more averse to innovations than ever. Had the Albanians been Catholics, they would probably have canonized Dom. Frielinghuysen, whom they considered as a martyr to levity and innovation. He prophesied a great deal; such prophecy as ardent and comprehensive minds have delivered, without any other inspiration but that of the sound, strong intellect, which augurs the future from a comparison with the past, and a rational deduction of probable consequences. The affection that was entertained for his memory induced people to listen to the most romantic stories of his being landed on an island, and become a hermit; taken up into a ship when floating on the sea, into which he had accidentally fallen, and carried to some remote country, from which he was expected to return, fraught with experience and faith. I remember some of my earliest reveries to have been occupied by the mysterious disappearance of this hard-fated pastor.[1]

In the meanwhile new events were unfolding

[1] There is an entry of a baptism by him on the 14th October, 1759, in the church *Doep Boek*, but strange to say, there is a letter in existence, written on the 10th October, 1759, by G. Abeel of New York to his relatives in Albany, in which he says that while he was writing, the ship in which Dom. Frielinghuysen had embarked was leaving the port, and according to custom the guns were firing parting salutes. That on the previous Sunday he preached in the new Dutch church, and when he sat down, after giving out the last psalm, the bench gave way and he fell to the floor, which was universally regarded as a bad omen. Among other gossip it was remarked that the ocean was fatal to his family, and the impression that he would never return pervaded the minds of the people standing about and discussing the matter. A letter to his wife is extant, showing that the domine was in London, expecting to embark on his return to America, since when nothing is known of him. Dr. Thomas De Witt says he went to Holland on business growing out of the impending controversy in the church, concerning the *cætus*, the ordination of the clergy; a party insisting that it was not imperative that the candidate should go to Holland to receive the rite there, as had been the practice. His child Eva, baptized 5 December, 1756, was buried 15 September, 1757 (*Munsell's Annals*). Another Eva was baptized 10 September, 1758 (*Pearson's Early Settlers*). These are the only children of Dom. Frielinghuysen, that are found recorded, and are said to have been grand-children of Geertruy Isabella Lydius, daughter of Domine John Lydius, pastor of the church 1700–9. Mrs. Frielinghuysen was a granddaughter of Lancaster Symes, an English officer, from whom and other relatives she inherited quite a fortune for the times. Office Secretary of State, Deeds, XVI.

more fully to the Albanians the characters of their lately acquired friends. Scandal of fifty years standing must by this time have become almost pointless. The house where the young colonel, formerly mentioned, was billeted, and made his quarters good by every art of seductive courtesy, was occupied by a person wealthy, and somewhat vain and shallow, who had an only daughter; I am not certain, but I think she was his only child. She was young, lively, bold, conceited and exceedingly well-looking. Artless and fearless of consequences, this thoughtless creature saw every day a person who was, no doubt, as much pleased with her as one could be with mere youth, beauty, and kindness, animated by vivacity, and distinguished from her companions by all the embellishments which wealth could procure in that unfashioned quarter; his heart, however, was safe, as will appear from the sequel. Madame foresaw the consequences likely to result from an intimacy daily growing, where there was little prudence on the one side, and as little of that honor which should respect unsuspecting innocence on the other. She warned the family, but in vain; they considered marriage as the worst consequence that could ensue; and this they could not easily have been reconciled to, notwithstanding the family and fortune of the lover, had not his address and attentions charmed them into a kind of tacit acquiescence; for, as a Roman citizen in the proud days of the republic would have refused his daughter to a king, an Albanian, at one period, would rather have his daughter married to the meanest of his fellow-citizens, than to a person, of the highest rank in the army, because they thought a young person, by such a marriage, was not only forever alienated from her family, but from those pure morals and plain manners, in which they considered the greatest possible happiness to exist. To return:

While these gaieties were going on, and the unhappy domine embarking on the voyage which terminated his career, an order came for the colonel to march; this was the only commander who had ever been in town who had not spent any time, or asked any counsel at the Flats. Meanwhile his Calista (for such she was) tore her hair in frantic agonies at his departure; not that she in the least doubted of his returning soon to give a public sanction to their union, but lest he should prove a victim to the war then existing; and because, being very impetuous, and unaccustomed to control, the object of her wishes had been delayed to a future period. In a short time things began to assume a more serious aspect; and her father came one day posting to the Flats, on his way to the lakes, seeking counsel too late, and requesting the aid of their influence to bring about a marriage, which should cover the disgrace of his family. They had little hopes of his success, yet he proceeded; and finding the colonel deaf to all his arguments, he had recourse to entreaty, and finally offered to divest himself of all but a mere subsistence, and give him such a fortune as was never heard of in that country. This, with an angel, as the fond father thought her, appeared irresistible; but no! heir to a considerable fortune in his own country, and perhaps inwardly despising a romp, whom he had not considered from the first as estimable, he was not to be soothed or bribed into compliance. The dejected father returned disconsolate; and the astonishment and horror this altogether novel occurrence occasioned in the town, was not to be described. Of such a circumstance there was no existing precedent; half the city were related to the fair culprit, for penitent she could hardly be called. This unexpected refusal threw the whole city into consternation. One would have thought there had been an earthquake; and all the insulted domine's predictions rose to remembrance, armed with avenging terrors.

Many other things occurred to justify the domine's caution; and the extreme reluctance which the elders of the land showed to all such associations. All this Madame greatly lamented, yet could not acquit the parties concerned, whose duty it was, either to keep their daughters from that society for which their undisguised simplicity of heart unfitted them, or give them that culture and usage of life, which enables a young person to maintain a certain dignity, and to revolt at the first trespass on decorum. Her own protégés were instances of this; who, having their minds early stored with sentiments, such as would enable them truly to estimate their own value, and to judge of the characters and pretensions of those who conversed with them; all conducted themselves with the utmost propriety, though daily mixing with strangers, and were solicited in marriage by the first people in the province, who thought themselves happy to select companions from such a school of intelligence and politeness, where they found beauty of the first order, informed by mind, and graced by the most pleasing manners.

PART TWO

Anne Grant

MEMOIRS
OF
AN AMERICAN LADY

Chapter I

DEATH OF COLONEL PHILIP SCHUYLER

THIS year (1757) was marked by an event that not only clouded the future life of Madame, but occasioned the deepest concern to the whole province. Colonel Schuyler was scarcely sensible of the decline of life, except some attacks of the rheumatism, to which the people of that country are peculiarly subject: he enjoyed sound health and equal spirits, and had upon the whole, from the temperance of his habits, and the singular equanimity of his mind, a more likely prospect of prolonging his happy and useful life, than falls to the lot of most people. He had, however, in very cold weather, gone to town to visit a relation, then ill of a pleurisy; and having sat a while by the invalid, and conversed with him both on his worldly and spiritual affairs, he returned very thoughtful. On rising the next morning, he began the day, as had for many years been his custom, with singing some verses of a psalm in his closet. Madame observed that he was interrupted by a most violent fit of sneezing; this returned again a little after, when he calmly told her, that he felt the symptoms of a pleuritic attack, which had begun in the same manner with that of his friend; that the event might possibly prove fatal; but that knowing as she did how long a period [1] of more than common felicity had been granted to their mutual affection, and with what tranquillity he was enabled to look forward to that event which is common to all, and which would be earnestly desired if withheld; he expected of her that, whatever might happen, she would look back with gratitude, and forward with hope; and in the meantime honor his memory, and her own profession of faith, by continuing to live in the manner they had hitherto done, that he might have the comfort of thinking that his house might still be an asylum to the helpless and the stranger, and a desirable place of meeting to his most valued friends; this was spoken with an unaltered countenance, and in a calm and even tone. Madame, however, was alarmed; friends from all quarters poured in, with the most anxious concern for the event. By this time there was an hospital built at Albany for the troops; with a regular medical establishment. No human aid was wanting, and the composure of Madame astonished every one. This, however, was founded on hope;

[1] Forty years. — *Mrs. Grant.*

for she never could let herself imagine the danger serious, being flattered both by the medical attendants, and the singular fortitude of the patient. He, however, continued to arrange all things for the change he expected; he left his houses in town and country, his plate, and in short all his effects, to his wife, at her sole disposal; his estates were finally left to the orphan son of his nephew, then a child in the family; but Madame was to enjoy the rents during her life.

His negroes, for whom he had a great affection, were admitted every day to visit him; and with all the ardor of attachment peculiar to that kind-hearted race, implored heaven day and night for his recovery. The day before his death, he had them all called round his bed, and in their presence besought Madame that she would upon no account sell any of them; this request he would not have made could he have foreseen the consequences. On the fifth day of his illness he quietly breathed his last; having expressed, while he was able to articulate, the most perfect confidence in the mercy of the God whom he had diligently served and entirely trusted; and the most tender attachment to the friends he was about to leave.[1]

It would be a vain attempt to describe the sorrow

---

[1] Col. Philip Schuyler died February 16, 1758. By his will he divided his large landed estate between his brothers and sisters, or their heirs. His personal property and a farm on the Mohawk river, with the use of the Flats for life, he gave to his widow.

of a family like his, who had all been accustomed from childhood to look up to him as the first of mankind, and the medium through which they received every earthly blessing; while the serenity of his wisdom, the sweet and gentle cast of his heartfelt piety, and the equal mildness of his temper, rendered him incapable of embittering obligations; so that his generous humanity and liberal hospitality, were adorned by all the graces that courtesy could add to kindness. The public voice was loud in its plaudits and lamentations. In the various characters of a patriot, a hero, and a saint, he was dear to all the friends of valor, humanity, and public spirit; while his fervent loyalty, and unvaried attachment to the king, and the laws of that country by which his own was protected, endeared him to all the servants of government; who knew they never should meet with another equally able, or equally disposed to smooth their way in the paths of duty assigned to them.

To government this loss would have been irreparable, had not two singular and highly meritorious characters a little before this time made their appearance, and by superiority of merit and abilities, joined with integrity seldom to be met with anywhere, in some degree supplied the loss to the public. One of these was Sir William Johnson, the Indian superintendent, formerly mentioned; the other was Cadwallader Colden,[1] for a very long

[1] Cadwallader Colden was born in Dunse, Scotland, February 17, 1688; died on Long Island, September 28, 1776.

AN AMERICAN LADY

period of years lieutenant-governor (indeed virtually governor) of New York; who in point of political sagacity, and thorough knowledge of those he governed, was fully capable to supply that place. This shrewd and able ruler, whose origin I believe was not very easily traced, was said to be a Scotchman, and had raised himself solely by his merit to the station he held. In this he maintained himself by indefatigable diligence, rigid justice, and the most perfect impartiality. He neither sought to be feared nor loved, but merely to be esteemed and trusted, and thus fixed his power on the broad foundation of public utility. Successive governors, little acquainted with the country, and equally strangers to business, found it convenient to leave the management with him; who confessedly understood it better than any one else, and who had no friends but a few personal ones, and no enemies but a few public ones, who envied his station. It was very extraordinary to see a man rule so long and so steadily where he was merely and coldly esteemed: with so few of the advantages that generally procure success in the world, without birth or alliance; he had not even the recommendation of a pleasing appearance, or insinuating address. He was diminutive, and somewhat more than high-shouldered; the contrast betwixt the wealth of his mind, and the poverty of his outward appearance, might remind one of Æsop, or rather of the faithful though ill-shaped herald of Ulysses:

> "Erubutes in whose large mind alone,
> Ulysses viewed the image of his own."

Thus was it with Colden. Among the number of governors who succeeded each other in his time, if by chance one happened to be a man of ability, he estimated his merit at its just rate; and whatever original measure he might find it necessary to take for the public good, left the common routine of business in the hands of that tried integrity and experience, in which he found them; satisfied with the state and the popularity of governor, on which the other had not a wish to encroach. Colden, however, enriched his own family, in a manner on the whole not objectionable; he procured from the successive governors various grants of land, which, though valuable in quality, were not, from the remoteness of their situation, an object of desire to settlers; and purchased grants from many, who had obtained the property of them, among which were different governors and military commanders. He allowed this mine of future wealth to lie quietly ripening to its value, till the lands near it were, in process of time, settled, and it became a desirable object to purchase or hold on lease.

Chapter II

MRS. SCHUYLER'S ARRANGEMENTS AND CONDUCT AFTER THE COLONEL'S DEATH

THE mind of our good aunt, which had never before yielded to calamity, seemed altogether subdued by the painful separation from her husband. Never having left her consort's bedside, or known the refreshment of a quiet sleep, during his illness, she sunk at first into a kind of torpor, which her friends willingly mistook for the effects of resignation. This was soon succeeded by the most acute sorrow, and a dangerous illness, the consequence of her mental sufferings. In spring she slowly recovered, and endeavored to find consolation in returning to the regulation of her family, and the society of her friends, for both which she had been for some months disqualified. Her nieces, the Miss Cuylers, were a great comfort to her, from their affectionate attention, and the pleasure she took in seeing them growing up to be all that her maternal affection could wish. In the social grief of Pedrom,[1] who gave all his time

---

[1] The colonel's brother Peter, so called. — *Mrs. Grant.* [Query, *Peteroom*, Uncle Peter? His portrait is preserved in the mansion of Madame Schuyler at the Flats, by Mr. Stephen Schuyler, the recent

to her during the early part of her widowhood, she also found consolation; and whenever she was able to receive them, her friends came from all quarters to express their sympathy and their respect. The colonel's heir and her own eldest nephew made, with one of her nieces, a part of her family; and the necessity of attending to such affairs as formerly lay within the colonel's province, served further to occupy her mind; yet her thoughts continually recurred to that loss, which she daily felt more and more. She had buried the colonel in a spot within a short distance of his own house, in which he had formerly desired to repose; that his remains might not quit a scene so dear to him; and that the place, rendered sacred by his ashes, might in future be a common sepulture to his family; that he might in death, as in life, be surrounded by the objects of his affection and beneficence. This consecrated spot, about the size of a small flower garden, was enclosed for this purpose, and a tombstone, with a suitable inscription erected over the grave, where this excellent person's relict proposed her ashes should mingle with his.[1] In the mean-

owner and occupant of the premises. The portrait had been artistically copied for the late Gen. John T. Cooper, and was among the rare objects of art at his residence in Albany].

[1] From the second bridge that spans the Erie canal north of the entrance to the Albany cemetery, on the Watervliet turnpike, a quiet lane leads to the ancient Schuyler bouwery, known in history as *The Flats*; and nearly equidistant between the canal and the river, in a cluster of locust trees, a few rods north of the lane, is the family burial

time, though by continually speaking of her deceased friend, she passed the day without much visible agitation, she had fallen into a habit of vigilance; rarely sleeping till morning, and suffering through the silent hours from a periodical agony, for such it might be called, with which she was regularly visited. She had a confidante in this secret suffering; a decent and pious woman, who, on the death of her husband, a sergeant in the army, had been received into this family as a kind of upper domestic; and found herself so happy, and made herself so useful in teaching reading and needle-work to the children, that she still remained. This good woman slept in aunt's

ground. The earliest dead were buried in the church on State Street, or in the graveyard on Beaver and Hudson Streets, now the site of the Middle Dutch Church. The Schuylers and Van Rensselaers frequently intermarried, and several of the former were entombed in the Van Rensselaer vault. This monument mentioned by Mrs. Grant, and alluded to on a previous page, is undoubtedly the oldest one in the ground, as well as the most conspicuous. Madame Schuyler's remains were buried by the side of those of her husband, but there is no monument or other object to mark her place of sepulture. The reason assigned for this neglect is, that she left a portion of her property in such a way as to give offence to some of the heirs, and a question of duty or a sense of dissatisfaction arising among the parties upon whom it was incumbent, neither of them would charge themselves with the undertaking. A large slab lies upon the ground near that of Colonel Philip, of the same size and material, having a cavity in its upper side, apparently designed for a metal tablet, which is supposed to have been abstracted. There is nothing remaining upon it to indicate its purpose; but it is traditional that it was not designed for Madame Schuyler. The slab is now believed to cover the dust of John Schuyler, Jr., the father of General Schuyler.

room; and when all the family were at rest, she used to accompany her to a small distance from the tomb which contained those remains so dear to her. Madame, in the meantime, entered alone into the hallowed enclosure, and there indulged her unavailing sorrow. This she continued to do for some time, as she thought unobserved; but being very tall, and become large as she advanced in life, her figure, arrayed in her night-clothes, was very conspicuous, and was on different occasions observed by neighbors, who occasionally passed by at night; the consequence was, that it was rumored that an apparition was seen every night near the colonel's grave. This came to the ears of the people of the house, some of whom had the curiosity to watch at a distance, and saw the dreaded form appear, and, as they thought, vanish. This they carefully concealed from their revered patroness. Every one else in the house, however, heard it; and a pensive air of awe and mystery overspread the whole family. Her confidante, however, told her of it; and the consequence of this improper indulgence of sorrow greatly increased the dislike which Madame had always expressed for mystery and concealment. She was unwilling to let a family, to whom she had always set such an example of self-command, know of her indulging a weakness so unsuitable to her character and time of life. At the same time, however, she was resolved not to allow the belief of a supernatural appearance to fasten on their minds; unwilling to mention the subject herself, she was forced to submit to the humiliation of having it revealed by her confidante, to quiet the minds of the children and domestics, and reconcile them to solitude and moonlight.

Her mind was at this time roused from her own peculiar sorrows, by an alarming event, which disturbed the public tranquillity, and awakened the fears of the whole province, by laying open the western frontier. This was the taking of Oswego by the French, which fortress was the only barrier, except the valor and conduct of Sir William Johnson and his Mohawk friends, by which the town was protected on that side. The poor people, who were driven by the terror of this event from the settlements in that quarter, excited the sympathy of liberal-minded persons : and the interest which she took in their distresses, was one of the first things that roused the attention of our good aunt to her wonted beneficent exertions. General Bradstreet, who had a high respect for her understanding, and consulted her on all emergencies, had a profound reverence for the colonel's memory, and continued his intimacy in the family. The critical situation of things at this time, occasioned Lord Loudon to be sent out as commander of the forces in America. Madame received this nobleman when he visited Albany, and gave him most useful information. He was introduced to her by General Bradstreet, whose power and consequence might be said to increase with the disasters of the country; his department was a very lucrative one, and enabled him first, greatly to enrich himself, and in process of time, his friend Philip Schuyler, who, from his deputy, became, in a manner, his coadjutor. Albany now swarmed with engineers, planners, architects, and boat-builders. Various military characters, since highly distinguished, whose names I do not recollect, though once familiar to me, obtained introductions to Madame, who began once more to occupy her mind with public matters, and to open her house to the more respected and well-known characters among the military. Her brother-in-law, whom I have so often mentioned under the affectionate appellation of Pedrom, by which he was known in the family, being within less than half an hour's walk, spent much of his time with her, and received her company. This he was well qualified to do, being a person of a comely, dignified appearance, and frank, easy manners, inferior only to his late brother in depth of reflection, and comprehension of mind.

Chapter III

MOHAWK INDIANS — SIR WILLIAM JOHNSON

BY this time matters had gradually assumed a new aspect on this great continent. The settlement at Albany was no longer an insulated region, ruled and defended by the wisdom and courage diffused through the general mass of the inhabitants, but begun, in the ordinary course of things, to incorporate with the general state. The Mohawk Indians were so engaged by treaties to assist the army, in its now regular operations to the westward, that they came less frequently to visit Albany. A line of forts had, at a prodigious expense, been erected, leading from Albany to Upper Canada, by the Mohawk river, and the lakes of Ontario, Niagara, etc. Many respectable engineers were engaged in constructing these; some of them I remember were Swedes, persons of a graceful appearance, polished manners, and very correct conduct. These strangers conducted matters better than our own countrymen; being more accommodating in their manners, and better accustomed to a severe climate, and inconveniences of every kind. They were frequent guests at the Flats, were a pleasing accession to the society, and performed their duty to the public with a degree of honor and fidelity that checked abuses in others, and rescued the service they were engaged in, from the reproach which it had incurred, in consequence of those fungi of society which had at first intruded into it.

By the advice of the Schuylers, there was now on the Mohawk river a superintendent of Indian affairs; the importance of which began to be fully understood. He was regularly appointed, and paid by government. This was the justly celebrated Sir William Johnson,[1] who held an office difficult both to execute and define. He might indeed be called the tribune of the Five Nations: whose claims he asserted, whose rights he protected, and over whose minds he possessed a greater sway than any other individual had ever attained. He was indeed calculated to conciliate and retain the affections of this brave people; possessing in common with them many of those peculiarities of mind and manners, that distinguished them from others. He was an uncommonly tall, well made man: with a fine countenance; which, however, had rather an expression of dignified sedateness, approaching to melancholy. He appeared to be taciturn, never wasting words on matters of no importance: but highly eloquent when the occasion called forth his powers. He possessed intuitive sagacity, and the

---

[1] See "Life and Times of Sir William Johnson, Baronet," 2 vols., 8vo, by William L. Stone, 1864.

most entire command of temper, and of countenance. He did by no means lose sight of his own interest, but on the contrary raised himself to power and wealth, in an open and active manner; not disdaining any honorable means of benefiting himself: but at the same time the bad policy, as well as meanness of sacrificing respectability, to snatching at petty present advantages, were so obvious to him, that he laid the foundation of his future prosperity on the broad and deep basis of honorable dealing, accompanied by the most vigilant attention to the objects he had in view; acting so as, without the least departure from integrity on the one hand, or inattention to his affairs on the other, to conduct himself in such a manner, as gave an air of magnanimity to his character, that made him the object of universal confidence. He purchased from the Indians (having the grant confirmed by his sovereign) a large and fertile tract of land upon the Mohawk river; where, having cleared and cultivated the ground, he built two spacious and convenient places of residence: known afterwards by the names of Johnson castle, and Johnson hall. The first was on a fine eminence, stockaded round, and slightly fortified; the last was built on the side of the river, on a most fertile and delightful plain, surrounded with an ample and well cultivated domain: and that again encircled by European settlers; who had first come there as architects, or workmen, and had been induced by Sir William's liberality, and the singular beauty of the district, to continue. His trade with the Five Nations was very much for their advantage; he supplying them on more equitable terms than any trader, and not indulging the excesses in regard to strong liquors which others were too easily induced to do. The castle contained the store in which all goods were laid up, which were meant for the Indian traffic, and all the peltry received in exchange. The hall was his summer residence, and the place round which his greatest improvements were made. Here this singular man lived like a little sovereign; kept an excellent table for strangers, and officers, whom the course of their duty now frequently led into these wilds, and by confiding entirely on the Indians, and treating them with unvaried truth and justice, without ever yielding to solicitation what he had once refused, he taught them to repose entire confidence in him; he, in his turn became attached to them, wore in winter almost entirely their dress and ornaments, and contracted a kind of alliance with them; for becoming a widower in the prime of life, he connected himself with an Indian maiden, daughter to a sachem, who possessed an uncommonly agreeable person, and good understanding: and whether ever formally married to him according to our usage, or not, contrived to live with him in great union and affection all his life. So perfect was his dependence on those people, whom his fortitude and other manly virtues had attached to him, that when they returned from their summer excursions, and exchanged the last year's furs for fire-arms, etc., they used to pass a few days at the castle; when his family and most of his domestics were down at the hall. There they were all liberally entertained by their friend; and five hundred of them have been known, for nights together, after drinking pretty freely, to lie around him on the floor, while he was the only white person in a house containing great quantities of everything that was to them valuable or desirable. While Sir William thus united in his mode of life, the calm urbanity of a liberal and extensive trader, with the splendid hospitality, the numerous attendance, and the plain though dignified manners of an ancient baron, the female part of his family were educated in a manner so entirely dissimilar from that of all other young people of their sex and station, that as a matter of curiosity, it is worthy a recital. These two young ladies inherited, in a great measure, the personal advantages and strength of understanding, for which their father was so distinguished. Their mother dying when they were young, bequeathed the care of them to a friend. This friend was the widow of an officer who had fallen in battle; I am not sure whether she was devout, and shunned the world for fear of its pollutions, or romantic, and despised its selfish bustling spirit; but so it was, that she seemed utterly to forget it, and devoted herself to her fair pupils. To these she taught needle-work of the most elegant and ingenious kinds, reading and writing; thus quietly passed their childhood; their monitress not taking the smallest concern in family management, nor indeed the least interest in any worldly thing but themselves; far less did she inquire about the fashions or diversions which prevailed in a world she had renounced; and from which she seemed to wish her pupils to remain for ever estranged. Never was anything so uniform as their dress; their occupations, and the general tenor of their lives. In the morning they rose early, read their Prayer-Book, I believe, but certainly their Bible, fed their birds, tended their flowers, and breakfasted; then were employed some hours with unwearied perseverance, at fine needle-work, for the ornamental parts of dress, which were the fashion of the day, without knowing to what use they were to be put, as they never wore them; and had not at the age of sixteen ever seen a lady, excepting each other and their governess; they then read, as long as they chose, the voluminous romances of the last century; of which their friend had an ample collection, or Rollin's ancient history, the only books they had ever seen; after dinner they, regularly in summer, took a long walk; or an excursion in the sledge, in winter, with their friend: and then returned and resumed their wonted occupations, with the sole variation of a stroll in the garden in summer, and a game at chess, or shuttlecock, in winter. Their dress was to the full as simple and uniform as everything else; they wore wrappers of the finest chintz, and green silk petticoats; and this the whole year round without variation. Their hair, which was long and beautiful, was tied behind with a simple ribbon; a large calash shaded each from the sun, and in winter they had long scarlet mantles that covered them from head to foot. Their father did not live with them, but visited them every day in their apartment. This innocent and uniform life they led, till the death of their monitress; which happened when the eldest was not quite seventeen. On some future occasion I shall satisfy the curiosity which this short but faithful account of these amiable recluses has possibly excited.[1]

[1] These ladies married officers, who in succession lived as aid-de-camps with their father. Their manners soon grew easy; they readily acquired the habits of society, and made excellent wives. — *Mrs. Grant.*

Chapter IV

GENERAL ABERCROMBIE — DEATH OF LORD HOWE

I MUST now return to Albany, and to the projected expedition.

General Abercrombie, who commanded on the northern lakes, was a brave and able man, though rather too much attached to the military schools of those days, to accommodate himself to the desultory and uncertain warfare of the woods, where sagacity, ready presence of mind, joined with the utmost caution, and condescension of opinion to our Indian allies, was of infinitely more consequence than rules and tactics, which were mere shackles and incumbrances in this contention, with difficulties and perplexities more harassing than mere danger. Indeed when an ambuscade or sudden onset was followed by defeat, here (as in Braddock's case) the result reminded one of the rout of Absalom's army; where, we are told, the wood devoured more than the sword. The general was a frequent guest with Madame, when the nature of his command would permit him to relax from the duties that occupied him. He had his men encamped below Albany, in that great field which I have formerly described, as the common pasture for the town. Many of the officers were quartered in the fort and town; but Lord Howe always lay in his tent, with the regiment which he commanded; and which he modelled in such a manner, that they were ever after considered as an example to the whole American army; who gloried in adopting all those rigid, yet salutary regulations, to which this young hero readily submitted, to enforce his commands by his example.

Above the pedantry of holding up standards of military rules, where it was impossible to practise them, and the narrow spirit of preferring the modes of his own country to those proved by experience to suit that in which he was to act, Lord Howe laid aside all pride and prejudice, and gratefully accepted counsel from those whom he knew to be best qualified to direct them. Madame was delighted with the calm steadiness with which he carried through the austere rules which he found it necessary to lay down. In the first place he forbade all displays of gold and scarlet, in the rugged march they were about to undertake, and set the example by wearing himself an ammunition coat, that is to say, one of the surplus soldier's coats cut short. This was a necessary precaution; because in the woods, the hostile Indians, who started from behind the trees, usually caught at the long and heavy skirts then worn by the soldiers; and for the same reason he ordered the muskets to be shortened, that they might not, as on former occasions, be snatched from behind by these agile foes. To prevent the march of his regiment from being descried at a distance, by the glittering of their arms, the barrels of their guns were all blackened; and to save them from the tearing of bushes, the stings of insects, etc., he set them the example of wearing leggins, a kind of buskin made of strong woolen cloth, formerly described as a part of the Indian dress. The greatest privation to the young and vain yet remained. Hair well dressed, and in great quantity, was then considered as the greatest possible ornament, which those who had it took the utmost care to display to advantage, and to wear in a bag or a queue, which ever they fancied. Lord Howe's was fine, and very abundant; he, however, cropped it, and ordered every one else to do the same. Every morning he rose very early, and after giving his orders, rode out to the Flats, breakfasted, and spent some time in conversing with his friends there; and when in Albany, received all manner of useful information from the worthy magistrate Cornelius Cuyler. Another point which this young Lycurgus of the camp wished to establish, was that of not carrying anything that was not absolutely necessary. An apparatus of tables, chairs, and such other luggage he thought highly absurd, where people had to force their way with unspeakable difficulty, to encounter an enemy free from all such incumbrances. The French had long learnt how little convenience could be studied on such occasions as the present.

When his lordship got matters arranged to his satisfaction, he invited his officers to dine with him in his tent. They gladly assembled at the hour appointed but were surprised to see no chairs or tables; there were, however, bear-skins, spread like a carpet. His lordship welcomed them, and sat down on a small log of wood; they followed his example; and presently the servants set down a large dish of pork and pease. His lordship, taking a sheath from his pocket, out of which he produced a knife and fork, began to cut and divide the meat. They sat in a kind of awkward suspense, which he interrupted, by asking if it were possible that soldiers like them, who had been so long destined for such a service, should not be provided with portable implements of this kind; and finally relieved them from their embarrassment, by distributing to each a case the same as his own, which he had provided for that purpose. The austere regulations, and constant self-denial which he imposed upon the troops he commanded, were patiently borne, because he was not only gentle in his manners, but generous and humane in a very high degree, and exceedingly attentive to the health and real necessities of the soldiery. Among many instances of this, a quantity of powdered ginger was given to every man; and the sergeants were ordered to see, that when, in the course of marching, the soldiers arrived hot and tired at the banks of any stream, they should not be permitted to stoop to drink, as they generally inclined to do, but obliged to lift water in their canteens, and mix ginger with it. This became afterwards a general practice; and in those aguish swamps, through which the troops were forced to march, was the means of saving many lives. Aunt Schuyler, as this amiable young officer familiarly styled his maternal friend, had the utmost esteem for him; and the greatest hope that he would at some future period redress all those evils that had formerly impeded the service; and perhaps plant the British standard on the walls of Quebec. But this honor another young hero was destined to achieve; whose virtues were to be illustrated by the splendor of victory, the only light by which the multitude can see the merits of a soldier.

The Schuylers regarded this expedition with a mixture of doubt and misery, knowing too well, from the sad retrospect of former failures, how little valor and discipline availed where regular troops had to encounter with unseen foes, and with difficulties arising from the nature of the ground, for which military science afforded no remedy. Of General Abercrombie's worth and valor they had the highest opinion; but they had no opinion of attacking an enemy so subtle and experienced on their own ground, in entrenchments, and this they feared he would have the temerity to attempt. In the meantime preparations were making for the

The Vanderhuyden Palace, erected on North Pearl Street in 1725

attempt. The troops were marched in detachments past the Flats, and each detachment quartered for a night on the common, or in the offices. One of the first of these was commanded by Lee, of frantic celebrity, who afterwards, in the American war, joined the opponents of government, and was then a captain in the British service. Captain Lee had neglected to bring the customary warrants for impressing horses and oxen, and procuring a supply of various necessaries, to be paid for by the agents of government on showing the usual documents; he, however, seized everything he wanted where he could most readily find it, as if he were in a conquered country; and not content with his violence, poured forth a volley of execrations on those who presumed to question his right of appropriating for his troops everything that could be serviceable to them: even Madame, accustomed to universal respect, and to be considered as the friend and benefactress of the army, was not spared; and the aids which she never failed to bestow on those whom she saw about to expose their lives for the general defence, were rudely demanded, or violently seized. Never did the genuine Christianity of this exalted character shine more brightly than in this exigency; her countenance never altered, and she used every argument to restrain the rage of her domestics, and the clamor of her neighbors, who were treated in the same manner. Lee marched on, after having done all the mischief in his power, and was the next day succeeded by Lord Howe, who was indignant on hearing what had happened, and astonished at the calmness with which Madame bore the treatment she had received. She soothed him by telling him, that she knew too well the value of protection from a danger so imminent, to grow captious with her deliverers on account of a single instance of irregularity, and only regretted that they should have deprived her of her wonted pleasure, in freely bestowing whatever could advance the service, or refresh the exhausted troops. They had a long and very serious conversation that night. In the morning his lordship proposed setting out very early; but when he rose was astonished to find Madame waiting, and breakfast ready; he smiled and said he would not disappoint her, as it was hard to say when he might again breakfast with a lady. Impressed with an unaccountable degree of concern about the fate of the enterprise in which he was embarked, she again repeated her counsels and her cautions; and when he was about to depart, embraced him with the affection of a mother, and shed many tears, a weakness which she did not often give way to.

Meantime, the best prepared and disciplined body of forces that had ever been assembled in America, were proceeding on an enterprise, that, to the experience and sagacity of the Schuylers, appeared a hopeless, or, at least, a very desperate one. A general gloom overspread the family; this, at all times large, was now augmented by several of the relations both of the colonel and Madame, who had visited them at that time, to be nearer the scene of action, and get the readiest and most authentic intelligence; for the apprehended consequence of a defeat was, the pouring in of the French troops into the interior of the province; in which case Albany might be abandoned to the enraged savages attending the French army.

In the afternoon a man was seen coming on horseback from the north, galloping violently, without his hat. Pedrom, as he was familiarly called, the colonel's only surviving brother, was with her, and ran instantly to inquire, well knowing he rode express. The man galloped on, crying out that Lord Howe was killed. The mind of our good aunt had been so engrossed by her anxiety and fears for the event impending, and so impressed by the merit and magnanimity of her favorite hero, that her wonted firmness sunk under this stroke, and she broke out into bitter lamentations. This had such an effect on her friends and domestics, that shrieks and sobs of anguish echoed through every part of the house. Even those who were too young or too old to enter into the public calamity, were affected by the violent grief of aunt, who, in general, had too much self-command to let others witness her sorrows. Lord Howe was shot from behind a tree, probably by some Indian : and the whole army were inconsolable for a loss they too well knew to be irreparable. This stroke, however, they soon found to be "portent and pain, a menace and a blow;" but this dark prospect was cheered for a moment by a deceitful gleam of hope, which only added to the bitterness of disappointment.

Chapter V

DEFEAT AT TICONDEROGA — GENERAL LEE — HUMANITY OF MADAME

THE next day they heard the particulars of the skirmish, for it could scarce be called a regular engagement, which had proved fatal to the young warrior, whose loss was so deeply felt. The army had crossed Lake George, in safety, on the 5th of July, and landed without opposition. They proceeded in four columns to Ticonderoga, and displayed a spectacle unprecedented in the New World. An army of sixteen thousand men, regulars and provincials, with a train of artillery, and all the necessary provisions for an active campaign or regular siege, followed by a little fleet of bateaux, pontoons, etc. They set out wrong, however, by not having Indian guides, who are alone to be depended on in such a place. In a short time the columns fell in upon each other, and occasioned much confusion. While they marched on in this bewildered manner, the advanced guard of the French which had retired before them, were equally bewildered, and falling in with them in this confusion, a skirmish ensued, in which the French lost above three hundred men, and we, though sucessful, lost as much as it was possible to lose, in one; for here it was that Lord Howe fell.

The fort is in a situation of peculiar natural strength; it lies on a little peninsular, with Lake George on one side, and a narrow opening, communicating with Lake Champlain, on the other. It is surrounded by water on three sides; and in front there is a swamp, very easily defended; and where it ceased the French had made a breast-work above eight feet high; not content with this, they had felled immense trees on the spot, and laid them heaped on each other, with their branches outward, before their works. In fine, there was no place on earth where aggression was so difficult, and defence so easy, as in these woods; especially when, as in this case, the party to be attacked had great leisure to prepare their defence. On this impenetrable front they had also a line of cannon mounted; while the difficulty of bringing artillery through this swampy ground, near enough to bear upon the place, was unspeakable. This garrison, almost impregnable from situation, was defended by between four and five thousand men. An engineer, sent to reconnoitre, was of opinion that it might be attacked without waiting for the artillery. The fatal resolution was taken without consulting those who were best qualified to judge. An Indian or native American were here better skilled in the nature of the ground, and probabilities of success. They knew better, in short, what the spade, hatchet, or musket could or could not do, in such situations, than the most skillful veteran from Europe, however replete with military science. Indeed, when system usurps the province of plain sound sense in unknown exigencies, the result is seldom favorable; and this truth was never more fatally demonstrated than in the course of the American war, where an obstinate adherence to regular tactics, which do not bend to time or place, occasioned, from first to last, an incalculable waste of blood, of treasure, and of personal courage. The resolution then was to attack the enemy without loss of time, and even without waiting for artillery. Alas! "What have not Britons dared?"

I cannot enter into the dreadful detail of what followed; certainly never was infatuation equal to this. The forty-second regiment was then in the height of deserved reputation; in which there was not a private man that did not consider himself as rather above the lower class of people, and peculiarly bound to support the honor of the very singular corps to which he belonged. This brave hard-fated regiment was then commanded by a veteran of great experience and military skill, Colonel Gordon Graham,[1] who had the first point

---

[1] Gordon Graham, of Dranie, entered the Black Watch as ensign 25 October, 1739; was promoted to lieutenant 24 June, 1743; served in Flanders and Fontenoy, 1745; obtained a company, 1747; was at the surrender of Fort William Henry, 1757, and wounded at Ticonderoga 8 July, 1758. On the death of Major Duncan Campbell, he

of attack assigned to him: he was wounded at the first onset. How many this regiment, in particular, lost of men and officers, I cannot now exactly say; but these were very many. What I distinctly remember, having often heard of it since, is, that, of the survivors, every single officer retired wounded off the field. Of the fifty-fifth regiment, to which my father had newly been attached, ten officers were killed, including all the field officers. No human beings could show more determined courage than this brave army did. Standing four hours under a constant discharge of cannon and musketry from barricades, on which it was impossible for them to make the least impression. General Abercrombie saw the fruitless waste of blood that was every hour increasing, and ordered a retreat, which was very precipitate, so much so, that they crossed the lake and regained their camp on the other side the same night. Two thousand men were killed, wounded, or taken on this disastrous day. On the next, those most dangerously wounded were sent forward in boats, and reached the Flats before evening; they in a manner brought (at least confirmed) the news of the defeat. Madame had her barn instantly fitted up into a temporary hospital, and a room in her house allotted for the

---

succeeded to his commission and made the campaign of 1759, '60 under Amherst; served in the West Indies in 1762, when he became lieutenant-colonel of his regiment. He retired from the service 12 December, 1770 (*Col. Doc.*, x, 728).

surgeon who attended the patients; among these was Lee, the same insolent and rapacious Lee, who had insulted this general benefactress, and deprived her of one of her greatest pleasures, that of giving a share of everything she had to advance the service. She treated him with compassion, without adverting, by the least hint, to the past. She tore up her sheets and table linen for bandages, and she and her nieces were constantly employed in attending and cheering the wounded, while all her domestics were busied in preparing food and everything necessary for those unhappy sufferers. Even Lee felt and acknowledged the resistless force of such generous humanity. He swore, in his vehement manner, that he was sure there would be a place reserved for Madame in heaven, though no other woman should be there, and that he should wish for nothing better than to share her final destiny. The active industrious beneficence she exercised at this time, not only towards the wounded, but the wretched widows and orphans who had remained here, and had lost their all in their husbands and parents, was beyond praise. Could I clearly recollect and arrange the anecdotes of this period, as I have often heard them, they would of themselves fill a volume; suffice it, that such was the veneration in which she was held in the army after this period, that I recollect, amongst the earliest impressions received in my mind, that of a profound reverence for Madame as these people were wont to call her. Before I ever saw her, I used to think of her as a most august personage, of a majestic presence, sitting on an elevated seat, and scattering bounty to wounded soldiers, and poor women and children.

Chapter VI

THE FAMILY OF MADAME'S SISTER — THE DEATH OF THE LATTER

AUNT found consolation for all her sorrows in the family of her favorite sister. The promise of uncommon merit, which appeared in the rising branches of that singularly fine family, was to her a peculiar gratification; for no mother could love her own children more tenderly than she did them. The two daughters, which were amongst the eldest, passed, by turns, much of their time with her, and were, from their beauty and their manners, the ornaments of her society; while their good sense, ripened by being called early into action, made these amiable and elegant young women more a comfort and assistance than a care or charge to their aunt, at a very early period. They had four brothers; three of whom are still living, and have, through life, done honor by their virtues, their manners, and their conduct, in the most trying exigencies, to the memory and example of their excellent parents, as well as to that collateral school of pure morality, and sound and genuine policy, of which they shared the benefit.

The history of this family, in the after vicissitudes in which the political changes in their country involved them, would furnish a very interesting detail, were it allowable to offend the delicacy of modest worth, or eligible to expose the depravity and fury of enraged factions. Of the brothers I shall only mention, that the third, in his childhood, showed uncommon fire and vivacity; not seeming to retain the smallest portion of that hereditary phlegm which could still be easily traced through many of the settlers of this peculiar colony. He could scarce be called an unlucky boy, for he never did harm designedly; yet he was so volatile, eccentric and original in the frolicsome excursions of his fancy, that many ludicrous and some serious consequences resulted from them. He showed, however, amidst all these gaieties, from a very early age, a steady and determined predilection towards a military life, which in due time was indulged, and has been since the means of leading him on to rank and distinction in the British service.[1] Of the eldest brother I shall have occasion to speak hereafter; the second and youngest were zealous partisans of government at the time of the revolution. Their loyalty occasioned the loss of their fortunes and their homes; but their worth and bravery procured them confidence and important commands in that painful service which was carried on during the American war, at the end of which they were par-

[1] The capture of Tobago was achieved by General Cuyler, who had for near forty years been engaged in the most active and hazardous departments of the service. — *Mrs. Grant.*

tially rewarded by grants of land in upper Canada.[1] Loyalty and courage seem hereditary in this family. Many sons of those expatriated brothers are now serving their country in different parts of the empire, undeterred by the losses and sufferings of their parents in the royal cause. It was a marked distinction of character to be observed in the conduct of aunt's protégés, that though she was equally attached to the children of her husband's relations and her own, these latter only adopted her political sentiments, with a single exception, which shall be mentioned in its place.

The defeat at Ticonderoga bore very hard upon the mind of Madame; public spirit was always an active principle in her strong and reflecting mind; and from the particular circumstances in which she had always been involved, her patriotism gained strength by exercise. The same ardent concern for the public good, which could produce no other effect but fruitless anxiety, would be as unavailing as unnecessary, in our secure and tranquil state; but with her it was an exercised and useful virtue. Her attachment to the British nation, which was to

[1] Cornelius Cuyler, Jr., entered the British army and rose to the rank of major-general; and for distinguished services he was created a baronet. Several of his descendants have been prominent in military and civil life, and some are now in the army. Abraham C. Cuyler was Mayor of Albany 1770–77; but towards the close of the Revolutionary War he emigrated to Canada, where he died in 1810. Philip Cuyler, the eldest of the three brothers, adhered to the patriot cause, and remained in the country of his birth.

the very last a ruling principle both of her actions and opinions, contributed to embitter this blow to her and her family. The taking of Frontenac on the western lakes, and the re-establishment of our power in that important quarter, were achieved by General Bradstreet, whom Abercrombie dispatched at the head of three thousand provincials. This was a cordial much wanted by all, and more particularly gratifying to the family at the Flats, as the colonel's nephew, Philip Schuyler, though his was not exactly a warlike department, had evinced much spirit, prudence, and resolution during that expedition; in which, without publicly arrogating command, he, under Bradstreet (who was indeed a very able man), directed most of the operations. In the mind of this extraordinary person, qualities, suited to all occasions, lay dormant and unsuspected, till called forth by the varying events of his busy though not bustling life; for he seemed to carry on the plans, public and private, which he executed with superior ability and success, by mere volition. No one ever saw him appear hurried, embarrassed, or agitated. The success of this expedition, and the rising distinction of her nephew Philip, was some consolation to Madame for the late disaster. Still friendly and hospitable, she was as kindly disposed towards the British as ever, and as indefatigable in promoting a good understanding between them and the natives; but the army was now on a larger scale. It was in a manner regularly organized, and more independent of such aid as individuals could bestow; and the many children educated by her, or left orphans to her care, became from their number, their marriages, and various pursuits, objects of more earnest solicitude.

At this period Aunt Schuyler, now everywhere spoken of by that affectionate designation, met with a severe affliction in the death of a sister,[1] whom she had always loved with more than common tenderness, and whose family she considered in a manner as her own. This was Mrs. Cuyler, the wife of that able and upright magistrate, Cornelius Cuyler, of whose family I have just been giving some account. Mrs. Cuyler, with a character more gentle and retiring, possessed the good sense and benevolence for which aunt was distinguished, though her sphere of action being entirely within the limits of her own family, she could not be so well known, or so much celebrated. The colonel had always had a great attachment to this valuable person; which still more endeared her to his widow. She, however, always found new duties resulting from her afflictions, so that she could not afford to sink under them. She now was at pains to console her sister's husband, who really seemed borne down by this stroke; and the exertions she made for the good of his singularly promising family, kept her mind occupied.

[1] Mrs. Cornelius Cuyler died February 21, 1758.

Chapter VII

**FURTHER SUCCESS OF THE BRITISH ARMS—
A MISSIONARY—CORTLANDT SCHUYLER**

THE conquest of Oswego, which was this year (1759) retaken from the French by General Bradstreet, contributed to revive the drooping spirits of the army and the patriots; and it was quickly succeeded by the dear-bought conquest of Quebec. Though Madame had never seen General Wolfe, she shared the general admiration of his heroism, and the general sorrow for his loss, in a very high degree. She, too, was conscious, that the security and tranquillity purchased by the conquest of Quebec, would, in a manner, loosen the bonds which held the colonists attached to a government which they only endured while they required its protection. This led to consequences which she too clearly foresaw.

The mind of Mrs. Schuyler, which had been greatly agitated by the sad events of Ticonderoga, now began, in consequence of the successes, to become more composed, and turn itself to objects of utility, as formerly. What she had done, and made others do, for the orphans and widows that had become such in consequence of the attack on the lines, could scarce be credited. No one would suppose a moderate fortune like hers could possibly be equal to it. She had at this time, too, much satisfaction in seeing the respective churches (in all which she was deeply interested), filled with persons who did honor to their profession. A young clergyman named Westerlo,[1] succeeded Domine Frielinghuysen, after an interval of three or four years, during which the charge was irregularly filled. This young man had learning, talent, and urbanity; he had all the sanctity of life and animated eloquence of his predecessor without his love of power, his bustling turn, or his eagerness for popularity; he was indeed a person of very singular merit, but studious and secluded, and unwilling to mix with strangers. To Madame, however, he was open and companionable, and knew and valued the attractions of her conversation. Dr. Ogilvie was the English Episcopal minister, who, under the

[1] Rev. Eilardus Westerlo was born in Groeningen in 1738, and received a thorough university education. It was still a custom with the American churches to send to Holland for ministers to supply their pulpits. He arrived in August, 1760, less than a year after Dom. Frielinghuysen left, and died 26 December, 1790, aged 53. He took a conspicuous part in severing the church from its dependence upon the mother country, and its reorganization upon the present plan. He took strong ground in favor of the cause of the Revolution, and at a most critical time when Burgoyne was advancing upon the city, he animated and inspired the people by having his church open daily for prayer and address. He left in manuscript a Hebrew and Greek lexicon in 2 vols., folio, which is preserved in the State Library at Albany.

name of Indian missionary, and with a salary allowed him as such, had the charge of performing duty in a church erected for that purpose in town, to strangers, and such of the military as chose to attend. The Christian Indians, who were his particular charge, lived at too great a distance to benefit by his labors. The province, however, allowed a salary to a zealous preacher, who labored among them with apostolic fervor, and with the same disregard to the things of this world. Dr. Ogilvie[1] was highly respected, and indeed much beloved by all who were capable of appreciating his merit. His appearance was singularly prepossessing; his address and manners entirely those of a gentleman. His abilities were respectable, his doctrine was pure and scriptural, and his life exemplary, both as a clergyman and in his domestic circle, where he was peculiarly amiable; add to all this a talent for conversation, extensive reading, and a thorough knowl-

[1] John Ogilvie was a native of New York. He was ostensibly an Indian missionary in the Mohawk valley, although he preached mostly at St. Peter's Episcopal Church in Albany, from his graduation at Yale College in 1748 until 1765, having been appointed to this mission on account of his being a Dutch scholar. In 1760 he joined the expedition against Niagara, and continued attached to the army until the close of the French war. After leaving Albany he was an assistant minister at Trinity Church in New York and a professor in Columbia College. On the death of Rev. Dr. Barclay in 1754, who had undertaken the supervision of the Book of Common Prayer in the Indian tongue, the work was continued by Dr. Ogilvie, who was also familiar with the language. The work seems to have been finished by him in 1769. He died 26 November, 1774, aged 51, leaving among other benefactions £300 to a charity school.

edge of life. The doctor was indeed a man after Madame's own heart; and she never ceased regretting his departure to New York, where he was settled two years after. For Stuart[1] she had the utmost veneration. Perfectly calculated for his austere and uncourtly duties, he was wholly devoted to them, and scarce cast a look back to that world which he had forsaken. Yet he was, on various accounts, highly valued by Madame; for since the appointment of the superintendent, and more particularly since the death of the colonel, he became more important to her, as the link which held her to the Mohawks, whom she now saw so much more seldom, but always continued to love. The comprehension of her mind was so great, and her desire for knowledge so strong, that she found much entertainment in tracing the unfoldings of the human mind in its native state, and the gradual progress of intellect when enlightened by the gentle influence of pure religion; and this good *Father of the deserts* gratified her more by the details he was enabled to give of the progress of devotion and of mind among his little flock, than he could have done by all that learning or knowledge of the world

[1] A pious missionary in the Mohawk country. — *Mrs. Grant.* [John Stuart, D.D., styled the father of the Episcopal Church in Upper Canada (See *N. Y. Doc. Hist.*, III, 1063), was the only Episcopal missionary among the Indians throughout the whole confederacy, which, we are informed by Sir Guy Johnson, "afforded an opportunity for introducing New England missionaries who diffused their evil principles with their religion!" (*Col. Doc.*, VIII., 657).

can bestow. Again the Flats began to be the resort of the best society. She had also her nephews in succession; one, a brother of that Philip so often mentioned, since better known to the world by the appellation of General Schuyler, had been long about the family. He was a youth distinguished for the gracefulness of his person, and the symmetry of his features. He was a perfect model of manly beauty, though almost as dark as an Indian. Indeed, both in looks and character, he greatly resembled the aborigines of the country. He seemed perfectly unconscious of the extraordinary personal advantages which be possessed; was brave, honorable, and possessed a very good understanding, but collected within himself; silent, yet eloquent when he chose to interest himself, or was warmed by the occasion; and had such stainless probity, that every one respected and trusted him. Yet he was so very indifferent to the ordinary pleasures and pursuits of life, and so entirely devoted to the sports of the field, that when his aunt afterwards procured him a commission in a marching regiment, hoping thus to tame and brighten him, he was known in Ireland by the name of the handsome savage. This title did not belong to him in the sense we most often use it in; for his manners were not rude and harsh in the least, though an air of cold austerity, which shaded his fine countenance, with his delight in solitary amusements, led the gay and social inhabitants of the country in which he resided, to consider

GENERAL PHILIP SCHUYLER'S RESIDENCE, BUILT IN 1760–61

him as unwillingly rescued from his native forests.[1] This youth was named Cortlandt, and will be more particularly mentioned hereafter. That eccentric and frolicsome boy, whose humorous sallies and playful flights were a continual source of amusement, was also a frequent guest, but did not stay so long as his elder brother, who certainly was, of all aunt's adopted, the greatest favorite, and became more endeared to her, from being less successful in life than the rest of his family.

In a council held between their relations and Madame, it was decided that both Cortlandt and Cornelius should try their fortune in arms. Cortlandt was made an ensign in an old regiment, and went over to Ireland. Cornelius, a year after, got a commission in the 55th, then commanded by that singularly worthy and benevolent character Sir Adolphus Oughton. The mayor was highly respected for his wisdom; yet his purchasing a commission for so mere a boy, and laying out for it a sum of money which appeared large in a country where people contrived to do very well with wonderfully little of that article, astonished all his countrymen. Conscious, however, of his son's military genius, and well knowing that the vivacity that filled his grave kinsmen with apprehension, was merely a lambent flame of youthful gaiety, which would blaze without scorching, he fearlessly launched him

[1] Capt. Cortlandt Schuyler returned from Ireland with his family in 1764, having resigned his commission.

into a profession in which he hoped to see him attain merited distinction. While the excellent patroness of all these young people had the satisfaction of seeing every one brought up under her auspices (and, by this time, they were not a few), do honor to her instructions, and fill up their different stations in a manner the most creditable and prosperous; and she was often surrounded by the children of those who had engaged her earliest cares.

Chapter VIII

BURNING OF THE HOUSE AT THE FLATS — MADAME'S REMOVAL — JOURNEY OF THE AUTHOR

IT was at this time, when she was in the very acme of her reputation, and her name never mentioned without some added epithet of respect or affection, that her house, so long the receptacle of all that was good or intelligent, and the asylum of all that was helpless and unfortunate, was entirely consumed before her eyes.

In the summer of this year, as General Bradstreet was riding by the Flats one day, and proposing to call on Madame, he saw her sitting in a great chair under the little avenue of cherry trees that led from her house to the road. All the way as he approached he saw smoke, and at last flames, bursting out from the top of her house. He was afraid to alarm her suddenly; but when he told her, she heard it with the utmost composure; pointed out the likeliest means to check the fire; and ordered the neighbors to be summoned, and the most valuable goods first removed, without ever attempting to go over the house herself, when she knew she could be of no service; but with the most admirable presence of mind, she sat still with a placid countenance, regulating and ordering everything in the most judicious manner, and with as much compos-

Madame Schuyler House at the Flats.

ure as if she had nothing to lose.[1] When evening came, of that once happy mansion not a single

[1] The house of Madame Schuyler was burnt in 1763. Her father in 1680, came in possession of two houses on the south-east corner of State and Pearl Streets in the city of Albany, one of which stood until recently, the other having been removed to widen Pearl Street. In one of these houses Madame Schuyler lived while her house at the Flats was in process of rebuilding. The house now occupied by the widow and daughter of Mr. Richard Schuyler is known to have been built upon the foundation of the old one, and of the same dimensions and style of architecture. That portion of the wall of the burnt house, forming the north-west corner, is still discernible in the present structure, of which an engraving is here presented. The house stands a few rods from the river bank, facing the east, and has the same aspect as when built more than a century ago. A handsome bay-window was placed over the porch in May, 1881, from which a fine view was obtained. The front door, which is divided laterally, in the fashion of the day, into an upper and lower door, still retains its quaint old brass knocker; and the same shutters, with their curious fastenings and hinges, remain as when it was built, in 1772, by the grandfather of the late Mr. John C. Schuyler, who leased the premises after

beam was left, and the scorched brick walls were all that remained to mark where it had stood.

Madame could not be said to be left without a dwelling, having a house[1] in Albany rather larger than the one destroyed. But she was fondly attached to the spot which had been the scene of so much felicity, and rendered more dear to her by retaining within its bounds the remains of her beloved partner. She removed to Pedrom's house for the night. The news of what had happened spread every where; and she had the comfort of knowing, in consequence of this misfortune, better than she could by any other means, how great a degree of public esteem and private gratitude she had excited. The next day people came from all quarters to condole, and ask her directions where and how she would choose to have another house built. And in a few days the ground was covered with bricks, timber, and other materials, brought there by her friends in voluntary kindness. It is to be observed that the people in the interior of New York were so exceedingly skillful in the use not only of the axe, but all ordinary tools used in

the fire. The scene looking south from this spot is one of great beauty, stretching over a level plain reaching to the site of the Van Rensselaer mansion about three or four miles below, skirted by the river on the east and the Erie Canal on its western border.

[1] This house was on the south side of State Street opposite North Pearl Street. It was owned and occupied by Madame's father, who directed in his will that she should have the use of it during life. Some years after the Revolution, it was removed for the opening of South Pearl Street.

planing and joining timber, that with the aid of a regular carpenter or two to carry on the nicer parts of the work, a man could build an ordinary house, if it were a wooden one, with very little more than his own domestics. It can scarce be credited that this house, begun in August, was ready for aunt's reception against winter, which here begins very early. But General Bradstreet[1] had sent some of the king's workmen, considering them as employed for the public service, while carrying on this building. The most unpleasant circumstance about this new dwelling, was the melancholy hiatus which appeared in front, where the former large house had stood, and where the deep and spacious cellars still yawned in gloomy desolation. Madame, who no longer studied appearance, but merely thought of a temporary accommodation, for a life which neither she nor any one expected to be a long one, ordered a broad wooden bridge, like those we see over rivers. This bridge was furnished with seats like a portico, and this with the high walls of the burnt house, which were a kind of screen before the new one,

---

[1] John Bradstreet was quarter-master general, whose career has been sketched by Dr. O'Callaghan in "Colonial Documents of New York," VIII, 379. His statement of Indian affairs in the war with Pontiac is to be found in the "Diary of the Siege of Detroit," published in IV, "Munsell's Hist. Series." His papers are preserved in the New York State Library at Albany. The house occupied by Gen. Philip Schuyler in Albany, one of the historical mansions of that city, was built by the wife of General Bradstreet during his absence at Oswego. He filled with distinguished ability various important offices, civil and military, and died 25 September, 1774, aged 63.

gave the whole the appearance of some ancient ruin.

Madame did not find the winter pass comfortably. That road, now that matters were regularly settled, was no longer the constant resort of her military friends. Her favorite nieces were too engaging, and too much admired, to leave room to expect they should remain with her. She found her house comparatively cold and inconvenient, and the winter long and comfortless. She could not now easily go the distance to church. Pedrom, that affectionate and respected brother, was now, by increasing deafness, disqualified from being a companion; and sister Susan, infirm and cheerless, was now, for the most part, confined to her chamber. Under these circumstances she was at length prevailed on to remove to Albany. The Flats she gave in lease to Pedrom's son Stephen. The house and surrounding grounds were let to an Irish gentleman, who came over to America to begin a new course of life, after spending his fortune in fashionable dissipation. On coming to America, he found that there was an intermediate state of hardship and self-denial to be encountered, before he could enter on that fancied Arcadia which he thought was to be found in every wood. He settled his family in this temporary dwelling, while he went to traverse the provinces in search of some unforfeited Eden, where the rose had no thorn, and the course of ceaseless labor had not begun to operate. Madame found reason to be highly satisfied with the change. She had mills[1] which supplied her with bread, her slaves cut and brought home fire wood, she had a good garden, and fruit and every other rural dainty came to her in the greatest abundance. All her former protégés and friends in different quarters delighted to send their tribute; and this was merely an interchange of kindness.

Soon after this removal, her eldest niece, a remarkably fine young woman, was married to Mr. C. of C.[2] manor, which was accounted one of the best matches, or rather the very best in the province. She was distinguished by a figure of uncommon grace and dignity, a noble and expressive countenance, and a mind such as her appearance led one to expect. This very respectable person is, I believe, still living, after witnessing, among her dearest connections, scenes the most distressing, and changes the most painful. She has ever con-

---

[1] Aunt Schuyler had a third share in the property left by her father at Saratoga (Schuylerville), consisting of lands, farms and mills. This large property afterwards came into the possession of General Philip Schuyler. The mills and other buildings were burned by Burgoyne.

[2] Elizabeth, eldest daughter of Cornelius Cuyler, married James Van Cortlandt, in 1654; and six years later her sister Elsie married Augustus Van Cortlandt, a brother of James. Elsie died eighteen months after her marriage. James and Augustus were the sons of Frederick Van Cortlandt and Frances Jay, his wife. They were descendants in the fourth generation of Olof Stevense Van Cortlandt, the Hollander. Margaret, youngest daughter of Cornelius Cuyler, married Isaac Low of New York. In the Revolution he hesitated, and was lost. His brother, Nicholas Low, was wiser, and saved himself and estate.

ducted herself, so as to do honor to the excellent examples of her mother and aunt, and to be a pattern of steadfast truth and generous friendship, in exigencies the most trying. Her younger sister, equally admired, though possessing a different style of beauty, more soft and debonair, with the fairest complexion, and most cheerful simplicity of aspect, was the peculiar favorite of her aunt, above all that ever she took charge of; she, too, was soon after married to that highly esteemed patriot the late Isaac L., revered, through the whole continent, for his sound good sense and genuine public spirit. He was, indeed, "happily tempered, mild, and firm;" and was finally the victim of steadfast loyalty.

It now remains to say how the writer of these pages became so well acquainted with the subject of these memoirs.

My father was at this time a subaltern in the 55th regiment. That body of men were then stationed at Oswego; but during the busy and warlike period I have been describing, my mother and I were boarded, in the country, below Albany, with the most worthy people imaginable; with whom we ever after kept up a cordial friendship. My father, wishing to see his family, was indulged with permission, and at the same time ordered to take the command of an additional company, who were to come up, and to purchase for the regiment all the stores they should require for the winter;

which proved a most extensive commission. In the month of October he set out on this journey, or voyage rather, in which it was settled that my mother and I should accompany him. We were, I believe, the first females, above the very lowest ranks, who had ever penetrated so far into this remote wilderness. Certainly never was joy greater than that which lulled my childish mind on setting out on this journey. I had before seen little of my father, and the most I knew of him was from the solicitude I had heard expressed on his account, and the fear of his death after every battle. I was, indeed, a little ashamed of having a military father, brought up as I had mostly been, in a Dutch family, and speaking that language as fluently as my own; yet, on the other hand, I had felt so awkward at seeing all my companions have fathers to talk and complain to, while I had none, that I thought upon the whole it was a very good thing to have a father of any kind. The scarlet coat, which I had been taught to consider as the symbol of wickedness, disgusted me in some degree; but then, to my great comfort, I found my father did not swear; and again, to my unspeakable delight, that he prayed. A soldier pray! was it possible? and should I really see my father in heaven! How transporting! By a sudden revolution of opinion I now thought my father the most charming of all beings; and the overflowings of my good will reached to the whole company, because they wore the same

color, and seemed to respect and obey him. I
dearly loved idleness too, and the more, because
my mother, who delighted in needle-work, confined me too much to it. What joys were mine!
to be idle for a fortnight, seeing new woods, rivers,
and animals, every day; even then the love of nature was, in my young bosom, a passion productive
of incessant delight. I had, too, a primer, two
hymns, and a ballad; and these I read over and
over with great diligence. At intervals my attention was agreeably engaged by the details the soldiers gave my father of their manner of living and
fighting in the woods, etc., and with these the
praises of Madame were often mingled. I thought
of her continually; every great thing I heard about
her, even her size, had its impression. She became
the heroine of my childish imagination; and I
thought of her as something both awful and admirable. We had the surgeon of the regiment,
and another officer with us; they talked too, of
Madame, of Indians, of battles, and of ancient
history. Sitting from morning to night musing in
the boat, contemplating my father, who appeared
to me a hero and a saint, and thinking of Aunt
Schuyler, who filled up my whole mind with the
grandeur with which my fancy had invested her;
and then having my imagination continually amused
with the variety of noble wild scenes which the
beautiful banks of the Mohawk afforded, I am
convinced I thought more in that fortnight, that is

to say, acquired more ideas, and took more lasting impressions, than ever I did, in the same space of time, in my life. This, however foreign it may appear to my subject, I mention, as so far connecting with it, that it accounts, in some measure, for that development of thought which led me to take such ready and strong impressions from aunt's conversation when afterwards I knew her.

Chapter IX

CONTINUATION OF THE JOURNEY — ARRIVAL AT OSWEGO

NEVER, certainly, was a journey so replete with felicity. I luxuriated in idleness and novelty; knowledge was my delight, and it was now pouring in on my mind from all sides. What a change from sitting pinned down to my samplar by my mother till the hour of play, and then running wild with children as young, and still simpler than myself. Much attended to by all my fellow travellers, I was absolutely intoxicated with the charms of novelty, and the sense of my new-found importance. The first day we came to Schenectady, a little town, situated in a rich and beautiful spot, and partly supported by the Indian trade. The next day we embarked, proceeded up the river with six bateaux, and came early in the evening to one of the most charming scenes imaginable, where Fort Hendrick was built; so called, in compliment to the principal sachem, or king of the Mohawks. The castle of this primitive monarch stood at a little distance, on a rising ground, surrounded by palisades. He resided, at the time, in a house which the public workmen, who had lately built this fort, had been ordered to erect for him in the vicinity. We did not fail to wait upon his majesty; who, not choosing to depart too much from the customs of his ancestors, had not permitted divisions of apartments, or modern furniture, to profane his new dwelling. It had the appearance of a good barn, and was divided across by a mat hung in the middle. King Hendrick, who had indeed a very princely figure, and a countenance that would not have dishonored royalty, was sitting on the floor beside a large heap of wheat, surrounded with baskets of dried berries of different kinds; beside him, his son, a very pretty boy, somewhat older than myself, was caressing a foal, which was unceremoniously introduced into the royal residence. A laced hat, a fine saddle and pistols, gifts of his good brother the great king, were hung round on the cross beams. He was splendidly arrayed in a coat of pale blue, trimmed with silver; all the rest of his dress was of the fashion of his own nation, and highly embellished with beads and other ornaments. All this suited my taste exceedingly, and was level to my comprehension. I was prepared to admire King Hendrick by hearing him described as a generous warrior, terrible to his enemies and kind to his friends: the character of all others calculated to make the deepest impression on ignorant innocence, in a country where infants learned the horrors of war from its vicinity. Add to all this, that the monarch smiled, clapped my head, and ordered me a little basket, very pretty, and filled by the officious kindness of his son with dried berries. Never did princely gifts, or the smile of royalty, produce more ardent admiration and profound gratitude. I went out of the royal presence overawed and delighted, and am not sure but what I have liked kings all my life the better for this happy specimen, to which I was so early introduced. Had I seen royalty, properly such, invested with all the pomp of European magnificence, I should possibly have been confused and over-dazzled. But this was quite enough, and not too much for me; and I went away, lost in a reverie, and thought of nothing but kings, battles, and generals for many days after.

This journey, charming my romantic imagination by its very delays and difficulties, was such a source of interest and novelty to me, that above all things I dreaded its conclusion, which I well knew would be succeeded by long tasks and close confinement. Happily for me we soon entered upon Wood creek, the most desirable of all places for a traveller who loves to linger if such another traveller there be. This is a small river, which winds irregularly through a deep and narrow valley of the most lavish fertility. The depth and richness of the soil here was evinced by the loftiness and the nature of the trees, which were, hickory, butter-nut, chestnut, and sycamores, of vast circumference as well as height. These became so top-heavy, and their roots were so often undermined by this insidious stream, that in every tempestuous night, some giants of the grove fell prostrate, and very frequently across the stream, where they lay in all their pomp of foliage, like a leafy bridge, unwitherd, and formed an obstacle almost invincible to all navigation. The Indian lifted his slight canoe, and carried it past the tree; but our deep-loaded bateaux could not be so managed. Here my orthodoxy was shocked, and my anti-military prejudices revived by the swearing of the soldiers; but then again my veneration for my father was if possible increased, by his lectures against swearing provoked by their transgression. Nothing remained for our heroes but to attack these sylvan giants axe in hand, and make way through their divided bodies. The assault upon fallen greatness was unanimous and unmerciful, but the resistance was tough, and the process tedious; so much so, that we were three days proceeding fourteen miles, having at every two hours' end at least, a new tree to cut through.

It was here, as far as I recollect the history of my own heart, that the first idea of artifice ever entered to my mind. It was, like most female artifices, the offspring of vanity. These delays were a new source of pleasure to me. It was October: the trees we had to cut through were often loaded with nuts, and while I ran lightly along the branches, to fill my royal basket with their spoils, which I had great pleasure in distributing, I met with multitudes of fellow plunderers in the squirrels of various colors and sizes, who were here numberless. This made my excursions amusing: but when I found my disappearance excited alarm, they assumed more interest. It was so fine to sit quietly among the branches, and hear concern and solicitude expressed about the child.

I will spare the reader the fatigue of accompanying our little fleet through

"Antres vast and deserts wild:"

only observing, that the munificent solitude through which we travelled was much relieved by the sight of Johnson hall, beautifully situated in a plain by the river; while Johnson castle, a few miles further up, made a most respectable appearance on a commanding eminence at some distance.

We travelled from one fort to another; but in three or four instances, to my great joy, they were so remote from each other, that we found it necessary to encamp at night on the bank of the river. This, in a land of profound solitude, where wolves, foxes, and bears abounded, and were very much inclined to consider and treat us as intruders, might seem dismal to wiser folks. But I was so gratified by the bustle and agitation produced by our measures of defence, and actuated by the love which all children have for mischief that is not fatal, that I enjoyed our night's encampment exceedingly. We stopped early wherever we saw the largest and most combustible kind of trees. Cedars were great favorites, and the first work was to fell and pile upon each other an incredible number, stretched lengthways, while every one who could was busied in gathering withered branches of pine, etc., to fill up the interstices of the pile, and make the green wood burn the faster. Then a train of gun-powder was laid along to give fire to the whole fabric at once, which blazed and crackled magnificently. Then the tents were erected close in a row before this grand conflagration. This was not merely meant to keep us warm, though the nights did begin to grow cold, but to frighten wild beasts and wandering Indians. In case any such Indians, belonging to hostile tribes, should see this prodigious blaze, the size of it was meant to give them an idea of a greater force than we possessed.

In one place, where we were surrounded by hills, with swamps lying between them, there seemed to be a general congress of wolves, who answered each other from opposite hills, in sounds the most terrific. Probably the terror which all savage animals have at fire was exalted into fury, by seeing so many enemies, whom they durst not attack. The bull frogs, the harmless, the hideous inhabitants of the swamps, seemed determined not to be out-done, and roared a tremendous bass to this bravura accompaniment. This was almost too much for my love of the terribly sublime: some women, who were our fellow-travellers, shrieked with terror: and finally, the horrors of that night were ever after held in awful remembrance by all who shared them.

The last night of this eventful pilgrimage, of which I fear to tire my readers by a farther recital, was spent at Fort Brewerton, then commanded by Captain Mungo Campbell,[1] whose warm and generous heart, whose enlightened and comprehensive mind, whose social qualities and public virtues I should delight to commemorate did my limits permit; suffice it, that he is endeared to my recollection by being the first person who ever supposed me to have a mind capable of culture, and I was ever after distinguished by his partial notice. Here we were detained two days by a premature fall of snow. Very much disposed to be happy any where, I was here particularly so. Our last day's journey, which brought us to Lake Ontario and Fort Oswego, our destined abode, was a very hard one; we had people going before, breaking the ice with paddles, all the way.

All that I had foreboded of long tasks, confinement, etc., fell short of the reality. The very deep snow confined us all; and at any rate the rampart or the parade would have been no favorable scene of improvement for me. One great source of entertainment I discovered here, was no other than

[1] Colonel Mungo Campbell was killed leading on the attack of Fort St. Anne, at the battle of White Plains, Anno 1777. — *Mrs. Grant.*

the Old Testament, which during my confinement I learned to read; till then having done so very imperfectly. It was an unspeakable treasure as a story book, before I learnt to make any better use of it, and became, by frequent perusal, indelibly imprinted on my memory. Wallace wight, and Welwood's memoirs of the history of England, were my next acquisitions. Enough of egotism, yet all these circumstances contributed to form that taste for solid reading which first attracted the attention of my invaluable friend.

I cannot quit Ontario without giving a slight sketch of the manner in which it was occupied and governed while I was there and afterwards, were it but to give young soldiers a hint how they may best use their time and resources, so as to shun the indolence and ennui they are often liable to in such situations. The 55th had by this time acquired several English officers; but with regard to the men, it might be considered as a Scotch regiment, and was indeed originally such, being raised but a very few years before, in the neighborhood of Stirling. There were small detachments in other forts; but the greatest part were in this, commanded by Major (afterwards Colonel) Duncan of Lundie, elder brother of the late Lord Duncan of Camperdown. He was an experienced officer, possessed of considerable military science, learned, humane, and judicious, yet obstinate, and somewhat of an humorist withal. Wherever he went a respectable

AN AMERICAN LADY

library went with him. Though not old he was gouty, and war-worn, and therefore allowably carried about many comforts and conveniences that others could not warrantably do. The fort was a large place, built entirely of earth and great logs; I mean the walls and ramparts, for the barracks were of wood, and cold and comfortless. The cutting down the vast quantity of wood used in this building had, however, cleared much of the fertile ground by which the fort was surrounded. The lake abounded with excellent fish and varieties of water-fowl, while deer and every kind of game were numerous in the surrounding woods. All these advantages, however, were now shut up by the rigors of winter. The officers were all very young men, brought from school or college to the army, and after the dreadful specimen of war which they had met with on their first outset, at the lines of Ticonderoga, they had gone through all possible hardships. After a march up St. Lawrence, and then through Canada here, a march indeed, considering the season, and the new road, worthy the hero of Pultowa, they were stationed in this new built garrison, far from every trace of civilization. These young soldiers were, however, excellent subjects for the forming hand of Major Duncan.[1] As

[1] Alexander Duncan, of the 55th regiment, obtained his company 28 October, 1755, was promoted to major 1760, and to lieutenant-colonel 1764. He was at Fort Ontario in October, 1763, and retired from the army in 1773.

I have said on a former occasion of others, if they were not improved, they were not spoiled, and what little they knew was good.

The major, by the manner in which he treated them, seemed to consider them as his sons, or pupils; only one might call him an austere parent, or a rigid instructor. But this semblance of severity was necessary to form his pupils to habitual veneration. Partaking every day of their convivial enjoyments, and showing every hour some proof of paternal care and kindness; all this was necessary to keep them within due limits. Out of regard to their own welfare he wanted no more of their love than was consistent with salutary fear; and yet made himself so necessary to them, that nothing could be so terrible to them as, by any neglect or imprudence, to alienate him. He messed with them, but lived in a house of his own. This was a very singular building divided into two apartments; one of which was a bedroom, in which many stores found place, the other, a breakfasting-parlor, and, at the same time, a library. Here were globes, quadrants, mathematical instruments, flutes, dumb-bells, and chess-boards; here, in short, was a magazine of instruction and amusement for the colonel's pupils, that is, for all the garrison. (Cornelius Cuyler, who had now joined the regiment, as youngest ensign, was included in this number.) This Scythian dwelling, for such it seemed, was made entirely of wood, and fixed upon wheels of the same material, so that it could be removed from one part of the parade to another, as it frequently was. So slight a tenement, where the winters were intensely cold, was ill calculated for a gouty patient; for this, however, he found a remedy; the boards, which formed the walls of his apartment, being covered with deer-skins, and a most ample bear-skin spread on the floor by way of carpet. When once the winter set fully in, Oswego became a perfect Siberia; cut off even from all intelligence of what was passing in the world. But the major did not allow this interval to waste in sloth or vacancy; he seemed rather to take advantage of the exclusion of all exterior objects. His library was select and soldier-like. It consisted of numerous treatises on the military art, ancient and modern history, biography, etc., besides the best authors in various sciences, of which I only recollect geography and the mathematics. All the young men were set to read such books as suited their different inclinations and capacities. The subalterns breakfasted with their commander in rotation every day, three or four at a time; after breakfast he kept them, perhaps two hours, examining them on the subject of their different studies. Once a week he had a supper party for such of the captains as were then in the fort; and once a week they entertained him in the same manner. To these parties such of the subalterns, as distinguished themselves by diligence and proficiency, were invited. Whoever was negligent, he made the subject of sarcasms so pointed at one time, and at another so ludicrous, that there was no enduring it. The dread of severe punishment could not operate more forcibly. Yet he was so just, so impartial, so free from fickleness and favoritism, and so attentive to their health, their amusements, and their economy, that every individual felt him necessary to his comfort, and looked up to him as his " guide, philosopher, and friend."

Chapter X

BENEFIT OF SELECT READING — HUNTING EXCURSION

UNSPEAKABLE benefit and improvement was derived from the course of reading I have described, which, in the absence of other subjects, furnished daily topics of discussion, thus impressing it more forcibly on the mind.

The advantages of this course of social study, directed by a mentor so respected, were such, that I have often heard it asserted that these unformed youths derived more solid improvement from it than from all their former education. Reading is one thing; but they learned to think and to converse. The result of these acquirements served to impress on my mind what I formerly observed with regard to Madame, that a promiscuous multitude of books always within reach retards the acquisition of useful knowledge. It is like having a great number of acquaintances and few friends; one of the consequences of the latter is to know much of exterior appearances, of modes and manners, but little of nature and genuine character. By running over numbers of books without selection, in a desultory manner, people, in the same way, get a general superficial idea of the varieties and nature of different styles, but do not comprehend or retain the matter with the same accuracy as those who have read a few books, by the best authors, over and over with diligent attention. I speak now of those one usually meets with; not of those commanding minds, whose intuitive research seizes on everything worth retaining, and rejects the rest as naturally as one throws away the rind when possessed of the kernel.

Our young students got through the winter pretty well; and it is particularly to be observed, that there was no such thing as a quarrel heard of among them. Their time was spent in a regular succession of useful pursuits, which prevented them from risking the dangers that often occur in such places; for, in general, idleness and confinement to the same circle of society produce such a fermentation in the mind, and such neglect of ceremonial observances, which are the barriers of civility, that quarrels and duels more readily occur in such situations than in any other. But when spring drew near, this paternal commander found it extremely difficult to rein in the impatience of the youths to plunge into the woods to hunt. There were such risks to encounter, of unknown morasses, wolves, and hostile Indians, that it was dangerous to indulge them. At last, when the days began to lengthen, in the end of February, a chosen party, on whose hardihood and endurance the major could depend, were permitted to go on a regular hunting excursion in the Indian fashion. This was become desirable on different accounts, the garrison having been for some time before entirely subsisting on salt provisions. Sheep and cows were out of the question, there not being one of either within forty miles. A Captain Hamilton, who was a practised wood ranger, commanded this party, who were clad almost like Indians, and armed in the same manner. They were accompanied by a detachment of ten men; some of whom having been prisoners with the Indians, were more particularly qualified to engage in this adventure. They were allowed four or five days to stay, and provided with a competent supply of bear-skins, blankets, etc., to make their projected wigwams comfortable. The allotted time expired, and we all begun to quarrel with our salt provisions, and to long for the promised venison. Another, and yet another day passed, when our longing was entirely absorbed in the apprehensions we begun to entertain. Volunteers now presented themselves to go in search of the lost hunters; but those offers were, for good reasons, rejected, and every countenance begun to lengthen with fears we were unwilling to express to each other. The major, conjecturing the hunters might have been bewildered in those endless woods, ordered the cannon to be fired at noon, and again at midnight, for their direction. On the eighth day, when suspense was wound up to the highest pitch, the party were seen approaching, and they entered in triumph, loaded with sylvan spoils; among which were many strange birds and beasts. I recollect, as the chief objects of my admiration, a prodigious swan, a wild turkey, and a young porcupine. Venison abounded, and the supply was both plentiful and seasonable.

"Spring returned with its showers," and converted our Siberia, frozen and forlorn, and shut out from human intercourse, into an uncultured Eden, rich in all the majestic charms of sublime scenery, and primæval beauty and fertility. It is in her central retreat, amidst the mighty waters of the west, that nature seems in solitary grandeur to have chosen her most favored habitation, remote from the ocean, whose waves bear the restless sons of Europe on their voyages of discovery, invasion, and intrusion. The coasts of America are indeed comparatively poor, except merely on the banks of great rivers, though the universal veil of evergreens conceals much sterility from strangers. But it is in the depth of those forests, and around these sea-like lakes, that nature has been profusely kind, and discovers more charms the more her shady veil is withdrawn from her noble features. If ever the fond illusions of poets and philosophers — that Atalantis, that new Arcadia, that safe and serene Utopia, where ideal quiet and happiness have so often charmed in theory; if ever this dream of social bliss, in some new-planted region, is to be realized, this unrivalled scene of grandeur and fer-

tame creature, dogs and cats excepted, to be seen here. But there was a great stock of palisadoes, which had been cut for the garrison, lying ready; and their pioneers and workmen still remaining there, the new erection being scarce complete. The new project was received with "curses not loud but deep." Were they to go all out to plod and drudge for others, who would neither pay nor thank them; for, at most, they argued they should stay only a year, and reap very little indeed of the fruit of their labors.

The major's plans, however, were deep laid; matters wore a peaceable aspect; and there was no knowing how long they might remain there. Except shooting in the woods, or fishing, they were without business, pleasure, or varied society. He feared the men would degenerate into savage wildness, and their officers into that sordid indifference which is too often the consequence of being, at the early season of life, without an aim or a pursuit. He wished to promote a common interest, and habits social and domestic. He wished too, that they might make some advantage of this temporary banishment, to lay by a little store to eke out their pittance when they returned to more expensive places; in short, he wished to give them habits of regular economy, which should be useful to them ever after. He showed them his plans; gave each of them a department in overseeing the execution of them; and, for that purpose, each had so many men allotted to his command. He made it obvious to them, that as the summer was merely to be occupied in gardening and the chase, the parade of military dress was both expensive and unnecessary. In the store was a great surplus of soldier's coats. These had been sent from Europe to supply the regiment, which had been greatly diminished in number by the fatal lines, and succeeding hard march. The major ordered the regimental tailor to fit these as a kind of short undress frock to the officers, to whom correspondent little round hats, very different from their regimental ones, were allotted. Thus equipped, and animated by the spirit of him who ruled their minds with unconscious yet unlimited sway, these young Cincinnati set out, nothing loath, on their horticultural enterprise. All difficulties soon vanished before them; and, in a very few days, they became enthusiastic in the pursuit of this new object. That large and fertile portion of ground, which had been cleared of the timber with which the garrison was built, was given in charge to a sagacious old sergeant, who knew something of husbandry, and who very soon had it enclosed in a palisade, dug up, and planted with beans, peas, and Indian corn, the food of future pigs and poultry. To the officers more interesting tasks were allotted. There was more than one gardener found in the regiment; and here the engineers and pioneers were particularly useful. The major, who had predestined a favorite spot for his ample garden, had it partially cleared, by cutting the winter firing of the garrison from it. Where a mulberry, a wild plum, or cherry tree was peculiarly well-shaped or large, he marked it to remain, as well as some lofty planes and chestnuts; and when the shrubs were grubbed up in spring, he left many beautiful ones peculiar to the country. To see the sudden creation of this garden, one would think the genius of the place obeyed the wand of an enchanter: but it is not every gardener who can employ some hundred men. A summer house in a tree, a fish-pond, and a gravel-walk, were finished before the end of May, besides having committed to the earth great quantities of every vegetable production known in our best gardens. These vegetables throve beyond belief or example. The size of the cabbages, the cucumbers, and melons, produced here was incredible. They used, in the following years, to send them down to astonish us at Albany. On the continent they were not equalled, except in another military garden, which emulation had produced at Niagara. The major's economical views were fully answered. Pigs and poultry in abundance were procured, and supported by their Indian corn crop; they even procured cows and made hay in the islands to feed them. The provisions allowed them by the public afforded a sufficiency of flour, butter, and salt meat, as also rice. The lake afforded quantities of excellent fish, much of which the soldiers dried for winter consumption; and fruit and vegetables, they had in profusion, from their gardens. In short, they all lived in a kind of rough luxury, and were enabled to save much of their pay. The example spread to all the line of forts; such is the power of one active liberal mind pursuing its object with undeviating steadiness.

We are now about to leave Ontario; but perhaps the reader is not willing to take a final farewell of Colonel Duncan. The Indian war then, which broke out after the peace of 1762, occasioned the detention of the regiment in America till 1765; and during all that time this paternal commander continued with six companies of the regiment at Ontario, improving both the soil and the inhabitants. He then returned with the regiment, of which he was become lieutenant-colonel, to Ireland. Soon after he retired from the army, and took up his residence on the family estate of Lundie, having previously married the woman of his heart, who had engaged his early affections, and corresponded with him during his long absence. Here he was as happy as a shattered invalid could be, highly respected by the neighborhood, and frequently visited by his old pupils, who still regarded him with warm attachment. He died childless, and was succeeded by the admiral, on whose merit it is needless to expatiate; for who has forgotten the victor of Camperdown?

A company of the 55th was this summer ordered to occupy the fort at Albany. This was commanded by a sagacious veteran called Winepress. My father did not exactly belong to this company, but he wished to return to Albany, where he was known and liked: and the colonel thought, from his steadiness and experience, he would be particularly useful in paying the detached parties, and purchasing for the regiment such stores as they might have occasion for. We set out in our bateaux; and I consoled myself for not only leaving Oswego, but what was nearer my heart, a tame partridge and six pigeons, by the hopes of wandering through Wood creek, and sleeping in the woods. In both these particulars I was disappointed. Our boats being lighter, made better way, and we were received in new settlements a little distant from the river. The most important occurrence to me happened the first day. On that evening we returned to Fort Brewerton;[1] I found Captain Campbell delighted with my reading, my memory, and my profound admiration of the friendship betwixt David and Jonathan. We staid the most of the next day. I was much captivated with the copper-plates in an edition of Paradise Lost, which, on that account, he had given me to admire. When I was coming away he said to me, "Keep that book, my dear child; I foretell that the time will come when you will take pleasure in it." Never did a present produce such joy and

[1] Fort Brewerton was one of the line of English fortifications between Oswego and the Mohawk valley, situated on the shore of Oneida outlet, opposite the present village of Brewerton, 144 miles north-west from Albany.

gratitude. I thought I was dreaming, and looked at it a hundred times, before I could believe anything so fine was really my own. I tried to read it and almost cried with vexation when I found I could not understand it. At length I quitted it in despair; yet always said to myself, I shall be wiser next year.

Chapter XII

MADAME'S FAMILY AND SOCIETY DESCRIBED

THE next year (1762) came, and found me at Albany; if not wiser, more knowing. Again I was shut up in a fort, solemn and solitary; I had no companion, and was never allowed to go out, except with my mother, and that was very seldom indeed. All the fine forenoons I sat and sewed; and when others went to play in the evening, I was very often sent up to a large waste room, to get a long task by heart of something very grave and repulsive. In this waste room, however, lay an old tattered dictionary, Bailey's I think, which proved a treasure to me; the very few books we had, being all religious or military. I had returned to my Milton, which I conned so industriously, that I got it almost by heart, as far as I went; yet took care to go no farther than I understood. To make out this point, when any one encouraged me by speaking kindly to me, I was sure to ask the meaning of some word or phrase; and when I found people were not at all willing or able to gratify me, I at length had recourse to my waste room and tattered dictionary, which I found a perpetual fountain of knowledge. Consequently the waste room, formerly a gloomy prison, which I thought of with horror, became now the scene of all my enjoyment; and the moment I was dismissed from my task, I flew to it with anticipated delight; for there were my treasure, Milton and the ragged dictionary, which was now become the light of my eyes. I studied the dictionary with indefatigable diligence; which I begun now to consider as very entertaining. I was extremely sorry for the fallen angels, deeply interested in their speeches, and so well acquainted with their names, that I could have called the roll of them with all the ease imaginable. Time run on, I was eight years old, and quite uneducated, except reading and plain-work; when company came I was considered as in the way, and sent up to my waste room; but here lay my whole pleasure, for I had neither companions nor amusement. It was, however, talked of, that I should go to a convent, at Trois Rivières, in Canada, where several officers had sent their daughters to be educated.

The fame of Aunt Schuyler every now and then reached my ears, and sunk deep in my mind. To see her I thought was a happiness too great for me; and I was continually drawing pictures of her to myself. Meanwhile the 17th regiment arrived; and a party of them took possession of the fort. During this interim, peace had been proclaimed; and the 55th regiment were under orders for Britain.

My father, not being satisfied with the single apartment allotted to him by the new comers, removed to the town; where a friend of his, a Scotch merchant, gave him a lodging in his own house, next to that very Madame Schuyler who had been so long my daily thoughts and nightly dreams. We had not been long there when aunt heard that my father was a good, plain, upright man, without pretensions, but very well principled. She sent a married lady,[1] the wife of her favorite nephew, who resided with her at the time, to ask us to spend the evening with her. I think I have not been on any occasion more astonished, than when, with no little awe and agitation, I came into the presence of Madame. She was sitting; and filled a great chair, from which she seldom moved. Her aspect was composed, and her manner such as was, at first, more calculated to inspire respect, than conciliate affection. Not having the smallest solicitude about what people thought of her, and having her mind generally occupied with matters of weighty concern, the first expression of her kindness seemed rather a lofty courtesy, than attractive affability; but she shone out by degrees; and she was sure eventually to please every one worth pleasing, her conversation was so rich, so various, so informing; everything she said bore such a stamp of reality; her character had such a grasp in it. Her expres-

[1] Aunt Schuyler's favorite nephew was Philip Cuyler, who married Sarah Tweedy of Newport, Rhode Island. Their daughter Cathaline Sophia, born January 19, 1766, was the wife of John Van Cortlandt, a great-grandson of Stephanus, first proprietor of Cortlandt Manor.

sions not from art and study, but from the clear perceptions of her sound and strong mind, were powerful, distinct, and exactly adapted to the occasion. You saw her thoughts as they occurred to her mind, without the usual bias rising from either a fear to offend, or a wish to please. This was one of the secrets in which lay the singular power of her conversation. When ordinary people speak to you, your mind wanders in search of the motives that prompt their discourse, or the views and prejudices which bias it; when those who excite (and perhaps solicit) admiration talk, you are secretly asking yourself whether they mean to inform, or dazzle you. All this interior canvass vanished before the evident truth and unstudied ease of aunt's discourse. On a nearer knowledge, too, you found she was much more intent to serve, than please you, and too much engrossed by her endeavors to do so, to stop and look round for your gratitude, which she heeded just as little as your admiration. In short, she informed, enlightened, and served you, without levying on you any tribute whatever, except the information you could give in return. I describe her appearance as it then struck me; and, once for all, her manners and conversation, as I thought of them when I was older and knew better how to distinguish and appreciate. Everything about her was calculated to increase the impression of respect and admiration; which, from the earliest dawn of reflection, I had been taught to entertain for her.

Her house was the most spacious and best furnished I had ever entered. The family pictures, and scripture paintings, were to me particularly awful and impressive. I compared them to the models which had before existed in my imagination, and was delighted or mortified, as I found they did or did not resemble them.

The family with which she was then surrounded, awakened a more than common interest. Her favorite nephew, the eldest son of her much beloved sister, had, by his father's desire, entered into partnership in a great commercial house in New York. Smitten with the uncommon beauty of a young lady of seventeen, from Rhode Island, he had married her without waiting for the consent of his relations. Had he lived in Albany, and connected himself with one of his fellow citizens, bred up in frugal simplicity, this step might have been easily got over. But an expensive and elegant style of living begun already to take place in New York; which was, from the residence of the governor and commander in chief, become the seat of a little court. The lady whom Philip had married, was of a family originally Scotch: and derived her descent at no great distance from one of the noblest families in that country.[1] Gay, witty, and very engaging, beloved and indulged, beyond measure, by a fond husband, who was generous and good-natured to excess, this young beauty became "the glass of fashion, and the mould of

[1] Earl of Crawford's. — *Mrs. Grant.*

form." And the house of this amiable couple was the resort of all that was gay and elegant, and the centre of attraction to strangers. The mayor, who was a person singularly judicious, and most impartial in the affection which he distributed among his large family, saw clearly that the young people trusted too much to the wealth he was known to possess, and had got into a very expensive style of living; which, on examining their affairs, he did not think likely to be long supported by the profits of the business in which his son was engaged. The probable consequence of a failure, he saw, would so far involve him as to injure his own family: this he prevented. Peace was daily expected: and the very existence of the business in which he was engaged, depended on the army; which his house was wont to furnish with everything necessary. He clearly foresaw the withdrawing of this army; and that the habits of open hospitality and expensive living would remain, when the sources of their present supplies were dried up. He insisted on his son's entirely quitting this line, and retiring to Albany. He loaded a ship on his own account for the West Indies, and sent the young man, as supercargo, to dispose of the lading. As house-keeping was given up in New York, and not yet resumed in Albany, this young creature had only the option of returning to the large family she had left, or going to her father-in-law's. Aunt Schuyler, ever generous and considerate, had every allowance to make for the

AN AMERICAN LADY

high spirit and fine feelings of this inexperienced young creature; and invited her, with her little daughter, to remain with her till her husband's return. Nothing could be more pleasing than to witness the maternal tenderness and delicate confidence, which appeared in the behavior of Madame to this new inmate, whose fine countenance seemed animated with the liveliest gratitude, and the utmost solicitude to please her revered benefactress. The child was a creature not to be seen with indifference. The beauty and understanding that appeared full blown in her mother seemed budding with the loveliest promise in the young Catalina; a child whom, to this day, I cannot recollect without an emotion of tenderness. She was then about three years old. Besides these interesting strangers, there was a grand-niece whom she had brought up. Such was her family when I first knew it. In the course of the evening, dreams began to be talked of; and every one in turn gave their opinion with regard to that wonderful mode, in which the mind acts independent of the senses, asserting its immaterial nature in a manner the most conclusive. I mused and listened, till at length the spirit of quotation (which very early began to haunt me) moved me to repeat, from Paradise Lost,

"When nature rests,
Oft in her absence mimic fancy wakes, to imitate her,
But misjoining shapes, wild work produces oft."

I sat silent when my bolt was shot; but so did not Madame. Astonished to hear her favorite author quoted readily, by so mere a child, she attached much more importance to the circumstance than it deserved. So much, indeed, that long after, she used to repeat it to strangers in my presence, by way of accounting for the great fancy she had taken to me. These partial repetitions of hers fixed this lucky quotation indelibly in my mind. Any person who has ever been in love, and has unexpectedly heard that sweetest of all music the praise of his beloved, may judge of my sensations when Madame began to talk with enthusiasm of Milton. The bard of Paradise was indeed "the dweller of my secret soul;" and it never was my fortune before to meet with any one who understood or relished him. I knew very well that the divine spirit was his Urania. But I took his invocation quite literally, and had not the smallest doubt of his being as much inspired as ever Isaiah was. This was a very hopeful opening; yet I was much too simple and too humble to expect that I should excite the attention of Madame. My ambition aimed at nothing higher than winning the heart of the sweet Catalina; and I thought if heaven had given me such another little sister, and enabled me to teach her, in due time, to relish Milton, I should have nothing left to ask.

Time went on; we were neighbors, and became intimate in the family. I was beloved by Catalina, caressed by her charming mother, and frequently noticed by aunt, whom I very much inclined to love, were it not that it seemed to me as if, in so doing, I should aspire too high. Yet in my visits to her, where I had now a particular low chair in a corner assigned me, I had great enjoyments of various kinds. First, I met there with all those strangers or inhabitants who were particularly respectable for their character or conversation. Then I was witness to a thousand acts of beneficence that charmed me, I could not well say why, not having learned to analyze my feelings. Then I met with the Spectator and a few other suitable books, which I read over and over with unwearied diligence, not having the least idea of treating a book as a plaything, to be thrown away when the charm of novelty was past. I was by degrees getting into favor with Aunt Schuyler, when a new arrival for a while suspended the growing intimacy. I allude to the colonel of my father's regiment, who had removed from Crown Point to Albany.

The colonel was a married man, whose wife, like himself, had passed her early days in a course of frivolous gaiety. They were now approaching the decline of life, and finding nothing pleasing in the retrospect nor flattering in prospect, time hung on their hands. Where nothing round them was congenial to their habits, they took a fancy to have me frequently with them as matter of amusement. They had had children, and when they died their mutual affection died with them. They had had a fortune, and when it was spent all their pleasures were exhausted. They were by this time drawing out the vapid dregs of a tasteless existence, without energy to make themselves feared, or those gentle and amiable qualities which attract love: yet they were not stained with gross vices, and were people of character as the world goes.

What a new world was I entered into! From the quiet simplicity of my home, where I heard nothing but truth, and saw nothing but innocence; and from my good friend's respectable mansion, where knowledge reflected light upon virtue, and where the hours were too few for their occupation; to be a daily witness of the manner in which these listless ghosts of departed fashion and gaiety drank up the bitter lees of misused time, fortune, and capacity. Never was lesson more impressive; and young as I was, I did not fail to mark the contrast, and draw the obvious inference. From this hopeful school I was set free the following summer (when I had entered on my ninth year), by the colonel's return to England. They were, indeed, kind to me; but the gratitude I could not but feel was a sentiment independent of attachment, and early taught me how difficult it is, nay how painful, to disjoin esteem from gratitude.

Chapter XIII

SIR JEFFREY AMHERST — MUTINY — INDIAN WAR

AT this time (1765) peace had been for some time established in Europe; but the ferment and agitation which even the lees and sediments of war kept up in the northern colonies, and the many regulations requisite to establish quiet and security in the new acquired Canadian territory, required all the care and prudence of the commander-in-chief, and no little time. At this crisis, for such it proved, Sir Jeffrey, afterwards Lord Amherst, came up to Albany.[1] A mutiny had broke out among the troops on account of withholding the provisions they used to receive in time of actual war; and this discontent was much aggravated by their finding themselves treated with a coldness, amounting to

[1] Jeffrey Amherst was born in England, 29 January, 1717, and early devoted himself to the profession of arms. He distinguished himself on the continent, and in 1758, was appointed to the American service with the rank of major-general, and captured Louisbourg. He succeeded Abercrombie, and in 1759 took Ticonderoga and Crown Point. It is related of him as an instance of his activity and energy, that he came down from Lake George on foot, 1st January, 1759, and proceeded on to New York afoot, with a few of his officers and soldiers ("Legacy of Historical Gleanings," I, 33). He saw the whole continent of North America reduced in subjection to Great Britain, and was loaded with title and honors by the government. He died 3 August, 1797, aged 81.

aversion, by the people of the country; who now forgot past services, and showed in all transactions a spirit of dislike bordering on hostility to their protectors, on whom they no longer felt themselves dependent.

Sir Jeffrey, however, was received like a prince at Albany, respect for his private character conquering the anti-military prejudice. The commander-in-chief was in those days a great man on the continent, having, on account of the distance from the seat of government, much discretionary power intrusted to him. Never was it more safely lodged than in the hands of this judicious veteran, whose comprehension of mind, impartiality, steadiness, and close application to business, peculiarly fitted him for his important station. At his table all strangers were entertained with the utmost liberality; while his own singular temperance, early hours, and strict morals, were peculiarly calculated to render him popular among the old inhabitants. Here I witnessed an impressive spectacle: the guard-house was in the middle of the street, opposite to Madame's; there was a guard extraordinary mounted in honor of Sir Jeffrey; at the hour of changing it all the soldiery in the fort assembled there, and laid down their arms, refusing to take them up again. I shall never forget the pale and agitated countenances of the officers; they being too well assured that it was a thing preconcerted; which was actually the case, for at Crown Point and Quebec the same thing was done on the same day. Sir Jeffrey came down, and made a calm dispassionate speech to them, promising them a continuance of their privileges till further orders from home, and offering pardon to the whole, with the exception of a few ringleaders, whose lives, however, were spared. This gentle dealing had its due effect; but at Quebec the mutiny assumed a most alarming aspect, and had more serious consequences, though it was in the end quelled. All this time Sir Jeffrey's visits to Madame had been frequent, both out of respect to her character and conversation, and to reap the benefit of her local knowledge on an approaching emergency. This was a spirit of disaffection, then only suspected, among the Indians on the Upper Lakes, which soon after broke suddenly out into open hostility. In consequence of her opinion he summoned Sir W. Johnson to concert some conciliatory measures. But the commencement of the war at this very crisis, detained him longer to arrange with General Bradstreet and Sir William the operations of the ensuing campaign.

This war broke out very opportunely in some respects. It afforded a pretext for granting those indulgences to the troops, which it would otherwise have been impolitic to give and unsafe to withhold. It furnished occupation for an army too large to lie idle so far from the source of authority, which could not yet be safely withdrawn till matters were on a more stable footing; and it made the inhabitants at once more sensible of their protection. Madame had predicted this event, knowing better than any one how the affections of these tribes might be lost or won. She well knew the probable consequences of the negligence with which they were treated, since the subjection of Canada made us consider them as no longer capable of giving us trouble. Pontiac, chief of those nations who inhabited the borders of the great lakes, possessed one of those minds which break through all disadvantages to assert their innate superiority.

The rise and conduct of this war, were I able to narrate them distinctly, the reader would perhaps scarce have patience to attend to; indistinct as they must appear, retraced from my broked recollections. Could I, however, do justice to the bravery, the conduct, and magnanimity in some instances, and the singular address and stratagem in others, which this extraordinary person displayed in the course of it, the power of untutored intellect would appear incredible to those who never saw man but in an artificial or degraded state, exalted by science or debased by conscious ignorance and inferiority. During the late war Pontiac occupied a central situation, bounded on each side by the French and English territories. His uncommon sagacity taught him to make the most of his local advantages, and of that knowledge of the European character which resulted from this neighborhood. He had that sort of consequence which in the last century raised the able and politic princes of the house of Savoy to the throne they have since enjoyed. Pontiac held a petty balance between two great contending powers. Even the privilege of passing through his territories was purchased with presents, promises and flatteries. While the court which was paid to this wily warrior, to secure his alliance, or at least his neutrality, made him too sensible of his own consequence, it gave him a near view of our policy and modes of life. He often passed some time, on various pretexts, by turns at Montreal and in the English camp. The subjection of Canada proved fatal to his power, and he could no longer play the skillful game between both nations which had been so long carried on. The general advantage of his tribe is always the uppermost thought with an Indian. The liberal presents which he had received from both parties, afforded him the means of confederating with distant nations, of whose alliance he thought to profit in his meditated hostilities.

There were at that time many tribes, then unknown to Europeans, on the banks of Lake Superior, to whom fire-arms and other British goods were captivating novelties. When the French insidiously built the fort of Detroit, and the still more detached one of Michilimackinac, on bounds hitherto undefined, they did it on the footing of having secure places of trade, not to overawe the natives, but to protect themselves from the English. They amply rewarded them for permission to erect these fortresses, and purchased at any expense that friendship from them without which it would have been impossible to have maintained their ground in these remote regions. All this liberality and flattery, though merely founded on self-interest, had its effect; and the French, who are ever versatile and accommodating, who wore the Huron dress, and spoke the Huron language when they had any purpose to serve, were without doubt the favored nation. We, too apt to despise all foreigners, and not over complaisant even when we have a purpose to serve, came with a high hand to occupy those forts which we considered as our right after the conquest of Canada, but which had been always held by the more crafty French as an indulgence. These troops, without ceremony, appropriated, and following Major Duncan's example, cultivated all the fertile lands around Detroit, as far as fancy or convenience led them. The lands round Ontario were in a different predicament, being regularly purchased by Sir William Johnson. In consequence of the peace which had taken place the year before, all the garrisons were considered as in a state of perfect security.

Pontiac, in the meantime, conducted himself with the utmost address, concealing the indignation which brooded in his mind under the semblance of the greatest frankness and good humor. Master of various languages, and most completely master of his temper and countenance, he was at home everywhere, and paid frequent friendly visits to Detroit, near which, in the finest country imaginable, was his abode. He frequently dined with the mess, and sent them fish and venison. Unlike other Indians, his manner appeared frank and communicative, which opened the minds of others and favored his deep designs. He was soon master, through their careless conversation, of all he wished to know relative to the stores, resources, and intentions of the troops. Madame, who well knew the Indian character in general, and was no stranger to the genius and abilities of Pontiac, could not be satisfied with the manner in which he was neglected on one hand, nor his easy admission to the garrison on the other. She always said they should either make him their friend, or know him to be their foe.

In the meanwhile no one could be more busy than this politic warrior. While the Indians were in strict alliance with the French, they had their wigwams and their Indian corn within sight of the fort, lived in a considerable kind of village on the border of the lake, and had a daily intercourse of traffic and civility with the troops. There was a large esplanade before the garrison, where the Indians and soldiers sometimes socially played at ball together. Pontiac had a double view in his intended hostility. The Canadian priests, with the wonted restless intriguing spirit of their nation, fomented the discontents of the Indians. They persuaded them, and perhaps flattered themselves, that if they (the Indians) would seize the chain of forts, the grand monarque would send a fleet to reconquer Canada, and guaranty all the forts he should take to Pontiac. Upon this he did not altogether depend: yet he thought if he could surprise Detroit, and seize a vessel which was expected up from Oswego with ammunition and stores, he might easily take the other small vessels, and so command the lake. This would be shut up by ice for the winter, and it would take no little time to build on its banks another fleet, the only means by which an army could again approach the place. I will not attempt to lead my reader through all the intricacies of an Indian war (entirely such), and therefore of all wars the most incomprehensible in its progress, and most difficult in its terms. The result of two master-strokes of stratagem, with which it opened, are such as are curious enough, however, to find a place in this detail.

Chapter XIV

PONTIAC — SIR ROBERT DAVERS

ALL the distant tribes were to join on hearing Pontiac was in possession of the fort. Many of those nearest, in the meanwhile, were to lie in the neighboring woods, armed and ready to rush out on the discharge of a cannon, on that day which was meant to be fatal to the garrison. Out of the intended massacre, however, the artillery were to be spared that they might work the guns. Near the fort lived a much admired Indian beauty, who was known in the garrison by the name of the Queen of Hearts. She not only spoke French, but dressed not inelegantly in the European manner, and being sprightly and captivating was encouraged by Pontiac to go into the garrison on various pretexts. The advantage the Indian chief meant to derive from this stratagem was, that she might be a kind of spy in the fort, and that by her influence over the commander, the wonted caution with regard to Indians might be relaxed, and the soldiers be permitted to go out unarmed and mingle in their diversions. This plan in some degree succeeded. There was at length a day fixed, on which a great match at football was to be decided between two parties of Indians, and all the garrisons were invited to be spectators.

It was to be played on the esplanade opposite to the fort. At a given signal the ball was to be driven over the wall of the fort, which, as there was no likelihood of its ever being attacked by cannon, was merely a pallisade and earthen breast-work. The Indians were to run hastily in, on pretence of recovering the ball, and shut the gate against the soldiers, whom Pontiac and his people were to tomahawk immediately.

Pontiac, jealous of the Queen of Hearts, gave orders, after she was let into the secret of this stratagem, that she should go no more into the fort. Whether she was offended by this want of confidence; whether her humanity revolted at the intended massacre, or whether she really felt a particular attachment prevailing over her fidelity to her countrymen, so it was; her affection got the better of her patriotism. A soldier's wife, who carried out to her the day before some article of dress she had made for her, was the medium she made use of to convey a hint of the intended treachery. The colonel was unwilling from the dark hint conveyed, to have recourse to any violent measures; and was, indeed, doubtful of the fact. To kindle the flames of war wantonly, surrounded, as he was, by hostile nations, who would carry their vengeance into the defenceless new settlements, was a dreadful expedient. Without betraying his informer he resolved to convince himself. The men were ordered to go out to see the ball played, but to keep under shelter of the fort; and if they saw the ball driven in, immediately to return and shut the gates. I cannot remember the exact mode in which this manœuvre was managed, but the consequence I know was, first, the repulsing of the Indians from the gate, and then the commencing of open hostilities on their side, while the garrison was for some time in a state of blockade.

Meantime the Indians had concerted another stratagem, to seize a vessel loaded with stores, which was daily expected from Niagara. Commodore Grant, a younger brother of the Glenmoriston family in Inverness-shire, was, and I believe still is, commander of the lakes; an office which has now greatly risen in importance. At that time his own vessel and two or three smaller were employed in that navigation. This little squadron was very interesting on a double account. It carried stores, troops, etc., which could not otherwise be transported, there being no way of proceeding by land; and again the size of the vessels and a few swivels or small cannon they carried enabled them to command even a fleet of canoes, should the Indians be disposed to attack them. Of this there was at the time not the least apprehension; and here I must stop to give some account of the first victim to this unlooked-for attack.

Sir Robert D———[1] was the representative of

[1] An account of the surprise and death of Sir Robert Davers, whose name Mrs. Grant hesitates to divulge, is given in "Munsell's Historical Series," IV, 2, 3, 128.

an ancient English family, of which he was originally the sixth brother. At a certain time of life, somewhere betwixt twenty-five and thirty, each was, in turn, attacked with a hypochondriac disorder, which finally proved fatal. Sir Robert, in turn, succeeded to the estate and title, and to the dreadful apprehension of being visited by the same calamity. This was the more to be regretted, as he was a person of very good abilities, and an excellent disposition. The time now approached when he was to arrive at that period of life at which the fatal malady attacked his brothers. He felt, or imagined he felt, some symptoms of the approaching gloom. What should he do? medicine had not availed. Should he travel; alas! his brothers had travelled, but the blackest despair was their companion. Should he try a sea voyage, one of them commanded a ship, and fate overtook him in his own cabin. It occurred to him that, by living among a people who were utter strangers to this most dreadful of all visitations, and adopting this manner of life, he might escape its influence. He came over to America, where his younger brother served in a regiment then in Canada. He felt his melancholy daily increasing, and resolved immediately to put in execution his plan of entirely renouncing the European modes of life, and incorporating himself in some Indian tribe, hoping the novelty of the scene, and the hardships to which it would necessarily subject him, might give an entire new turn to his spirits.

He communicated his intention to Sir William Johnson, who entirely approved of it, and advised him to go up to the great lake among the Hurons, who were an intelligent and sensible race, and inhabited a very fine country, and among whom he would not be liable to meet his countrymen, or be tempted back to the mode of life he wished for a while entirely to forsake. This was no flight of caprice, but a project undertaken in the most deliberate manner, and with the most rational views. It completely succeeded. The Hurons were not a little flattered to think that a European of Sir Robert's rank was going to live with them, and be their brother. He did not fail to conciliate them with presents, and still more by his ready adoption of their dress and manners. The steadiness he showed in adhering to a plan where he had not only severe hardships, but numberless disgusts to encounter, showed him possessed of invincible patience and fortitude; while his letters to his friends, with whom he regularly corresponded, evinced much good sense and just observation. For two years he led this life, which habit made easy, and the enjoyment of equal spirits agreeable. Convinced that he had attained his desired end, and conquered the hereditary tendency so much dreaded, he prepared to return to society, intending if his despondency should recur, to return once more to his Indian habit, and rejoin his Huron friends. When the intention was formed by Pontiac and his associates of attacking the commodore's vessel, Sir Robert, who wished now to be conveyed to some of the forts, discerned the British ship from the opposite shore of the great lake, and being willing to avail himself of that conveyance, embarked in a canoe with some of his own Indian friends, to go on board the commodore. Meanwhile a very large canoe, containing as many of Pontiac's followers as it could possibly hold, drew near the king's ship, and made a pretext of coming in a friendly manner, while two or three others filled with warriors, hovered at a distance. They had fallen short of their usual policy; for they were painted red, and had about them some of those symbols of hostility, which are perfectly understood amongst each other. Some friendly Indians, who happened to be by accident on board the commodore's vessel, discerned these, and warned him of the approaching danger. On their drawing near the vessel they were ordered to keep off. Thinking they were discovered, and that things could be no worse, they attempted to spring on board armed with their tomahawks and scalping-knives, but were very soon repulsed. The other canoes, seeing all was discovered, drew near to support their friends, but were soon repulsed by a discharge of the six-pounders. At this crisis, the canoe, containing Sir Robert, began to advance in another direction. The Indians who accompanied him had not been apprised of the proposed attack; but being Hurons, the commodore never doubted of their hostility. Sir Robert sat in the end of the canoe dressed in all the costume of a Huron, and wrapped up in his blanket. He ordered his companions to approach the ship immediately, not deterred by their calling to them to keep off, intending, directly, to make himself known; but in the confusion he was accidently shot.

To describe the universal sorrow diffused over the province in consequence of this fatal accident would be impossible. Nothing since the death of Lord Howe had excited such general regret. The Indians carried the body to Detroit, and delivered it up to the garrison for interment. He had kept a journal during his residence on the lakes, which was never recovered, and must certainly have contained (proceeding from such a mind so circumstanced) much curious matter. Sir Charles, his younger brother, then a captain in the 17th, succeeded him, but had no visitation of the depression of mind so fatal to his brothers.

Rumors, enlarged by distance, soon reached Albany of this unlooked-for attack of the Indians. Indeed, before they had any authentic details, they heard of it in the most alarming manner from the terrified back settlers, who fled from their incursions. Those who dwell in a land of security, where only the distant rumor of war can reach them, would know something of the value of safety could they be but one day transported to a region where this plague is let loose; where the timorous and the helpless are made to

"Die many times before their death,"

by restless humor, cruel suspense, and anticipated misery. Many of the regiments employed in the conquest of Canada had returned home, or gone to the West Indies. Had the Canadians had spirit and cohesion to rise in a body and join the Indians, 't is hard to say what might have been the consequence. Madame, whose cautions were neglected in the day of prosperity, became now the public oracle, and was resorted to and consulted by all. Formerly she blamed their false security and neglect of that powerful chief, who, having been accustomed to flattery and gifts from all sides, was all at once made too sensible that it was from war he derived his importance. Now she equally blamed the universal trepidation, being confident in our resources, and well knowing what useful allies the Mohawks, ever hostile to the Canadian Indians, might prove.

Never was our good aunt more consulted or more respected. Sir Jeffrey Amherst planned at Albany an expedition to be commanded by General Bradstreet, for which both New York and New England raised corps of provincials.

Chapter XV

DEATH OF CAPTAIN DALYELL — MADAME — HER PROTÉGÉS

MEANTIME an express arrived with the afflicting news of the loss of a captain and twenty men of the 55th regiment. The name of this lamented officer was Dalziel,[1] of the Carnwath family. Colonel Beckwith had sent for a reinforcement. This Major Duncan hesitated to send, till better informed as to the mode of conveyance. Captain Dalziel volunteered going. I cannot exactly say how they proceeded; but, after having penetrated through the woods till they were in sight of Detroit, they were discovered and attacked by a party of Indians, and made their way with the utmost difficulty, after the loss of their commander and the third part of their number.

Major Duncan's comprehensive mind took in everything that had any tendency to advance the

---

[1] This was Captain James Dalyell, of the 2d battalion of the Royals, who perished in a brave but indiscreet attack on the Indians soon after his arrival at Detroit, August 31, 1763. He marched out with 247 men, intending to surprise the enemy about three miles from the fort, but was himself surprised and killed. See IV "Munsell's Hist. Series," 54, 56, et seq. ; also a biographical sketch "Colonial Hist. N. Y.," VI, 547 ; "Parkman's Pontiac," 275.

general good, and cement old alliances. He saw none of the Hurons, whose territories lay far above Ontario, but those tribes whose course of hunting or fishing led them to his boundaries, were always kindly treated. He often made them presents of ammunition or provision, and did everything in his power to conciliate them. Upon hearing of the outrage which the Hurons[1] had been guilty of, the heads of the tribe, with whom the major had cultivated the greatest intimacy, came to assure him of their good wishes and hearty co-operation. He invited them to come with their tribe to celebrate the birth-day of the new king (his present majesty), which occurred a few days after, and there solemnly renew, with the usual ceremonies, the league offensive and defensive made between their fathers and the late king. They came accordingly in their best arms and dresses, and assisted at a review, and at a kind of feast given on the occasion, on the outside of the fort. The chief and his brother, who were two fine noble looking men, were invited in to dine with the major and officers. When they arrived, and were seated, the major called for a glass of wine to drink his sovereign's health; this was no sooner done, than the sachem's brother fell lifeless on the floor. They thought it was a fainting

[1] The author, perhaps, uses the term Huron, where that of Algonquin would have been more correct. She does not recollect the distinctive terms exactly, but applies the epithet, in general, to the Indians who then occupied the banks of the Huron Lake, and the adjacent country. — *Mrs. Grant.*

fit, and made use of the usual applications to recover him, which to their extreme surprise proved ineffectual. His brother looked steadily on while all those means were using; but when convinced of their inefficacy, sat down, drew his mantle over his face, sobbed aloud, and burst into tears. This was an additional wonder. Through the traces of Indian recollection no person had been known to fall suddenly dead without any visible cause, nor any warrior to shed tears. After a pause of deep silence, which no one felt inclined to break, the sachem rose with a collected and dignified air, and thus addressed the witnesses of this affecting accident: "Generous English, misjudge me not; though you have seen me for once a child, in the day of battle you will see a man, who will make the Hurons weep blood. I was never thus before. But to me my brother was all. Had he died in battle, no look of mine would change. His nation would honor him, but his foes should lament him. I see sorrow in your countenances; and I know you were not the cause of my brother's death. Why, indeed, should you take away a life that was devoted to you? Generous English, ye mourn for my brother, and I will fight your battles." This assurance of his confidence was very necessary to quiet the minds of his friends; and the concern of the officers was much aggravated by the suspicious circumstances attending his death so immediately after drinking the wine they had given him.

The major ordered this lamented warrior to be interred with great ceremony. A solemn procession, mournful music, the firing of cannon, and all other military honors, evinced his sympathy for the living, and his respect for the dead; and the result of this sad event, in the end, rather tended to strengthen the attachment of those Indians to the British cause.

I have given this singular occurrence a place in these memoirs, as it serves to illustrate the calm good sense and steady confidence, which made a part of the Indian character, and added value to their friendship when once it was fairly attended.

The 55th, which had been under orders to return home, felt a severe disappointment in being, for two years more, confined to their sylvan fortresses. These, however, they embellished, and rendered comfortable, with gardens and farm-grounds, that, to reside in them, could no longer be accounted a penance. Yet, during the Indian war, they were, from motives of necessary caution, confined to very narrow limits; which, to those accustomed to pursue their sports with all that wild liberty and wide excursion peculiar to savage hunters, was a hardship of which we can have no idea. Restrained from this unbounded license, fishing became their next favorite pursuit, to which the lakes and rivers on which these forts were built, afforded great facility. Tempted by the abundance and excellence of the productions of these copious waters, they were led to endanger their health by their assiduity in this amusement. Agues, the disease of all new establishments, became frequent among them, and were aggravated by the home-sickness. To this they were more peculiarly liable; as the regiment, just newly raised before they embarked for America, had quitted the bosom of their families, without passing through the gradation of boarding-schools and academies, as is usual in other countries.

What an unspeakable blessing to the inhabitants were the parish schools of the north, and how much humble worth and laborious diligence has been found among their teachers. In those lowly seminaries boys not only attained the rudiments of learning, but the principles of loyalty and genuine religion, with the abatement of a small tincture of idolatry; of which their household gods were the only objects. Never surely was a mode of education so calculated to cherish attachment to those tutelar deities. Even the laird's son had often a mile or two to walk to his day school; a neighboring tenant's son carried the basket which contained his simple dinner; and still as they went along they were joined by other fellow-travellers in the paths of learning. How cordial were those intimacies, formed in the early period of life and of the day, while nature smiled around in dewy freshness! How gladdening to the kind and artless heart were these early walks through the wild varieties of a romantic country, and among the peaceful cottages of simple peasants,[1] from whence the incense of praise, "in sounds by distance made more sweet," rose on the morning breeze! How cheering was the mid-day sport, amid their native burns and braes, without the confinement of a formal play-ground! How delightful the evening walk homeward, animated by the consciousness of being about to meet all that was dearest to the artless and affectionate mind! Thus the constitution was improved with the understanding; and they carried abroad into active life, the rigid fibre of the robust and hardy frame, and the warm and fond affections of the heart, uncorrupted and true to its first attachments. Never sure were youth's first glowing feeling more alive than in the minds of those young soldiers. From school they were hurried into the greatest fatigues and hardships, and the horrors of the most sanguinary war; and from thence transported to the depth of those central forests, where they formed to themselves a little world, whose greatest charm was the cherished recollection of the simple and endeared scenes of their childhood, and of the beloved relations whom they had left behind, and to whom they languished to return. They had not gone through the ordeal

---

[1] The Scottish peasants, when they return to breakfast from their early labors, always read a portion of Scripture, sing some part of a psalm, and pray. This practice is too general, either to diminish cheerfulness, or convey the idea of superior sanctity; while the effect of vocal music, rising at once from so many separate dwellings, is very impressive. — *Mrs. Grant.*

of the world, and could not cheer their exile by retracing its ways, its fashions, or its amusements. It is this domestic education, that unbroken series of home joys and tender remembrances, that render the natives of the north so faithful to their filial and fraternal duties, and so attached to a bleak and rugged region, excelled in genial warmth of climate, and fertility of soil, in every country to which the spirit of adventure leads them.

I was now restored to my niche at Aunt Schuyler's and not a little delighted with the importance which, in this eventful crisis, seemed to attach to her opinions. The times were too agitated to admit of her paying much attention to me: but I, who took the deepest interest in what was going on, and heard of nothing, abroad or at home, but Indians, and sieges, and campaigns, was doubly awake to all the conversation I heard at home.

The expedition proceeded under General Bradstreet, while my father, recommended to his attention by Madame, held some temporary employment about mustering the troops. My friend had now the satisfaction of seeing her plans succeed in different instances.

Philip, since known by the title of General Schuyler, whom I have repeatedly mentioned, had now, in pursuance of the mode she pointed out to him, attained to wealth and power; both which were rapidly increasing. His brother Cortlandt[1]

[1] These were the sons of Johannes Schuyler, Jr., and Cornelia Van Cortlandt, and the nephews of Madame Schuyler. General Philip,

(the handsome savage) who had, by her advice, gone into the army, was returned from Ireland, the commander of a company;[1] and married to a very pleasing and estimable woman, whose perpetual vivacity and good humor threw a ray of light over the habitual reserve of her husband; who was amiable in domestic life, though cold and distant in his manner. They settled near the general, and paid a degree of attention to Madame that showed the filial tie remained in full force.

The colonel, as he was then called, had built a house near Albany,[2] in the English taste, comparatively magnificent, where his family resided, and where he carried on the business of his department. Thirty miles or more above Albany, in the direction of the Flats, and near the far-famed Saratoga, which was to be the scene of his future triumph, he had another establishment.[3] It was here that the colonel's political and economical genius had full scope. He had always the com-

born 1733, died 18 November, 1804, aged 71, distinguished by his revolutionary services, which have been made the subject of two volumes by Benson J. Lossing.

[1] She was an Irish lady whose first name was Barbara. After the death of her husband and eldest son, she returned to Ireland with her younger children; and it is said, that some of her descendants bearing the name of Schuyler are yet (1901) living in the Emerald Isle.

[2] This house, still standing at the head of Schuyler Street, is said to have been built by General Bradstreet.

[3] The place is now known as Schuylerville. The land had been in the family nearly a century, when Burgoyne occupied the house, built on the site of the one burned by the French in 1745, for his headquarters both on his advance and retreat.

mand of a great number of those workmen who were employed in public buildings, etc. Those were always in constant pay; it being necessary to engage them in that manner, and were, from the change of seasons, the shutting of the ice, and other circumstances, months unemployed. All these seasons, when public business was interrupted, the workmen were employed in constructing squares of buildings in the nature of barracks, for the purpose of lodging artisans and laborers of all kinds. Having previously obtained a large tract of very fertile lands from the crown, on which he built a spacious and convenient house; he constructed those barracks at a distance, not only as a nursery for the arts which he meant to encourage, but as the materials of a future colony, which he meant to plant out around him. He had here a number of negroes well acquainted with felling of trees and managing saw-mills; of which he erected several. And while these were employed in carrying on a very advantageous trade of deals and lumber, which were floated down on rafts to New York, they were at the same time clearing the ground for the colony the colonel was preparing to establish.

This new establishment was an asylum for every one who wanted bread and a home: from the variety of employments regularly distributed, every artisan and laborer found here lodging and occupation: some hundreds of people, indeed, were employed at once. Those who were in winter engaged at the saw-mills, were in summer equally busied at a large and productive fishery. The artisans got lodging and firing for two or three years, at first, besides being well paid for everything they did. Flax was raised, and dressed, and finally spun and made into linen there; and as artisans were very scarce in the country, every one sent linen to weave, flax to dress, etc., to the colonel's colony. He paid them liberally; and having always abundance of money in his hands, could afford to be the loser at first, to be amply repaid in the end. It is inconceivable what dexterity, address, and deep policy were exhibited in the management of this new settlement; the growth of which was repaid beyond belief. Every mechanic ended in being a farmer, that is a profitable tenant to the owner of the soil; and new recruits of artisans from the north of Ireland chiefly supplied their place, nourished with the golden dews which this sagacious projector could so easily command. The rapid increase and advantageous result of this establishment were astonishing. 'T is impossible for my imperfect recollection to do justice to the capacity displayed in these regulations. But I have thus endeavored to trace to its original source that wealth and power which became, afterwards, the means of supporting an aggression so formidable.

Chapter XVI

MADAME'S POPULARITY — EXCHANGE OF PRISONERS

IN the front of Madame's house was a portico, towards the street. To this she was supported, in fine evenings, when the whole town were enjoying themselves on their respective seats of one kind or other. To hers there were a few steps of ascent, on which we used humbly to seat ourselves; while a succession of "the elders of that city" paid their respects to Madame, and conversed with her by turns. Never was levee better attended. "Aunt Schuyler is come out," was a talismanic sentence that produced pleasure in every countenance, and set every one in motion who hoped to be well received: for, as I have formerly observed, aunt knew the value of time much too well to devote it to every one. We lived all this time next door to her, and were often of these evening parties.

The Indian war was now drawing to a close, after occasioning great disquiet, boundless expense, and some bloodshed. Even when we had the advantage which our tactics and artillery in some instances gave, it was a warfare of the most precarious and perplexing kind. It was something like hunting in a forest at best; could you but have supposed the animals you pursued armed with missile weapons, and ever ready to start out of some unlooked for place. Our faithful Indian confederates, as far as I can recollect, were more useful to us on this occasion than all the dear bought apparatus, which we collected for the purpose of destroying an enemy too wise and too swift to permit us to come in sight of them; or, if determined to attack us, sufficiently dextrous to make us feel before we saw them. We said, however, that we conquered Pontiac, at which no doubt he smiled; for the truth of the matter was, the conduct of this war resembled a protracted game of chess. He was as little able to take our forts, without cannon, as we were able without the feet, the eyes, and the instinctive sagacity of Indians, to trace them to their retreats. After delighting ourselves for a long while with the manner in which we were to punish Pontiac's presumption, "*could we but once catch him*," all ended in our making a treaty, very honorable for him, and not very disadvantageous to ourselves. We gave both presents and promises, and Pontiac gave — permission to the mothers of those children who had been taken away from the frontier settlements to receive them back again, on condition of delivering up the Indian prisoners.

The joyful day when the congress was held for concluding peace I never shall forget. Another memorable day is engraven in indelible characters upon my memory. Madame, being deeply interested in the projected exchange, brought about a scheme for having it take place at Albany, which was more central than any other place, and where her influence among the Mohawks could be of use in getting intelligence about the children, and sending messages to those who had adopted them, and who, by this time, were very unwilling to part with them. In the first place because they were growing very fond of them ; and again, because they thought the children would not be so happy in our manner of life, which appeared to them both constrained and effeminate. This exchange had a large retrospect. For ten years back there had been, every now and then, while these Indians were in the French interest, ravages upon the frontiers of the different provinces. In many instances these children had been snatched away while their parents were working in the fields, or after they were killed. A certain day was appointed, on which all who had lost their children, or sought those of their relations, were to come to Albany in search of them ; where, on that day, all Indians possessed of white children were to present them. Poor women, who had travelled some hundred miles from the back settlements of Pennsylvania and New England, appeared here, with anxious looks and aching hearts, not knowing whether their children were alive, or how exactly to identify them if they should meet them. I observed these apprehensive and tender mothers were, though poor people, all dressed with peculiar neatness and attention, each wishing the first impression her child should receive of her might be a favorable one. On a gentle slope near the fort, stood a row of temporary huts, built by retainers to the troops; the green before these buildings was the scene of these pathetic recognitions; which I did not fail to attend. The joy of even the happy mothers was overpowering, and found vent in tears; but not like the bitter tears of those who, after long travel, found not what they sought. It was affecting to see the deep and silent sorrow of the Indian women, and of the children, who knew no other mother, and clung fondly to their bosoms, from whence they were not torn without the most piercing shrieks; while their own fond mothers were distressed beyond measure at the shyness and aversion with which these long lost objects of their love received their caresses. I shall never forget the grotesque figures and wild looks of these young savages; nor the trembling haste with which their mothers arrayed them in the new clothes they had brought for them, as hoping that, with the Indian dress, they would throw off their habits and attachments. It was in short a scene impossible to describe, but most affecting to behold. Never was my good friend's considerate liberality and useful sympathy more fully exerted than on this occasion, which brought so many poor travellers from their distant homes on this pilgrimage to the shrine of nature. How many traders did she persuade to take them gratis in their boats! How many did she feed and lodge! and in what various ways did she serve or make others serve them all. No one indeed knew how to refuse a request of Aunt Schuyler, who never made one for herself.

Chapter XVII

RETURN OF THE 55TH REGIMENT TO EUROPE
— PRIVATES SENT TO PENSACOLA

THE 55th now left their calm abodes amidst their lakes and forests, with the joy of children breaking up from their school; little aware that they were bidding adieu to quiet, plenty and freedom, and utter strangers to the world, into which they were about to plunge. They all came down to Albany. Captain Mungo Campbell was charmed to find me so familiar with his Milton; while I was equally charmed to find him a favorite with Aunt Schuyler, which was with me the criterion of merit. Colonel Duncan, for such he was now, marched proudly at the head of his pupils, whom he had carried up raw youths, but brought back with all the manly and soldierly openness of manner and character that could be wished, and with minds greatly improved. Meanwhile Madame's counsels had so much influence on my father, that he began seriously to think of settling in America. To part with his beloved 55th was very trying; yet his prospects of advantage in remaining among a people by whom he was esteemed, and to whom he had really become attached, were very flattering; for by the aid of aunt and the old inhabitants, and friendly Indians, who were at her powerful bidding, he could expect to get advantageously some lands which he, in common with other officers who served in America, was entitled to. He, having a right to apply for the allotted quantity wherever he found it vacant, that is, in odd unoccupied places, between different patents, which it required much local knowledge of the country to discover, had greatly the advantage of strangers; because he could get information of those secluded spots here and there that were truly valuable; whereas other officers belonging to regiments disbanded in the country, either did not find it convenient to go to the expense of taking out a patent and surveying the lands, and so sold their rights for a trifle to others; or else half a dozen went together, and made a choice, generally an injudicious one, of some large tract of ground, which would not have been so long unsolicited had it been of real value. My father bought the rights of two young officers who were in a hurry to go to Europe, and had not perhaps wherewithal to go through the necessary forms used to appropriate a particular spot, the expense of that process being considerable. Accordingly he became a consequential landholder, and had his half-pay to boot.

The 55th were now preparing to embark for that home which they regarded with enthusiasm; this extended to the lowest ranks, who were absolutely home-sick. They had, too, from the highest to the lowest, been enabled, from their unexpensive mode of living, to lay up some money. Never was there a body of men more uncorrupted and more attached to each other. Military men contract a love of variety in their wandering manner of life, and always imagine they are to find some enjoyment in the next quarters that they have not had in this; so that the order for march is generally a joyful summons to the younger officers at least. To these novices, who, when they thought the world of variety, glory, and perferment was open before them, were ordered up into the depth of unexplored forests, to be kept stationary for years without even the amusement of a battle, it was sufficiently disappointing. Yet afterwards I have been told that, in all the changes to which this hapless regiment was subjected, they looked back on the years spent on the lakes as the happiest of their lives.

My father parted with them with extreme regret, but he had passed the Rubicon; that is to say, taken out his patent, and stay he must. He went however to New York with them, and here a very unexpected scene opened. Many of the soldiers who had saved little sums had deposited them in my father's hands, and, when he gave every one his own at New York, he had great pleasure in seeing their exultation, and the purchases they were making. When, all of a sudden, a thunderbolt burst among these poor fellows, in the shape of an order to draft the greatest part of them to Pensacola: to renew regiments who, placed on a bar of burning sand, with a salt marsh before and a swamp behind were lingering out a wretched and precarious existence, daily cut short by disease in some new instance. Words are very inadequate to give an idea of the horror that pervaded this band of veterans. When this order was most unexpectedly read at the head of the regiment, it was worse to the most of them than a sentence of immediate death; they were going to a dismal and detested quarter, and they were going to become part of a regiment of no repute; whom they themselves had held in the utmost contempt when they had formerly served together. The officers were not a little affected by this cruel order, to part with the brave well disciplined men; who, by their singular good conduct, and by the habits of sharing with their officers in the chase, and in their agricultural amusements, fishing-parties, etc., had acquired a kindly nearness to them not usually subsisting between those who command and they who must implicitly obey. What ties were broken! what hopes were blasted by this fatal order! These sad exiles embarked for Pensacola at the same time that their comrades set out for Ireland. My father returned, sunk in the deepest sadness, which was increased by our place of abode; for we had removed to the forsaken fort, where there was no creature but ourselves and three or four soldiers who chose to stay in the country, and for whom my father had procured their discharge.

I was in the meantime more intimate than ever at Aunt Schuyler's; attracted not only by her kindness, but my admiration for Mrs. Cuyler, and attachment for her lovely little girl. The husband of the former was now returned from his West India voyage, and they retired to a house of their own, meaning to succeed to that business which the mayor, now wealthy and infirm, was quitting. Cortlandt Schuyler, the general's brother, and his sprightly agreeable wife, were now, as well as the couple formerly mentioned, frequent visitors at aunt's, and made a very pleasing addition to her familiar circle. I began to be considered as almost a child of the family, and Madame took much pains in instructing me, hoping that I would continue attached to her, and knowing that my parents were much flattered by her kindness, and fully conscious of the advantages I derived from it. With her aid my father's plan of proceeding was fully digested. He was to survey and *locate* his lands (that was the phrase used for such transactions), and at leisure (as the price of lands was daily rising), to let them out on lease. He was to reserve a good farm for himself, but not to reside upon it till the lands around it were cultivated; and so many settlers gone up as would make the district in a degree civilized and populous; a change which was like to take place very rapidly, as there were daily emigrations to that neighborhood, which was become a favorite rallying point, on account of a flourishing and singularly well conducted settlement which I have already mentioned, under the auspices of Colonel Schuyler in this quarter.

Chapter XVIII

PROPERTY AT CLARENDON — VISIONARY PLANS

MY father went up in summer with a retinue of Indians, and disbanded soldiers, etc., headed by a land-surveyor. In that country, men of this description formed an important and distinct profession. They were provided with an apparatus of measuring-chains, tents, and provisions. It was upon the whole an expensive expedition; but this was the less to be regretted as the object proved fully adequate. Never was a *location* more fertile or more valuable, nor the possessor of an estate more elated with his acquisition: a beautiful stream passed through the midst of the property; beyond its limits on one side rose a lofty eminence covered with tall cedar, which being included in no patent, would be a common good, and offered an inexhaustible supply of timber and firing after the lands should be entirely cleared. This sylvan scene appeared, even in its wild state, to possess singular advantages: it was dry lying land without the least particle of swamp, great part of it was covered with chestnuts, the sure indication of good wheat-land, and the rest with white oak, the never-failing forerunner of good Indian corn and pasture. The ground, at the time of the survey, was in a great measure covered with strawberries, the sure sign of fertility. And better and better still, there was, on a considerable stream which watered this region of benediction, a beaver-dam, that was visibly of at least fifty years standing. What particular addition our overflowing felicity was to derive from the neighborhood of these sagacious buildings, may not be easily conjectured. It was not their society, for they were much too wise to remain in our vicinity, nor yet their example, which, though a very good one, we were scarce wise enough to follow. Why then did we so much rejoice over the dwelling of these old settlers? Merely because their industry had saved us much trouble: for, in the course of their labors, they had cleared above thirty acres of excellent hay-land; work which we should take a long time to execute, and not perform near so well; the truth was, this industrious colony, by whose previous labor we were thus to profit, were already extirpated, to my unspeakable sorrow, who had been creating a *beaver* Utopia ever since I heard of the circumstance. The protection I was to afford them, the acquaintance I was to make with them, after conquering the first shyness, and the delight I was to have in seeing them work, after convincing them of their safety, occupied my whole attention, and helped to console me for the drafting of the 55th, which I had been ever since lamenting.

How buoyant is the fancy of childhood! I was mortified to the utmost to hear there were no beavers remaining; yet the charming, though simple, description my father gave us of this "vale of bliss," which the beavers had partly cleared, and the whole Township of Clarendon (so was the new laid out territory called), consoled me for all past disappointments. It is to be observed that the political and economical regulations of the beavers make their neighborhood very desirable to new settlers. They build houses and dams with unwearied industry, as every one that has heard of them must needs know; but their unconquerable attachment to a particular spot is not so well known; the consequence is, that they work more, and of course clear more land in some situations than in others. When they happen to pitch upon a stream that overflows often in spring, it is apt to carry away the dam, formed of large trees laid across the stream, which it has cost them unspeakable pains to cut down and bring there. Whenever these are destroyed they cut down more trees and construct another; and, as they live all winter on the tender twigs from the underwood and bark which they strip from poplar and alder, they soon clear these also from the vicinity. In the day-time they either mend their houses, lay up stores in them, or fish, sitting upon their dams made for that purpose. The night they employ in cutting down trees, which they always do so as to make them fall towards the stream, or in dragging them to the dam. Meanwhile they have always sentinels placed near to give the alarm, in case of any intrusion. It is hard to say when these indefatigable animals refresh themselves with sleep. I have seen those that have been taken young and made very tame, so that they followed their owner about; even in these the instinct which prompts their nocturnal labors was apparent. Whenever all was quiet they began to work. Being discontented and restless, if confined, it was usual to leave them in the yard. They seemed in their civilized, or rather degraded state, to retain an idea that it was necessary to convey materials for building to their wonted habitation. The consequence was, that a single one would carry such quantities of wood to the back door, that you would find your way blocked up in the morning to a degree almost incredible.

Being very much inclined to be happy, and abundant in resources, the simple felicity which was at some future period to prevail among the amiable and innocent tenants we were to have at Clarendon, filled my whole mind. Before this flattering vision, all painful recollections, and even all the violent love which I had persuaded myself to feel for my native Britain, entirely vanished.

The only thing that disturbed me, was Aunt Schuyler's age, and the thoughts of outliving her, which sometimes obtruded among my day dreams of more than mortal happiness. I thought all this could scarce admit of addition; yet a new source of joy was opened, when I found that we were actually going to live at the Flats. The spot, rendered sacred by the residence of aunt, where I should trace her steps wherever I moved, dwell under the shadow of her trees, and, in short, find her in everything I saw. We did not aspire to serious farming, reserving that effort for our own estate, of which we talked very magnificently, and indeed had some reason, it being as valuable as so much land could be; and from its situation in a part of the country which was hourly acquiring fresh inhabitants, its value daily increased, which consideration induced my father to refuse several offers for it; resolved either to people it with highland emigrants, or retain it in his own hands till he should get his price.

Sir Henry Moore, the last British governor of New York that I remember, came up this summer to see Albany, and the ornament of Albany — Aunt Schuyler; he brought Lady Moore and his daughter with him. They resided for some time at General Schuyler's, I call him so by anticipation; for sure I am, had any gifted seer foretold then what was to happen, he would have been ready to answer, "Is thy servant a dog, that he should do this thing." Sir Harry, like many of his predecessors, was a mere show governor, and old Cadwallader Colden, the lieutenant governor, continued to do the business, and enjoy the power in its most essential branches, such as giving patents for lands, etc. Sir Harry, in the meantime, had never thought of business in his life; he was honorable as far as a man could be so, who always spent more than he had; he was, however, gay, good natured, and well bred, affable and courteous in a very high degree, and if the business of a governor was merely to keep the governed in good humor, no one was fitter for that office than he, the more so, as he had sense enough to know two things of great importance to be known: one was, that a person of tried wisdom and good experience like Colden, was fitter to transact the business of the province, than any dependant of his own: the other, that he was totally unfit to manage it himself. The government house was the scene of frequent festivities and weekly concerts, Sir Henry being very musical, and Lady Moore peculiarly fitted for doing the honors of a drawing-room or entertainment. They were too fashionable, and too much hurried to find time for particular friendships, and too good natured and well bred to make invidious distinctions, so that, without gaining very much either of esteem or affection, they pleased every one in the circle around them; and this general civility of theirs, in the storm which was about to rise, had its use.[1] In the beginning, before the tempest broke loose in all its fury, it

[1] See Appletons' "Cyclopaedia of American Biography," vol. IV., and Wilson's "History of New York," vol. II.

was like oil poured on agitated waters, which produces a temporary calm immediately round the ship. As yet the storm only muttered at a distance, but Madame was disturbed by anxious presages. In her case,

> "Old experience actually did attain
> To something like prophetic strain."

But it was not new to her to prophesy in vain. I, for my part, was charmed with these exalted visitors of aunt's, and not a little proud of their attention to her, not knowing that they showed pretty much the same attention to every one.

While I was dancing on air with the thoughts of going to live at the Flats, of the beauties of Clarendon, and many other delights which I had created to myself, an event took place that plunged us all in sorrow; it was the death of the lovely child Catalina, who was the object of much fondness to us all, for my parents, bating the allowance to be made for enthusiasm, were as fond of her as I was; Madame had set her heart very much on this engaging creature; she mustered up all her fortitude to support the parents of her departed favorite, but suffered much notwithstanding. Here began my acquaintance with sorrow. We went, however, to the Flats in autumn. Our family consisted of a negro girl, and a soldier, who had followed my father's fortunes from Scotland, and stuck to him through every change. We did not mean to farm, but had merely the garden, orchard, and enclosure for hay, two cows, a horse for my father, and a colt, which, to my great delight, was given me as a present. Many sources of comfort and amusement were now cut off from Madame, her nephew and his lively and accomplished wife had left her, Dr. Ogilvie was removed to New York, and had a successor no way calculated to supply his place. This year she had lost her brother-in-law Cornelius Cuyler,[1] whose sound sense and intelligence made his society of consequence to her,

[1] This estimable character had for the space of forty years (which included very important and critical conjunctures) been chief magistrate of Albany, and its district. A situation calculated to demand the utmost integrity and impartiality, and to exercise all the powers of a mind, acute, vigilant, and comprehensive. The less he was amenable to the control and direction of his superiors, the more liable was he to the animadversions of his fellow citizens, had he in the least departed from that rectitude which made him the object of their confidence and veneration. He administered justice, not so much in conformity to written laws, as to that rule of equity within his own breast, the application of which was directed by sound sense, improved by experience. I by no means insinuate, that he either neglected or disobeyed those laws, by which, in all doubtful cases he was certainly guided; but that the uncorrupted state of public morals, and the entire confidence which his fellow citizens reposed in his probity, rendered appeals to the law, for the most part, superfluous. I have heard that the family of the Cuylers was originally a German one of high rank. Whether this can or cannot be ascertained, is of little consequence. The sterling worth of their immediate ancestor, and his long and faithful services to the public, reflect more honor on his descendants than any length of pedigree. — *Mrs. Grant.* [Cornelius Cuyler was an Albany merchant, some years alderman of the second ward, mayor of Albany, commissioner of Indian affairs, and held the office of magistrate some time, which long service in various capacities led Mrs. Grant to attribute to him forty years of chief magistracy.]

independent of the great esteem and affection she had for him. The army, among whom she always found persons of information and good breeding, in whose conversation she could take pleasure which might be truly called such, were gone. Nothing could compensate, in her opinion, for the privation of that enjoyment; she read, but then the people about her had so little taste for reading, that she had not her wonted pleasure in that, for want of some one with whom she could discuss the topics suggested by her studies. It was in this poverty of society such as she was accustomed to enjoy, that she took a fancy to converse much with me, to regret my want of education, and to take a particular interest in my employments and mental improvement. That I might more entirely profit by her attention, she requested my parents to let me pass the winter with her; this invitation they gladly complied with.

The winter at the Flats was sufficiently melancholy, and rendered less agreeable by some unpleasant neighbors we had. These were a family from New England, who had been preparing to occupy lands near those occupied by my father. They had been the summer before recommended to aunt's generous humanity, as honest people, who merely wanted a shelter in a room in her empty house, till they should build a temporary hut on those new lands which they were about to inhabit. When we came, the time permitted to them had long elapsed, but my father, who was exceedingly humane, indulged them with a fortnight more after our arrival, on the pretence of the sickness of a child; and there they sat, and would not remove for the winter, unless coercion had been used for that purpose. We lived on the road side; there was at that time a perpetual emigration going on from the provinces of New England to our back settlements. Our acquaintance with the family who kept possession beside us, and with many of even the better sort, who came to bargain with my father about his lands, gave us more insight than we wished into the prevalent character of those people, whom we found conceited, litigious, and selfish beyond measure. My father was told that the only safe way to avoid being overreached by them in a bargain, was to give them a kind of tacit permission to sit down on his lands, and take his chance of settling with them when they were brought into some degree of cultivation; for if one did bargain with them, the custom was to have three years free for clearing, at the end of which, the rents or purchase money was paid. By that time, any person who had expended much labor on land, would rather pay a reasonable price or rent for it, than be removed.

In the progress of his intercourse with these very vulgar, insolent, and truly disagreeable people, my father began to disrelish the thoughts of going up to live among them. They flocked indeed so fast, to every unoccupied spot, that their malignant and envious spirit, their hatred of subordination, and their indifference to the mother country, began to spread like a taint of infection.

These illiberal opinions, which produced manners equally illiberal, were particularly wounding to disbanded officers, and to the real patriots, who had consulted in former times the happiness of the country, by giving their zealous coöperation to the troops sent to protect it. These two classes of people began now to be branded as the slaves of arbitrary power, and all tendencies to elegance or refinement were despised as leading to aristocracy. The consequence of all this was, such an opposition of opinions, as led people of the former description to seek each other's society exclusively. Winter was the only time that distant friends met there, and to avoid the chagrin resulting from this distempered state of society, veterans settled in the country were too apt to devote themselves to shooting and fishing, taking refuge from languor in these solitary amusements.

We had one brave and royal neighbor, however, who saw us often, and was "every inch a gentleman;" this was Pedrom,[1] aunt's brother-in-law, in whom lived the spirit of the Schuylers, and who

[1] Pedrom's residence was on the Kromme kil, near the late residence of Robert Dunlop, opposite the cemetery. This crooked (*kromme*) stream, which had formerly a considerable flow, has, like all the currents from the neighboring hills, shrunk to a feeble brooklet, only noticeable in time of freshet.

was our next neighbor and cordial friend. He was now old, detached from the world, and too hard of hearing, to be an easy companion: yet he had much various information, and was endeared to us by similarity of principle.

Matters were beginning to be in this state the first winter I went to live with aunt. Her friends were much dispersed; all conversation was tainted with politics, Cromwellian politics too, which of all things, she disliked. Her nephew, Cortlandt Schuyler, who had been a great Nimrod ever since he could carry a gun, and who was a man of strict honor and nice feelings, took such a melancholy view of things, and so little relished that stamp act, which was the exclusive subject of all conversation, that he devoted himself more and more to the chase, and seemed entirely to renounce a society which he had never greatly loved. As I shall not refer to him again I shall only mention here, that this estimable person was taken away from the evil to come two years after, by a premature death, being killed by a fall from his horse in hunting. What sorrows were hid from his eyes by this timely escape from scenes, which would have been to him peculiarly wounding!

If Madame's comforts in society were diminished, her domestic satisfactions were not less so. By the time I came to live with her, Mariamat and Dianamat[1] were almost superannuated, and had lost, in

[1] Mat, or mater, mother or superior of the negroes.

a great measure, the restraining power they used to exercise over their respective offspring. Their woolly heads were snow white, and they were become so feeble, that they sat each in her great chair at the opposite side of the fire; their wonted jealousy was now embittered to rancor, and their love of tobacco greater than ever. They were arrived at that happy period of ease and indolence, which left them at full liberty to smoke and scold the whole day long; this they did with such unwearied perseverance, and in a manner so ludicrous, that to us young people they were a perpetual comedy.

Sorely now did aunt lament the promise she had kept so faithfully, never to sell any of the colonel's negroes. There was so little to do for fourteen persons, except the business they created for each other, and it was so impossible to keep them from too freely sharing the plenty of her liberal house, that idleness and abundance literally began to corrupt them.

All these privations and uneasinesses will in some measure account for such a person as Madame taking such pleasure in the society of an overgrown child. But then she was glad to escape from dark prospects and cross politics, to the amusement derived from the innocent cheerfulness, natural to that time of life. A passion for reading, and a very comprehensive memory too, had furnished my mind with more variety of knowledge, than fell to the lot of those, who living in large families, and sharing the amusements of childhood, were not, like me, driven to that only resource. All this will help to account for a degree of confidence and favor, daily increasing, which ended in my being admitted to sleep in a little bed beside her, which never happened to any other. In the winter nights our conversations often encroached on the earlier hours of morning. The future appeared to her dubious and cheerless, which was one reason, I suppose, that her active mind turned solely on retrospection. She saw that I listened with delighted attention to the tales of other times, which no one could recount so well. These, too, were doubly interesting, as, like the sociable angel's conversation with our first father, they related to the origin and formation of all I saw around me; they afforded food for reflection, to which I was very early addicted, and hourly increased my veneration for her whom I already considered as my polar star. The great love I had for her first gave interest to her details; and again, the nature of these details increased my esteem for the narrator. Thus passed this winter of felicity, which so much enlarged my stock of ideas, that in looking back upon it, I thought I had lived three years in one.

Chapter XIX

RETURN TO THE FLATS — SUMMER AMUSEMENTS

SUMMER came, and with it visitors, as usual, to Madame from New York and other places; among whom, I remember, were her nieces Mrs. L. and Mrs. C. I went to the Flats, and was, as usual, kept very close to my needle-work; but though there was no variety to amuse me, summer slid by very fast. My mind was continually occupied with aunt, and all the passages of her life. My greatest pleasure was to read over again the books I had read to her, and recollect her observations upon them. I often got up and went out to the door to look at places where particular things had happened. She spent the winter's nights in retrospections of her past life; and I spent the summer days in retrospections of these winter nights. But these were not my only pleasures. The banks of the river and the opposite scenery delighted me; and, adopting all aunt's tastes and attachments, I made myself believe I was very fond of Pedrom and Susanna Muet, as the widow of Jeremiah was called. My attention to them excited their kindness; and the borrowed sentiment, on my part, soon became a real one. These old friends were very amusing. But then I had numberless young friends, who shared my attention, and were in their own way very amusing too. These were the objects of my earliest cares in the morning, and my needless solicitude all day. I had marked down in a list, between thirty and forty nests of various kinds of birds. It was an extreme dry summer; and I saw the parent birds, whom I diligently watched, often panting with heat, and, as I thought, fatigued. After all I had heard and seen of aunt, I thought it incumbent on me to be good and kind to some being that needed my assistance. To my fellow-creatures my power did not extend; therefore I wisely resolved to adapt my mode of beneficence to the sphere of action assigned to me, and decided upon the judicious scheme of assisting all these birds to feed their young. My confederate Marian (our negro girl), entered heartily into this plan; and it was the business of the morning, before tasks commenced, to slaughter innumerable insects, and gather quantities of cherries and other fruit for that purpose. Portions of this provision we laid beside every nest, and then applauded ourselves for saving the poor birds' fatigue. This, from a pursuit, became a passion. Every spare moment was devoted to it, and every hour made new discoveries of the nature and habits of our winged friends, which we considered as amply recompensing our labors.

The most eager student of natural philosophy

could not be more attentive to those objects, or more intent on making discoveries. One sad discovery we made, that mortified us exceedingly. The mocking-bird is very scarce and very shy in this northern district. A pair came, however, to our inexpressible delight, and built a nest in a very high tree in our garden. Never was joy like ours. At the imminent risk of our necks we made shift to ascend to this lofty dwelling during the absence of the owners; birds we found none; but three eggs of a color so equivocal, that, deciding the point whether they were green or blue, furnished matter of debate for the rest of the day. To see these treasures was delightful, and to refrain from touching them impossible. One of the young we resolved to appropriate, contrary to our general humane procedure; and the next weighty affair to be discussed, was the form and size of the cage which was to contain this embryo warbler. The parents, however, arrived. On examining the premises, by some mysterious mode of their own, they discovered that their secret had been explored, and that profane hands had touched the objects of all their tenderness. Their plaintive cries we too well understood. That whole evening and all the next day they were busied in the orchard; while their loud lamentations, constantly reiterated, pierced us with remorse. We soon saw the garden nest forsaken: and a little further examination soon convinced us, that the violated eggs had been transported to another, where, however, they were not hatched; the delicate instincts, which directed these creatures to form a new nest, and carry off their eggs, on finding they had been handled, did not, at the same time, inform them, that eggs carried away, and shaken by that motion during the process of incubation, cannot produce anything.

The great barn, which I formerly described, afforded scope for our observations of this nature; and here we remarked a phenomenon, that I am still at a loss to account for. In the highest part of that spacious and lofty roof, multitudes of swallows, of the martin species, made their nests. These were constructed of mud or clay as usual, and, in the ordinary course of things, lasted, with some repairs, from year to year. This summer, however, being unusually hot and dry, the nests, in great numbers, cracked and fell down on the floor, with the young ones in them. We often found them in this situation, but always found the birds in them alive and unhurt; and saw the old ones come to feed them on the floor, which they did with such eager confidence, that they often brushed so near as to touch us. Now we could no other way account for the nests always coming down with the birds unhurt in them, but by supposing that the swallows watched the fracture of the nests, and when they saw them about to fall, came round the descending fabric, and kept it in a kind of equilibrium. Of these birds we stood in such profound awe, that we never profited by the accident which put them in our power; we would not indeed, for any consideration, have touched them, especially after the sad adventure of the mocking bird, which hung very heavy upon our consciences.

Autumn came, and aunt came at the appointed day, the anniversary of his death, to visit the tomb of her beloved consort. This ceremony always took place at that time. She concluded it with a visit to us, and an earnest request for my returning with her, and remaining the winter.

Chapter XX

MELANCHOLY PRESAGES — TURBULENCE OF THE PEOPLE

THE conversations between my father and aunt assumed a melancholy cast. Their hopes of a golden age in that country (now that the flames of war were entirely quenched) grew weaker. The repeal of the stamp act occasioned excessive joy, but produced little gratitude. The youth of the town, before that news arrived, had abandoned their wonted sports, and begun to amuse themselves with breaking the windows and destroying the furniture of two or three different people, who had, in succession, been suspected of being stamp-masters in embryo. My father grew fonder than ever of fishing and shooting, because birds and fish did not talk of tyranny or taxes. Sometimes we were refreshed by a visit from some of aunt's nephews, the sons of the mayor. They always left us in great good humor, for they spoke respectfully of our dear king, and dearer country. But this sunshine was transient; they were soon succeeded by Obadiah or Zephaniah, from Hampshire or Connecticut, who came in without knocking; sat down without invitation; and lighted their pipe without ceremony; then talked of buying land; and, finally, began a discourse on politics, which would have done honor to Praise God Barebones, or any of the members of his parliament. What is very singular, is, that though the plain-spoken and manly natives of our settlement had a general dislike to the character of those litigious and loquacious pretenders, such are the inconsistencies into which people are led by party, that they insensibly adopted many of their notions. With Madame I was quite free from this plague. None of that chosen race ever entered her door. She valued time too much to devote it to a set of people whom she considered as greatly wanting in sincerity. I speak now of the Hampshire and Connecticut people. In towns and at sea-ports the old leaven had given way to that liberality which was produced by a better education, and an intercourse with strangers. Much as aunt's loyal and patriotic feelings were hurt by the new mode of talking which prevailed, her benevolence was not cooled, nor her mode of living changed.

I continued to grow in favor with aunt this winter; for the best possible reasons, I was the only one of the family that would sit still with her. The young people in the house were by no means congenial with her; and each had a love affair in hand fast ripening into matrimony, that took up all their thoughts. Mr. H. our chaplain, was plausible, but superficial, vain, and ambitious. He too was busied in hatching a project of another kind. On pretence of study, he soon retired to his room after meals, dreading no doubt that aunt might be in possession of Ithuriel's spear, or to speak without a figure, might either fathom his shallowness or detect his project. One of these discoveries he knew would sink him in her opinion, and the other exclude him from her house. For my own part, I was always puzzling myself to consider, why I did not more love and reverence Mr. H., who I took it for granted must needs be good, wise, and learned; for I thought a clergyman was all but inspired. Thus thinking, I wondered why I did not feel for Mr. H. what I felt for aunt in some degree; but unfortunately Mr. H. was a true bred native of Connecticut, which perhaps helped more than any intuitive penetration to prevent any excess of veneration. Aunt and I read Burnet's memoirs and some biography this winter, and talked at least over much geography and natural history. Here indeed, I was in some degree obliged to Mr. H. I mean for a few lessons on the globe. He had too an edition of Shakespeare. I have been trying but in vain to recollect what aunt said of this. Not much certainly, but she was much pleased with the Essay on Man, etc. Yet I somehow understood that Shakespeare was an admired author, and was not a little mortified when I found myself unable to appreciate his merits. I suppose my taste had been vitiated by bombast tragedies I had read at Colonel

E's. I thought them grossly familiar, and very inferior to Cato, whom aunt had taught me to admire; in short I was ignorant, and because I could read Milton, did not know my own ignorance. I did not expect to meet nature in a play, and therefore did not recognize her. 'T is not to be conceived how I puzzled over Hamlet, or how his assumed madness and abuse of Ophelia confounded me. Othello's jealousy, and the manner in which he expressed it, were quite beyond my comprehension.

I mention these things as a warning to other young people not to admire by rote, but to wait the unfolding of their own taste, if they would derive real pleasure from the works of genius. I rather imagine I was afraid aunt would think I devoted too much time to what I then considered as a *trifling book*. For I remember reading Hamlet the third or fourth time, in a frosty night, by moonlight, in the back porch. This reiterated perusal was not in consequence of any great pleasure it afforded me; but I was studiously laboring to discover the excellence I thought it must needs contain; yet with more diligence than success. Madame was at this time, I imagine, foreseeing a storm, and trying to withdraw her mind as much as possible from earthly objects.

Forty years before this period, a sister of the deceased colonel had married a very worthy man of the name of Wendell.[1] He being a person of an

[1] Jacob Wendell, a half-brother of Aunt Schuyler, settled in Boston as a merchant, and attained to a high position in business and civil life.

AN AMERICAN LADY

active, enterprising disposition, and possessing more portable wealth than usually fell to the share of the natives there, was induced to join some great commercial company near Boston, and settled there. He was highly prosperous and much beloved, and for a while cultivated a constant commerce with the friends he left behind. When he died, however, his wife, who was a meek, benevolent woman, without distrust, and a stranger to business, was very ill-treated: her sons, who had been married in the country, died. Their connections secured the family property for their children. In the primitive days of New York, a marriage settlement was an unheard of thing. Far from her native home, having out-lived her friends, helpless and uncomplaining, this good woman, who had lived all her days in the midst of deserved affluence and affection, was now stripped by chicanery of all her rights, and sinking into poverty without a friend or comforter. Aunt, immediately upon hearing this, set on foot a negotiation to get Mrs. Wendell's affairs regulated, so that she might have the means of living with comfort in a country in which long residence had naturalized her; or that failing, to bring her home to reside with herself. Perhaps in the whole course of her life, she had not experienced so much of the depravity of human nature as this inquiry unfolded to her. The negotiation, however, cheered and busied her at a time when she greatly needed some exertion of mind to check the current of thought produced by the rapid and astonishing change of manners and sentiments around her. But in our province there were two classes of people who absolutely seemed let loose by the demon of discord, for the destruction of public peace and private confidence. One of these was composed of lawyers, who multiplied so fast that one would think they rose like mushrooms from the earth. For many years one lawyer was sufficient for the whole settlement. But the swarm of these, which had made so sudden and portentous an appearance, had been encouraged to choose that profession, because a wide field was open for future contention, merely from the candor and simplicity of the last generation.

Not in the least distrusting each other, nor aware of the sudden rise of the value of lands, these primitive colonists got large grants from government, to encourage their efforts in the early stages of cultivation; these lands being first purchased, for some petty consideration, from the Indians, who alone knew the land marks of that illimitable forest.

The boundaries of such large grants, when afterwards confirmed by government, were distinguished by the terms used by the Indians, who pointed them out; and very extraordinary marks they were. For instance, one that I recollect. " We exchange with our brother Cornelius Rensselaer, for so many strouds, guns, etc., the lands beginning at the beaver creek, going on northward, to the great fallen plane tree, where our tribe slept last summer; then eastward, to the three great cedars on the hillock; then westward, strait to the wild duck swamp; and strait on from the swamp to the turn in the beaver creek where the old dam was."[1]

Such are the boundaries seriously described in this manner, in one of the earliest patents. The only mode, then existing, of fixing those vague limits was to mark large trees which grew at the corners of the property, with the owner's name deeply cut, along with the date of the patent, etc., after blazing, that is to say, cutting deeply into the tree, for a plain space to hold this inscription.

In this primitive manner were all the estates in the province bounded. Towards the sea this did very well, as the patents, in a manner, bounded each other; and every one took care to prevent the encroachments of his neighbor. But in the interior people took great stretches of land here and there, where there were not patented lands adjoining; there being no continuity of fertile ground except on the banks of streams. The only security the public had against these trees being cut down, or others at a greater distance marked in their stead, was a law which made such attempts penal. This was a very nugatory threat; it being impossible to

[1] The boundless wilderness was thought to afford such an inexhaustible region for townships, domains, settlements, farms, etc., that boundaries were loosely described, whether for large or small tracts. See note, vol. I. p. 56.

prove such an offence. Crimes of this nature encroaching on the property of individuals, I believe, rarely happened: but to enlarge one's boundary, by taking in a little of King George's ground, to use a provincial phrase, was considered as no great harm; and, besides, many possessed extensive tracts of land unquestioned, merely on the strength of Indian grants unsanctioned by government. One in particular, the proudest man I ever knew, had a law-suit with the king, for more land than would form a German principality. Now that the inundation of litigious new settlers, from Massachusetts' bounds, had awakened the spirit of inquiry, to call it no worse, every day produced a fresh law-suit, and all of the same nature, about ascertaining boundaries. In one instance, where a gentleman was supposed to be unfairly possessed of a vast tract of fine land, a confederacy of British officers, I must confess, questioned his right;[1] applying beforehand for a grant of such lands as they could prove the possessor entitled to; and contributing among them a sum of money to carry on this great law-suit, which having been given against them in the province, they appealed to the board of trade and plantations at home. Here the uncertainty of the law

[1] After the conquest of Canada some British officers, wishing to settle in the country, applied for a patent of lands in Claverack, N. Y., belonging to Col. John Van Rensselaer, father of General Schuyler's wife. The lands had been in possession of the Van Rensselaers an hundred and thirty years, secured to them by purchase of the Indians, and by royal patents. The application was eventually denied.

was very glorious indeed; and hence, from the gainful prospect opening before them, swarms of petulant, half-educated young men, started one knew not whence. And as these great law-suits were matter of general concern, no one knowing whose turn might be next, all conversation begun to be infected with litigious cant; and everything seemed unstable and perplexed.

Chapter XXI

SETTLERS OF A NEW DESCRIPTION — MADAME'S CHAPLAIN

ANOTHER class of people contributed their share to destroy the quiet and order of the country. While the great army, that had now returned to Britain, had been stationed in America, the money they spent there, had, in a great measure, centred in New York, where many ephemeral adventurers began to flourish as merchants, who lived in a gay and even profuse style, and affected the language and manners of the army on which they depended. Elated with sudden prosperity, those people attempted every thing that could increase their gains; and, finally, at the commencement of the Spanish war, fitted out several privateers, which, being sent to cruise near the mouth of the gulf of Florida, captured several valuable prizes. Money so easily got was as lightly spent, and proved indeed ruinous to those who shared it; they being thus led to indulge in expensive habits, which continued after the means that supplied them were exhausted. At the departure of the army, trade languished among these new

AN AMERICAN LADY

people; their British creditors grew clamorous; the primitive inhabitants looked cold upon them; and nothing remained for them but that self-banishment, which, in that country, was the usual consequence of extravagance and folly, a retreat to the woods. Yet, even in these primeval shades, there was no repose for the vain and the turbulent. It was truly amusing to see those cargoes of rusticated fine ladies and gentlemen going to their new abodes, all lassitude and chagrin; and very soon after, to hear of their attempts at finery, consequence, and preëminence, in the late invaded residence of bears and beavers. There, no pastoral tranquillity, no sylvan delights awaited them. In this forced retreat to the woods they failed not to carry with them those household gods whom they had worshiped in town; the pious Æneas was not more careful of his Penates, nor more desirous of establishing them in his new residence. These are the persons of desperate circumstances, expensive habits, and ambitious views; who, like the " tempest-loving raven," delight in changes, and anticipate, with guilty joy, the overturn of states in which they have nothing to lose, and have hopes of rising on the ruins of others. The lawyers, too, foresaw that the harvest they were now reaping from the new mode of inquiry into disputed titles, could not be of long duration. They did not lay a regular plan for the subversion of the existing order of things; but they infected the once plain and primitive conversation of the people with law jargon, which spread like a disease, and was the more fatal to elegance, simplicity, and candor, as there were no rival branches of science, the cultivation of which might have divided people's attention with this dry contentious theme.

The spirit of litigation, which narrowed and heated every mind, was a great nuisance to Madame, who took care not to be much troubled with it in conversation, because she discountenanced it at her table, where, indeed, no petulant upstarts were received. She was, however, persecuted with daily references to her recollections with regard to the traditionary opinions relative to boundaries, etc. While she sought refuge in the peaceable precincts of the gospel, from the tumultuous contests of the law, which she always spoke of with dislike, she was little aware that a deserter from her own camp was about to join the enemy. Mr. H. our chaplain, became, about this time, very reserved and absent; law and politics were no favorite topics in our household, and these alone seemed much to interest our divine. Many thought aunt was imposed on by this young man, and took him to be what he was not; but this was by no means the case. She neither thought him a wit, a scholar, nor a saint; but merely a young man, who, to very good intentions and a blameless life, added the advantages of a better education than fell to the lot of laymen there; simplicity of manners, and some powers of conversation, with a little dash of the coxcomb, rendered tolerable by great good nature.

Vanity, however, was the rock on which our chaplain split; he found himself, among the circle he frequented, the one-eyed king in the kingdom of the blind; and thought it a pity such talents should be lost in a profession where, in his view of the subject, bread and peace were all that was to be expected. The first intelligence I heard was, that Mr. H. on some pretence or other, often went to the neighboring town of Schenectady, now rising into consequence, and there openly renounced his profession, and took out a license as a practising lawyer. It is easy to conjecture how Madame must have considered this wanton renunciation of the service of the altar for a more gainful pursuit, aggravated by simulation at least; for this seeming open and artless character took all the benefit of her hospitality, and continued to be her inmate the whole time that he was secretly carrying on a plan he knew she would reprobate. She, however, behaved with great dignity on the occasion; supposing, no doubt, that the obligations she had conferred upon him, deprived her of a right to reproach or reflect upon him. She was never after heard to mention his name; and when others did, always shifted the conversation.

All these revolutions in manners and opinion helped to endear me to aunt, as a pupil of her own school; while my tenacious memory enabled me to entertain her with the wealth of others' minds, rendered more amusing by the simplicity of my childish comments. Had I been capable of flattery, or rather had I been so deficient in natural delicacy, as to say what I really thought of this exalted character, the awe with which I regarded her would have deterred me from such presumption; but as I really loved and honored her, as virtue personified, and found my chief happiness in her society and conversation, she could not but be aware of this silent adulation, and she became indeed more and more desirous of having me with her. To my father, however, I was now become, in some degree, necessary, from causes somewhat similar. He, too, was sick of the reigning conversation; and being nervous, and rather inclined to melancholy, began to see things in the darkest light, and made the most of a rheumatism, in itself bad enough, to have a pretext for indulging the chagrin that preyed upon his mind, and avoiding his Connecticut persecutors, who attacked him everywhere but in bed. A fit of chagrin was generally succeeded by a fit of homesickness, and that by a paroxysm of devotion exalted to enthusiasm; during which all worldly concerns were to give way to those of futurity. Thus melancholy and thus devout I found my father; whose pure and upright spirit was corroded with the tricks and chicanery he was forced to observe in his new associates, with whom his singular probity and simplicity of character rendered him very unfit to contend. My mother, active, cheerful, and constantly occupied with her domestic affairs, sought pleasure nowhere, and found content everywhere. I had begun to taste the luxury of intellectual pleasures with a very keen relish. Winter, always severe, but this year armed with tenfold vigor, checked my researches among birds and plants, which constituted my summer delights; and poetry was all that remained to me. While I was, "in some diviner mood," exulting in these scenes of inspiration, opened to me by the "humanizing muse," the terrible decree went forth, that I was to read no more "idle books or plays." This decree was merely the momentary result of a fit of sickness and dejection, and never meant to be seriously enforced. It produced, however, the effect of making me read so much divinity, that I fancied myself got quite "beyond the flaming bounds of space and time;" and thought I could never relish light reading more. In this solemn mood, my greatest relaxation was a visit now and then to aunt's sister-in-law, now entirely bedridden, but still possessing great powers of conversation, which were called forth by the flattering attention of a child to one whom the world had forsaken. I loved indeed play, strictly such, thoughtless, childish play, and next to that, calm reflection and discussion. The world was too busy and too artful for me; I found myself most at home with those who had not entered, or those who had left it.

My father's illness was much aggravated by the conflict which began to arise in his mind regarding his proposed removal to his lands, which were already surrounded by a new population, consisting of these fashionable emigrants from the gay world at New York, whom I have been describing, and a set of fierce republicans, if anything sneaking and drawling may be so called, whom litigious contention had banished from their native province, and who seemed let loose, like Samson's foxes, to carry mischief and conflagration wherever they went. Among this motley crew there was no regular place of worship, nor any likely prospect that there should, for their religions had as many shades of difference as the leaves of autumn; and every man of substance who arrived, was preacher and magistrate to his own little colony. To hear their people talk, one would think time had run back to the days of the levellers. The settlers from New York, however, struggled hard for superiority, but they were not equal in chicane to their adversaries, whose power lay in their cunning. It was particularly hard for people who acknowledged no superior, who had a thorough knowledge of law and scripture, ready to wrest to every selfish purpose, it was particularly hard, I say, for such all-sufficient personages to hold their land from such people as my father and others, of "King George's red coats," as they elegantly styled them. But they were fertile in expedients. From the original establishment of these provinces, the Connecticut river had been accounted the boundary, to the east, of the province of New York, dividing it from the adjoining one; this division was specified in old patents, and confirmed by analogy. All at once, however, our new tenants at will made a discovery, or rather had a revelation, purporting, that there was a twenty mile line, as they called it, which in old times had been carried thus far beyond the Connecticut river, into the bounds of what had ever been esteemed the province of New York. It had become extremely fashionable to question the limits of individual property, but for so bold a stroke at a whole province, people were not prepared. The consequence of establishing this point was, that thus the grants made by the province of New York, of lands not their own, could not be valid; and thus the property, which had cost the owners so much to establish and survey, reverted to the other province, and was no longer theirs. This was so far beyond all imagination, that though there appeared not the smallest likelihood of its succeeding, as the plea must in the end be carried to Britain, people stood aghast, and saw no safety in living among those who were capable of making such daring strides over all established usage, and ready, on all occasions, to confederate where any advantage was in view, though ever engaged in litigious contentions with each other in their original home. This astonishing plea, during its dependence, afforded these dangerous neighbors a pretext to continue their usurped possession till it should be decided to which province the lands really belonged. They even carried their insolence so far, that when a particular friend of my father's, a worthy, upright man, named Munro,[1] who possessed a large tract of land adjoining to his; when this good man, who had established a settlement, saw-mills, etc., came to fix some tenants of his on his lands, a body of these incendiaries came out, armed, to oppose them, trusting to their superior numbers and the peaceable disposition of our friend. Now, the fatal twenty mile line ran exactly through the middle of my father's property. Had not the revolution followed so soon, there was no doubt of this claim being rejected in Britain; but in the meantime it served as a pretext for daily encroachment and insolent bravadoes. Much of my father's disorder was owing to the great conflict of his mind. To give up every prospect of consequence and afflu-

[1] John Munro, who for several years was very troublesome to the New Hampshire settlers, was a Scotchman, a New York justice of the peace, and resided in Shaftsbury, within a few rods of the New York line. After the year 1772, the threats of the Green Mountain boys appear to have kept him quiet; but on the approach of Burgoyne in 1777 he joined the British, and his personal property in Vermont was confiscated. He had been the agent of Duane, and from a desponding letter which he wrote to the latter in 1786, it appears that he was on his return to Canada from England, where he had been prosecuting his claims on the British government for his services and losses as a loyalist, without much success, and was returning to his family, penniless, and friendless, and appealed to his former friend and employer, for sympathy and aid. See "Hiland Hill's Early History of Vermont."

ence, and return to Britain, leaving his property afloat among these ungovernable people (to say no worse of them), was very hard. Yet to live among them, and by legal coercion force his due out of their hands, was no pleasing prospect. His good angel, it would seem in the sequel, whispered to him to return. Though, in human prudence, it appeared a fatal measure to leave so valuable a property in such hands, he thought, that he would stay two or three years; and then, when others had vanquished his antagonists, and driven them off the lands, which they, in the meantime, were busily clearing, he should return with a host of friends and kinsmen and form a chosen society of his own. He however waited to see what change for the better another twelvemonth might produce. Madame, who was consulted on his plans, did not greatly relish this; he, at length, half promised to leave me with her, till he should return from this expedition.

Returning for a short time to town in spring I found aunt's house much enlivened by a very agreeable visitor; this was Miss W., daughter to the Honorable Mr. W., of the council.[1] Her elder

[1] Archibald Kennedy, captain in the royal navy, married, first, Catharine, only child of Col. Peter Schuyler of New Jersey, by whom he received a large fortune; and, secondly, Anne, daughter of John Watts, member of the King's Council. The mother of Miss Watts was a Van Cortlandt, and related to Aunt Schuyler. Kennedy in the Revolutionary War saved his large estate, returned to England, and inherited the earldom of Cassilis. The sister of Anne Watts married

sister was afterwards Countess of Cassilis, and she herself was long afterwards married to the only native of the continent, I believe, who ever succeeded to the title of baronet. She possessed much beauty, and understanding, and vivacity. Her playful humor exhilarated the whole household. I regarded her with admiration and delight; and her fanciful excursions afforded great amusement to aunt, and were like a gleam of sunshine amidst the gloom occasioned by the spirit of contention which was let loose among all manner of people.

The repeal of the stamp act having excited new hopes, my father found all his expectations of comfort and prosperity renewed by this temporary calm, and the proposed return to Britain was deferred for another year. Aunt, to our great joy, as we scarce hoped she would again make so distant a visit, came out to the Flats with her fair visitor, who was about to return to New York. This lady, after going through many of the hardships to which persecuted loyalists were afterwards exposed, with her husband, who lost an immense property in the service of government, is now with her family settled in Upper Canada, where Sir J. Johnson has obtained a large grant of lands as a partial retribution for his great losses and faithful service.

Aunt again requested and again obtained permission for me to pass some time with her; and

John Johnson, who on the death of his father, Sir William Johnson, Bart., succeeded to the title. Sir John died in Montreal in 1830.

golden dreams of felicity at Clarendon, again began to possess my imagination. I returned however soon to the Flats, where my presence became more important, as my father became less eager in pursuit of field sports.

Chapter XXII

MODE OF CONVEYING TIMBER IN RAFTS DOWN THE RIVER

I BROUGHT out some volumes of Shakespeare with me, and, remembering the prohibition of reading plays promulgated the former winter, was much at a loss how to proceed. I thought rightly that it was owing to a temporary fit of spleen. But then I knew my father was, like all military men, tenacious of his authority, and would possibly continue it merely because he had once said so. I recollected that he said he would have no plays brought to the house; and that I read them unchecked at Madame's, who was my model in all things. It so happened that the river had been higher than usual that spring, and, in consequence, exhibited a succession of very amusing scenes. The settlers, whose increase above towards Stillwater had been for three years past incredibly great, set up saw-mills on every stream, for the purpose of turning to account the fine timber which they cleared in great quantities off the new lands. The planks they drew in sledges to the side of the great river; and when the season arrived that swelled the stream to its greatest height, a whole neighborhood assembled, and made their joint stock into a large raft, which was floated down the river with a man or two on it, who with long poles were always ready to steer it clear of those islands or shallows which might impede its course. There is something serenely majestic in the easy progress of those large bodies on the full stream of this copious river. Sometimes one sees a whole family transported on this simple conveyance; the mother calmly spinning, the children sporting about her, and the father fishing on one end, and watching its safety at the same time. These rafts were taken down to Albany, and put on board vessels there, for conveyance to New York; sometimes, however, it happened that, as they proceeded very slowly, dry weather came on by the time they reached the Flats, and it became impossible to carry them further; in that case they were deposited in great triangular piles opposite our door. One of these, which was larger than ordinary, I selected for a reading closet. There I safely lodged my Shakespeare; and there in my play hours I went to read it undisturbed, with the advantage of fresh air, a cool shade, and a full view of the road on one side, and a beautiful river on the other. While I enjoyed undisturbed privacy, I had the prohibition full in my mind, but thought I should keep to the spirit of it by only reading the historical plays, comforting myself that they were true.

These I read over and over with pleasure ever new; it was quite in my way, for I was familiarly acquainted with the English history; now, indeed, I began to relish Shakespeare, and to be astonished at my former blindness to his beauties. The contention of the rival roses occupied all my thoughts, and broke my rest. "Wind-changing Warwick" did not change oftener than I, but at length my compassion for holy Henry, and hatred to Richard, fixed me a Lancastrian. I began to wonder how any body could exist without reading Shakespeare, and at length resolved, at all risks, to make my father a sharer in my new found felicity. Of the nature of taste I had not the least idea; so far otherwise, that I was continually revolving benevolent plans to distribute some of the poetry I most delighted in among the Bezalees and Habakkuks, of the twenty mile line. I thought this would make them happy as myself, and that when they once felt the charm of "musical delight," the harsh language of contention would cease, and legal quibbling give way before the spirit of harmony. How often did I repeat Thompson's description of the golden age, concluding,

"For music held the whole in perfect peace."

At home, however, I was in some degree successful. My father did begin to take some interest in the roses, and I was happy, yet kept both my secret and my closet, and made more and more advances in the study of these "wood notes wild." *As you like it,* and the *Midsummer Night's Dream* enchanted me; and I thought the comfort of my closet so great, that I dreaded nothing so much as a flood, that should occasion its being once more set in motion. I was one day deeply engaged in compassionating Othello, sitting on a plank, added on the outside of the pile for strengthening it, when happening to lift my eyes, I saw a long serpent on the same board, at my elbow, in a threatening attitude, with its head lifted up. Othello and I ran off together with all imaginable speed; and as that particular kind of snake seldom approaches any person, unless the abode of its young is invaded, I began to fear I had been studying Shakespeare in a nest of serpents. Our faithful servant examined the place at my request. Under the very board on which I sat, when terrified by this unwished associate, was found a nest with seven eggs. After being most thankful for my escape, the next thing was to admire the patience and good humor of the mother of this family, who permitted such a being as myself so long to share her haunt with impunity. Indeed, the rural pleasures of this country were always liable to those drawbacks; and this place was peculiarly infested with the familiar garter-snake, because the ruins of the burnt house afforded shelter and safety to these reptiles.

Chapter XXIII

THE SWAMP—PATRICK COONIE

THIS adventure made me cautious of sitting out of doors, yet I daily braved a danger of the same nature, in the woods behind the house, which were my favorite haunts, and where I frequently saw snakes, yet was never pursued or annoyed by them. In this wood, half a mile from the house, was a swamp, which afforded a scene so totally unlike any thing else, that a description of it may amuse those who have never seen nature in that primitive state.

This swamp, then, was in the midst of a pine wood, and was surrounded on two sides by little hills, some of which were covered with cedar, and others with the silver fir, very picturesque, and finely varied with shrubs, and every gradation of green. The swamp sunk into a hollow, like a large basin, exactly circular; round half of it, was a border of maple, the other half was edged with poplar.[1] No creature ever entered this place in

---

[1] From the southern border of this swamp issued a small brook called the Vleykil, which emptied into the Kramkil, the southern boundary of the old Schuyler farm. From the northern boundary of the swamp issued another Vleykil which emptied into a creek called the Steenbrookkil forming the northern bounds of the farm. The

summer, its extreme softness kept it sacred from every human foot, for no one could go, without the risk of being swallowed up; different aquatic plants grew with great luxuriance in this quagmire, particularly bulrushes, and several beautiful species of the iris, and the alder and willow; much of it, however, was open, and in different places the water seemed to form stagnant pools; in many places large trees had fallen of old, which were now covered with moss, and afforded a home to numberless wild animals. In the midst of this aquatic retreat, were two small islands of inconceivable beauty, that rose high above the rest, like the oasis of the deserts, and were dry and safe though unapproachable. On one of these, I remember, grew three apple trees, an occurrence not rare here; for a squirrel, for instance, happens to drop the seeds of an apple in a spot at once sheltered and fertile; at a lucky season, they grow and bear, though with less vigor and beauty than those which are cultivated. That beautiful fruit, the wild plum, was also abundant on these little sanctuaries, as they might be called, for, conscious of impunity, every creature that flies the pursuit of man, gambolled in safety here, and would allow one to gaze at them from the brink of this natural fortress. One would think a congress of birds and animals had assembled here; never was a spot

swamp was drained long since, and is now occupied in part by nurseries, flower gardens, country mansions, and a railroad track.

more animated and cheerful. There was nothing like it in the great forests; creatures here, aware of their general enemy, man, had chosen it as their last retreat. The black, the large silver grey, the little striped, and nimble flying squirrel, were all at home here, and all visible in a thousand fantastic attitudes. Pheasants and woodpeckers in countless numbers, displayed their glowing plumage, and the songsters of the forest, equally conscious of their immunity, made the marsh resound with their blended music, while the fox, here a small auburn colored creature, the martin, and racoons occasionally appeared and vanished through the foliage. Often, on pretence of bringing home the cows in the morning (when in their own leisurely way they were coming themselves), I used to go, accompanied by my faithful Marian, to admire this swamp, at once a menagerie and aviary, and might truly say with Burns,

"My heart rejoic'd in nature's joys."

Not content, however, with the contemplation of animated nature, I began to entertain a fancy, which almost grew into a passion, for explaining

"Every herb that sips the dew."

The ordinary plants of that country differ very much from those most frequent here; and this thirst for herbalizing, for I must dignify my humble researches with the name of botanical ones, was a pleasing occupation. I made some progress in discovering the names and natures of these plants, I mean their properties; but unfortunately they were only Indian or Dutch names. This kind of knowledge, in that degree, is easily acquired there, because every one possesses it in some measure. Nothing surprised me so much, when I came to Britain, as to see young people so incurious about nature.

The woods behind our dwelling had been thinned to procure firing, and were more open and accessible than such places generally are. Walking one fine summer's evening, with my usual attendant, a little further into the wood than usual, but far from any known inhabitant, I heard peals of laughter, not joyous only, but triumphant, issue from the bottom, as it seemed, of a large pine. Silence succeeded, and we looked at each other with a mixture of fear and wonder, for it grew darkish. At last we made a whispered agreement to glide nearer among the bushes, and explore the source of all this merriment. Twilight, solemn everywhere, is awful in these forests; our awe was presently increased by the appearance of a light, that glimmered and disappeared by turns. Loud laughter was again reiterated, and at length a voice cried, "How pretty he is!" while another answered in softer accents, "See how the dear creature runs!" We crept on, cheered by these sounds, and saw a handsome, good-natured looking man, in a ragged provincial uniform, sitting on a stump of a tree. Opposite, on the ground, sat a pretty little brunette woman, neatly though meanly clad, with sparkling black eyes, and a countenance all vivacity and delight. A very little, very fair boy, with his mother's brilliant black eyes contrasting his flaxen hair and soft infantine complexion, went with tottering steps, that showed this was his first essay, from one to the other, and loud laughter gratulated his safe arrival in the arms of either parent. We had now pretty clearly ascertained the family, the next thing was to discover the house; this point was more difficult to establish; at last, we found it was barely a place to sleep in, partly excavated from the ground, and partly covered with a slight roof of bark and branches : never was poverty so complete or so cheerful. In that country, every white person had inferiors, and therefore being merely white, claimed a degree of respect, and being very rich, or very fine, entitled you to very little more. Simplicity would be a charming thing, if one could strain it from grossness, but that, I believe is no easy operation. We now, with much consideration and civility, presented ourselves; I thought the cows would afford a happy opening for conversation. "Don't be afraid of noise, we are driving our three cows home; have you any cows?" "Och no, my dare child, not one, young miss," said the soldier. "O, but then mamma will give milk to the child, for we have plenty and no child." "O dear pretty miss, don't mind that at all, at all." "Come," said the mistress of the hovel, "we have got fine butter-milk here, from Stephen's, come in and take a drink." I civilly declined this invitation, being wholly intent on the child, who appeared to me like a smiling love, and at once seized on my affection. Patrick Coonie, for such was the name of our new neighbor, gave us his history in a very few words; he had married Kate in Pennsylvania, who, young as she looked, had three children, from ten to fourteen, or thereabouts; he had some trade which had not thriven, he listed in the provincials, spent what he had on his family; hired again, served another campaign, came down penniless, and here they had come for a temporary shelter, to get work among their neighbors; the excavation existed before, Patrick happily discovered it, and added the ingenious roof which now covered it.[1] I asked for their other children; they were in some mean service. I was all anxiety for Patrick: so was not he; the lilies of the field did not look gayer, or more thoughtless of to-morrow, and Kate seemed equally unconcerned.

Hastily were the cows driven home that night, and to prevent reproaches for delay, I flew to communicate my discovery. Eager to say how ill off we often were for an occasional hand, to assist with our jobs, and how well we could spare a certain neglected log-house on our premises, etc. This was treated as very chimerical at first, but when Patrick's

[1] If it will gratify any one's curiosity to know where the site of the humble cot of Patrick Coonie was located, it is pointed out as in the now populous village of West Troy, and in the immediate vicinity of the residence of the late wealthy manufacturer James Roy.

VOL. II.— 12

family had undergone a survey, and Kate's accomplishments of spinning, etc., were taken into consideration, to my unspeakable joy, the family were accommodated as I wished, and their several talents made known to our neighbors, who kept them in constant business. Kate spun and sung like a lark, little Paddy was mostly with us, for I taught every one in the house to be fond of him.

I was at the utmost loss for something to cherish and caress, when this most amusing creature, who inherited all the gaiety and good temper of his parents, came in my way, as the first of possible playthings. Patrick was, of all beings, the most handy and obliging; he could do everything, but then he could drink too, and the extreme cheapness of liquor was a great snare to poor creatures addicted to it; Patrick, however, had long lucid intervals, and I had the joy of seeing them comparatively happy. To this was added, that of seeing my father recover his spirits, and renew his usual sports, and moreover, I was permitted to return to Aunt Schuyler's. I did not fail to entertain her with the history of my discovery, and its consequences, and my tale was not told in vain. Aunt weighed and balanced all things in her mind, and drew some good out of everything.

White servants, whom very few people had, were very expensive here; but there was a mode of meliorating things. Poor people who came adventurers from other countries, and found a settlement a slower process than they were aware of, had got into a mode of apprenticing their children. No risk attended this in Albany; custom is all-powerful; and lenity to servants was so much the custom, that to ill-use a defenceless creature in your power was reckoned infamous, and was indeed unheard of. Aunt recommended the young Coonies, who were fine well-looking children, for apprentices to some of the best families in town, where they were well bred and well-treated, and we all contributed decent clothing for them to go home in. I deeply felt this obligation, and little thought how soon I was to be deprived of all the happiness I owed to the friendship of my dear benefactress. This accession occupied and pleased me exceedingly; my attachment to the little boy grew hourly, and I indulged it to a degree I certainly would not have done, if I had not set him down for one of the future inhabitants of Clarendon; that region of fancied felicity, where I was building log-houses in the air perpetually, and filling them with an imaginary population, innocent and intelligent beyond comparison. These visions, however, were soon destined to give way to sad realities. The greatest immediate tribulation I was liable to, was Patrick's coming home now and then gay beyond his wonted gaiety; which grieved me both on Kate's account and that of little Paddy: but in the fertile plains of Clarendon, remedies were to be found for every passing evil; and I had not the least doubt of having influence enough to prevent the admission of spirituous liquors into that " region of calm delights." Such were the dreams from which I was awakened (on returning from a long visit to aunt) by my father's avowing his fixed intention to return home.

A very worthy Argyleshire friend of his, in the meantime, came and paid him a visit of a month; which month was occupied in the most endearing recollections of Lochawside, and the hills of Morven. When I returned, I heard of nothing but the Alpine scenes of Scotland, of which I had not the smallest recollection; but which I loved with borrowed enthusiasm: so well that they at times balanced with Clarendon. My next source of comfort was, that I was to return to the land of light and freedom, and mingle, as I flattered myself I should, with such as those whom I had admired in their immortal works. Determined to be happy, with the sanguine eagerness of youth, the very opposite materials served for constructing another ideal fabric.

Chapter XXIV

MRS. SCHUYLER'S VIEW OF THE CONTINENTAL POLITICS

AUNT was extremely sorry when the final determination was announced. She had now her good sister-in-law, Mrs. Wendell, with her, and seemed much to enjoy the society of that meek, pious woman, who was as happy as any thing earthly could make her. As to public affairs their aspect did not please her; and therefore she endeavored, as far as possible, to withdraw her attention from them. She was too well acquainted with the complicated nature of human affairs, to give a rash judgment on the political disputes then in agitation. She saw indeed reason for apprehension whatever way she turned. She knew the prejudices and self-opinion fast spreading through the country too well, to expect quiet submission, and could see nothing on all hands but a choice of evils. Were the provinces to set up for themselves, she thought they had not cohesion nor subordination enough among them to form, or to submit to any salutary plan of government. On the other hand she saw no good effect likely to result from a reluctant dependence on a distant people, whom they already began to hate, though hitherto nursed and protected by them. She clearly foresaw that no mode of taxation could be invented to which they would easily submit; and that the defence of the continent from enemies, and keeping the necessary military force to protect the weak and awe the turbulent, would be a perpetual drain of men and money to Great Britain, still increasing with the increased population. In short, she held all the specious plans that were talked over very cheap; while her affection for Britain made her shudder at the most distant idea of a separation; yet not as supposing such a step very hurtful to this country, which would be thus freed of a very costly incumbrance. But the dread of future anarchy, the horrors of civil war, and the dereliction of principle which generally results from tumultuary conflicts, were the spectres with which she was haunted.

Having now once for all given (to the best of my recollection) a faithful sketch of aunt's opinions on this intricate subject, I shall not recur to them, nor by any means attempt to enter into any detail of the dark days that were approaching. First, because I feel unspeakable pain in looking back upon occurrences that I know too well, though I was not there to witness; in which the friends of my early youth were greatly involved, and had much indeed to endure, on both sides. Next, because there is little satisfaction in narrating transactions where there is

FORT FREDERICK, STATE STREET, ALBANY, ABOUT 1765

AN AMERICAN LADY

no room to praise either side. That waste of personal courage and British blood and treasure, which were squandered to no purpose on one side in that ill-conducted war, and the insolence and cruelty which tarnished the triumph of the other, form no pleasing subject of retrospection: while the unsuccessful and often unrewarded loyalty of the sufferers for government, cannot be recollected without the most wounding regret. The years of Madame, after I parted with her, were involved in a cloud raised by the conflicts of contending arms, which I vainly endeavored to penetrate. My account of her must therefore, in a great measure, terminate with this sad year. My father taking in spring decided measures for leaving America, intrusted his lands to the care of his friend John Munro, Esq., then residing near Clarendon, and chief magistrate of that newly peopled district; a very worthy friend and countryman of his own, who was then in high triumph, on account of a fancied conquest over the supporters of the twenty mile line; and thought, when that point was fully established, there would be no further obstruction to their realizing their property to great advantage, or colonizing it from Scotland, if such should be their wish. Aunt leaned hard to the latter expedient, but my father could not think of leaving me behind to await the chance of his return; and I had been talked into a wish for revisiting the land of my nativity.

I left my domestic favorites with great pain, but

took care to introduce them to aunt, and implored her, with all the pathos I was mistress of, to take an interest in them when I was gone; which she very good naturedly promised to do. Another very kind thing she did. Once a year she spent a day or two at General Schuyler's, I call him by his later acquired title, to distinguish him from the number of his namesakes I have had occasion to mention. She now so timed her visit (though in dreadful weather) that I might accompany her, and take my last farewell of my young companions there: yet I could not bring myself to think it a final one. The terrible words, *no more*, never passed my lips. I had too buoyant a spirit to encounter a voluntary heart-ache by looking on the dark side of anything, and always figured myself returning, and joyfully received by the friends with whom I was parting.

Chapter XXV

DESCRIPTION OF THE BREAKING UP OF THE ICE ON HUDSON'S RIVER

SOON after this I witnessed, for the last time, the sublime spectacle of the ice breaking up on the river; an object that fills and elevates the mind with ideas of power, and grandeur, and, indeed, magnificence; before which all the triumphs of human art sink into contemptuous insignificance. This noble object of animated greatness, for such it seemed, I never missed: its approach being announced, like a loud and long peal of thunder, the whole population of Albany were down at the river side in a moment; and if it happened, as was often the case, in the morning, there could not be a more grotesque assemblage. No one who had a nightcap on waited to put it off; as for waiting for one's cloak, or gloves, it was a thing out of the question; you caught the thing next you, that could wrap round you, and run. In the way you saw every door left open, and pails, baskets, etc., without number, set down in the street. It was a perfect saturnalia. People never dreamt of being obeyed by their slaves, till the ice was past. The houses were left quite empty: the meanest slave, the youngest child, all were to be found on the shore. Such as could walk, ran; and they that could not, were carried by those whose duty it would have been to stay and attend them. When arrived at the *show place*, unlike the audience collected to witness any spectacle of human invention, the multitude with their eyes all bent one way, stood immovable, and silent as death, till the tumult ceased, and the mighty commotion was passed by; then every one tried to give vent to the vast conceptions with which his mind had been distended. Every child, and every negro, was sure to say, " Is not this like the day of judgment?" and what they said every one else thought. Now to describe this is impossible; but I mean to account, in some degree, for it. The ice, which had been all winter very thick, instead of diminishing, as might be expected in spring, still increased, as the sunshine came, and the days lengthened. Much snow fell in February; which, melted by the heat of the sun, was stagnant, for a day, on the surface of the ice; and then by the night frosts, which were still severe, was added, as a new accession to the thickness of it, above the former surface. This was so often repeated, that in some years the ice gained two feet in thickness, after the heat of the sun became such, as one would have expected should have entirely dissolved it. So conscious were the natives of the safety this accumulation of ice afforded, that the sledges continued to drive on the ice, when the trees were budding, and everything looked like spring; nay, when there was so much melted on the surface that the horses were knee deep in water, while travelling on it; and portentous cracks, on every side, announced the approaching rupture. This could scarce have been produced by the mere influence of the sun, till midsummer. It was the swelling of the waters under the ice, increased by rivulets, enlarged by melted snows, that produced this catastrophe; for such the awful concussion made it appear. The prelude to the general bursting of this mighty mass, was a fracture, lengthways, in the middle of the stream, produced by the effort of the imprisoned waters, now increased too much to be contained within their wonted bounds. Conceive a solid mass, from six to eight feet thick, bursting for many miles in one continued rupture, produced by a force inconceivably great, and, in a manner, inexpressibly sudden. Thunder is no adequate image of this awful explosion, which roused all the sleepers, within reach of the sound, as completely as the final convulsion of nature, and the solemn peal of the awakening trumpet, might be supposed to do. The stream in summer was confined by a pebbly strand, overhung with high and steep banks, crowned with lofty trees, which were considered as a sacred barrier against the encroachments of this annual visitation. Never dryads dwelt in more security than those of the vine clad elms, that extended their ample branches over this mighty stream. Their tangled nets laid bare by the impetuous torrents, formed caverns ever fresh and fragrant; where the most delicate plants flourished, unvisited by scorching suns, or snipping blasts; and nothing could be more singular than the variety of plants and birds that were sheltered in these intricate safe recesses. But when the bursting of the crystal surface set loose the many waters that had rushed down, swollen with the annual tribute of dissolving snow, the islands and low lands were all flooded in an instant; and the lofty banks, from which you were wont to overlook the stream, were now entirely filled by an impetuous torrent, bearing down, with incredible and tumultuous rage, immense shoals of ice; which, breaking every instant by the concussion of others, jammed together in some places, in others erecting themselves in gigantic heights for an instant in the air, and seemed to combat with their fellow giants crowding on in all directions, and falling together with an inconceivable crash, formed a terrible moving picture, animated and various beyond conception; for it was not only the cerulean ice, whose broken edges combating with the stream, refracted light into a thousand rainbows, that charmed your attention, lofty pines, large pieces of the bank torn off by the ice with all their early green and tender foliage, were drove on like travelling islands, amid this battle of breakers, for such it seemed. I am absurdly attempting to paint a scene, under which the powers of language sink. Suffice it, that this year its solemnity was increased by an unusual quantity of snow, which the last hard winter had accumulated, and the dissolution of which now threatened an inundation.

Solemn indeed it was to me, as the memento of my approaching journey, which was to take place whenever the ice broke, which is here a kind of epoch. The parting with all that I loved at the Flats was such an affliction, as it is even yet a renewal of sorrows to recollect. I loved the very barn and the swamp I have described so much that I could not see them for the last time without a pang. As for the island and the bank of the river, I know not how I should have parted with them, if I had thought the parting final; the good kind neighbors, and my faithful and most affectionate Marian, to whom of all others this separation was most wounding, grieved me not a little. I was always sanguine in the extreme, and would hope against hope; but Marian, who was older, and had more common sense, knew too well how little likelihood there was of my ever returning. Often with streaming eyes and bursting sobs she begged to know if the soul of a person dying in America could find its way over the vast ocean to join that of those who rose to the abodes of future bliss from Europe: her hope of a reunion being now entirely referred to that in a better world. There was no truth I found it so difficult to impress upon her mind as the possibility of spirits being instantaneously transported from one distant place to another; a doctrine which seemed to her very comfortable. Her agony at the final parting I do not like to think of. When I used to obtain permission to pass a little time in town, I was transported with the thoughts of the enjoyments that awaited me in the society of my patroness, and the young friends I most loved.

Chapter XXVI

DEPARTURE FROM ALBANY — ORIGIN OF THE STATE OF VERMONT

AFTER quitting the Flats we were to stay for some days at Madame's, till we should make a circular visit, and take leave. Having lulled my disappointment with regard to Clarendon,[1] and filled all my dreams with images of Clydesdale and Tweedale, and every other vale or dale that were the haunts of the pastoral muse in Scotland, I grew pretty well reconciled to my approaching journey; thinking I should meet piety and literature in every cottage, and poetry and music in every recess, among the sublime scenery of my native mountains.

[1] Duncan MacVicar was a staff-officer of the 55th Scotch Highlanders of the rank of lieutenant. As such officer he was entitled to 2,000 acres of land, and by the purchases which Mrs. Grant speaks of, became the proprietor of 4,000 more, all of which he located in a body, partly in the town of Shaftsbury and partly in what is now White Creek, N. Y., the twenty-mile line running exactly through the centre of it. This property he called a township, and gave it the name of Clarendon, and anticipated, as Mrs. Grant says, great enjoyment of a baronial estate. Becoming disgusted with the surroundings of his property, unable to obtain a suitable tenantry, and alarmed at the spread of republicanism and disloyalty, he embarked in the summer of 1770, with his daughter, then about fifteen years old, for his native Scotland. See Hiland "Hall's History of Vermont," p. 80, note. Mrs. Annie Laggan Dewar, a member of Mrs. Grant's family, writes from Dunfermline, Scotland, under date of 20 Sept., 1901: "I am

At any rate, I was sure I should hear the larks sing, and see the early primrose deck the woods, and daisies enamel the meadows. On all which privileges I had been taught to set the due value, yet I wondered very much how it was that I could enjoy nothing with such gay visions opening before me; my heart, I supposed, was honester than my imagination, for it refused to take pleasure in anything; which was a state of mind so new to me that I could not understand it. Everywhere I was caressed, and none of these caresses gave me pleasure; at length the sad day came that I was to take the last farewell of my first best friend, who had often in vain urged my parents to leave me till they should decide whether to stay or return. About this they did not hesitate; nor, though they had, could I have divested myself of the desire now waked in my mind, of seeing once more my native land, which I merely loved upon trust, not having the faintest recollection of it.

Madame embraced me tenderly with many tears, at parting; and I felt a kind of prelusive anguish, as if I had anticipated the sorrows that awaited; I do not mean now the painful vicissitudes of after life, but merely the cruel disappointment that I felt in finding the scenery and its inhabitants so different from the Elysian vales and Arcadian swains, that I had imagined.

unable to tell you much of my great-grandfather MacVicar: he held a commission in the 77th Fort under Col. Archibald Montgomerie, afterwards Earl of Eglinton, and I imagine he was a Captain. Later he was transferred to the 55th regiment, and retired on half pay in 1765."

When we came away, by an odd coincidence, aunt's nephew Peter was just about to be married to a very fine young creature, whom his relations did not, for some reason that I do not remember, think suitable; while, at the very same time, her niece, Miss W. had captivated the son of a rich but avaricious man, who would not consent to his marrying her, unless aunt gave a fortune with her; which, being an unusual demand, she did not choose to comply with. I was the proud and happy confidant of both these lovers; and before we left New York we heard that each had married without waiting for the withheld consent. And thus for once Madame was left without a *protégé*, but still she had her sister W. and soon acquired a new set of children, the orphan sons of her nephew Cortlandt Schuyler, who continued under her care for the remainder of her life.[1]

My voyage down the river, which was by contrary winds protracted to a whole week, would have been very pleasant, could anything have pleased me. I was at least soothed by the extreme beauty of many scenes on the banks of this fine stream, which I was fated never more to behold.

Nothing could exceed the soft, grateful verdure that met the eye on every side as we approached New York: it was in the beginning of May, the

[1] Peter Schuyler, fourth of the name, married his cousin, Gertrude Lansing, and Miss W. married John Johnson. The widow and children of Cortlandt Schuyler until they returned to Ireland lived much of the time in the house with Aunt Schuyler on State Street, Albany.

great orchards which rose on every slope were all in bloom, and the woods of poplar beyond them had their sprouting foliage tinged with a lighter shade of the freshest green. Staten Island rose gradual from the sea in which it seemed to float, and was so covered with innumerable fruit trees in full blossom, that it looked like some enchanted forest. I shall not attempt to describe a place so well known as New York, but merely content myself with saying that I was charmed with the air of easy gaiety, and social kindness, that seemed to prevail everywhere among the people, and the cheerful, animated appearance of the place altogether. Here I fed the painful longings of my mind, which already began to turn impatiently towards Madame, by conversing with young people whom I had met at her house, on their summer excursions. These were most desirous to please and amuse me; and, though I knew little of good breeding, I had good nature enough to try to seem pleased, but, in fact, I enjoyed nothing. Though I saw there was much to enjoy had my mind been turned as usual to social delight, fatigued with the kindness of others and my own simulation, I tried to forget my sorrows in sleep; but night, that was wont to bring peace and silence in her train, had no such companions here. The spirit of discord had broke loose. The fermentation was begun that had not yet ended. And at midnight, bands of intoxicated electors, who were then choosing a member for the assembly, came thundering to the doors, demanding a vote for their favored candidate. An hour after another party equally vociferous, and not more sober, alarmed us, by insisting on our giving our votes for their favorite competitor. This was mere play; but before we embarked, there was a kind of prelusive skirmish, that strongly marked the spirit of the times. These new patriots had taken it in their heads that Lieut. Gov. Colden sent home intelligence of their proceedings, or in some other way betrayed them, as they thought, to government. In one of these fits of excess and fury, which are so often the result of popular elections, they went to his house, drew out his coach, and set fire to it. This was the night before we embarked, after a week's stay in New York.

My little story being no longer blended with the memoirs of my benefactress, I shall not trouble the reader with the account of our melancholy and perilous voyage. Here, too, with regret I must close the account of what I knew of Aunt Schuyler. I heard very little of her till the breaking out of that disastrous war, which every one, whatever side they may have taken at the time, must look back on with disgust and horror.

To tell the history of aunt during the years that her life was prolonged to witness scenes abhorrent to her feelings, and her principles, would be a painful task indeed; though I were better informed than I am, or wish to be, of the transactions of those perturbed times. Of her private history I only know, that, on the accidental death, formerly mentioned, of her nephew Capt. Cortlandt Schuyler, she took home his two eldest sons, and kept them with her till her own death, which happened 28 August, 1782. I know too, that like the Roman

Margret Schuyler

A Facsimile of Aunt Schuyler's Signature, from her Will.

Atticus, she kept free from the violence and bigotry of party, and like him too, kindly and liberally assisted those of each side, who, as the tide of success ran different ways, were considered as unfortunate. On this subject I do not wish to enlarge, but shall merely observe, that all the colonel's relations were on the republican side, while every one of her own nephews [1] adhered to the royal cause, to their very great loss and detriment; though some of them have now found a home in Upper Canada, where, if they are alienated from their native province, they have at least the consolation

---

[1] When the war of independence commenced there were three, and possibly five, nephews of her deceased husband, Stephen, Philip, and Peter Schuyler, Peter Lansing and Barent Staats, of whom Philip S. was a colonel in the State line. Madame's nephews were Philip and Stephen Schuyler, the one a major-general, the other a colonel under the Congress; Philip, Abraham, and Cornelius Cuyler, of whom Philip was loyal to his country, while his two brothers were royalists.

of meeting many other deserving people, whom the fury of party had driven there for refuge.[1]

Though unwilling to obtrude upon my reader any further particulars, irrelevant to the main story I have endeavored to detail, he may perhaps be desirous to know how the township of Clarendon was at length disposed of. My father's friend, Captain Munro, was engaged for himself and his

---

[1] Since writing the above, the author of this narrative has heard many particulars of the later years of her good friend, by which it appears, that to the last her loyalty and public spirit burned with a clear and steady flame. She was by that time too venerable as well as respectable to be insulted for her principles; and her opinions were always delivered in a manner firm and calm, like her own mind, which was too well regulated to admit the rancor of party, and too dignified to stoop to disguise of any kind. She died full of years, and honored by all who could or could not appreciate her worth; for not to esteem Aunt Schuyler was to forfeit all pretensions to estimation. — *Mrs. Grant.*

The American Lady survived her brothers and sister, and those of her deceased husband; indeed, she was for many years the sole survivor in the third generation of Philip (Pieterse) Schuyler's descendants. Her estate, derived from her father, from her brother Philip, who was killed by the French at Saratoga in 1745, and from her husband, was more considerable than Mrs. Grant supposed. By her will, dated February 21, 1762, she gave it to her ten nephews and nieces, children of her brother John and of her sister Mrs. Cuyler, to each one-tenth. Her affections were loyal to her family, and she did not discriminate because of political differences. She had leased the Flats to a nephew of her late husband, a son of Pedrom, Stephen Schuyler, who rebuilt the house on the foundations of the one destroyed by fire; and it was while on a visit to the new-old place, she died, August 28, 1782, in the eighty-third year of her age. She was buried in the private cemetery between the graves of her husband and her brother John. It is greatly to be regretted that Mrs. Schuyler's last resting-place is unmarked. *Vide* note on p. 9, Vol. II.

military friends, in a litigation, or I should rather say, the provinces of New York and Connecticut continued to dispute the right to the boundary within the twenty mile line, till a dispute still more serious gave spirit to the new settlers from Connecticut, to rise in arms, and expel the unfortunate loyalists from that district, which was bounded on one side by the Green mountains, since distinguished, like Rome in its infancy, as a place of refuge to all the lawless and uncontrollable spirits who had banished themselves from general society.

It was a great mortification to speculative romance and vanity, for me to consider that the very spot, which I had been used fondly to contemplate as the future abode of peace, innocence, and all the social virtues, that this very spot should be singled out from all others, as a refuge for the vagabonds and banditti of the continent. They were, however, distinguished by a kind of desperate bravery, and unconquerable obstinacy. They, at one time, set the states and the mother country equally at defiance, and set up for an independence of their own; on this occasion they were so troublesome, and the others so tame, that the last mentioned were fain to purchase their nominal submission by a most disgraceful concession. There was a kind of provision made for all the British subjects who possessed property in the alienated provinces, provided that they had not borne arms against the Americans; these were permitted to sell their lands, though not for their full value, but at a limited price. My father came precisely under this description; but the Green mountain boys, as the irregular inhabitants of the disputed boundaries were then called, conscious that all the lands they had forcibly usurped were liable to this kind of claim, set up the standard of independence. They indeed positively refused to confederate with the rest, or consent to the proposed peace, unless the robbery they had committed should be sanctioned by a law, giving them a full right to retain, unquestioned, this violent acquisition.

It is doubtful, of three parties, who were most to blame on this occasion. The depredators, who, in defiance of even natural equity, seized and erected this little petulant state. The mean concession of the other provinces, who, after permitting this one to set their authority at defiance, soothed them into submission by a gift of what was not theirs to bestow; or the tame acquiescence of the then ministry, in an arrangement which deprived faithful subjects, who were at the same time war-worn veterans, of the reward assigned them for their services.

Proud of the resemblance which their origin bore to that of ancient Rome, they latinized the common appellation of their territory, and made wholesome laws for its regulation. Thus began the petty state of Vermont, and thus ends the *history of an heiress.*

Chapter XXVII

PROSPERITY OF ALBANY—GENERAL REFLECTIONS

I HOPE my readers will share the satisfaction I feel, in contemplating, at this distance, the growing prosperity of Albany, which is, I am told, greatly increased in size and consequence, far superior, indeed, to any inland town on the continent, so important from its centrical situation, that it has been proposed as the seat of congress, which, should the party attached to Britain ever gain the ascendancy over the southern states, would very probably be the case; the morality, simple manners, and consistent opinions of the inhabitants, still bearing evident traces of that integrity and simplicity which once distinguished them. The reflections which must result from the knowledge of these circumstances are so obvious, that it is needless to point them out.

A reader that has patience to proceed thus far, in a narration too careless and desultory for the grave, and too heavy and perplexed for the gay, too minute for the busy, and too serious for the idle; such a reader must have been led on by an interest in the virtues of the leading character, and will be sufficiently awake to their remaining effects.

AN AMERICAN LADY

Very different, however, must be the reflections that arise from a more general view of the present state of our ancient colonies.

> "O for that warning voice, which he who saw
> Th' Apocalypse, heard cry, That a voice, like
> The deep and dreadful organ-pipe of Heaven,"

would speak terror to those whose delight is in change and agitation; to those who wantonly light up the torch of discord, which many waters will not extinguish. Even when peace succeeds to the breathless fury of such a contest, it comes too late to restore the virtues, the hopes, the affections that have perished in it. The gangrene of the land is not healed, and the prophets vainly cry peace! peace! where there is no peace.

However upright the intentions may be of the first leaders of popular insurrection, it may be truly said of them, in the end, instruments of cruelty are in their habitations: nay, must be, for when they have proceeded a certain length, conciliation or lenity would be cruelty to their followers, who are gone too far, to return to the place from which they set out. Rectitude, hitherto upheld by laws, by custom, and by fear, now walks alone, in unaccustomed paths, and like a tottering infant, falls at the first assault, or first obstacle it meets; but falls to rise no more. Let any one who has mixed much with mankind, say, what would be the consequence if restraint were withdrawn, and impunity offered to all whose probity is not fixed on the basis of real piety, or supported by singular fortitude, and that sound sense which, discerning remote consequences, preserves integrity as armor of proof against the worst that can happen.

True it is, that amidst these convulsions of the moral world, exigencies bring out some characters that sweep across the gloom like meteors in a tempestuous night, which would not have been distinguished in the sunshine of prosperity. It is in the swell of the turbulent ocean that the mightiest living handy-works of the author of nature are to be met with. Great minds no doubt are called out by exigencies, and put forth all their powers. Though Hercules slew the Hydra and cleansed the Augæan stable, all but poets and heroes must have regretted that any such monsters existed. Seriously beside the rancor, the treachery, and the dereliction of every generous sentiment and upright motive, which are the rank production of the blood manured field of civil discord, after the froth and feculence of its cauldron have boiled over, still the deleterious dregs remain. Truth is the first victim to fear and policy; when matters arrive at that crisis, every one finds a separate interest; mutual confidence, which cannot outlive sincerity, dies next, and all the kindred virtues drop in succession. It becomes a man's interest that his brothers and his father should join the opposite party, that some may be applauded for steadiness or enriched by confiscations; to such temptations the mind, fermenting with party hatred, yields with less resistance than could be imagined by those who have never witnessed such scenes of horror darkened by duplicity. After so deep a plunge in depravity, how difficult, how near to impossible is a return to the paths of rectitude! This is but a single instance of the manner in which moral feeling is undermined in both parties. But as our nature, destined to suffer and to mourn, and to have the heart made better by affliction, finds adversity a less dangerous trial than prosperity, especially where it is great and sudden, in all civil conflicts the triumphant party may, with moral truth, be said to be the greatest sufferers. Intoxicated as they often are with power and affluence, purchased with the blood and tears of their friends and countrymen, the hard task remains to them of chaining up and reducing to submission the many headed monster, whom they have been forced to let loose and gorge with the spoils of the vanquished. Then, too, comes on the difficulty of dividing power where no one has a right, and every one a claim; of ruling those whom they have taught to despise authority; and of reviving that sentiment of patriotism, and that love of glory, which faction and self-interest have extinguished.

When the white and red roses were the symbols of faction in England, and when the contest between Baliol and Bruce made way for invasion and tyranny in Scotland, the destruction of armies and of cities, public executions, plunder and confiscations, were the least evils that they occasioned. The annihilation of public virtue and private confidence; the exasperation of hereditary hatred; the corrupting the milk of human kindness, and breaking asunder every sacred tie by which man and man are held together; all these dreadful results of civil discord are the means of visiting the sins of civil war on the third and fourth generation of those who have kindled it. Yet the extinction of charity and kindness in dissensions like these, is not to be compared to that which is the consequence of an entire subversion of the accustomed form of government. Attachment to a monarch or line of royalty, aims only at a single object, and is at worst loyalty and fidelity misplaced; yet war once begun on such a motive, loosens the bands of society, and opens to the ambitious and the rapacious the way to power and plunder. Still, however, the laws, the customs, and the frame of government stand where they did. When the contest is decided, and the successful competitor established, if the monarch possesses ability and courts popularity, he, or at any rate his immediate successor, may rule happily, and reconcile those who were the enemies, not of his place, but of his person. The mighty image of sovereign power may change its "head of gold" for one of silver; but still it stands firm on its basis, supported by all those whom it protects. But when thrown from its pedestal by an entire subversion of government, the wreck is far more fatal and the traces indelible. Those who on each side support the heirs claiming a disputed crown, mean equally to be faithful and loyal to their rightful sovereign; and are thus, though in opposition to each other, actuated by the same sentiment. But when the spirit of extermination walks forth over prostrate thrones and altars, ages cannot efface the traces of its progress. A contest for sovereignty is a whirlwind, that rages fiercely while it continues, and deforms the face of external nature. New houses, however, replace those it has demolished; trees grow up in the place of those destroyed; the landscape laughs, the birds sing, and everything returns to its accustomed course. But a total subversion of a long established government is like an earthquake, that not only overturns the works of man, but changes the wonted course and operation of the very elements; makes a gulf in the midst of a fertile plain, casts a mountain into a lake, and in fine produces such devastation as it is not in the power of man to remedy. Indeed it is too obvious that, even in our own country, that fire which produced the destruction of the monarchy, still glows among the ashes of extinguished factions; but that portion of the community who carried with them across the Atlantic, the repugnance to submission which grew out of an indefinite love of liberty, might be compared to the Persian Magi. Like them, when forced to fly from their native country, they carried with them a portion of the hallowed fire, which continued to be the object of their secret worship. Those who look upon the revolution, of which this spirit was the prime mover, as tending to advance the general happiness, no doubt consider these opinions as a rich inheritance, productive of the best effects. Many wise and worthy persons have thought and still continue to think so. There is as yet no room for decision, the experiment not being completed. Their mode of government, anomalous and hitherto inefficient, has not yet acquired the firmness of cohesion, or the decisive tone of authority.

The birth of this great empire is a phenomenon in the history of mankind. There is nothing like it in reality or fable, but the birth of Minerva, who proceeded full armed and full grown out of the head of the thunderer. Population, arts, sciences, and laws, extension of territory, and establishment of power, have been gradual and progressive in other countries, where the current of dominion went on increasing as it flowed, by conquests or other acquisitions, which it swallowed like rivulets in its course: but here it burst forth like a torrent, spreading itself at once into an expanse, vast as their own superior lake, before the eyes of the passive generation which witnessed its birth. Yet it is wonderful how little talent or intellectual preëminence of any kind has appeared in this new-born world, which seems already old in worldly craft, and whose children are indeed "wiser in their generation than the children of light." Self-interest, eagerly grasping at pecuniary advantages, seems to be the ruling principle of this great continent.

Love of country, that amiable and noble sentiment, which by turns exalts and softens the human mind, nourishes enthusiasm, and inspires alike the hero and the sage, to defend and adorn the sacred land of their nativity, is a principle which hardly exists there. An American loves his country, or prefers it rather, because its rivers are wide and deep, and abound in fish; because he has the forests to retire to, if the god of gainful commerce should prove unpropitious on the shore. He loves it because if his negro is disrespectful, or disobedient, he can sell him and buy another; while if he himself is disobedient to the laws of his country, or disrespectful to the magistracy appointed to enforce them, that shadow of authority, without power to do good, or prevent evil, must possess its soul in patience.

We love our country because we honor our ancestors; because it is endeared to us not only by early habit, but by attachments to the spots hallowed by their piety, their heroism, their genius, or their public spirit. We honor it as the scene of noble deeds, the nurse of sages, bards, and heroes. The very aspect and features of this blest asylum of liberty, science, and religion, warm our hearts, and animate our imaginations. Enthusiasm kindles at the thoughts of what we have been, and what we are. It is the last retreat, the citadel, in which all that is worth living for is concentrated. Among the other ties which were broken, by the detachment of America from us, that fine ligament, which binds us to the tombs of our ancestors (and seems to convey to us the spirit and the affections we derive from them), was dissolved: with it perished all generous emulation. Fame,

> "That spur which the clear mind doth raise
> To live laborious nights and painful days,"

has no votaries among the students of Poor Richard's almanac, the great *Pharos* of the states. The land of their ancestors, party hostility has taught them to regard with scorn and hatred. That in which they live calls up no images of past glory or excellence. Neither hopeful nor desirous of that after-existence, which has been most coveted by those who do things worth recording, they not only live, but thrive; and that is quite enough. A man no longer says of himself with exultation, "I belong to the land where Milton sung the song of seraphims, and Newton traced the paths of light; where Alfred established his throne in wisdom, and where the palms and laurels of renown shade the tombs of the mighty and the excellent." Thus dissevered from recollections so dear, and so ennobling, what ties are substituted in their places? Can he regard with tender and reverential feelings, a land that has not only been deprived of its best ornaments, but become a receptacle of the outcasts of society from every nation in Europe? Is there a person whose dubious or turbulent character has made him unwelcome or suspected in society, he goes to America, where he knows no one, and is of no one known; and where he can with safety assume any character. All that tremble with the consciousness of undetected crimes, or smart from the consequence of unchecked follies; fraudulent bankrupts, unsuccessful adventurers, restless projectors, or seditious agitators, this great Limbus Patrum has room for them all; and to it they fly in the day of their calamity. With such a heterogeneous mixture a transplanted Briton of the original stock, a true old American, may live in charity, but can never assimilate. Who can, with the cordiality due to that sacred appellation, "my country," apply it to that land of Hivites and Girgashites, where one cannot travel ten miles, in a stretch, without meeting detachments of different nations, torn from their native soil and first affections, and living aliens in a strange land, where no one seems to form part of an attached, connected whole.

To those enlarged minds, who have got far beyond the petty consideration of country and kindred, to embrace the whole human race, a land, whose population is like Joseph's coat, of many colors, must be a peculiarly suitable abode. For in the endless variety of the patchwork, of which society is composed, a liberal philosophic mind might meet with the specimens of all those tongues and nations which he comprehends in the wide circle of his enlarged philanthropy.

Chapter XXVIII

FURTHER REFLECTIONS — GENERAL HAMILTON

THAT some of the leaders of the hostile party in America acted upon liberal and patriotic views can not be doubted. There were many, indeed, of whom the public good was the leading principle; and to these the cause was a noble one: yet even these little foresaw the result. Had they known what a cold, selfish character, what a dereliction of religious principle, what furious factions, and wild unsettled notions of government, were to be the consequences of this utter alienation from the parent state, they would have shrunk back from the prospect. Those fine minds who, nurtured in the love of science and of elegance, looked back to the land of their forefathers for models of excellence, and drank inspiration from the production of the British muse, could not but feel this rapture as " a wrench from all we love, from all we *are.*" They, too, might wish, when time had ripened their growing empire, to assert that independence which, when mature in strength and knowledge, we claim even of the parents we love and honor. But to snatch it with a rude and bloody grasp, outraged the feelings of those gentler children of the common parent. Mildness of manners, refinement of mind, and all the softer virtues that spring up in the cultivated paths of social life, nurtured by generous affections, were undoubtedly to be found on the side of the unhappy loyalists; whatever superiority in vigor and intrepidity might be claimed by their persecutors. Certainly, however necessary the ruling powers might find it to carry their system of exile into execution, it has occasioned to the country an irreparable privation.

When the revocation of the Edict of Nantz gave the scattering blow to the protestants of France, they carried with them their arts, their frugal regular habits, and that portable mine of wealth which is the portion of patient industry. The chasm produced in France by the departure of so much humble virtue, and so many useful arts, has never been filled.

What the loss of the Huguenots was to commerce and manufactures in France, that of the loyalists was to religion, literature, and *amenity*, in America. The silken threads were drawn out of the mixed web of society, which has ever since been comparatively coarse and homely. The dawning light of elegant science was quenched in universal dulness. No ray has broken through the general gloom except the phosphoric lightnings of her cold blooded philosopher, the deistical Franklin, the legitimate father of the American "age of calculation." So well have "the children of his *soul*" profited by the frugal lessons of this apostle of Plutus, that we see a new empire blest in its infancy with all the saving virtues which are the usual portion of cautious and feeble age; and we behold it with the same complacent surprise which fills our minds at the sight of a young miser.

Forgive me, shade of the accomplished Hamilton [1] while all that is lovely in virtue, all that is honorable in valor, and all that is admirable in talent, conspire to lament the early setting of that western star; and to deck the tomb of worth and genius with wreaths of immortal bloom:

> "Thee Columbia long shall weep;
> Ne'er again thy kindness see;"

fain would I add,

> "Long her strains in sorrows steep,
> Strains of immortality."— *Gray.*

but alas!

> "They have no poet, and they die." — *Pope.*

His character was a bright exception; yet, after all, an exception that only confirms the rule. What must be the state of that country where worth, talent, and the disinterested exercise of every faculty of a vigorous and exalted mind, were in vain devoted to the public good? Where, indeed, they

[1] General Alexander Hamilton, killed in a duel, into which he was forced by Col. Aaron Burr, Vice-President of the United States, at New York, in 1804. — *Mrs. Grant.*

only marked out their possessor for a victim to the shrine of faction? Alas! that a compliance with the laws of false honor (the only blemish of a stainless life), should be so dearly expiated! Yet the deep sense expressed by all parties of this general loss, seems to promise a happier day at some future period, when this chaos of jarring elements shall be reduced by some pervading and governing mind into a settled form.

But much must be done, and suffered, before this change can take place. There never can be much improvement till there is union and subordination; till those strong local attachments are formed, which are the basis of patriotism, and the bonds of social attachment. But, while such a wide field is open to the spirit of adventure; and, while the facility of removal encourages that restless and ungovernable spirit, there is little hope of any material change. There is in America a double principle of fermentation, which continues to impede the growth of the arts and sciences, and of those gentler virtues of social life, which were blasted by the breath of popular fury. On the sea-side there is a perpetual importation of lawless and restless persons, who have no other path to the notoriety they covet, but that which leads through party violence; and of want of that local attachment, I have been speaking of, there can be no stronger proof, than the passion for emigration so frequent in America.

Among those who are neither beloved in the vicinity of their place of abode, nor kept stationary by any gainful pursuit, it is incredible how light a matter will afford a pretext for removal!

Here is one great motive, for good conduct and decorous manners, obliterated. The good opinion of his neighbors is of little consequence to him, who can scarce be said to have any. If a man keeps free of those crimes which a regard to the public safety compels the magistrate to punish, he finds shelter in every forest from the scorn and dislike incurred by petty trespasses on society. There, all who are unwilling to submit to the restraints of law and religion, may live unchallenged, at a distance from the public exercise of either. There all whom want has made desperate, whether it be the want of abilities, of character, or the means to live, are sure to take shelter. This habit of removing furnishes, however, a palliation for some evils, for the facility with which they change residence becomes the means of ridding the community of members too turbulent or too indolent to be quiet or useful. It is a kind of voluntary exile, where those whom government want power and efficiency to banish, very obligingly banish themselves; thus preventing the explosions which might be occasioned by their continuing mingled in the general mass.

It is owing to this salutary discharge of peccant humors that matters go on so quietly as they do, under a government which is neither feared nor loved, by the community it rules. These removals are incredibly frequent; for the same family, flying as it were before the face of legal authority and civilization, are often known to remove farther and farther back into the woods, every fifth or sixth year, as the population begins to draw nearer. By this secession from society, a partial reformation is in some cases effected. A person incapable of regular industry and compliance with its established customs will certainly do least harm, when forced to depend on his personal exertions. When a man places himself in the situation of Robinson Crusoe, with the difference of a wife and children for that solitary hero's cats and parrots, he must of necessity make exertions like his, or perish. He becomes not a regular husbandman, but a hunter, with whom agriculture is but a secondary consideration. His Indian corn and potatoes, which constitute the main part of his crop, are, in due time, hoed by his wife and daughters; while the axe and the gun are the only implements he willingly handles.

Fraud and avarice are the vices of society, and do not thrive in the shade of the forests. The hunter, like the sailor, has little thought of coveting or amassing. He does not forge, nor cheat, nor steal, as such an unprincipled person must have done in the world, where, instead of wild beasts, he must have preyed upon his fellows, and he does not drink much, because liquor is not attainable. But he becomes coarse, savage, and totally negligent of all the forms and decencies of life. He grows wild and unsocial. To him a neighbor is an encroacher. He has learnt to do without one; and he knows not how to yield to him in any point of mutual accommodation. He cares neither to give or take assistance, and finds all the society he wants in his own family. Selfish, from the over-indulged love of ease and liberty, he sees in a new comer merely an abridgement of his range, and an interloper in that sport on which he would much rather depend for subsistence than on the habits of regular industry. What can more flatter an imagination warm with native benevolence, and animated by romantic enthusiasm, than the image of insulated self-dependant families, growing up in those primeval retreats, remote from the corruptions of the world, and dwelling amidst the prodigality of nature. Nothing however can be more anti-Arcadian. There no crook is seen, no pipe is heard, no lamb bleats, for the best possible reason, because there are no sheep. No pastoral strains awake the sleeping echoes, doomed to sleep on till the bull-frog, the wolf, and the quackawary [1] begin their nightly concert. Seriously, it is not a place that can, in any instance, constitute happiness. When listless indolence or lawless turbulence fly to shades the most tranquil, or scenes the most beautiful, they degrade nature instead of improving or enjoying

[1] Quackawary is the Indian name of a bird, which flies about in the night, making a noise similar to the sound of its name. — *Mrs. Grant.*

her charms. Active diligence, a sense of our duty to the source of all good, and kindly affections towards our fellow-creatures, with a degree of self-command and mental improvement, can alone produce the gentle manners that ensure rural peace, or enable us, with intelligence and gratitude, to " rejoice in nature's joys."

Chapter XXIX

SKETCH OF THE SETTLEMENT OF PENNSYLVANIA

FAIN would I turn from this gloomy and uncertain prospect, so disappointing to philanthropy, and so subversive of all the flattering hopes and sanguine predictions of the poets and philosophers, who were wont to look forward to a new Atlantis,

> "Famed for arts and laws derived from Jove."

in this western world. But I cannot quit the fond retrospect of what once was in one favored spot, without indulging a distant hope of what may emerge from this dark, disordered state.

The melancholy Cowley, the ingenius bishop of Cloyne, and many others, alike eminent for virtue and for genius, looked forward to this region of liberty as a soil, where peace, science, and religion could have room to take root and flourish unmolested. In those primeval solitudes, enriched by the choicest bounties of nature, they might (as these benevolent speculators thought) extend their shelter to tribes no longer savage, rejoicing in the light of evangelic truth, and exalting science. Little did these amiable projectors know how much is to be done before the human mind, debased by habitual vice, and cramped by artificial manners in the old world, can wash out its stains and resume its simplicity in a new; nor did they know through how many gradual stages of culture the untutored intellect of savage tribes must pass before they become capable of comprehending those truths which to us habit has rendered obvious, or which at any rate we have talked of so familiarly, that we think we comprehend them. These projectors of felicity were not so ignorant of human nature, as to expect change of place could produce an instantaneous change of character; but they hoped to realize an Utopia, where justice should be administered on the purest principles; from which venality should be banished, and where mankind should, through the paths of truth and uprightness, arrive at the highest attainable happiness in a state not meant for perfection. They "talked the style of gods," making very little account of "chance and sufferance." Their speculations of the result remind me of what is recorded in some ancient writer, of a project for building a magnificent temple to Diana in some one of the Grecian states. A reward was offered to him who should erect, at the public cost, with most taste and ingenuity, a structure which should do honor both to the goddess and her worshippers. Several candidates appeared. The first that spoke was a self-satisfied young man, who, in a long florid harangue, described the pillars, the porticoes, and the proportions of this intended building, seeming all the while more intent on the display of his elocution, than on the subject of his discourse. When he had finished, a plain, elderly man came from behind him, and leaning forwards, said in a deep hollow voice, "All that he has said I will do."

William Penn was the man, born to give "a local habitation and a name," to all that had hitherto only floated in the day dreams of poets and philosophers.

To qualify him for the legislator of a new born sect, with all the innocence and all the helplessness of infancy, many circumstances concurred, that could scarce ever be supposed to happen at once to the same person; born to fortune and distinction, with a mind powerful and cultivated, he knew, experimentally, all the advantages to be derived from wealth or knowledge, and could not be said ignorantly to despise them. He had, in his early days, walked far enough into the paths of folly and dissipation, to know human character in all its varieties, and to say experimentally — all is vanity. With a vigorous mind, an ardent imagination, and a heart glowing with the warmest benevolence, he appears to have been driven, by a repulsive abhorrence of the abuse of knowledge, of pleasure, and preëminence, which he had witnessed, into the opposite extreme; into a sect, the very first principles of which, clip the wings of fancy, extinguish ambition, and bring every struggle for superiority, the result of uncommon powers of mind, down to the dead level of tame equality; a fact, that reminds one of the exclusion of poets from Plato's fancied republic, by stripping off all the many-colored garbs with which learning and imagination have invested the forms of ideal excellence, and reducing them to a few simple realities, arrayed as soberly as their votaries.

This sect, which brings mankind to a resemblance of Thomson's Laplanders,

"Who little pleasure know, and feel no pain,"

might be supposed the last to captivate, nay, to absorb, such a mind as I have been describing. Yet so it was: even in the midst of all this cold humility, dominion was to be found. That rule, which of all others, is most gratifying to a mind conscious of its own power, and directing it to the purposes of benevolence, the voluntary subjection of mind, the homage which a sect pays to its leader, is justly accounted the most gratifying species of power; and to this lurking ambition everything is rendered subservient by those, who have once known this native and inherent superiority. This man, who had wasted his inheritance, alienated his relations, and estranged his friends, who had forsaken the religion of his ancestors, and in a great measure the customs of his country, whom some charged with folly, and others with madness, was, nevertheless, destined to plan with consummate wisdom, and execute with indefatigable activity and immovable firmness, a scheme of government, such as has been the wish, at least, of every enlarged and benevolent mind (from Plato, downwards), which has indulged speculations of the kind. The glory of realizing, in some degree, all these fair visions was, however, reserved for William Penn alone.

Imagination delights to dwell on the tranquil abodes of plenty, content, and equanimity, that so quickly "rose like an exhalation," in the domains of this pacific legislator. That he should expect to protect the quiet abodes of his peaceful and industrious followers, merely with a fence of olive (as one may call his gentle institutions), is wonderful; and the more so, when we consider him to have lived in the world, and known too well, by his own experience, of what discordant elements it is composed. A mind so powerful and comprehensive as his, could not but know, that the wealth which quiet and blameless industry insensibly accumulates, proves merely a lure to attract the armed spoiler to the defenceless dwellings of those, who do not think it a duty to protect themselves.

"But when divine ambition swell'd his mind,
Ambition truly great, of virtue's deeds,"

he could no otherwise execute his plan of utility, than by the agency of a people who were bound together by a principle, at once adhesive and exclusive, and who were too calm and self-subdued, too benignant and just to create enemies to themselves among their neighbors. There could be no motive but the thirst of rapine, for disturbing a community so inoffensive; and the founder, no doubt, flattered himself that the parent country would not fail to extend to them that protection, which their useful lives and helpless state both needed and deserved.

Never, surely, were institutions better calculated for nursing the infancy of a sylvan colony, from which the noisy pleasures, and more bustling varieties of life, were necessarily excluded. The serene and dispassionate state, to which it seems the chief aim of this sect to bring the human mind, is precisely what is requisite to reconcile it to the privations that must be encountered, during the early stages of the progression of society, which, necessarily excluded from the pleasures of refinement, should be guarded from its pains.

Where nations, in the course of time become civilized, the process is so gradual from one race to another, that no violent effort is required to break through settled habits, and acquire new tastes and inclinations, fitted to what might be almost styled a new mode of existence. But when colonies are first settled, in a country so entirely primitive as that to which William Penn led his followers, there is a kind of retrograde movement of the mind, requisite to reconcile people to the new duties and new views that open to them, and to make the total privation of wonted objects, modes, and amusements, tolerable.

Perfect simplicity of taste and manners, and entire indifference to much of what the world calls pleasure, were necessary to make life tolerable to the first settlers in a trackless wilderness. These habits of thinking and living, so difficult to acquire, and so painful when forced upon the mind by inevitable necessity, the Quakers brought with them, and left, without regret, a world from which they were already excluded by that austere simplicity which peculiarly fitted them for their new situation. A kindred simplicity, and a similar ignorance of artificial refinements and high seasoned pleasures, produced the same effect in qualifying the first settlers at Albany to support the privations, and endure the inconveniences of their noviciate in the forests of the new world. But to return to William Penn; the fair fabric he had erected, though it speedily fulfilled the utmost promise of hope, contained within itself the principle of dissolution, and, from the very nature of the beings which composed it, must have decayed, though the revolutionary shock had not so soon shaken its foundations. Sobriety and prudence lead naturally to wealth, and wealth to authority, which soon strikes at the root of the short lived principle of equality. A single instance may occur here and there, but who can ever suppose nature running so contrary to her bias that all the opulent members of a community should acquire or inherit wealth for the mere purpose of giving it away? Where there are no elegant arts to be encouraged, no elegant pleasures to be procured, where ingenuity is not to be rewarded, or talent admired or exercised, what is wealth but a cumbrous load, sinking the owner deeper and deeper into grossness and dullness, having no incitement to exercise the only faculties permitted him to use, and few objects to relieve in a community from which vice and poverty are equally excluded by their industry, and their wholesome rule of expulsion. We all know that there is not in society a more useless and disgusting character than what is formed by the possession of great wealth without elegance or refinement, without, indeed, that liberality which can only result from a certain degree of cultivation. What then would a community be, entirely formed of such persons, or, supposing such a community to exist, how long would they adhere to the simple manners of their founder, with such a source of corruption mingled with their very existence? Detachment from pleasure and from vanity, frugal and simple habits, and a habitual close adherence to some particular trade or employment, are circumstances that have a sure tendency to enrich the individuals who practise them. This in the end is " to give humility a coach and six," that is, to destroy the very principle of adhesion which binds and continues the sect.

Highly estimable as a sect, these people were respectable and amiable in their collective capacity as a colony. But then it was an institution so constructed, that, without a miracle, its virtues must have expired with its minority. I do not here speak of the necessity of its being governed and protected by those of different opinions, but merely of wealth stagnating without its proper application. Of this humane community it is but just to say, that they were the only Europeans in the new world who always treated the Indians with probity like their own, and with kindness calculated to do honor to the faith they professed. I speak of them now in their collective capacity. They too are the only people that, in a temperate, judicious (and, I trust, successful), manner, have endeavored, and still endeavor to convert the Indians to Christianity; for them too was reserved the honorable distinction of being the only body who sacrificed interest to humanity, by voluntarily giving freedom to those slaves whom they held in easy bondage. That a government so constituted could not, in the nature of things, long exist, is to be regretted; that it produced so much good to others and so much comfort and prosperity to its subjects while it did exist, is an honorable testimony of the worth and wisdom of its benevolent founder.

Chapter XXX

PROSPECTS BRIGHTENING IN AMERICA

HOWEVER discouraging the prospect of society on this great continent may at present appear, there is every reason to hope time, and the ordinary course of events, may bring about a desirable change; but in the present state of things, no government seems less calculated to promote the happiness of its subjects, or to ensure permanence to itself, than that feeble and unstable system which is only calculated for a community comprising more virtue, and more union than such a heterogeneous mixture can be supposed to have attained. States, like individuals, purchase wisdom by suffering, and they have probably much to endure before they assume a fixed, determined form.

Without partiality it may be safely averred, that notwithstanding the severity of the climate, and other unfavorable circumstances, the provinces of British America are the abode of more present safety and happiness, and contain situations more favorable to future establishments, than any within the limits of the United States.

To state all the grounds upon which this opinion is founded, might lead me into discussions, narratives, and description which might swell into a volume, more interesting than the preceding one. But being at present neither able or inclined to do justice to the subject, I shall only briefly observe first, with regard to the government, it is one to which the governed are fondly attached, and which like religion becomes endeared to its votaries, by the sufferings they have endured for their adherence to it. It is consonant to their earliest prejudices, and sanctioned by hereditary attachment. The climate is indeed severe, but it is steady and regular, the skies in the interior are clear, the air pure. The summer, with all the heat of warm climates to cherish the productions of the earth, is not subject to the drought that in such climates scorches and destroys them. Abundant woods furnish shelter and fuel, to mitigate the severity of winter; and streams rapid and copious flow in all directions to refresh the plants and cool the air, during their short but ardent summer.

The country, barren, at the sea-side, does not afford an inducement for those extensive settlements which have a tendency to become merely commercial from their situation. It becomes more fertile as it recedes further from the sea. Thus holding out an inducement to pursue nature into her favorite retreats, where on the banks of mighty waters, calculated to promote all the purposes of social traffic among the inhabitants, the richest soil, the happiest climate, and the most complete detachment from the world, promises a safe asylum to those who carry the arts and the literature of Europe, hereafter to grace and enlighten scenes where agriculture has already made rapid advances.

In the dawning light which already begins to rise in these remote abodes, much may be discovered of what promises a brighter day. Excepting the remnant of the old Canadians, who are a very inoffensive people, patient and cheerful, attached to monarchy, and much assimilated to our modes of thinking and living, these provinces are peopled, for the most part, with inhabitants possessed of true British hearts and principles. Veterans who have shed their blood, and spent their best days in the service of the parent country, and royalists who have fled here for a refuge, after devoting their property to the support of their honor and loyalty; who adhere together and form a society graced by that knowledge, and those manners, which rendered them respectable in their original state, with all the experience gained from adversity; and that elevation of sentiment which results from the consciousness of having suffered in a good cause. Here, too, are clusters of emigrants, who have fled, unacquainted with the refinements, and uncontaminated by the old world, to seek for that bread and peace, which the progress of luxury and the change of manners denied them at home. Here they come in kindly confederation, resolved to cherish in those kindred groups, which have left with social sorrow their native mountains, the customs and traditions, the language and the love of their ancestors, and to find comfort in that religion, which has been ever their support and their shield, for all that they have left behind.[1]

It is by tribes of individuals intimately connected with each other by some common tie, that a country is most advantageously settled; to which the obvious superiority in point of principle and union that distinguishes British America from the United States, is chiefly owing. Our provinces afford no room for wild speculations either of the commercial or political kind; regular, moderate trade, promising little beyond a comfortable subsistence, and agriculture, requiring much industry and settled habits, are the only paths open to adventurers; and the chief inducement to emigration is the possibility of an attached society of friends and kindred, finding room to dwell together, and meeting, in the depth of these fertile wilds, with similar associations. Hence solitary and desperate adventurers, the vain, the turbulent, and the ambitious, shun these regulated abodes of quiet industry, for scenes more adapted to their genius.

I shall now conclude my recollections, which circumstances have often rendered very painful; but

---

[1] It is needless to enlarge on a subject, to which Lord Selkirk has done such ample justice, who wanted nothing but a little experience and a little aid, to make the best practical comments on his own judicious observations. — *Mrs. Grant.*

will not take upon me to enlarge on those hopes that stretch a dubious wing into temporal futurity, in search of a brighter day, and a better order of things. Content if I have preserved some records of a valuable life; thrown some glimmering light upon the progress of society in that peculiar state, which it was my fate to witness and to share, and afforded some hours of harmless amusement to those lovers of nature and of truth, who can patiently trace their progress through a tale devoid alike of regular arrangement, surprising variety, and artificial embellishment.

The reader, who has patiently gone on to the conclusion of these desultory memoirs, will perhaps regret parting with that singular association of people, the Mohawk tribes, without knowing where the few that remain have taken up their abode. It is but doing justice to this distinguished race to say, that, though diminished, they were not subdued; though voluntary exiles, not degraded. Their courage and fidelity were to the last exerted in the most trying exigencies. True to their alliance with that nation with whom they had ever lived in friendship, and faithful to that respectable family, who had formed at once the cement and the medium by which that alliance was confirmed, and through which assurances of attachment and assistance had been transmitted, all that remained of this powerful nation followed Sir John Johnson (the son of their revered

Sir William) into Upper Canada, where they now find a home around the place of his residence. One old man alone, having no living tie remaining, would not forsake the tombs of his ancestors, and remains like "a watchman on the lonely hill;" or rather like a sad memento of an extinguished nation.

APPENDIX

MRS. ANNE GRANT'S LETTERS TO DR. JOSEPH GREEN COGSWELL, 1819–1821

CORRESPONDENCE BETWEEN MRS. ALEXANDER HAMILTON AND MRS. GRANT IN 1834

COMMUNICATIONS FROM MRS. GRANT TO MRS. DOUGLAS CRUGER, 1837–1838

LETTERS TO MRS. GRANT FROM ROBERT SOUTHEY AND OTHERS, 1811–1834

"THE INDIAN WIDOW," AND LINES ADDRESSED TO AN AMERICAN LADY BY MRS. GRANT

A LIST OF MRS. GRANT'S WRITINGS

APPENDIX

LETTERS TO DR. JOSEPH GREEN COGSWELL[1]

AMENDELL HOUSE, Dec. 12, 1819.

MY DEAR SIR, — I must begin by assuring you that very soon after the receipt of your letter from Leipsic I bestowed all my tediousness upon you in a long and minute epistle, and though I were as tedious as a queenlike Dogberry, I made your honor very welcome. You may believe, I regret exceedingly that what I took so much pains to write should never have reached you. But there is no intellectual treasure lost, for I remember merely that it was a gossiping letter, containing all the little occurrences of the town, which I thought would be as acceptable to you as any wit or wisdom of mine, if I had such to bestow. I was much amused in the meantime with your letter, and all the lazy luxury and rural lounges of your Leipsic friends. I should exempt the ladies from this charge, who seem to have been like the little busy bee in the children's hymn. I cannot now recollect or arrange all that I told you in my former letter, but go on to say how much we were amused by a visit from young John Lowell and a good-natured heavy friend of his, Porter by name, as unlike himself as possible. I might tell you too of the pains I took to amuse them, and par-

[1] Joseph Green Cogswell (1786–1871) spent two years with George Ticknor at Göttingen University, and later the two young New Englanders were guests of Sir Walter Scott at Abbotsford. Becoming the friend and companion of Halleck and Irving, he was appointed with them a Trustee of the Astor Library, later becoming its Superintendent, and purchasing the books in Europe. Dr. Cogswell had met Goethe, Humboldt, Byron, Béranger, and almost all of the brilliant Edinburgh literary circle of Mrs. Grant's era, having spent the winter of 1818–19 there. He was perhaps the greatest favorite among her many American friends and correspondents.

ticularly how I did go down to Stirling with them, including in the party a very admirable English clergyman who was here upon a tour through Scotland, Ryland by name; also Miss Steven and Miss North, to both of whom Stirling was new. How fine the weather was, how smooth the motion of the steamboat, and how beautiful, grand, and classical the scenery, I shall not attempt to say. Nor yet — for that would prove difficult — how much my fellow-travellers — your countrymen — were particularly delighted. Of the hospitality of good old friends to so large a party I could not say enough. Suffice that, after three days of much enjoyment, both lively and serene, we proceeded homewards, Mr. Ryland westward, and the Bostonians to Loch Katrine, all parting with much mutual regret. A period follows of which I have a very confused recollection from the rapid succession of strangers, with letters of introduction, to whom I felt obliged, as best I could, to do the honors of Edinburgh. They were persons whom it was a pleasure to see and serve, but came in such quick succession that they have not kept the place they deserved in my memory. Mrs. Fletcher had gone with her family to visit her relations in Yorkshire. Every one else that strangers care for was out of town, by which means I stood alone to do these duties of hospitality. In August Mrs. F., with her daughters, went to London. My son was pressed to spend his holidays with our friends the Ruckers, and Angus Fletcher being to go up at the same time, they went together. Mrs. Fletcher's journey proved very interesting, from her present intercourse with persons whom to name is to praise, — Joanna Baillie, Lady Byron, Thomas Campbell, Mrs. Barbauld, Mrs. Fry, and numberless names of less renown, the rest unknown to fame. John [Mrs. Grant's son] was very fortunate in the kindness of his friends. Not content with showing him all that could amuse or improve him, they went purposely to Oxford, staying two days to show it to him, and carried him on a tour they were making to the Isle of Wight. He staid six or seven weeks. Meantime, we too had an enjoyment. I must go back to tell you Miss North, a little before this time, went reluctantly to London; that Miss Futher, a very fine girl, and her brothers, two handsome, modest, and well informed young man, were among our summer guests — that they wished her to return, but she implored and

APPENDIX

obtained a respite for another year — that they carried her with them all over the Highlands for a fortnight, which delighted them not a little, and confirmed her Scottish mania; also that Moore [Mrs. Grant's daughter], taking a fancy to spend a little time in the sheltering retreats of beautiful Dunkeld, we proceeded there early in August, and though pressed by many Highland friends to stay with them, and within a day's journey of Laggan, I took lodgings in the pretty little town of Dunkeld. I received a letter from the Duchess of Athol, then at Blair, giving free access to all her walks and gardens in that delightful spot. The clergy of the place (there are two) are both learned and most agreeable men, and made to us the most pleasant neighbors imaginable. We were overwhelmed with kindness by the gentry in the vicinity, and certainly before the cordiality of Highland kindness that of others sinks into mere civility. Seeing we would not come, they sent us everything you could think of — among the rest a pretty little pony for Moore to ride as long as pleased her, of which she made great use. The only thing like an event that occurred to us was my meeting with Prince Leopold, which took place in consequence of a visit I paid to the Izetts of Kinnaird. Mrs. Izett, a very amiable woman, with a highly cultivated mind, was the particular friend of the late Mrs. Brunton, to whom her published letters are chiefly addressed. Staying a few very pleasant days with her, half-way betwixt Dunkeld and Blair, we heard the Prince, who had dined the day before with the Duke, was to pass through the Kinnaird grounds on his way to Lord Breadalbane's. Resolved on getting a complete view of him, we went down to the River Tummel, where he must needs cross. He left his horses to be fed in the village, and crossed with the intention to walk on, attended by only three or four gentlemen. He met us, and spoke to us. I was formally introduced to him, conversed with him a little, and might have prolonged that pleasure had I not been doubtful of encroaching on his politeness. I was charmed with his appearance. Yet his singular fate — the sudden elevation and more sudden depression of "this husband of a year, this father of a day" — pressed so heavily on my mind, that I spoke to him with a hesitation that the sense of superior rank would never have produced. Do you remember Colonel Stuart? Now I think of it, he was not in Edinburgh in your day.

He was the Prince's cicerone in his native Breadalbane, and a very fit one, for a truer or braver Highlander breathes not. Three weeks, three little weeks, I spent in Athol, and then removed to Dumblane, on account of its medicinal waters, recommended to Moore. This abode too I liked exceedingly — the old Cathedral, the solemn walks, the good Bishop Leighton's memory and his library, had all charms for me; but the greatest charm was that leisure and perfect freedom to which in general I am so much a stranger, and living for the time merely with and for my dear girls. We lived a great deal within that fortnight, and sadly reluctant was I to leave, though a call of duty as well as of friendship summoned me at the time, and I left Isabella and Moore to enjoy the quiet and the waters a week longer. I found my sick friend better, and then went to spend three happy weeks at Jordanhill, with that dear family whose firm and tender attachment has been the cordial of my life for forty years past, and whose excellent children inherit their parents' feelings towards me and mine. Three other weeks passed here, I need not say how pleasantly. I was then obliged to return home, having to meet a gentleman who had placed a daughter with me, Ildeton by name. I should have staid on the way with the Hon. Mrs. Erskine at Amendell, whom you must remember. She remembers you perfectly. We had agreed to pass the week of the musical festival, which we both wished to avoid, in this retreat, but it could not be. What I dreaded took place. I was obliged to go to the festival, and to see a balloon fly over the Calton Hill, etc. The consequence was that I caught a violent cold, attended with other unpleasant symptoms. I was seriously ill, and kept the house six weeks. I began to go out a very little, and was really much better, when Mrs. Erskine prevailed on me, very easily indeed, to accompany her, with one other lady. Here I am so very well, so perfectly quiet, spending my time so much to my wish, and in such congenial society. Hearing too such good accounts of Moore, that I dread next week, when I must fly this abode of pensive peace to mingle with the crowd, and be at cross purposes about various engagements. Now, after all this egotism, it is time to speak of other people. We have Miss Stanger, very much improved, and Miss Ildeton, from England; Miss Steven, much come out and handsome, and a fine, good girl; Miss Crochs from the West Country. Miss Edward and Mr. Crawford fell out violently, — he went to London, and she to old friends near Leith, who brought her up. They wished to seclude her among them from a fear that she would, doubtless, marry Captain Macdonald. I understand she is about to leave them, and think it is likely she will marry the Captain after all. Do you remember the Captain's pretty sister, Jacobina? She is lately married to a very ill-looking and very silly Yorkshire baronet, under age, — some years younger than herself, but possessed of twelve thousand a year. Her sister is gone up with her. A marriage has just taken place which gives the utmost concern to the friends of both parties. It is that of the thrice beautiful Miss Maclean with a very idle and shallow young man, Clark, a younger brother of Clark of Comrie, totally unprovided, and without any feasible prospect. They say the glory of carrying her off privately was the chief motive. I was thunderstruck at hearing this to-day, having imagined that she was on the way to India with Lady Loudon or Hastings. You hardly know so much of young Lady Thomas Cochran as would make you sorry for her death, which happened a month ago, after the birth of a child. You remember the Stotts. Their son is gone to Oxford this season, and they are very sensibly gone too — to watch over him. Do you remember Mr. Frederic Grant? He is just married to a very lovely and accomplished girl of his own name, who was a while our very pleasant inmate. They are gone, accompanied by her sister, to spend a year on the Continent. You may possibly meet them in Paris; pray be on the lookout for them. How much I should admire the taste of Augustus [Thorndike] if it led him to fall in love with her! He will see few so elegant, none more amiable or accomplished. I heard of a loss with much regret to-day, though not with more concern than the news of Miss Maclean's marriage. It is the death of that of an excellent and much loved person, Mrs. Col. Gerrard, the daughter of Rev. Mr. Allison, and the mother of five children. It took place in Lausanne, where she went in full health, and caught this fatal typhus fever. I thank you for translating to me in idea the great sublime of nature, which carried you "Beyond the visible Diurnal sphere," while the Alps in all their lofty grandeur and snowy purity lay before you. I have much curiosity about Bohemia. Why did you not tell me more of my long admired and much approved Tyrolese? I would tell you much of Edinburgh, and all the architectural wonders that have been wrought in your absence, but I have a strong hope that you will see it again, and wish you to be agreeably surprised. Mr. Arthur, a gentleman of family with a strong taste for literature, is with his family at Tours. His wife is a sister of Mrs. Gillies, and was a visitor of mine. Will you deliver my compliments to her? I know some other people at Tours, but forget at this moment who they are. Crawford is coarse, but not malicious. I take it that Miss Edward, who has a great relish for the pleasure of giving pain, took particular pains to make him jealous of you. He said to me that you were full of nonsensical German romance, and I do not think he said more to any one. All reporters, whether in or out of the House of Commons, are given to exaggerate. I say nothing of the acts of Radicals — you will find them all in the papers — only that I view them with a countenance more in sorrow than in anger, and not in the least in fear. I am glad Augustus goes home. My good wishes follow him. I wish they could overtake him with the effect of making him do justice to a very good heart and respectable understanding. Write from Paris, and believe me, with sincere good will and much regard,

Yours,   ANNE GRANT.

P. S. — Answered instantly upon receipt. Mrs. Erskine sends her compliments to you, and wishes much that you were here again with us.

101, PRINCES STREET, [EDINBURGH] 24th May, 1819.

MY DEAR SIR, — I received your letter with very great pleasure, for I do love to be remembered, and were I writing of you instead of addressing yourself to you, I should describe the sort of persons by whom I most desire to be remembered. But you are so tenderly cherished by friends whose praise is fame, that my mite of approbation would scarce be noticed amidst the abundance of these testimonies of affection, sweetened with encomiums (more sincere than most such), that you receive from others. Now, I purposely delayed writing that I might not send fear or sorrow over the sea. Yet I have begun very meritoriously in the pangs of a rheumatic toothache, but this is merely pain, which you know some philoso-

APPENDIX

phers considered as no evil. So do not I. But you know too well when we have felt the extremity of mental agony how lightly mere bodily pain appears in comparison. But now to my narration. Soon after I received your letter I was seized with an influenza, which has for some weeks past been epidemical in town. Isabella had it before, in her meek, quiet way saying very little about it. Nor should I have said much had it not come in a questionable hour, with so violent and continual a cough, that I had not an interval of quiet. This lasted three weeks. I am thankful to say I am now quite well. But a much greater alarm awaited me. Moore, my dear Moore, whose sound and powerful mind has been so long and severely tried with illness, was recovering very fast and preparing her dress to go out, when she was seized so very severely with this influenza that we were terrified for the result. It came in the shape of fever, and has reduced her very much, but, thank God, she is now decidedly recovering, though still confined to bed, and her medical attendant thinks that this will be the means of curing her tedious rheumatism. I have been the fuller in these details to account for my silence. I do not like to practise on the feelings of my absent friends, and therefore seldom acquaint them with any crisis of this nature till it determines one way or other. Before I close this list of calamities I must call forth your sympathy for one in which your countryman has been involved, — not being so selfish as to demand it all for Scottish suffering. The all-accomplished Mr. Livingston, like many other distinguished characters, prides himself most on that in which he excels least; namely, horsemanship, which he seems (or did seem) to class with the moral virtues. He came to us one night in a state of visible perturbation. We thought something terrible had happened, and so it proved. For a little horse, a most treacherous, deceitful animal, had run off with him for some miles. Preserving his balance without being thrown off and arriving safe in town, appeared to him such an exploit as to deserve an ovation at least. Meantime he had evidently come to tell us lest we should have heard it reported to his disadvantage, and was most anxious to show us it was from no defect in his skill that this happened. In less than a fortnight, as he was riding past the post office, his horse fell with him and broke his arm at the elbow in the most painful and shattering way imaginable. You can conceive nothing more distressing, and he has not even the consolation of looking like a hero of a duel, with his arm in a scarf. He is forced to hold it perpendicularly down, and will have no use of his arm for many months. I am quite seriously vexed for him. He is not in visiting condition, you may suppose. I heard to-day that the accident happened by his throwing himself in a fright from the horse. Though he does not visit in general he comes often here, and we are at pains to amuse him. Miss Edmund has left us for some time to stay with old friends at the seaside. Of literary news I have little. Dr. Brunton has published a short, modest, and very well written memoir of his admirable wife, with a fragment of a tale beautifully executed, as far as it goes, which she left unfinished, and some partial extracts of a journal in which her vigorous mind and sound discernment are very obvious. Campbell's Specimens of English Poetry, with short critical notices, appeared, I think, before you left us. The little of himself that intervenes between these specimens is exquisite. I read them over and over with ever new delight, and when I cease reading a sensation remains on my mind that makes me think of what Milton says:

> "The Angel ended, but in Adam's ear
> So charming left his voice, that he awhile
> Still thought him speaking, still stood fixed to hear."

So much refinement without fastidiousness, such perfect delicacy and truth of taste, and moreover so much truth and wisdom conveyed in language of classical purity and unequalled sweetness. People growl at there being so little of these precious strictures. Would they drink champagne out of tumblers? The Blackwood has lost all shame. The last number is perfectly vindictive against the Whig observances in the bitterest satire and the keenest ridicule. There is, for instance, an Alphabet on the plan of A. was an archer and shot at a frog, etc., in which each name has some undesirable attribute. There are such complaints as might remind one of "Cocytus named for lamentation loud." They meantime sell four thousand numbers and laugh at censure. The Rev. Mr. Morehead has undertaken Constable's Magazine, the Crafty man having as usual quarrelled with his Editors and dismissed them.

APPENDIX 245

Wordsworth has published a Peter Bell, enough to make the gravest laugh, the worthiest weep; it is so absurd, and the worthless waste of an amiable man's talents is so lamentable. It is a kind of sequel to the Lyrical Ballads. The White Doe was below zero, and this is below the White Doe. Some wag anticipated without seeing it, and published a very comical Peter Bell of his own, assuring his readers that this was the real Simon pure, and that any appearing after, must be a counterfeit. There is also a very witty Examiner published in ridicule of Leigh Hunt's, as written by himself. The Edinburgh Review has come out two days ago, duller than I have ever known it, containing, however, very just praise of Campbell and quite sufficiently laudatory of Samuel Rogers, whose poems I like better than I thought I should. All the other articles are medical, surgical or Broughamical. That is, it is loaded with a long bitter defence of Brougham about the schools, defending him from the strictures in the Quarterly. The hostility between these rival powers grows daily warmer. I compare them to two champions in the lists, while Blackwood and Constable appear in their respective magazines as the attendant squires of these doughty knights. Walter Scott called the other day to take leave, saying he could not go away without shaking hands with me, but was afraid so much had he been shaken that I would scarcely know him, but mistake him for a Potato Bogle! Pity an image so thoroughly Scotch, and so untranslatable, should be lost on you![1] It is time now to do what a well-bred person would have done at first, *i.e.*, advert to your letter. I was aware that your voyage would be neither short nor pleasant. I am charmed with your intelligent peasant that loved his own ugly country so well. Such countries are always best loved by such of the natives as are capable of loving anything. You know better than I can tell you what an added demonstration this affords of the benevolent wisdom that governs all. But you cannot know so well as I could tell you, how many endearing virtues often flourish best in barren soils. But having been already "as tedious as a King," I do not feel

[1] A dozen years later Sir Walter made use of the same expression when Washington Irving called on the illustrious author then in London, on his way to Italy, in the vain hope of restoring his shattered health. *Vide* "Bryant and his Friends," p. 163, New York, 1886.

inclined to bestow much more of my tediousness upon your worship. I might have addressed you in terms sentimental or metaphysical considering where this will find you. But you will meet so much of both these commodities where you are, that it is needless to send over the sea what you have in abundance, and I wish merely to amuse you. You are far too well governed, I trust, in all that is right, to seek advice from me, and I have no ambition to be considered a fine letter writer, so you must accept a little harmless gossip. Lady Buchan has been dead about a week, to his Lordship's undissembled joy, and he has already asked and been refused by a young lady, but will learn to be satisfied with some more humble choice. The Fletchers are very well and inquire of you very tenderly. The young ones talk of a short tour to the Continent. I beg to be kindly remembered to Augustus [Thorndike], for whom I retain no small kindness, though I am provoked at his not doing more justice to himself. He is the prey of self-distrust, while others with neither his goodness of heart nor abilities, being themselves forward by mere dint of self-opinion and confident address. I am glad that you will return less Germanized than formerly. Herman is a very honest and willing and laborious drudge in the mine of science. But his taste is bad and his notions crude and unformed. His religion is very sentimental, mystic, and approaching to Deistical. And good that doubleth has a little trimming of French tinsel of which he is himself insensible. Then he will talk — ye gods, how he will talk ! — and after all his talk is " rendered heavily, heavily " by the enthusiastic German philosopher Sir William Hamilton, who spoke much and very kindly of you. Now that this paper is done, I think of things I should have told you. Let me hear how you get on. All this family send affectionate remembrances to you.

I am, with sincere regard, very much yours,

ANNE GRANT.

Never was May so mild, so showery and so flowery as this.

MOUNT ANNAN, 22 August, 1820.

MY DEAR SIR, — You have escaped from me while my hands were stretched out in all directions to seize upon you. It grieved me not a little, in the first place, that I was forced to leave Edinburgh while you were there. Then I flattered myself with having enough of antiquated attraction to keep you a day at Moffat on your way up. Then being engaged to make a visit to General Direm's at Mount Annan, I went with the intention of returning to bonny Moffat when I should hear that you were in Edinburgh, that I might meet you. John wrote to me that you were leaving Edinburgh on the ensuing Friday. I was bustling about my preparations for departure. My friends, understanding my motive, persuaded me that by leaving them at the time, I should pass you on the road. I wrote to Isabella at their request to direct you and your companion, if such you had, to come here on your way to Mount Annan, just overlooking the town of Annan, through which you must necessarily pass. Not content with authorizing this invitation, the General, who is an excellent person, sent a note himself to the inn where the coach stops, inviting you. We meanwhile thought every person less than six feet high who came up the avenue must needs be you. After all, need I add words to convince you of your importance in my eyes, or of the excess of disappointment when informed by a letter from Isabella this evening, saying you had been hastily called to London, and if I wished to give you the last remaining proof of my tenderness, I must write to you there immediately. This, you see, I am doing with all my might, though the man is hurrying to the post office, and though this fine house of Mount Annan, which abounds in pleasant people and good things, does not after all afford a tolerable pen. Judge how eloquent I should be if I had a very good one. In this inspiring place, where the Cumberland mountains are in full sight of my window, and where every town and stream speak of the "Bold Buccleuch" and Willy of Kinmont, of belted knights and desperate forays, I cannot so much as walk among these beautiful shades by moonlight for fear of meeting one of the Wardens of the English Border. When will so many associations and so many dignified spectres meet you on the other side of the Atlantic? The most you have to look at is the angry spirit of some old sachem who died of new rum or the smallpox, given him by his white friends. For Washington and Patrick Henry must be at east a hundred years dead before they can

> " Revisit thus the glimpses of the moon,
> Making night hideous."

248 APPENDIX

For a ghost to appear impressive must be as long dead before he is awful, as a Catholic saint before he is canonized.

You are perhaps shocked at all this levity in a farewell letter, but pray observe, I do not consider it such. You cannot do less after all my solicitude than write to me from London. Answer you I shall, though

> "Broad seas between us roll and roar."

And see you I will, having already a "second sight" of you landing at Greenock. I dare say, however, you may take a fancy to see your new western world first. In that case you will meet Mr. Preston, and be sure you tell him that in consideration of all the good I have heard of him since he went westward, I forgive his breach of promise to me. This kind message will at once prove my constancy, my clemency, and my high esteem for even imperfect virtue, for, had his been perfect, he would have kept his word. I will not say how sorry I shall be not to see you more, or allow myself to think the separation final. I thought (what did I not think?) of the many letters I was to send by you to my many American friends, but you see that cannot be. Remember me, however, tenderly to Mrs. Jackson, whom I highly esteem, and fondly to Sarah Lowell, whom I truly love, centering in her and her brother the regard now exalted into veneration, which I felt for the departed worthies of their family. If you see Mr. Bigelow, pray tell him that I did not receive his long letter of last year, though I acknowledged it in a hurry by mistake. Augustus [Thorndike] has been too long in France to care about old friends or early recollections, else I should send him my kind regards. Present them, however, to Mr. Ticknor.[1]

---

[1] The following extract from a letter addressed to a Transatlantic correspondent, also alludes to Mr. George Ticknor of Boston, and several other friends and visitors from the new world : "The American character has been much raised among our literary people here, by a constellation of persons of brilliant talents and polished manners, by whom we were dazzled and delighted last winter. A Mr. Preston of Virginia (South Carolina) and his friend from Carolina, whose name I cannot spell, for it is French (Hugh S. Legarè), Mr. Ticknor and Mr. Cogswell were the most distinguished representatives of your new world. A handsome and high bred Mr. Ralston, from Philadelphia, whose mind seemed equal to his other attractions, left also a very favorable impression of Transatlantic accomplishments. These

APPENDIX

The Post calls. Pray write from London, and believe, wherever you go, you will be followed by the affectionate good wishes of, dear sir,

Yours most cordially,   ANNE GRANT.

101 PRINCES STREET, April 14, 1821.

MY DEAR SIR, — You cannot suppose me to have forgotten you, though perhaps I have been too long in telling you so. Your affectionate and most valued letter on the eve of departure from the old world filled me with regret at your departure and concern for your health. That seemed too good an excuse for your not coming to Moffat. You cannot imagine how we all luxuriated in the simple, pastoral, and mild tranquillity of our most desirable abode there. I wished you to have a picture of that green dale of many pure streams with its sheltering mountains, and the friends who so often spoke and thought of you there, to sooth your imagination where you could only see meeting seas and skies. I thank you for the affectionate expression of your regard, because I know it to be perfectly sincere. So Hamlet says to Horatio : " Why should the poor be flattered ? " Amidst very many and very deep afflictions the consolation has been vouchsafed to me of dwelling in comfort with the excellent of the earth, and breathing in such an atmosphere of the warmest friendship and purest virtue that I must have been something more " Than fables e'er have feigned or been conceived " not to profit by such an association. I was certainly very anxious to know of your health after your arrival, and did hear good accounts of you, but I cannot remember how. Indeed my recollections have been a good deal confused in consequence of an accident which endangered my life, and has confined me to the house in a very helpless state all winter. I am really tired of answering inquiries about this same fall, and most unwilling to sink into the habits too frequent among invalids of my age and sex — that of making myself and my personal calamities the subject of wearisome details. I have been obliged to tell the sad story of the fall and its conse-

were all very agreeable persons, Mr. Ticknor pre-eminently so, and I can assure you ample justice was done to their merits here."

quences so frequently that I revolt at the repetition of it, but from our mutual friends, the Sewells, you can hear all the painful particulars. The enjoyment of last summer and autumn, the tranquil freedom and domestic comforts of Moffat, and the succeeding delights of the Southern Border more vivid and more varied required a counterbalance, and they have found it.

I do not exactly recollect whether you traced the classic streams of the Tweed, the Jed, and the Teviot in the same direction that I did when paying a visit to an old friend in September last. Yet from your ardent curiosity about things worth seeing, I think you must have gone there were it but to see the fine skeleton of Melrose Abbey, beautiful in decay and commemorated in all its pristine dignity in "The Monastery," which I take it for granted you have read, and which I value much more than most readers do, because it contains an accurate and pleasing sketch of a mode of life hitherto nondescript, yet very interesting. That the church vassals were indeed the only vassals in those troublous times who quietly enjoyed the fruits in the stormy bounds of the restless Borders, such a peaceful and comparatively free community is as refreshing to the mind that contemplates it as a green oasis must have been in the wastes of Arabia Deserta. Glendearg did not live merely in my imagination, for before quitting the fair region of shadowy recollections I spent two or three days at the house of a gentleman who lives a mile from the Abbey, and by the individual ford where the white hind mounted behind the mule of the bewildered priest. On the other side of the Tweed opposite is a very narrow glen, terrific for the common people from the noise of winds and falling waters heard fitfully through its narrow winding bounds. The common people call it the fairy glen. It has indeed no other. It ascends slowly through Lord Somerville's grounds till it reaches the boundary hills and wild moorlands, at which termination are still remaining the ruins of a small fortalice. My friends and I tried this romantic and gloomy recess as far as we could go without a carriage, but the path to the ruin is only fit for mules or foot passengers. We went, however, further than we ought, for it was so late that we made out our way with difficulty, and this under thick shades by the gleams of a clouded moon. We returned very weary and very charitably disposed toward the credulous peasantry, considering too that the musical contests of rival owls were at the same time making night hideous. The Magician of the Border has always originals in view, which is one reason that his pictures seem always about to walk out of their frames.

I had great pleasure in my visit to this famous Minstrel, not only from the cordiality of my reception, but from seeing him look so much better than I hoped, for his health had been very indifferent before, but seems now quite restored. That happy pair (then happy), John Lockhart and his wife, were there, — indeed her father could not live without Sophie, and is almost equally fond of her husband. Poets and Prophets were said to have been, neither indeed can exist, without an inspiration. We talked of that most outrageous affair about the atrocious Queen which raged like a pestilence, and was spread both by the deceivers and the deceived. He said that of these fits of national excitement there had been various instances, though none so extravagant as the present. He added that these fits had always a crisis, and were generally succeeded by a great revulsion of opinion, attended by shame and remorse. I was glad to have his sanction of my own opinion, and the end has justified his prediction. People here who from the mere spirit of party (never a moral spirit had supported the canonization of Saint Caroline) are now so much ashamed that I could not be so cruel as to remind them of their folly or worse. Indeed the party begin to look very foolish and crestfallen. They had one short triumph of malignity lately occasioned by the fatal duel which poor John Scot brought upon himself by his most unwarranted and outrageous attack upon John Lockhart. John went up to London in consequence of Scot's telling his friend there that he was willing and ready to give him satisfaction. When Lockhart very unexpectedly made his appearance in London John Scot shrunk from the contest in a manner which in the fashionable world was considered evasive, as poor Scot could not take credit for having avoided the combat from a religious scruple. He began to feel most bitterly the obloquy that must follow a most gross and unprovoked insult followed by an evasion from either making a due acknowledgment or having recourse to the usual resource for wounded honor. In a fit of desperation he flew to John Lockhart's friend and dragged him out by moonlight to find means of recovering the honor he was considered to have lost. Chrystie fired purposely past him, but by some fatal misapprehension he, Scot, continued the combat, and fell. When the news arrived here Lockhart fainted upon hearing it, and was with difficulty recovered. When the party saw he was so sensitive upon the occasion, they spared no artifice to put his feelings and those of his family to torture. But no more of this ungracious theme. Offences must come, but woe to those by whom they come. And one has some shame of the woe in resisting them.

At this moment an universal shade of woe hangs over Edinburgh from a very different cause. Dr. Gregory is gone, lamented by all, and has left no adequate successor. I mourn for him not merely as a person I always admired and revered, but as a noble specimen of genius and unblemished virtue, cast in a most peculiar mould. . . . What an ancestry he had to look back had not his own individual greatness been sufficient. On his Father's side a race of Sages and Saints, eminent for science and beloved for goodness. He was the fifth distinguished Gregory of his line — I mean in the paths of science. That ancestor who was the favored friend of Sir Isaac Newton had three sons who, at the same time, held the three mathematical chairs of Oxford, Edinburgh, and Aberdeen. Dr. Gregory's mother was a daughter of Lord Forbes, the eldest Scotch Baron. On that side nobles and heroes graced the line to which he gave additional lustre. He was not a man to die rich, but added to the inheritance of such a name his family will have what will support them. Very rich he might have been.

You mentioned in your letter the possibility, or more, of your being here in the Spring, and perhaps this letter may miss you. It is sent by a very amiable person, the Rev. Matthias Bruen,[1] whom you would like very much if you knew him, and who has contributed, with others you know, to leave a most favorable impression

---

[1] A clergyman who for many years was in charge of the Bleecker Street Presbyterian Church, New York. His widow survived until the last decade of the nineteenth century, and a short time before her death Mrs. Bruen sent her granddaughter, now the wife of Admiral Beaumont, R.N., for a certain small box, and taking from it a sheaf of silvered hair, presented it to her friend Mrs. Pruyn of Albany. Mrs. Grant had cut it off and given it to Mrs. Bruen more than half a century previous. A part of it is among my most valued relics.

of the American character among us. I assure you it never stood so high as it does at present. Mr. Ticknor, Mr. Preston, and yourself are tenderly remembered and often inquired after, especially by the whole of the Clan Fletcher. Indeed among all our friends the Sketch Book has greatly increased this prepossession. It is universally read and admired beyond measure. In short, I think we are all very much inclined at present, like good old people as we are, to dote on our grand-children in the western world. Now, if they had any such sympathy as that Milton tells us of, Eve's shadow in the Lake which came forward to meet her with answering looks of love, all would be well. But while you are all seduced from your first and best love by the godless gaieties and the dreaming and sceptical metaphysics of Germany, we hope in vain to attract you. There is a very fine young man here now whom I and every one else admires very much — a Mr. Middleton from South Carolina, very cultivated, with pleasing manners, but I fear, like all from the Southern states, no true Anti-Gallican.

If you came here now you would be astonished at the extension and improvement of Edinburgh since you saw it. The Fletchers [1] are well, and frequent in their inquiries for you. Now you must write immediately, and tell me a great deal about Mr. Ticknor, to whom I will address a few lines by Mr. Bruen, if he does not go till the mail-coach departs to-morrow. In any event I will write to him soon. You will be sorry to hear that my poor Moore has lost during the winter all that she gained in summer. But I hope this season will do much for her. She shall not be another winter in this climate, if God graciously pleases to spare her to me. All the rest are well, and I look forward with humble hope to a complete recovery, though still a prisoner of hope. Accept the cordial good wishes of the whole family, also of all the Fletchers, and

[1] Mrs. Grant and Mrs. Eliza Fletcher (1770–1858) were the two most distinguished literary ladies of Edinburgh, who received visits from almost all strangers of note. Both were fine conversationalists. Mrs. Grant, an extreme Tory, rejoiced in a wide Tory coterie, and Mrs. Fletcher, an equally staunch Whig, was surrounded by a large Whig circle, but, notwithstanding their differing politics, they were most cordial and sincere friends. The latter was a lovable lady, who seems, according to her portraits at fifteen and eighty, to prove that there is a beauty for every age. Her surviving child, the widow of Sir John Richardson, the Arctic explorer, edited her mother's autobiography. 8vo, London, 1874.

others whom I cannot enumerate. Offer the same to Mr. Ticknor, and believe me, with esteem and affection,

Yours truly, ANNE GRANT.

101 PRINCES STREET, June 24, 1821.

MY DEAR SIR, — When my mind is easier, I will endeavor to write you an entertaining letter, not depending on the exertion of my own powers, but from having the means of telling you much of a tribe and people, both which I give you credit for remembering very kindly. At present my communications must be very limited, even confined to that domestic circle by which as by some magic spell my thoughts have been for some time circumscribed. I cannot tell you of moving accidents of flood and field, like poor Othello, nor yet of those strange people who each other eat, though I could tell you of several who seemed much inclined to do so, and of many singular characters which came in my way last summer. I must allow that, however singular in other respects, their heads do grow above their shoulders, and very extraordinary heads some of them are. Certainly I could make an amusing letter of the transactions of last summer if I were not obliged to furnish a very sombre one from the events succeeding these pleasant scenes and people which memory delights to cherish. When then after my most quiet and enjoyable residence at sweet pastoral Moffat, where I wish much you had seen me, and where I cultivated an intimacy with Dr. Ryerson, a wonderful evergreen sage, who flourished nearly fifty years as first physician in the great court of not good Catherine and that of her mad grandson of Russia. I have rarely met at any time with a person of such a sound and lively intellect — well bred, well informed, and most particularly judicious in laying among his humble friends in Dumfries the fruits of his own industry, and the munificence of his Imperial mistress. I wish I could tell you of a fortnight I spent at Gen. Direm's, at his beautiful seat at Mount Annan, which overlooks the Solway Firth, and where I met some much valued companions of my early days, meanwhile feeling that my dear Moore was getting better ; and that my no less dear Isabella and she were very much enjoying the calm delights of Moffat gave me spirit to relish every circumstance contributing to enjoyment. In the beginning of September I came down a month before they returned to show Edinburgh to a very pleasing guest from Ireland, who here made a pilgrimage from Harrowgate to see me. After giving ten days to her I went to Roxburgh, where for years past I promised to visit an old friend at Jedburgh and where I passed a fortnight in wakening dreams and reveries in that land of recollections where the Tweed and Teviot flow through the greenest pastoral vales sung by the sweetest of pastoral, really pastoral poets. While the dark heaths, the battlefields of old, renowned in Scottish classics and heroic ballads, as well as the fine remains of castles and abbeys, preserve the memory of sages, saints, and patriot, heroes that live in every truly Scottish breast. But I cannot wait to describe my pilgrimage through this land of memorials or how high my national spirit soared when I came to the spot consecrated of old and rising in renewed celebrity —

" Where Tweed flows round holy Melrose,
And Eldon slopes to the plain."

I did indeed think the scene very sad and fair, and required all the fraternal cordiality with which I was received at Abbotsford to revive my spirits. I never saw the Great Magician look so well, and regretted that I deferred my visit till my return homewards, when my time was very limited.

. . . .

You will probably have heard of John Wilson's violent struggle for the chair of moral philosophy and of his ultimate success.[1] Sir William Hamilton was the unsuccessful candidate, though very well qualified and abounding in friends, but the Scotchman had loaded poor John with so many slanderous accusations that proved

[1] Mrs. Grant contributed to " Christopher North's " success by writing a strong letter in his behalf, dwelling particularly on his excellent private character, which had been attacked. It was to the Professor that our author was indebted for the title of " Queen of the Blue-Stockings." Scott on one occasion said, " She was so very cerulean," and Lockhart described her as " a shrewd and sly observer." Alluding to one of the series of Scott's novels that appeared about this period (1822), Mrs. Grant wrote to a friend, " I had a letter informing me that ' The Fortunes of Nigel,' in England, is accounted a failure. Honest John Bull has not seen such a failure on his side of the Tweed since Shakespeare's time."

unfounded, that he was elected to clear his character, and mortify his enemies. His class is large, and his lectures said to be very elegant. Sir William next winter takes the historical chair. Perhaps I do not express it right. Prof. Seresby is prosecuting Blackwood for accusing him of ignorance in the Hebrew tongue, and Lord Archibald Hamilton, the Corypheus of the Scotch Whigs, prosecutes the Beacon for saying that he and his brother, the Duke, deserted their part at Hamilton last year for fear of the very Radicals whom their croaking had encouraged. As they actually did run away the trial is likely to be a merry one, at least his Lordship, like Falstaff, will be the cause of wit in others. The Beacon is a paper offered to the Scotchmen, abounding in coarse humor. It is the Scotch John Bull. Who are right and wrong in this contest I pretend not to say, yet I think I can apprehend pretty clearly who are witty and who dull. Twenty years ago the triumphs of intellect were all on the side of the Whigs. They said, "We are the People, and Wisdom shall die with us." Many of these meteors have been quenched in the darkness of the grave, and the few survivors are grown worldly, dry and dull enough. The light troops of imagination seem all engaged on the other side, and the rising brood of young Tories sparkle with no common effulgence. The King's promised visit, if it takes place, will increase the number of deserters from the ancient faith. They will be stigmatized as Rats, but will find comfort in supposing that their adversaries look as small as mice on that occasion. Tom Hamilton, Sir William's brother, who is the O'Doherty of Blackwood, was, to the wonder of all beholders, married. His wife was a Miss Campbell, elegant in person and manners, highly cultivated, and possessed of a considerable fortune, of which the standard bearer had great need. Gillies, to whose political fame you can be no stranger, has gone with his family, by way of doing something original, to Germany. The Fletchers are away for a year's residence to Yorkshire, on account of some old Aunt they have there. I grieve to say that James Wilson, who certainly has more real genius than any man in Edinburgh, has been for a twelve-month past with his sisters in Italy, on account of his health. They went to take care of him, but he is coming home very little if any-

APPENDIX

thing better. Tell Mr. Jay,[1] with my compliments, that Miss Glassel,[2] that was, who lived with me for some years and is now Lady John Campbell, has a son who will some time be Duke of Argyll. All that shire was in a blaze with bonfires and illuminations on the occasion. You will receive this from Mr. Greenwood, whom we all consider a very pleasing specimen of Transatlantic manners and abilities. I have made in my present state of mind no small effort for your amusement. Pray do as much for mine. You know how many of your fellow-citizens are to me most interesting. Adieu, dear sir. Accept the kind regards of all here, as well as those of

Yours very truly,   ANNE GRANT.

[1] Peter Augustus Jay, eldest son of Governor John Jay. He was a prominent member of the New York Bar, a gentleman of many accomplishments, and exceedingly active in the social affairs of the city during the first third of the nineteenth century. As a young man, Mr. Jay accompanied his father as Secretary, when he was appointed Minister to the Court of St. James, by Washington, in 1794.

[2] Miss Glassel, who spent several years with Mrs. Grant, and later married Lord John Campbell, was the mother of the eighth Duke of Argyll, who expressed to the editor of this volume, both in conversation and correspondence, much admiration for the literary ability of the author of "The American Lady."

APPENDIX

CORRESPONDENCE BETWEEN MRS. ALEXANDER HAMILTON AND MRS. GRANT

MRS. HAMILTON TO MRS. GRANT

NEW YORK, June 13, 1834.

DEAR MADAM,—The kindness with which you have recollected all your early associations with my family, and the interest with which your genius has created in the name of Schuyler, have prompted me to address you this note. You will perhaps derive pleasure from learning the state of our family. My brother Philip resides in this city, in easy opulence, enjoying the respect of the community with which our hereditary disease, the gout, does not permit him often to mingle. He has two sons, one a confirmed bachelor, the other secretly engaged to marry with one of my granddaughters. Philip, the son of my brother John, lives at the family seat of Saratoga, and is happily married to a beautiful woman. They have eight daughters and a son. My brother Rensselaer resides not far from him on the upper waters of the Hudson. My only surviving sister married Mr. Cochran and lives at Oswego, where also resides a daughter of my sister Angelica.[1] The home of her brother Philip

---

[1] Among a sheaf of Mrs. Grant's unpublished correspondence, I find the following letter, dated New York, August 19th, 1811, signed "Angelica Church, born Schuyler," and addressed, "Mrs. Grant, authoress of the Memoirs of an American Lady, Edinburgh." As it has no postmark, it was probably sent by private hand. Mrs. Church writes: "I have read with so much pleasure the Memoirs of my aunt, whose virtues and manners you have so faithfully delineated, that I feel myself impressed with a fervid desire to recall myself to your remembrance. But whether you recollect or not, Miss A. Schuyler, the eldest daughter of Colonel, afterwards General Schuyler, she remembers with endeared recollections the first time she saw you, in company with her governess, Mrs. Ross, at the old home on the Flats. She then felt the emanations of your genius, and naturally contrasted your conversation with that of the good, but unintelligent, young persons

APPENDIX

Church is at Angelica, in the Geneseo County, where he has been a Judge and has around him extensive possessions, a charming wife, and many children.

At the age of seventy-six I am still in the enjoyment of perfect health, seeing my sons established in life and in prosperous circumstances. Of these my third son, John,[1] has recently published the first volume of the biography of his father, of which I beg to present you a copy. Although it relates to subjects chiefly of American interest, yet you will, I hope, find many things to amuse you, showing the moral and intellectual development of a mind always exerted to promote the honor of his country and the happiness of his fellow-creatures, but of a character perhaps too frank and independent for a Democratic people. The subsequent volumes will embrace topics of high national interest and display traits of character which will make even Scotland, so fertile in genius and virtue, proud to enumerate him among her descendants. The work you will see requires every indulgence. I may hope if it comes before the Reviewers it may not receive too severe a criticism.

---

of her narrow circle. A letter from my nephew, Mr. Van Rensselaer, to his father, mentions your kind inquiries after all my family; let this also, dear Madam, excuse me for wishing to know whatever relates to you and yours. As I pass many hours at Laggan, and always visit it with renewed delight, your sorrows are my sorrows, your friends and occupations are mine, and the "Letters from the Mountains" exalt and fill the mind. But they make me sadly regret that during my long residence in London I did not know that Miss MacVickar was Mrs. Grant, and on the same island with myself, or I should have braved the bad roads over the rude mountains to have conversed with the acquaintance of my youth, and have met with her in the performance of those serious duties she so feelingly describes. If ever you do me the favor to write, pray tell me sincerely if you recalled me. There has been a most terrible flood in your former *Castle Building* Estate, Clarendon, but what gives me a peculiar interest in Clarendon, it is made classic by your enchanting pen. Adieu, dear Madam, whatever taste I have found pleasure in your writings, I have still more in the contemplation and example of your excellence, and with many recollections of times long past, I am, etc., etc.

[1] John Church (1792–1882) was Hamilton's *fourth* son, his seniors being Philip, Alexander, and James A. A second Philip was born the year after the eldest son was killed in a duel on the same spot, at Weehawken, where Burr shot his father three years later. In calling John the *third* son, Mrs. Hamilton presumably referred to the living, with all of whom the writer was acquainted.

I have received from Mrs. Douglas Cruger many interesting incidents concerning you to which I have listened with my heart. Indeed, at our age we can only enjoy life by cultivating our affections, and in no mode can we receive more lively pleasure than by continuing with a christian confidence in the future — the recollections of the days of our hopes.

With sentiments of great respect and regard, I remain, dear Madam,

Faithfully yours,   ELIZABETH HAMILTON.[1]

P. S. — Mr. O. Rich, agent for American books, Red Lion Square, London, has received instructions to deliver the volume to your order.

EDINBURGH, COATES CRESCENT, 18 November, 1834.

DEAR MADAM, — It is not easy to say how much I was delighted with the kind feeling which dictated your most welcome and gratifying letter. So many grateful and affectionate recollections of

---

[1] Born but two years after Mrs. Grant, the friend of her early days, she survived her for sixteen years. When, as a youth, the writer visited the widow of the illustrious Hamilton, she was residing with a daughter in the city of Washington, and was then in her ninety-seventh year. The venerable lady was much affected at meeting with the godson of the companion of her childhood, speaking of Mrs. Grant and the Memoir of "Aunt Schuyler," with the warmest interest. "It is eighty-six years since Anne MacVicar and Elizabeth Schuyler parted as girls of thirteen and eleven," said Mrs. Hamilton. Another of her remarks that has been cherished in her visitor's memory for almost half a century, was made after he had kissed her dainty little hand in bidding her a final farewell : " It may interest you, my dear young friend, to remember that Washington's lips frequently pressed the same hand that yours have pressed." Writing to Miss Harriet Douglas in January, 1833, before her marriage, Mrs. Grant remarks: " There is a lady in New York who was my playmate in childhood, whom you may chance to meet in society, Mrs. Hamilton, the widow of the distinguished General Hamilton, better known to me as 'Betsy Schuyler.' There were three sisters: Angelica, elegant and dignified, whom I used to look up to with great awe as a fine lady, and such in after life she proved. I had a letter from her twenty years since, introducing one of her countrymen. Then there was Betsy, good natured and unpretending ; and Margaret, very pretty, and a kind of wicked wit. I have a sort of pleasure in referring to this gossip of early days. I never forget one of those once familiarly known to me, and would not like to be forgotten by them."

your family have accompanied me through life that to think that at this advanced period I still continue to excite any interest like that which I feel for those to whom I have owed much of life's best comforts and enjoyments, soothes the decline of a life in which the severest sufferings were mingled with the purest enjoyments indulged to mortals. What has been said of the French emigrants by way of reproach, that they forgot nothing, may be truly said of me. That they learnt nothing, I hope is less applicable. I hope the wholesome chastening of affliction has not been lost on me. I remember most accurately all the little intercourse I ever had with your sisters — first at a little school in Albany, where, I suppose, we were all placed more to keep us quiet than for any other purpose — then I remember your kindness in calling on us on your way to and from Saratoga when we lived at the Flats. I remember as it were yesterday the awe and admiration with which I looked to your sister Angelica's early air of elegance and dignity when she first returned from New York. We returned to Europe in the sixty-eight, just when the clouds that presaged the Revolution, which proved in the end so happy for both countries, were gathering thick. I went out from Aunt Schuyler's to take a final leave of you all and an old friend, Mrs. Ross, who had the charge of you and of whose fate since I never could hear. To my unpractised eye your house appeared supereminently fine and spacious. The little brother you had then I hope still survives. I heard with much interest of your marriage with that highly distinguished individual who I find has left with you sons worthy of their Father, whose merits and prosperity are the greatest to you of all earthly consolations. It gives me great pleasure to hear that you desire consolation from still higher sources, and that your exemplary life is mentioned with applause by all I ever heard speak of you.

I once had a letter from Mrs. Church introducing her nephew, who was here for a good while, and have seen a little of the other young Rensselaer during their short stay here, and once of Mrs. Church, then residing in Paris, who came to see me; thus my frequent inquiries after you all still kept present to my mind the early years of happiness and improvement, for both which I am chiefly indebted to your excellent Aunt Schuyler, whom I was wont fondly to call mine. She admitted me at a childish age into a companionship very unusual in such a disparity of years, and her cordial kindness in treating me above my years produced in my mind a solidity of thought and a habit of reflection not usual in the early spring of life, which may have been an advantage to an active mind at home. I saw nothing but uprightness and piety. By the bye, I saw in a Transatlantic publication a mistake about my Father's occupation, not of the smallest consequence further than it recalls to my mind a stirring period in which he was concerned. He was a subaltern officer in the 55th, and a kind of favorite with your Father, at whose desire he was appointed Muster Master to the troops raised in New England and New York at the time of the Indian war, which broke out after the general peace. I am exceedingly glad to hear that you have a brother living in affluence and general esteem so near you. The gout which detracts from his enjoyments had, I thought, been quite a European disease. The rheumatism, I supposed, simply supplied its place with you. I am glad to hear of his son's proposed marriage. It would be a pity the direct male line should not be continued. I can easily suppose the family seat at Saratoga by this time improved into a princely residence. I see Mr. Church has piously perpetuated his mother's name in the place of his residence. Your nephew seems likely to rear a large supply of beauty to enrich my early residence. I spent most of my sixth year at Oswego when it was merely a fort, and the first thing that attracted my regard was a cow, the only existing one on that side of Johnson Hall. My surprise and admiration is continually renewed by the accounts I hear of rapid population and splendid improvements in that boundless forest that I remember. Your countrymen have indeed made the wilderness to blossom as the rose. Your wide extending populations and towns that rise like exhalations excite no little wonder, not to say envy, here. A hardy and adventurous population not tied down to fond localities and associations seem so made to promote the task of spreading knowledge and population over so ample a portion of the globe, refinement will follow too soon for peace or exertion. At present it might prove only a stumbling-block in the way of the vigor and dexterity that surmounts so many difficulties with a speed that appears to us unendible, limited as we are by the boundaries of our comparatively little island. Many of us look eagerly forward to sharing your privileges of immeasurable space and unbounded freedom. I hardly suppose the Fathers of the Revolution contemplated anything like equality such as seems the object of general aspiration with you, and in which our lower class begin very fast to emulate yours. Such certainly were not the views of Generals Washington and Hamilton, and it does not appear that any of their successors have been braver or wiser.

There is one family of your alliance that I cannot trace — that of Courtlandt Schuyler. He was a captain in our army, and married a good little Irishwoman. When I came away our good Aunt, who like the Popes, indulged much in hospitality, had taken the eldest boy, the little Courtlandt, a child of five, to domesticate with her. I met in England our favorite niece Mrs. Low in the undesirable state of an exiled loyalist with no liberal substitute for all she had lost and left behind. I met also one of Aunt's nephews, the son of a favorite sister, Cornelius Cuyler, who at a very early age, full of exuberant spirits and boyish playfulness, was sent as an ensign into my Father's regiment — I mean the same regiment. He made me a sort of plaything, but the pleasure of teasing me soon ceased. He went to England, with his regiment still, sooner than myself. At least fifty years ago, when I was on a visit in Hertfordshire, he heard and came a good distance to see me and bring me and my daughter to visit him at his newly purchased estate at St. John's Hill. He had a very pleasing wife, Grant by name, two fine youths entering upon manhood, and a pretty daughter, who just married the rector of Wellwyn, where Young died, and where the "Night Thoughts" were born. The Church and Rectory were very near the house, and I was much urged by my besetting sin to remain alone and indulge myself in some thoughts near his tomb and Lady Betty's, but having long lived under a strict regimen of self-denial I contented myself with admiring Lady Betty's needlework on the altarpiece. A large vine and full clusters were wrought upon fawn-colored satin. Beneath it a few sheep seemed sheltered. The texts inscribed were: "I am the true vine, and ye are the branches," "My sheep hear my voice," etc. General, now Sir, Cornelius Cuyler had been engrossed in a successful pursuit of ambition, had long been chief commander in the West, and was in short like the first Thane of Cawdor, a prosperous gentleman. But it did not appear that Albany, with its attractions and endearments, lived nearly so fresh in his memory as it did in mine. He was become a grave, rich, worldly man, and took little delight in my lively reminiscences. His sons, I think, are in the army. People in this country, even of distinction, are so much at a loss what to do with their sons. One of the most enviable advantages you possess over us is that you have ample room and scope enough to establish your sons in your own boundless country, while the tenderest Mothers wait anxiously for the power of sending their sons to encounter all the dangers of those fatal climates, from which so few return. Years elapsed during which I could not see without shrinking the name of that country where my beautiful, my brave, perished in the bloom of his years and of his virtues. Of my daughters I will only say that with every external advantage of form, with more than common capacities, and all that a mother could hope or pray for, they were prematurely ripened for the tomb. They indeed gave their Mother grief but when they died. Yet do not call me Mara. I did feel bitterly when all these faded in succession, but I was enabled to bear these strokes silently and consider that their constitutional fragility and great delicacy of mind fitted them so ill for the rough world they might have to encounter, as removed from the evil to come, and safely sheltered in that peaceful harbor towards which their earliest aspirations were directed. If the sympathies and kindness of the worthy and excellent could alleviate, and they did soften the sense of these privations, all that my fellow beings could do they did. I have known many whom it was an honor as well as a pleasure to know. Now my son and his wife do all that is possible to cheer my decline, and I am, I hope, truly thankful for what remains.

I should sooner have acknowledged the great favor of yours, but have waited till last week for the arrival of the Memoirs which your son has undertaken the pious task of arranging and thus doing honor both to himself and to the parent whose memory reflects so much lustre on his descendants. I immediately wrote with directions to deliver the volume to a friend of mine in London. Happening about that time to go to a distant part of the country where I staid three months, I found it had come to Edinburgh in my absence, and I am now engaged in reading it with more interest than many others could, from the assistance I derive from my recollection of what caused so much suffering and produced so much to us as well as to you. I will not affect any modesty about style ; for I think the best authors and the best conversation have in this respect made me a tolerable judge. To me the book seems to possess every advantage that many perspicuous and unaffected languages can, and quite free of that finery which I consider my old friends to have borrowed from the French, our new friends. Have the goodness, dear Madam, to transmit my best acknowledgments, and to believe that I am, with much gratitude for your kind letter,

Dear Madam, yours with respect and esteem,

ANNE GRANT.

LETTERS TO MRS. DOUGLAS CRUGER OF NEW YORK

EDINBURGH, 9th February, 1837.

MY DEAR HARRIET, — Your compliments are not acceptable to a spirit in much need of all the consolation that real and well-tried friendship can give. I have read your letter at last, with some attention, which I could not do when it arrived, my whole mind being occupied with my son's full cup of fear about his dear wife's protracted illness. She has had the influenza, which rages here like a plague, and has already cost many valuable lives, though I hope hers (the subject of many prayers) is now out of danger.

Your cousin Miss Abercromby, called on me lately with some message from Lady Abercromby, and without intending (for she is a sweet artless creature), won my heart. She seemed gratified by the acquaintance, and said she would come often to see me if agreeable. Both in her instance, and in that of a younger one who came here, I was struck with the frugal simplicity of dress which is now become fashionable even among distinguished young ladies. Two years ago, a young girl of ten or twelve was in dress just a facsimile of her mother; now, the simplest straw-bonnet, in the cottage form, shades the fairest face, and the homely gray tartan the figure is mantled in, gives you the idea of a pretty rustic at best. But all that disguise breaks off when the young lady appears in full dress, as Miss Abercromby did at a late Highland ball, where she was allowed to be the fairest of the fair.

I am glad to find you so captivated with the character of my Aunt Schuyler. You cannot form to yourself a better model of female excellence. I have, in one sense, outlived her too long; that is, I have outlived those who, at the time the book was written, remembered her, and bore testimony to the fidelity of the picture. An odd circumstance occurred when I was in London in 1808, about the period of the publication of the book. You know how partial I had ever been to the North American Indians, over whose injuries and oppressions I still mourn. My respect for the pure and peaceable doctrines and spotless lives of the Quakers was much heightened by their just and upright dealings with the Indians. William Penn was a legislator quite to my taste, admiring, as I did, the wisdom and humanity of his ordinances. It had not occurred to me, or rather I had not heard it, but it seems the Governor of Pennsylvania, the last William Penn,[1] had come over to England to seek rest from the storms of the Revolution. He was about fifty years old, with the genuine dress and air of a Quaker, yet, with this gravity, he placed his affections on Lady Juliana Fermor, daughter of the Earl of Pomfret, a young lady who, on account of her beauty and talents, was considered the ornament of the British Court. This ambitious flame was encouraged by the lady's mother, and finally by herself. It was settled, as usual in such cases, that the boys should be Quakers, and the girls of the National Church. One of the daughters, who proved afterwards a distinguished personage, was married to the Hon. William Stuart, Primate of Ireland. She took some pains to cultivate my acquaintance, as did several others of the same very agreeable family. I was rather surprised at all this kindness, until it occurred to me that some of it might be owing to a partiality for the topics in my American book. Speaking of Quakers, I have often thought it something odd, that though we are so ready to acknowledge the merit of these people, — their self-command and placid manners, — none of us would much approve of having a son a member of that amiable fraternity.

I am very glad for your own sake as well as theirs, you take so kindly to those youths whom their father left to you as a kind of legacy. The more our best affections are called forth, the happier we are. These are the treasures of the heart, and may prove invaluable. I remember, on coming first to this country from America, I used to tell people, with a kind of triumph, of the certainty of always finding children in that country about a Dutch house. Whether they were their own or not, they seemed to be

---

[1] John (not William) Penn, who was born in London, 14 July, 1729, and died in Bucks County, Pennsylvania, 9 February, 1795. His beautiful country-seat, "Lansdowne," is now a part of Fairmount Park, Philadelphia.

an article quite indispensable : whatever enlarges the circles of our affections must add to our enjoyments. . . .

I have over-written myself, and merely add every affection for Mr. Cruger and Mrs. Hasell, from

Yours, very truly,   ANNE GRANT.

EDINBURGH, 9th April, 1838.

MY DEAR HARRIET, — I am beginning to make a feeble attempt to write after recovering from a rather dangerous illness. I was tempted to make this a kind of valedictory letter, but having an impression on my mind that this long protracted life may yet continue while I can be of any use to my fellow-creatures, I will not address you for the last time. I was very much gratified to find my shadow[1] so kindly welcomed by my American friends, partly on my son's account, who was eager about forwarding it, but more particularly on that of Mr. Watson Gordon, who is by no means a mere artist, but a gentleman of refined taste, and quiet, unambitious character. I owe something to the picture for procuring me the pleasure of his acquaintance. He wrought *con amore*, and was no doubt pleased that his powers should be distinguished beyond the mighty waters of the West.

I am going to ask some questions of you, but before I begin, must entreat you to send my benediction to Mr. Preston,[2] who has done honor to himself, and given me great pleasure by advocating the cause of those noble creatures, the deeply injured Indians. Your country people used to offend me very much by the apathy with which they listened to all I could say of these "Stoics of the Woods." Often I said to myself, —

> "Forgiveness to the injured does belong,
> But they ne'er pardon who have done the wrong."

---

[1] The portrait appears as a frontispiece to this volume, for which it has been reproduced for the first time. Another of Sir John's pictures, painted for Mrs. Grant, is that of her young poet friend William Wilson, now in the possession of his son, General Wilson, of New York.

[2] William C. Preston (1794–1860) of South Carolina, who became intimate with Mrs. Grant during several years' residence in Edinburgh in early life. Many letters were afterwards exchanged between them.

APPENDIX

One of my sweetest recollections of my venerated Aunt Schuyler is, that she always spoke with sympathy and kindness of the Indians, thoroughly understood and justly appreciated their character. . . .

Tell that charming writer Mrs. Jameson [1] that I (being a little prudish) took great offence at seeing so much beautiful praise lavished on the beauties of Charles the Second's Court, whom I considered no better than they should be. But, afterwards, her stricture on Shakespeare's female characters delighted me. She invested them with all the properties that I had long studied and admired, without a hope of meeting with any one that would understand, far less explain, my feelings. Pray thank her for me for melting the frost of age about my heart, and restoring to me the delights of loving and admiring excellence. I can never do her any good, but she did a great deal to me: thank her for me, I earnestly entreat you.

With a confused head and chilled fingers, you must make allowance for something more than my usual incoherence. I understand well who the daughter-in-law of the late Lord Chancellor Erskine was, to whom you referred. She was a Colden, of an old Scottish family long resident in New York. Who has not heard of Cadwallader Colden, the clear-sighted oracle of all the successive governors of that Province? Lady Erskine called on me frequently when she was in Edinburgh. She was accounted a person of singular mildness and prudence; she was beautiful, and continued to be so for a longer period than is usually allotted to the fair Americans, who are chiefly a kind of spring flower. I must now give you in charge to tell Mr. Stephens,[2] the traveller in the Holy Land, with how much pleasure my son and I read his travels, or whatever else he calls them. We thought him quite original and unpretending, and liked very much his respectful and proper mode of expressing himself on sacred subjects; not pre-

---

[1] Mrs. Anne Jameson (1797-1860), author of "The Beauties of the Court of Charles II," "Legends of the Madonna," and many other works on art, was then on a visit to the United States.

[2] John L. Stephens (1805-1852), who wrote many interesting books of travel, chief among them being his popular volumes on Central America and Yucatan, perhaps the most important contributions yet made by any one writer on the subject of American Antiquities.

tending to be "wiser than what is written," as the poor pretenders to philosophy invariably do, but speaking with modest reverence of those things "which the angels desire to look into." We give him credit, too, for a talent not liberally bestowed on his countrymen; I mean humor. His dinner on the banks of the Nile with his English friends diverted me exceedingly. I hope success will not mislead or spoil a person of such good abilities and sound opinions.

I trust this letter will find you beginning to look forward with pleasant anticipation to your summer retreat, where, if a wish would waft me, I should like to meet you. I hope your commercial panics have, in some degree, subsided, and that you begin to discover that an alarm of this kind is as useful to the general good as the thunder storm that clears and purifies the air. If we look in a right spirit at what is passing round us, we shall daily find the Great Alchymist at work, producing permanent good out of transient passing evils. For instance, the obstructions to public credit in your affairs were met with so much candor and good feeling on our side of the water as, I think, will lay the foundation of more confidence and a better understanding hereafter. Then, with regard to that crazy war in Canada, the fair dealing and sincere desire of your government to repress the attempts of the ignorant mob on the borders, will establish friendly and confidential feelings on our side.

Deaths have been fearfully frequent this winter. I seldom rise without hearing of the death of some one younger than myself; but every added day, if it is well spent, is an added blessing. I suffer no pain, have equal spirits, and take pleasure in nameless trifles, birds, flowers, etc. If more months or years be allotted to me, I shall write to you again. My true love to Mrs. Hasell, and most kind remembrance to Mr. Cruger. Adieu, affectionately, says your faithful

ANNE GRANT.[1]

[1] So far as the Editor is aware, the only American letter of later date than the above was written by Mrs. Grant in August (she passed away in November), to Mrs. Jane Sibbald Wilson of Poughkeepsie, N. Y., in which she replies to an inquiry, "My mother, *née* Catherine Mackenzie, was not a connection of my gifted

APPENDIX

LETTERS TO MRS. GRANT FROM ROBERT SOUTHEY AND OTHERS

Among a number of unpublished letters written by Mrs. Grant's distinguished correspondents, the following are selected at random from the originals, in the writer's possession. The first is from the pen of William Hayley, the friend of Gibbon and the biographer of the poet Cowper, who was born in the year of 1745 and died in 1820. "The sublime Mr. Hayley," Thackeray calls him in his Roundabout Paper " On Ribbons." Hayley, it appears, was considerably worried over the question as to whether he or Cowper was the greater man. In an epistle to Hayley, included in Mr. Thomas Wight's collection of " Unpublished Letters of William Cowper," the poet says: " Whether you or I have the most genius, I know not, nor care a fig. God gives to every man as He pleases, and I should make Him a very unsuitable return for the little He has given me did I allow myself to repine that He has given others more. And now that I have once called you my friend, I defy even you to shine at such a rate as to excite in me any other sentiments than those of pleasure and congratulation."

FELPHAM, NEAR CHICHESTER, December 26, 1811.

DEAR MADAM, — I trust you will forgive my intrusion, as it arises from the pleasure you have afforded me by your writings, and particularly by the interesting account of your American lady.[1]

and good friend, Henry Mackenzie ; " alludes to a recent meeting with " Christopher North," who had good-naturedly called her " Queen of the Blue-Stockings ; " expresses the hope that " my little godson, James Grant, is growing strong," adding, " Please purchase for him, with the accompanying gold coin, a suitable gift," and concluding with the parting words, " Farewell, for I cannot expect to linger here much longer."

[1] In one of her early letters, written at the age of eighteen, Miss MacVicar remarks that whatever culture her mind had received she owed to Madame Schuyler,

APPENDIX

The delight you felt at a very early age from an unexpected present of Milton has tempted me to try if I can gratify your lively and tender feelings by a similar offering.

> "In childhood thy quick, piercing eyes,
>   When Milton chanced to meet,
> The stranger bard how didst thou prize !
>   His Paradise how sweet !
> Hoping thou may'st a new surprise
>   With equal kindness greet,
> To thee thy grateful fav'rite flies.
>   Behold him at thy feet."

Accept the little volumes that accompany this billet as a kind though a petty proof that your talents have excited esteem at the southern extremity of our island, and believe me, with hearty good wishes for your happiness and for your literary renown,
Very sincerely, dear madam, your friend,

W. HAYLEY.

In the following letter from Henry Smyth, Esq., of Mount Henry, Ireland, is contained an announcement of his sister's legacy of a thousand pounds to Mrs. Grant, not previously mentioned in this volume, as a mark of appreciation of her admirable character and writings.

MOUNT HENRY, September 7, 1814.

MY DEAR MADAM, — My lamented sister Isabella having left a paper behind her containing her wishes upon various particulars,

and says, "Many particulars relative to this excellent person's life and manners would be well worth preserving ; and if I outlive her, I think I will, some time or other, endeavor to please myself at least by preserving a memoir of a life so valuable and important." As has been seen, thirty years passed before this project of her youth was successfully carried out. Writing in June, 1808, to Sir Henry Steuart, Mrs. Grant says : "At the request of particular friends, I have, since the beginning of this year, been busily engaged in preparing for the press Memoirs of a deceased worthy well known in her time not only all over the Continent, but to all distinguished persons who in her day led the British army to the Canadian frontier. But I shall refer for particulars to the Memoirs themselves, which will very soon appear."

and as those wishes are to a certain extent considered as sacred by her family, it falls to my lot in our joint names to desire your acceptance of the sum of £1000, the interest thereon to commence from the first day of next August at the rate of six per cent. I must take the liberty of assuring you that the disposition entirely accords with the feelings of every branch of her family, that we entertain a mournful pleasure in offering this imperfect testimony of her gratitude and esteem, and I shall consider your acceptance as not only grateful to the memory of the departed, but complimentary to those who survive.

I shall await your commands as to the disposition of this sum; if it shall suit your convenience to suffer it to remain for any time in its present security, I shall send you mine or my brother's bond for the principal, the interest to be paid half yearly, or if you should judge that it might be more advantageously vested elsewhere, I shall take immediate steps for raising the money.

With the warmest wishes for the family, I have the honor to be, my dear madam, with very great esteem,

Your faithful and affectionate servant,

HENRY SMYTH.

The following letter was addressed to Mrs. Grant by her friend, Robert Southey, perhaps the most laborious literary worker of any age. Who that had the privilege of listening to the brave words of the large-hearted Thackeray, on the occasion of his last visit to the United States, can ever forget his allusion, in the course of his lecture on George the Third, to the great and good Southey? Writing to a friend in 1817, Mrs. Grant says: "Southey has the finest poetical countenance, features unusually high, and somewhat strong though regular, and a quantity of bushy black hair. I have heard Southey called silent and constrained; I did not find him so. He talked easily and much, without seeming in the least consequential, or saying a single word for effect."

KESWICK, 24th July, 1824.

MY DEAR MADAME, — If I had any influence with Colburn, it could not be better employed than on this occasion. I have

VOL. II. — 18

never had any communication with him but once, which was many years ago, when he wrote to request that I would lend him a portrait of myself, to be engraved for his magazine, and also communicate to him some particulars of my life. It happened that a most methodistical mis-likeness of me had been exhibited some little time before in the "European Magazine," and I was willing to supersede it by something better. I told Colburn where he might borrow a bust which was the only satisfactory resemblance that existed. At the same time, I stated, in as few words as possible, the time and place of my birth and the course of my education, saying that this would suffice for his purpose, and that the public had no business to expect anything more in the way of memoirs while the subject in question was alive. Mr. Colburn, however, was not satisfied with this. He borrowed the bust and got some one to attempt the impossible task of making a portrait from it, which he engraved as an original picture — a physiognomy between assassin and hangman. And he produced a long memoir of my private life, evidently written by some person who must once have been my guest, or he could not have known so much, and yet had been in no degree intimately acquainted with me, or he could not have made so many grossly erroneous statements. Of course, I thought myself ill-used; but that sort of usage is too common to excite either surprise or anger.

This has been my whole intercourse with Mr. Colburn. Campbell is the person who is most likely to have influence with him. But, surely, you can stand in need of no such interference. There has been but one opinion of all your writings, and they are of a character always to excite as much interest as when they were first published.

As to the form of publication, booksellers ought to be the best advisers. To me, the common octavo is the least agreeable form in which a book can appear, as being too large to be held conveniently in the hand and yet not large enough to require a table. The crown octavo is a much pleasanter size; but I believe the other is the more economical way of printing. In either shape, two duodecimo volumes may very well be comprised in one volume. When the books are published, it may be in my power to render them some little service; and that opportunity I will gladly take

— glad, indeed, of any occasion to show with what sincere respect I regard Mrs. Grant and her writings.

Dear Madame, believe me yours, very faithfully,
ROBERT SOUTHEY.

Miss Baillie, the writer of the following letter and the intimate friend of Sir Walter Scott, who frequently spoke of her as "the immortal Joanna," was distinguished as the author of numerous plays and poems in an age prolific of great writers. She spent a large share of her long life in a pretty cottage at Hampstead, near London, where she died, February 23, 1851 :

HAMPSTEAD, April 12, 1828.

DEAR MADAM, — Though with no disparagement to the memory of your young mountaineer, my answer to your obliging letters shall be conveyed to you in a more direct manner. I am gratified by hearing from you and having an opportunity of renewing my acquaintance with a member of your family ; and I beg you to accept my thanks. That the stream of your existence — which, you say, never did run smooth — should be at present disturbed by the protracted illness of Miss Grant I am very sorry to learn ; but, in the skillful hands of my good and kind friend, Dr. Thomson, and the favorable season of the year before her, I hope you will ere long have the happiness to see her restored to perfect health. Pray have the goodness to present my kind remembrances to her, in which my sister begs hers to be included. I am sure Mrs. Baillie, who is at present pretty well and recovering her wonted spirits by degrees, will be pleased with your mention of her, which I shall take care to communicate.

It has given me pleasure to hear that you are interested for Lady Byron and can do justice to her character, which, for genuine worth, disinterested generosity, and Christian forbearance and charity, is one of the most excellent I have ever known. She has been our near neighbor in Hampstead for nearly a year, and her occupation has been to assist all her friends who have any claim upon her, in every way in her power, either by her fortune or her interest. I wish I could give you a satisfactory answer to your inquiries as far as her health is concerned. She has been very unwell and confined almost entirely to the house all the winter, and the affliction she has suffered from the recent death of her father has checked her recovery. But she is somewhat better, and proposes soon to go to the seaside, which I hope will be of great benefit to her. You will be pleased to know that she has had the comfort of having two of her oldest and dearest friends in the house with her for some months past, who helped her to cheer her poor father under the weight of his infirmities and supported her in many various distresses.

I am glad to hear from your son that Mr. Mackenzie [1] continues to enjoy such good health at his advanced age, and beg to be kindly — I should also say gratefully — remembered to him. Farewell dear Madam, and believe me

Very truly yours,   J. BAILLIE.

David Stewart, of Garth, writer of the accompanying letter, a gallant soldier, and Governor of the West Indian Island of St. Lucia, was the author of " Sketches of the Character, Manners, and Present State of the Highlands of Scotland, with details of the Military Service of the Highland Regiments." Sir Walter Scott says : " Therein Mrs. Grant of Laggan has drawn the manners, customs, and superstitions of the mountains in their unsophisticated state, and my friend, General Stewart, of Garth, in giving the real history of the Highland Regiments has rendered any attempt to fill up the sketch with fancy coloring extremely rash and precarious ! " [2] Elsewhere Sir Walter writes : " The late lamented General Stewart, of Garth, in his account of the battle of Killiekrankie, informs us that Lochiel was attended on the field by the son of his foster-brother. This faithful adherent followed him like his shadow, ready to assist him with his sword, or cover him from the shot of the enemy. Suddenly the chief missed his friend from his side, and turning round to look what had become of him, saw him lying on his back with his breast pierced by an arrow. He had hardly breath, before he expired, to tell Lochiel, that see-

---

[1] Author of "The Man of Feeling," "Man of the World," etc. He was born in 1745 and died in 1831.
[2] Chronicles of the Canongate.

ing an enemy, a Highlander in General Mackay's army, aiming at him with a bow and arrow, he sprung behind him, and thus sheltered him from instant death. "This," observes the gallant David Stewart, "is a species of duty not often practised, perhaps, by our aide-de-camps of the present day."[1]

GOVERNMENT HOUSE, ST. LUCIA, July 3, 1829.

MY DEAR MADAM, — Far from friends and homes as I am here, one of the best sources of mental satisfaction is retiring as it were within myself and thinking of them. When fatigued by business or by violent exercise, I find these recollections as great, if not greater relief than rest to the body. If I could add some of our native music to these recollections of old friends and past times, the recreation would be complete. But a person must be long and far separated from friends to be able to enjoy such a mixture of melancholy and pleasing recollections as I frequently do. For several days past I have thought much of you. If I had not been so much in the world and forgotten some of my native country's beliefs, I would be as [illegible] or whether anything has happened, as a few nights ago I was in deep conversation with you in one of my waking dreams. One might forget such things in this land of heathens, of pestilence, of slavery, and of poisonous plants, and such poisonous ailments, and with people of many religious beliefs and many without any religion or belief — and of colors as various as their religions, some having no color at all, being white as this sheet of paper, and the rest composing all the intermediate shades down — or up — to jet black.

In such a country, with much to occupy my mind, I still find my original attachments and recollections unchanged. With these feelings I am very anxious to learn if you are in good health, and a letter cannot be more gratefully received than by me.

My official duties are a mixture of civil and military. To-day, in a garrison being among soldiers, to-morrow holding council and busy making new laws, also mending old ones. The laws of France which we have here are favorable to colonists and those who wished to encourage the colonies, made them more so, and a proprietor

[1] Preface to the Fair Maid of Perth.

of land cannot be compelled to pay his just debts — that is, his land is not liable, and cannot be sold for debt under the French laws. The Governor has great powers. This I now exercise, and hope, as I intend, to good purpose. A new law is passed, and every man must now pay what he owes. . . . I have to beg the favor of you to write at your convenience, and do let me entreat that it may be a long letter. It is only those who live at a distance that can fully appreciate the satisfaction and delight of receiving letters from dear and valued friends.

I remain, with great regard and esteem,

Ever faithfully yours, DAVID STEWART.

The following letter, written by Professor Andrews Norton, (1786–1852), author of an admirable article on Mrs. Grant and her writings contributed to the "North American Review," in 1845, is introduced here chiefly because of the truthful indorsement by Mrs. Grant which accompanies it, — "a very beautiful letter from Professor Norton of New England." His article of thirty pages in the "North American," concludes with these appreciative lines : " We have succeeded but ill in these imperfect notices of Mrs. Grant, if we have not given the impression of a woman of extraordinary good sense, and of uncommon powers of mind ; whose letters, embracing a wide variety of subjects, are as truly valuable as those of any other writer, and likely to be of as permanent interest, and to afford as lasting gratification ; but especially of a woman of great strength of character, formed by religious principle and penetrated by religious sentiment, the vital principle of whose moral being was faith in God and immortality, whose sympathies were warm and diffusive, and who was full of disinterested kindness."

CAMBRIDGE [NEW ENGLAND], Dec. 29, 1829.

MY DEAR MADAM, — You can hardly estimate how much pleasure your kind and cordial letter gave Mrs. Norton and myself. I fear you will think it strange that I have not sooner expressed my gratitude for it. I have twice begun a letter to you: but since receiving yours, I have been suffering from almost constant ill health, and am now but just recovering from a severe fit of sickness. My health promises now, I think, to be better than it has been.

It was a great satisfaction to have the pleasure of seeing you in Edinburgh. It is among my choicest remembrances of that most interesting and beautiful city. We had long known you through your writings and through our common friends; and it was like meeting one with whom we had been acquainted in youth, and with whom were associated some of its most agreeable recollections. We had been with you during your eventful life in the Highlands of Scotland and on the banks of the Hudson. The scenes and characters to which you had introduced us are such as give their charm to life, presenting a far more delightful aspect of the world than that which appears to him who is toiling on its frequented and careworn highways. It was delightful to find you, in old age, after such severe trials, so supported and strengthened by the power of God; not resigned only, but cheerful; possessing not the calm benevolence of age alone, but all the kinder feelings in their freshness and flower, which, beautiful as they are in youth, become so much more deeply interesting, when we know that care and sorrow have had no power to wither them, and that they will soon form a part of that crown of glory which fadeth not. If we could have forgotten the blessings which God has for a time taken to himself and is reserving for you in his keeping, we might have thought of you only as one —

> Whose cheerful day benevolence endears,
> Whose night congratulating conscience cheers,
> The general favorite, as the general friend.

Your meeting with Mrs. Hemans, and still more your parting with her, must have been very interesting to you both. Her visit to Scotland was to her highly exciting and gratifying, and could not, I think, but give her an impression of the estimate formed of her poetry by the best capable of feeling and judging of its excellence, which she had not received before. It must have been delightful to her to visit a country so peopled with romantic associations, where one familiar with its history and poetry, and possessing the gifted eye of genius, everywhere sees forms and hears voices which another cannot perceive, and is able to read and understand the handwriting on the ruined wall of other days. But since her return I have received a letter from her apparently written in much dejection of spirits. They are greatly affected without doubt by her very uncertain health, by the fact that her means of support depend much on its continuance, by the gloom which hangs over the prospects of her children, by her unfitness to struggle in this working-day world, and by the want of any one on whom she can naturally rely as a household friend for daily encouragement, assistance, and strength. She is as much an object of compassion as of admiration and love.

All our common friends in this country — though it is a very comprehensive term — are, I believe, well. Mrs. Norton begs you to think of her as one who remembers you always with the sincerest respect and affection. Her mother, than whom few ever had more power of attracting others, has lately been taken from us. The light of Heaven shone free on the days which preceded her death, and she has left a treasury of consolation and hope to her children. The little traveller, our boy Charles, in whom you took so kind an interest while in Edinburgh, is now as hearty and rosy, good tempered and noisy, as any boy ought to be. Our two little girls are well. Miss Guild, who is on a visit to us, desires to be respectfully remembered to you.

And now, my dear Madam, farewell. Accept my best thanks for all your kindness. May the close of your life be peaceful and happy, and lead you gently on to that infinitely happier state which, with my firm faith in the goodness of God, I can have no doubt that you are approaching. Perhaps you may find an opportunity to gratify and honor me by another letter. If not, will you remember me as one who thinks of you with the highest respect and regard.

ANDREWS NORTON.

The following "notelet," with which we shall conclude our selections, was written by Mrs. Opie, of whom Mrs. S. C. Hall said: "Her manners would have graced a court and not encumbered a cottage." She was a native of Norwich, and died in 1853, at the age of 84. Her note bears this indorsement, written by Mrs. Grant:

"From Mrs. Opie, once a belle, a beauty, and an authoress, who is remembered as the author of 'The Father and the Daughter.' She has become a Quaker, and the sect are very vain of such a convert."

RESPECTED FRIEND, — I hope I shall be more fortunate than I was in 1816, and that this time of my being in Edinburgh I shall be able to see thee. I intend to set off to-morrow to Perth, on my way with Mrs. Fry[1] and other friends, to the General Meeting at Aberdeen, and thence I shall go to the Highlands; but I hope to be here again, and at No. 2 South Castle Street (where I arrived on the 11th at night), and here I mean to remain till the beginning of the 10th month [October]. On my return, I shall be truly glad to receive a welcome from thee.

Thine very respectfully, AMELIA OPIE.

SOUTH CASTLE STREET, 8th month, 13th, 1834.

[1] Mrs. Elizabeth Fry, among the most eminent of modern philanthropists.

THE INDIAN WIDOW.[1]

Thy looks speak compassion, thy language a friend,
Yet think not, kind stranger, my purpose to bend;
Nouraddin's blest spirit awaits me the while
And hovers around his pale corpse on the pile.

He whispers — he call me — he passes like wind —
Oh, why should I linger in anguish behind?
Through this desolate Earth should I wander alone,
When my light was all quenched with Nouraddin's last groan?

Beloved and endear'd, in his shadow I dwelt,
In his tender protection no sorrow I felt;
As our souls were united, our pleasures the same,
So our ashes shall mingle and hallow the flame.

Like a vine without prop shall I sink on the ground,
And low in the dust spread my tendrils around?
While the beasts of the forest shall trample with scorn
The plant they neglected, despised and forlorn!

You tell me my children forsaken will pine, —
(What a wound to a bosom so tender as mine!)
That their innocent cries shall ascend in the air,
And drown with their clamor, my last dying prayer.

Oh, still, my loved babes, ye cling close to my heart;
But, alas! with your father I never can part;
Yet Bramah, in pity, my truth to reward,
Unseen, will permit me my children to guard.

Adieu, gentle stranger! Oh, linger not here,
Nor force me my triumph to stain with a tear;
The flames as they kindle I view with a smile —
How blest when our ashes shall mix on yon pile!

---

[1] The original manuscript of this poem was presented by Mrs. Grant in May, 1829, to the Editor's father, William Wilson, Esq., of Poughkeepsie, N. Y., who at the same time sent Mrs. Grant his lines on "Richard Cœur de Lion," said by Bryant to be "more spirited than any of the ballads of Aytoun."

APPENDIX

LINES ADDRESSED TO AN AMERICAN LADY

"I was born where men are proud to be —
The inviolate Island of the Sage and Free."
— LORD BYRON.

AND must we bid a last adieu,
    Fair Pilgrim of the Western clime?
And wilt thou with indulgence view
    This unpremeditated rhyme

That bidst thee, ere thou leavest her strand
    O'er Europe's ancient realms to rove,
Bequeath a blessing to the Land
    That Science and the Muses love?

Land of thy Sires. The parent stem,
    Whose vigorous branches spread so wide —
Fair freedom's shrine, Old Ocean's gem,
    Embraced and cherished by his tide —

While wandering through her sacred Fanes
    Did no low whisper meet thy ear?
Where sleep thy ancestors' remains
    Didst thou no aërial voices hear?

Blest in thy gentle bosom's Lord,
    Whose every care and wish is thine,
Did ye not bend with one accord,
    As listening to some voice divine?

The sounds that murmur from the Tomb
    Die indistinctly on the air;
The pensive Muse can pierce the gloom
    And find their secret meaning there.

APPENDIX

Hear her in mortal strains rehearse
    The words of each ancestral shade,
While thus in rude and artless verse
    Their solemn counsel seems conveyed.

Welcome from o'er the Atlantic wave,
    Blest children of heroic sires ;
Your presence in the silent Grave
    Relumes affection's faded fires.

Tho' on your happy native coast
    Her banner Liberty displays ;
Tho' equal Laws you justly boast,
    And Nations envy while they gaze ;

Tho' earth, in virgin bloom arrayed,
    Her lavish gifts profusely pours ;
Tho' with interminable shade
    The dark primeval forest lours,

That forest doomed so soon to yield
    Before the sturdy sons of toil,
Where in each cultured mead or field
    Shall fruits and flowers abundant smile.

For you a brighter, warmer sun
    Sheds lustre thro' a purer sky ;
Like mighty floods your rivers run,
    And plenty to their stores supply.

Yet from these bleak, inclement skies,
    Where Winter's lingering chills delay,
Ye bore away the matchless prize
    That kindles darkness into day.

The glorious intellectual light
    That shone from Bacon's wondrous mind,
That played round Shakespeare's varied flight,
    And Newton, nature's Priest, enshrined ;

Thence too ye bore the Torch of truth
    That lights the Altar's hallowed fire —
The hope of age, the guide of youth,
    That heavenward leads us to aspire.

While Seraphs' Hallelujahs sing,
    While Martyrs bear the immortal palm,
The heart which mortal sorrows wring
    Shall find these truths a healing balm.

Then while through gayer scenes you rove,
    Where pleasure leads the laughing hours,
Bids music wake in every grove,
    And fancy deck her Syren bowers.

Still steadfast holds that radiant light
    That pierces superstition's gloom,
Puts gay delusion's train to flight,
    And sheds its lustre o'er the Tomb.

Think kindly of the far-famed Isle
    From which your sires their lineage drew;
So may the Fates propitious smile
    When you your happy home renew.

May friends, a kind, unbroken band,
    With dewy eyes and glowing hearts,
Receive you on your native strand,
    And fondly meet, no more to part.[1]

Written below, by the lady to whom this farewell is addressed:
"Edinburgh, 16th. By Mrs. Grant of Laggan, from whom we have received every kindness imaginable since our arrival in this delightful town," and who in the following page of quotations from Scott, Goldsmith, and others, records her impressions of her fatherland: —

[1] The original manuscript of this poem, believed to have been written by Mrs. Grant in 1836, when she had passed fourscore, may be seen in the Lenox Library, New York. It is neatly written on four quarto pages, and is in excellent preservation. The name of the American lady to whom the poem was addressed does not appear on the manuscript. So far as known, it has never before appeared in print.

"O Caledonia, stern and wild !
Meet nurse for a poetic child ;
Land of brown heath and shaggy wood —
Land of the mountain and the flood."

"It may not be — it will not last —
The vision of Enchantment's past.
Like frostwork on the morning ray
The gilded fabric melts away."

"Like some tall cliff which lifts its awful form,
Swells from the vale, and midway leaves the storm ;
Though round its breast the rolling clouds are spread,
Eternal sunshine settles on its head !"

"How very desolate that breast must be
Whose only joyance is in memory !"

ARMS OF THE SCHUYLER FAMILY

APPENDIX

A LIST OF MRS. ANNE GRANT'S WRITINGS

"Poems on Various Subjects." By Mrs. Grant, Laggan. 1 vol., 8vo. Printed for the author by John Moir, Royal Bank Close. Edinburgh. 1803.

The same. Second edition. 1804.

"The Highlanders, and Other Poems." By Mrs. Grant, Laggan. Third edition. 18mo. Edinburgh : Printed by James Ballantyne & Co. for Longman, Hurst, & Orme, London. 1810.

"Letters from the Mountains : Being the real Correspondence of a Lady Between the Years 1773 and 1807." 3 vols., 18mo. London : Longman, Hurst, Rees & Orme. 1806.

The same. Second edition. 1807.

The same. Boston : Greenough & Stebbins. 2 vols., 12mo.

"Memoirs of an American Lady, with Sketches of Manners and Scenes in America as they existed previous to the Revolution." By the author of "Letters from the Mountains." 2 vols., 12mo. London : Longman, Hurst, Rees & Orme. 1808.

The same. Second edition. 1809.

The same. 1 vol., 12mo. Boston : B. W. Wells; New York : Samuel Campbell. 1809.

The same. Third edition. London : A. K. Newman & Co. 2 vols., 12mo. 1817.

The same. 1 vol., 12mo. New York : George Dearborn. 1836. (Contains Preface by Fitz-Greene Halleck.)

The same. 1 vol., 12mo. New York : D. Appleton & Co. 1846. (Has Introduction by Grant Thorburn.)

"Essays on the Superstitions of the Highlanders of Scotland. To which are added Translations from the Gaelic, and Letters connected with those formerly published." By the author of "Letters from the Mountains." 2 vols., 12mo. London : Longman, Hurst, Rees, Orme & Brown. 1811. (The presentation copy before the writer contains these words in the Author's handwriting : "By Anne Grant, who has here embodied recollections precious to memory, the only valuable to the thoughtful and imaginative, such as the owner of this book, Mr. William Wilson.")

APPENDIX

The same. 2 vols., 12mo. New York. 1813.

"Eighteen Hundred and Thirteen: A Poem in Two Parts," 8vo. London: Longman, Hurst, Rees & Co. 1814.

"Popular Models and Impressive Warnings for the Sons and Daughters of Industry." 2 vols., 12mo. London. 1815.

"Letters from the Mountains, Being the real Correspondence of a Lady Between the Years 1773 and 1803." Edited by her son, John Peter Grant, Esq. 2 vols., 12mo. London: Longman, Brown, Green & Longmans. 1845.

"Memoir and Correspondence of Mrs. Grant of Laggan," Author of "Letters from the Mountains," "Memoirs of an American Lady," &c. Edited by her son, John Peter Grant, Esq., with a steel portrait. 3 vols., post 8vo. London: Longman, Brown, Green & Longmans. 1844.

The same. Second edition. 1845.

The same. Third edition. 1853.

"Memoirs of an American Lady, with Sketches of Manners and Scenes in America as they Existed Previous to the Revolution." By Mrs. Anne Grant, author of "Letters from the Mountains," &c., with a memoir of Mrs. Grant, by Gen. Jas. Grant Wilson. 1 vol., 8vo, with steel portrait of the author, and other illustrations. Albany: Joel Munsell. 1876.

"Letters Written by Mrs. Grant of Laggan, concerning Highland Affairs and Persons connected with the Stuart Cause in the Eighteenth Century." Edited by J. R. N. Macphail. Edinburgh: Printed at the University Press by T. & A. Constable for the Scottish History Society. 1896. 8vo, cloth. Privately-printed edition, 40 copies. Extracted from Vol. XXVI. of the Publications of the Scottish History Society.

Also numerous contributions in prose and verse to the Scottish journals and magazines, during her twenty-eight years' residence in Edinburgh. Among the most important American articles on Mrs. Grant's writings, may be mentioned those in the North American Review, vol. 60; in Wilson's "Poets and Poetry of Scotland," vol. 1; and in "Appletons' Cyclopædia of American Biography," vol. 2.

INDEX

INDEX

The Contents of the Memoir of Mrs. Grant of Laggan, the Notes, and also the Appendix, are included in the Index.

ABBOTSFORD, Scotland, II. 237, 255
Abercrombie, General, II. 20, 24, 32, 38, 91
Abercromby, Lady, II. 266
Abercromby, Miss, II. 266
Addison, Joseph, 64
African servants, 265
Aged Bard's Wish, The, 18
Agricola and Mentor, II. 74
Albanians, The, 78, 88
Albany, 16, 26, 47, 54
Albany, Munsell's Annals of, 303
Algonquins, The, II. 108
Amendell House, II. 237, 240
American Indians, 132
American Manners, 25
American War, II. 36
Americans worth knowing, 32
Amherst, Lord, II. 32, 91, 92, 106
Amusements of Albany, 112
Anbury, Capt. Thomas, 132
Appian Way, Rome, 22
Appletons' Cyclopædia of American Biography, II. 288
Arbuthnot, Dr. John, 64
Argyll, Duke of, 21 ; II. 257
Astor Library, New York, II. 237

Athol, Duchess of, II. 239
Auld West Kirk, 31
Austrian Succession, 184
Aytoun, William E., II. 282

BACON, Lord, II. 284
Baillie, Joanna, 32 ; II. 238, 275, 276
Ballantyne and Co., II. 287
Bancroft, George, 9
Barbauld, Mrs. Anna L., II. 238
Barclay, Rev. Dr., II. 42
Baron of Bradwardine, 13
Beaumont, Admiral, II. 252
Beaux Stratagem, The, 294
Beckwith, Colonel, II. 107
Beekman Family, The, 46
Béranger, Pierre Jean de, II. 237
Black Watch, The, II. 31
Blackie, Prof. John Stuart, 18
Blackwood's Magazine, II. 244, 256
Bleecker Street Church, N. Y., II. 252
Blue Bells of Scotland, The, 20
Bold Buccleuch, The, II. 247
Bolingbroke, Lord, 64
Bostonians, The, II. 238
Braddock, General, II. 20
Braddock's Defeat, 239

INDEX

Bradstreet, Gen. John, 280, 281;
  II. 11, 38, 40, 47, 50, 106,
  113, 114
Brainard, David, 225
Breadalbane, Lord, II. 239
Brewerton, N. Y., II. 79
British America, II. 228, 231
British cause, II. 110
British government, 28, 33
British officers, II. 154
Brown, Dr. John, 32
Browne, Sir Thomas, 19
Bruce, King Robert, 298
Bruen, Mrs. Matthias, II. 252
Bruen, Rev. Matthias, II. 252, 253
Brunton, Doctor, II. 244
Brunton, Mrs. Mary, II. 239
Bryant and Friends, II. 245
Bryant, William Cullen, II. 282
Buchan, Lady, II. 246
Buffalo Exposition of 1901, 25
Bull, Honest John, II. 255
Bull, Scotch John, II. 256
Burgoyne, Gen. John, II. 114, 164
Burns, Robert, 40; II. 174
Burr, Col. Aaron, II. 213
Byron, Lady, II. 238, 275
Byron, Lord, II. 237, 283

CALEDONIANS, 142
Calton Hill, Edinburgh, II. 240
Calvinist Tracts, 66
Campbell, Major Duncan, II. 31
Campbell, Lady John, II. 257
Campbell, Capt. Mungo, II. 63, 79, 122
Campbell, Thomas, 32; II. 238, 245, 274
Camperdown, Lord, 16; II. 78

Canada, Conquest of, 16
Canadian priests, II. 97
Canadians, The, II. 106, 230
Cardaraqui, 231
Cassilis, Countess of, II. 166
Cassilis, Earl of, II. 165
Cawdor, Thane of, II. 264
Celtic language, The, 18
Centennial and Columbian Expositions, 25
Central America, II. 269
Charles the Second, 45, 47
Charles II., Beauties of Court, II. 269
Chaucer's Oxford Scholar, 30
Christian Indians, II. 42
Church, Miss Angelica, II. 258
Church, Mrs. Angelica, II. 258, 260, 261
Clarendon, Vt., II. 128, 129, 130, 131, 167, 179, 191, 197
Clark of Comrie, II. 241
Claverack on the Hudson, 15
Clydesdale, II. 190
Cochran, Dr. John, 253, 254; II. 258
Cochran, Lady Thomas, II. 241
Cockburn, Lord Henry, 33
Cogswell, Joseph G., 10; II. 237, 248
Colburn, Henry, II. 274
Colden, Cadwallader, II. 4, 6, 132, 133, 195, 269
Colden's History Five Nations, 232
Colonial History, II. 107
Constable, T. and A., II. 288
Constable's Magazine, II. 244
Coonie Children, II. 179
Coonie, Patrick, II. 177
Cooper, James Fenimore, 16

INDEX

Cooper, Gen. John T., II. 8
Corlaer, or governor, 226, 232
Cortlandts and Cuylers, 45
Cowper, William, II. 271
Crawford, Earl of, II. 85
Cromwell, Oliver, 189
Crown Point, 184; II. 89, 91, 92
Cruger, Mrs. Douglas, 21, 22; II. 260, 266, 268
Cuyler, General, II. 36, 37, 263
Cuyler, Misses, II. 7
Cuyler, Abraham C., II. 37
Cuyler, Abraham N., 148
Cuyler, Cornelius, 66, 274; II. 22, 66, 135
Cuyler, Mrs. Cornelius, 276; II. 39, 126
Cuyler, Elizabeth, II. 52
Cuyler, Johannes, 274
Cuyler, Philip, II. 37, 83, 196
Cuyler Family, II. 135

DALYELL, Capt. James, II. 107
Davers, Sir Charles, II. 105
Davers, Sir Robert, II. 99, 101, 102, 103, 104, 105
Dean, Capt. Steward, 47
D'Este, Colonel, 35
De la Barre, M., 229
De Lancey Family, 45, 46, 163
De Quincy, Thomas, 26, 31
Detroit, Siege of, II. 50
Dewar, Mrs. Annie Laggan, II. 191
DeWitt, Dr. Thomas, 303
Dianamat, II. 139
Diren, General, II. 247, 254
Douglas, George, of New York, 22
Douglas, Harriet. See Mrs. Douglas Cruger

Duncan, Colonel, 16; II. 64, 65, 78, 96, 107, 122
Duncan, Lord, II. 64
Dunfermline, II. 191
Dunlop, Robert, II. 138
Dutchman's Fireside, The, 10, 25

EDINBURGH, 23, 26, 30, 32; II. 280, 287
Edinburgh Castle, 31
Edinburgh Review, II. 245
Eglinton, The Earl of, II. 192
Eighteen-Hundred-and-Thirteen, The poem of, 27
English Border, The, II. 247
English History, II. 170
Erskine, Chancellor, II. 269
Erskine, Mrs., II. 240, 242
Esmond, Henry, by Thackeray, 9
"Ettrick Shepherd." See James Hogg

FAIR MAID OF PERTH, II. 277
Fairmount Park, Philadelphia, II. 267
Falstaff's Soldiers, 188, 295
Fermor, Lady Juliana, II. 267
Fifty-fifth Highlanders, II. 122, 123, 129, 191, 192
Fingal, a poem, II. 64
Five Nations, The, 62, 63; II. 14, 16, 232, 233
Fletcher, Mrs. Eliza, 26; II. 238, 253
Fontenoy, battle of, II. 31
Forbes, Lord, II. 252
Fort Augustus, Scotland, 17
Fort Brewerton, II. 63, 79
Fort Frontenac, 229
Fort Hendrick, II. 57
Fort Mackinaw, II. 95

INDEX

Fort Ontario, II. 65
Fort Orange (Albany), 48
Fort Oswego, II. 63
Fort St. Frederick, 184
Fort William, Inverness-shire, 13
Fort William Henry, II. 31
Franklin, Benjamin, II. 212
French Canadians, 156, 182
French Protestants, 246
French War, The, 186
Frielinghuysen, Dominie, 285, 289, 291, 297, 302, 303
Frontenac, Count, 229
Fry, Mrs. Elizabeth, II. 238, 281

GAELIC translations, 28
Garth, David Stewart of, II. 276
Gay, John, poet, 64
George the Fourth, 26; II. 256
Glassel, Miss, II. 257
Glenmoriston family, II. 101
Godolphin, Lord, 64
Goethe, J. W. von, II. 237
Goldsmith, Oliver, II. 285
Gordon, The Duchess of, 20
Gordon, Sir John Watson, 21; II. 268
Graham, Capt. Gordon, II. 31
Grant, Commodore, II. 101
Grant, Mrs. Anne — Memoir of, 13; mentioned, 38, 42, 45, 148, 149, 217, 226; II. 9, 53, 74, 108, 135, 191, 237, 253, 255, 259, 268, 270, 271, 272, 273, 278, 282, 285; Bibliography, 287, 288
Grant, Mrs. Elizabeth, 13
Grant, Mrs., of Carron, 13
Grant, Frederic, II. 241
Grant, The Rev. James, 17, 19, 31
Grant, John Andrew, 21

Grant, Mrs. John Peter, 21, 33
Grant, John Peter, 33; II. 238, 288
Grant, Captain Walter, 33
Grant, Sir William, 23, 37
Green Mountain Boys, II. 164, 199
Green Mountains, II. 198
Great Britain, II. 91
Gregory, Dr. John, II. 252
Groesbeck, Catherine, 161
Guild, Miss, II. 280

HAMILTON, Duke of, II. 256
Hamilton, Alexander, II. 213, 263
Hamilton, Mrs. Alexander, 10; II. 258, 259, 260
Hamilton, Lord Archibald, II. 256
Hamilton, Mrs. Elizabeth, 33
Hamilton, John C., II. 259
Hamilton, Philip, II. 259
Hamilton, Thomas, II. 256
Hamilton, Sir William, II. 255, 256
Hall, Mrs. S. Carter, II. 280
Hall's History of Vermont, II. 164, 191
Halleck, Fitz-Greene, II. 237, 287
Harrowgate, England, II. 255
Hasell, Mrs., II. 268, 270
Hastings, Lady, II. 241
Hayley, William, 32; II. 271, 272
Hemans, Mrs. Felicia, 32; II. 279
Henry, Patrick, II. 247
Henry the Fifth, 34
Highland Regiments, II. 276

INDEX

Highland Society, The, 28
Highlanders and other Poems, 20, 34
Highlanders of Scotland, 18
Highlands of Scotland, II. 276
Highlands, Poetry of, 18
Hogg, James, 27
Holy Land, The, II. 269
Horses, unknown in Oswego, II. 74
Howe, Lord, II. 21, 22, 23, 26, 27, 105
Hudson River, The, 47; II. 185, 279
Huguenots, The, 25, 73, 191; II. 212
Humboldt, Baron von, II. 237
Hunter, Robert, 162
Hunting Excursions, II. 70
Hurons, 230; II. 103, 108, 109

Indian Beauty, II. 99, 100
Indian corn, II. 76
Indian language, 134
Indian Sachems, 184
Indian Traders, 96
Indian War, II. 110, 113, 117
Indian Widow, The, II. 282
Indian Wigwams, 178
Indian Women, 138; II. 119
Iroquois, or Five Nations, 55
Irving, Washington, 9, 32; II. 237, 245
Isle of Wight, II. 238

Jameson, Mrs. Anne, II. 269
Jay, Frances, II. 52
Jay, John, II. 257
Jay, Peter Augustus, II. 257
Jeffrey, Lord Francis, 9, 27, 33
Johnson, Sir Guy, II. 43

Johnson, Sir John, II. 166, 193, 232
Johnson, Dr. Samuel, 54
Johnson, Sir William, II. 4, 11, 14, 17, 93, 96, 103, 233
Johnson Hall, II. 15, 262
Jordanhill, Scotland, II. 240

Kennedy, Archibald, II. 165
Killiekrankie, battle of, II. 276
King George the Third, 124, 227
King Hendrick, 62; II. 57, 58
King William the Third, 46
Kings Arms, New York Inn, 124
Kinrara, The Estate of, 20

Laggan, Inverness-shire, 17, 19, 20, 26
Lake Champlain, 148
Lake George, II. 29, 30
Lake Huron, II. 108
Lake Ontario, 229
Lambert, Major William H., 9
Lansing, Gertrude, 253; II. 193
Lansing, Johannes, 245
Lansing, Peter, II. 196
Laplanders, The, II., 222
Lee, Gen. Charles, II. 25, 33
Legarè, Hugh Swinton, II. 248
Legends of the Madonna, II. 269
Leggins, of deer skin, 132
Leighton, Bishop, II. 240
Lennox, Mrs. Charlotte, 54
Lenox Library, II. 285
Letters from the Mountains, 17, 23, 24
Lines to a Lady, II. 283
Literary Reminiscences, 26
Livingston, Mr., Edinburgh, II. 243
Livingston, Walter, 253

INDEX

Livingston Family, 163
Loch Katrine, II. 238
Lochawside, Scotland, II. 180
Lochiel, Cameron of, II. 276
Lockhart, John Gibson, II. 251, 255
Longman & Co., London, 22, 24, 34 ; II. 287, 288
Lorne, The Marquis of, 21
Loudon, Lady, II. 241
Loudon, Lord, II. 11
Louis Fourteenth, 56, 192
Louisburgh, Capture of, II. 91
Lovelace, Governor, 162
Low, Nicholas, II. 52
Lowell, Miss Anne Cabot, 23, 24
Lowell, John, Junior, 23
Lowell, Judge John, 24
Lowell, Miss Sarah, II. 248
Lydius, The Rev. John, 303

MACDONALD, Captain, II. 241
Mackay, General, II. 277
Mackenzie, Catherine, II. 270
Mackenzie, Henry, 27, 35 ; II. 271, 276
Macphail, J. R. N., II. 288
MacVicar, Capt. Duncan, 13, 15, 16, 17 ; II. 122, 124, 147, 160, 162, 164, 166, 180, 191, 192
MacVicar, Mrs. Duncan, 15
Mariamat, II. 139
Marlborough, Duke of, 64
Marriages in Albany, 108
Middleton, Mr., of S. C., II. 253
Milton, John, 16, 19 ; II. 88, 122, 150
Moccasins, of deer skin, 132
Mohawk language, 143
Mohawk Valley, II. 79

Mohawks, The, 55, 100, 156, 159, 183, 189
Mohicans, The Last of the, 16
Montague, Lady Mary, 141
Montgomerie, Colonel, II. 192
Moore, Lady Henry, II. 132
Moore, Sir Henry, II. 132, 133
Mount Annan, II. 246, 247, 254
Mount Henry, II. 272
Mount Seir, 206
Munhattoes, The, 45, 47
Munro, John, II. 164, 183
Munsell, Joel, 10 ; II. 288
Murray, Lady Augusta, 35

NEW ENGLAND, II. 119, 136, 278
New Hampshire, 236
New Jersey College, 252
New York City, II. 115, 124, 193, 195
New York troops, 188, 194
Newton, Sir Isaac, II. 284
Niagara Falls, II. 101
Nigel, Fortunes of, II. 255
North, Christopher. See Prof. John Wilson
North America, 141 ; II. 91
North American Review, II. 278, 288
Norton, Andrews, II. 278, 280
Norton, Mrs. Andrews, II. 278, 280
Norton, Charles Eliot, II. 280,

O'CALLAGHAN, Dr. Edmund Bailey, II. 50
O'Doherty, The, II. 256
Ogilvie, Dr. John, II. 42, 135
Onnonthio, or Governor, 226, 230, 231
Onondagas, The, 55, 229

INDEX

Ontario Lands, II. 96
Opie, Mrs. Amelia, II. 280, 281
Ossian, The poem of, 18
Oughton, Sir Adolphus, II. 45
Oxford, Lord, 64

PARADISE LOST, 16, 65 ; II. 79, 87
Parkman's Pontiac, II. 107
Paulding, James Kirke, 10, 25
Pearson's Albany Settlers, 164
Penn, Gov. John, II. 267
Penn, William, II. 221, 223, 225, 267
Pennsylvania, II. 219
Philipse, Frederick, and Manor Confiscated, 50
Plays represented, 293
Pontiac War, The, II. 50, 93, 95, 96, 97, 98, 99, 103, 118
Potato Bogle, II, 245
Poughkeepsie, N. Y., II. 270, 282
Preston, William C., of South Carolina, II. 248, 253, 268
Prince Leopold, II. 239
Pruyn, Col. Augustus, 10
Pruyn, Mrs. John V. L., II. 252
Pultowa, Battle of, II. 65

QUACKAWARY, II. 217
Quakers, The, II. 225, 227, 267
Queen Anne, 63
Queen of Hearts, II. 99
Quincy, Mrs. Josiah, 23

RALSTON, Robert, of Philadelphia, II. 248
Recruiting Officer, The, 297
Rensselaerwyck, 46
Revolutionary Fathers, II. 263

Rhode Island, 271
Richard Cœur de Lion, II. 282
Richardson, Sir John, II. 253
Rogers, Samuel, II. 245
Roman Atticus, II. 196
Ross, Mrs. Schuyler, governess, II. 258, 261
Roy, James, II. 177
Roy's Wife of Aldivalloch, 13
Royal Americans, 285
Ryerson, Doctor, II. 254

SAINT CAROLINE, II. 251
St. Lawrence River, II. 65
St. Lucia Island, II. 276, 277
Schenectady, II. 57, 159
Schuyler, Catalina, 66 ; II. 87
Schuyler, Cornelius, II. 45
Schuyler, Cortlandt, II. 45, 126, 139, 193, 196, 263
Schuyler, George L., 21
Schuyler, George W., 10
Schuyler, Gertrude, 245
Schuyler, Jeremiah, 148, 152, 161, 185, 247, 250
Schuyler, Johannes, 66, 180 ; II. 113
Schuyler, John, 55
Schuyler, John, Jr., II. 9
Schuyler, John C., 166 ; II. 48
Schuyler, Margaretta ("Aunt"), 24, 66, 128, 129, 131, 146, 147, 162, 166, 180, 195, 198, 200, 237, 243, 244, 249, 286, 287, 306 ; II. 2, 3, 9, 10, 24, 25, 33, 35, 47, 48, 82, 86, 92, 97, 106, 113, 117, 119, 121, 122, 126, 131, 132, 134, 135, 139, 150, 158, 165, 178, 179, 191, 192, 194, 195, 196, 197, 260, 261, 266, 271

INDEX

Schuyler, Peter, Colonel, 128, 146, 161, 184, 185, 220, 246; II. 165
Schuyler, Peter (Pedrom), 148, 152; II. 12, 138
Schuyler, Col. Peter S., 128
Schuyler, Col. Philip, 24, 146, 147, 152, 155, 245, 280; II. 1, 3, 9
Schuyler, Gen. Philip, 55; II. 9, 12, 44, 50, 52, 113, 126, 132, 184, 258
Schuyler, Pieter, Col., 59, 60, 64, 73, 86
Schuyler, Rensselaer, II. 258
Schuyler, Mrs. Richard, II. 48
Schuyler, Stephen, II. 51
Schuyler, Susan, 248
Schuyler Flats, II. 8, 136
Schuyler house burned, II. 48
Schuylerville, N. Y., II. 114
Scot, John, killed in duel, II. 252
Scott, Sir Walter, 9, 22, 27, 35; II. 237, 245, 255, 275, 276, 285
Scottish Highlanders, 27
Scottish Highlands, II. 279
Scottish History Society, II. 288
Scottish Literary World, 27
Scottish Peasants, II. 112
Selkirk, Earl of, II. 231
Seresby, Professor, II. 256
Seventy-Seventh Highlanders, 13
Shakespeare, 30, 295; II. 149, 168, 169, 255, 269
Shirley, Governor, 186
Smyth, Henry and Isabella, II. 272
Solway Firth, II. 254
Somerville, Lord, II. 250
Southey, Robert, 9; II. 273, 275
Spectator, of London, 59, 64

Staats, Drs. Abraham and Samuel, 131
Staats, Barent, II. 196
Stealing turkeys, 122
Steamboats, Newton and Rochester, 47
Steenhoek kill, 154
Stephens, John L., II. 269
Steuart, Sir Henry, II. 272
Stewart, Gen. David, II. 276, 277, 278
Stewart, Alexander of Invernahyle, 13
Stoics of the Woods, II. 268
Stuart, Colonel, II. 239
Stuart, Dr. John, II. 43
Stuart, Hon. William, II. 267
Stuart Cause, The, II. 288
Superstitions of Highlanders, 27
Symes, Lancaster, 303

Ten Broeck, Gen. Abraham, 45
Ten Broeck, Dirk (Mayor), 45
Ten Broeck, Dirk Wesselse, 45, 274
Ten Broeck, Mrs. Elizabeth, 46
Thackeray, William M., 9, 32; II. 271, 273
Thorburn, Grant, II. 287
Thorndike, Augustus, II. 242, 246, 248
Ticknor, George, II. 64, 237, 248, 253
Ticonderoga, 15; II. 29, 40, 91
Trees, 76, 103; elms and sycamores, 150
Trinity Church, New York, II. 42
Trois Rivières, II. 82
Tweedy, Sarah, II. 83
Tyte, a Schuyler servant, 268

INDEX

United States, The, II. 228, 231, 273
Upper Canada, II. 233; Mohawks removed to, II. 233
Upper Lakes, II. 93; Indian War of the, II. 93, 94
Utopia, A Serene, II. 72
Utrecht, Treaty of, 184

Van Cortlandt, Augustus and James, II. 52
Van Cortlandt, Cornelia, II. 113
Van Cortlandt, John, II. 83
Van Cortlandt, Olof S., II. 52
Van Cortlandt, Stephanus, II. 83
Van Cortlandt Manor, 50; II. 83
Van Rensselaer, Cornelius, II. 152
Van Rensselaer, Jeremiah, 146
Van Rensselaer, John, 280; II. 154
Van Rensselaer, Maria, 146
Van Rensselaer, Stephen (Patroon), 46, 48
Van Rensselaer Family, The, II. 9
Van der Poel, Johannes and Mrs., 201
Venice and Oswego, II. 74
Venison, abundance of, 271; II. 71
Voice of Cona, 44

Wallace, by Blind Harry, 15
Wampum preferred to beads, 217
Warrior, refractory, 186, 187
Washington, Gen. George, II. 247, 257, 260, 263

Watts, John and Anne, II. 165
Waverley, by Sir Walter Scott, 13, 14
Waverley Novels, attributed to Mrs. Grant, 27
Welwood's "Memoirs of England," II. 64
Wendell, Jacob, II. 150
Wendell, Mrs. Jacob, II. 151, 181
West Friesland, 289
West India Girls, 20
West India Productions, 273
Westminster, Peace of, 47
West Troy, N. Y., II. 177
Westerlo, Rev. Eilardus, II. 41
Weyman, New York printer, 289
White Creek, N. Y., II. 191
White Plains, N. Y., II. 63; battle of, II. 63
White's History of Selborne, 197
Whittington and his Cat, 197
Wigwams at the Flats, 178, 185
Wild turkeys, II. 72
Wilson, James, II. 256
Wilson, James Grant, 9, 25, 27, 32, 36; II. 260, 268, 271, 288
Wilson, Prof. John ("Christopher North"), 27; II. 255
Wilson, Mrs. Jane Sibbald, 34; II. 270
Wilson, William, 9, 30, 34; II. 268, 282, 288
Wilson's Poets and Poetry of Scotland, 27; II. 288
Winds, mild Southern, 93
Windsor Forest, 64
Winepress, Captain, commands Albany fort, II. 79
Winter amusements, 117

INDEX

Winters, coldness of, 92, 93; II. 161
Wolf, a favorite horse, stratagem of, 268
Wolfe, General James, II. 40
Wolves of America, 68, 101, 217; II. 61, 62
Wolves, foxes, and bears, II. 61
Women Slaves, 142, 143
Wood Creek, II. 59, 60

Wood rangers, practical, II. 71
Worcester's Rebellion, 241
Wordsworth, William, II. 245
Wrens, and their nests, 167, 172
Wynant's Kill, and Islands, 148

YUCATAN, II. 269
Yonnondio, 231, 232

ZEPHANIAH and Obadiah, II. 147